PHYSICAL EDUCATION AND SPORT

A CONTEMPORARY INTRODUCTION

FOURTH EDITION

ANGELA LUMPKIN B.S.E., M.A., M.B.A., Ph.D.

Dean, College of Education
State University of West Georgia

Boston, Massachusetts   Burr Ridge, Illinois   Dubuque, Iowa   Madison, Wisconsin
New York, New York   San Francisco, California   St. Louis, Missouri

WCB/McGraw-Hill

A Division of The **McGraw·Hill** Companies

PHYSICAL EDUCATION AND SPORT: A CONTEMPORARY INTRODUCTION

1 2 3 4 5 6 7 8 9 0 DOC/DOC 9 0 9 8 7

ISBN 0-8151-4488-1

Publisher: *Edward E. Bartell*
Sponsoring editor: *Vicki Malinee*
Developmental editor: *Sarah Reed*
Marketing manager: *Pamela S. Cooper*
Project manager: *Jane C. Morgan*
Production supervisor: *Sandra Hahn*
Designer: *Cindy Crampton*
Compositor: *Interactive Compositon Corporation*
Typeface: *10/12 Garamond*
Printer: *R. R. Donnelley & Sons Company*

Library of Congress Cataloging-in-Publication Data
Lumpkin, Angela.
    Physical education and sport : a contemporary introduction /
  Angela Lumpkin.—4th ed.
      p.   cm.
  Includes bibliographical references and index.
  ISBN 0-8151-4488-1
  1. Physical education and training. 2. Sports. 3. Physical
  education and training—Vocational guidance—United States.
  I. Title.
  GV341.L85 1998
  613.7'1'023—dc21   97-20737

www.mhhe.com

Contents

UNIT TWO

HISTORY AND DEVELOPMENT OF PHYSICAL EDUCATION AND SPORT PROGRAMS

UNIT THREE

ISSUES, TRENDS, AND THE FUTURE OF PHYSICAL EDUCATION AND SPORT

Preface

Physical Education and Sport: A Contemporary Introduction provides students with an exciting opportunity to discover the diversity of physical education and sport and the wealth of careers available in this field. Students will be introduced to the heritage, current programs, and future potential of the field that they are considering entering. The purpose of this book is to introduce students to this multifaceted field and to involve students in assessing potential careers in physical education and sport.

The intent of this book is to broaden students' understanding of how the philosophies and programs of physical education and sport evolved as well as to present the current status of these fields. Inherent within the changing nature of physical education and sport is a need to examine how Title IX of the 1972 Education Amendments, the inclusion into classrooms of physically- and mentally-challenged individuals, the increased emphasis on physical activity for all ages, past programs in this country and in Europe, and traditional philosophies have affected and will influence what you do as a professional in this field in the twenty-first century.

No longer are physical education and sports just for schools or colleges, although teaching in these settings is certainly an important endeavor. By learning about careers in leisure services, athletic training, corporate fitness, sport management, fitness club instruction and management, recreation for all ages and abilities, coaching, and a variety of other activity-related pursuits, students will gain a clearer perspective of the future role physical education and sport should play in American society. Individuals who accept the challenges of these careers will help women, minorities, senior citizens, individuals in lower socioeconomic classes, students, and many others benefit from active, fit lifestyles. Practical suggestions are provided to students as you choose and prepare for careers. To enhance this process, throughout the book the importance of physical education and sport as an expanding and diverse field of service, enjoyment, and employment is emphasized.

NEW TO THIS EDITION

- A greater focus on nonteaching-related careers in physical education and sport is presented.

- New boxes are added throughout the text to help reinforce important information (for example: NASPE's National Standards for Physical Education, Title IX time line of important events, and a guide to careers).

- Chapter 3: "Physical Education and Sport as an Academic Discipline" now includes an "Applied Sciences Quiz" to help reinforce the information presented concerning the 12 applied sciences of physical education and sport. This chapter has also expanded the discussions of adapted physical education, motor learning, sport management, sport psychology, and sport sociology.

- Chapter 4: "The Profession of Physical Education and Sport" contains a decreased emphasis on teaching to give equal importance to other growing specializations, such as athletic training and sport management. A new box containing certification requirements for NATA is also included.

- Chapter 6: "Preparation for a Career" includes an expanded discussion of the importance of internships and an updated list of certifications and their prerequisites.

- Chapter 9: "Twentieth-Century Physical Education and Sport" has been revised to include expanded discussions of "intramurals" outside of education (e.g., company sport tournaments), inclusion and "least restrictive environment" for adapted physical education students into nondisabled classrooms, and movement education (child-centered curricula).

- Chapter 10: "The Changing Nature of Physical Education and Sport" contains an expanded discussion of fitness, exercise, and sport science trends. There is also additional information presented concerning accreditation standards in nonschool settings.

- Chapter 11: "Trends and Issues in Physical Education-Related Careers" has been expanded a great deal. Some issues are stressed in greater depth, including standards and assessment, teacher-coach role conflict, burnout, and instructional challenges. Several new boxes appear, including NASPE's "Content Standards for Physical Education," "Performance-Based Assessment," and "Program Adherence Factors." Also, a new discussion of quality in education, business, and government (quality fitness programs) is presented to reinforce the call for standards in all disciplinary fields. Finally, the chapter has been reorganized to begin with the section "The Value of Physical Education for Everyone." This helps to target all physical education careers, not only teaching.

- Chapter 13: "Living in the Twenty-First Century" contains new scenarios from the year 2000 and after. It also includes a new section on physical activity throughout life, as well as ways to promote physical activity and sport. The chapter also stimulates thinking with new information concerning school programs, higher education, athletics, and sport and fitness careers.

- New student activities are included throughout the text to help students understand and apply the information learned in each chapter.

- New photos are integrated throughout to enhance and update the text.

CONTENT FEATURES

Written in a conversational and personal style, *Physical Education and Sport: A Contemporary Introduction* is designed for students enrolled in their first course related to exercise science, sport management, physical education, athletic training, or other related majors.

An overview of the field is stressed rather than an in-depth examination of the disciplinary areas. Some of these relevant topics discussed include practical suggestions for selecting and obtaining a job in the chosen career; current issues affecting job selection; girls and women in sport; minorities in physical education and sport; the standards and assessment movement; teacher, coach, athletic trainer, and exercise specialist certifications; educational values of sports; and the future of fitness for Americans.

A career emphasis is integrated throughout, and given special attention in Chapters 5 and 6. Chapter 5 describes more than 50 careers in education, recreation, fitness, sports, business, and athletics. Students can learn about job responsibilities, prerequisite education and preparation, and the potential availability of positions. Chapter 6 provides practical ideas for preparing for careers, with an emphasis on the importance of volunteer experiences, internships, and obtaining certifications.

The book's three units are self-contained and may be read in any order, although each is important to a full understanding of the field. Unit One provides foundational information in the first four chapters before focusing on careers. As defined in Chapter 1, *physical education is a process through which an individual obtains optimal physical, mental, and social skills and fitness through physical activity.* Sport is operationally defined as *physical activities governed by formal or informal rules that involve competition against an opponent or oneself and are engaged in for fun, recreation, or reward.* The cognitive, affective, and physical fitness and motor skill development objectives of physical education and sport indicate how physical education and sport can contribute to improvements in quality of life for all. The five traditional philosophies and discussion of ethics presented in Chapter 2 provide reference points for the development of a personal philosophy. Chapter 3 examines the 12 applied sciences that constitute the academic discipline of physical education and sport. An explanation of organizations in the field precedes a discussion about preparation programs for school and nonschool careers in Chapter 4.

In order to assist students in the career selection process, Chapter 5 describes a variety of available career options, while Chapter 6 provides practical suggestions for career preparation.

Unit Two covers the history and development of physical education and sport from early cultures through today. Athletics in Athens and Sparta, European gymnastics programs, and English sports and games are emphasized in Chapter 7 in terms of their influence on programs in the United States. In Chapter 8, early American physical education and sport is traced from early sporting diversions through the formalized gymnastics programs of the late 1800s. Chapter 9 completes the chronology of evolving programs that are diverse in philosophy, clientele, and activity.

Unit Three describes issues and trends in physical education and sport. Chapter 10, examining the changing nature of this field, discusses fitness and exercise and sport science program developments, unique features of elementary, middle, and secondary school physical education, certification and accreditation, legal liability, and other factors impacting program delivery. Issues such as the value of physical activity for everyone, consumer education, public relations, career burnout, merit pay, standards and assessments, and teacher-coach conflict that currently affect individuals in physical education and sport careers are the focus of Chapter 11. The beneficial outcomes and associated issues of sports for girls and women, minorities, youth, school and college students, and Olympic athletes are addressed in Chapter 12. The final chapter looks at the image and role of physical education and sport in all settings in the twenty-first century.

KEY CONCEPTS

Each chapter begins with statements that highlight the major topics to be discussed. These provide students with both a focus and direction as they read.

INTRODUCTIONS

The first paragraphs in the chapters briefly set the stage for and preview the text. They help students gain further perspective on the relevance of the content.

ILLUSTRATIONS

More than 150 photographs help students see the diversity of physical education and sport and potential careers therein. These photographs also reemphasize the popularity of sports and activities for all and help teach important concepts.

BOXED MATERIAL

Throughout the text, specially highlighted information is designed to enhance students' understanding and provide additional insights into the profession.

SUMMARIES

A summary paragraph at the conclusion of each chapter emphasizes the primary areas of importance, thus complementing the initial key concepts. These summaries help students focus on the major items discussed.

CAREER PERSPECTIVES

A unique feature of this book is the integration of biographical sketches of sport and physical educators in several diverse careers. The featured individuals list their job responsibilities, hours, course work, and degrees, discuss experience needed for their careers, satisfying aspects of their careers, and job potential, and offer suggestions for students.

REVIEW QUESTIONS

To enhance retention of each chapter's content, students are encouraged to answer the review questions. Rather than seeking rote memorization of facts, these questions stress understanding the concepts.

STUDENT ACTIVITIES

Like the review questions, student activities encourage students to think about and use the chapter content in greater depth and to extract practical ideas for career application. These activities also encourage an active participation in the learning process.

SUGGESTED READINGS

Suggested readings furnish students with additional information and potential resources for further study. The annotations are especially beneficial to expanding students' knowledge.

GLOSSARY

A comprehensive glossary of important terms reinforces students' understanding of the terminology used in the book and in physical education and sport.

APPENDICES

An appendix of professional journals and addresses provides easy references for purchasing these periodicals or learning more about their availability. A second appendix gives addresses for several organizations that certify coaches, athletic trainers, and fitness leaders.

SUPPLEMENTS

An *Instructor's Manual and Test Bank* accompanies the text and is available to those who adopt it. The manual includes practical teaching suggestions, chapter overviews, instructional objectives, additional annotated readings, more than 450 multiple choice, true/false, matching, and essay test items with separate answer keys, suggested audiovisual materials, and transparency masters of important drawings, tables, and charts from the text. These were chosen to help explain difficult concepts within the text.

Available to qualified adopters, a computerized test bank allows the instructor to select, edit, delete, or add questions, as well as construct and print tests and answer keys. It is available in IBM Windows and Macintosh formats.

ACKNOWLEDGMENTS

Without the help of numerous individuals, this book would not exist. First and foremost, my parents, Janice and Carol Lumpkin, instilled in me a love for learning, provided me with many educational opportunities through personal sacrifice, and continually encourage all of my endeavors. I dedicate this book to them with my love. My sister, Vernell Berry, and my brother, Phillip Lumpkin, who are dear friends, and their families provide me with love and encouragement too.

I am also appreciative of the invaluable help given to me by the reviewers and other colleagues, who have provided valuable suggestions for this revision:

Viola Bahls
University of Nebraska—Lincoln

Cathy Buell, Ph.D.
San Jose State University

Mark Harvey, Ed.D.
Metropolitan State College

DawnElla Rust, Ed.D.
Northeastern State University

Beverly Yerg, Ph.D.
Florida State University

Lastly, but significantly, I want to thank the outstanding professionals at McGraw-Hill Higher Education. It has been a pleasure to be associated with each of them. Their commitment to the publishing of quality books is unmatched. It is the desire of the author that this book will awaken and kindle the interest of those who read it to select careers in physical education and sports.

Angela Lumpkin

PHYSICAL EDUCATION AND SPORT

UNIT ONE

Principles and Scope of Physical Education and Sport

(Photo courtesy Julianne Foster.)

CHAPTER 1

Physical Education and Sport—A Dynamic Field

KEY CONCEPTS

- Today's physical education and sport programs have the potential to improve the quality of life for everyone.
- The purpose of physical education and sport is to enhance lives through participation in physical activity. The growing interest in health and fitness contributes to the achievement of this purpose.
- Cognitive development, affective development, and physical fitness and motor skill development objectives are achieved through today's physical education and sport programs.
- The allied fields of health, recreation, and dance overlap in some curricula and for some purposes with physical education and sport programs.
- The continual challenge facing physical educators and leaders in sport programs remains instilling in Americans of all ages the importance of participating in regular physical activity.

Children love to move because it is fun. Adults choose to engage in physical activity because they find it enjoyable. With increased leisure time, people of all ages are seeking out instructional, recreational, and competitive physical education and sport programs. This interest promises a dynamic future for professionals who want to contribute to the well-being and quality of life of others. The millions who enroll in aerobic dance classes, join fitness clubs, bowl in leagues, hike, camp, swim, jog, climb, sail, walk, skate, and engage in many other activities already have determined that these activities are fun. Many also value the mental, social, and physical development resulting from their regular participation.

Although maintaining a physically active and fit lifestyle is highly esteemed by many, others have not been convinced. Motivating this latter group is the challenge awaiting you when you begin your physical education and sport career.

Aerobic activities are important. (Photo courtesy Lisa Sense.)

The term physical educator is often used to encompass professionals in various careers who teach fitness and skills. This inclusive term is a highly respected one because it describes those individuals who are committed to using physical activities to develop the whole person.

To help you meet this challenge to become an enthusiastic physical educator who can contribute to the wellness of others, this text will introduce you to both the current concepts and objectives in the field of physical education and sport and to the field's rich heritage. Past physical education programs provide the foundation for today's programs in the United States, shaping the way we structure and describe the field. Understanding the definition and objectives of physical education, today and in the past, will help you conceptualize the breadth and depth of this field. Understanding current affective, cognitive, and psychomotor domains of learning will ensure that you know what physical education and sport programs seek to accomplish today.

QUALITY OF LIFE—THE CONTRIBUTION OF PHYSICAL EDUCATION AND SPORT

What does "quality of life" mean? Is it happiness, wellness, health, fitness, or fun? Maybe it refers to leisure time, relief from stress, safety from harm, or the absence of disease. Quality of life, although defined individually, in today's world increasingly means a long and healthy life. Inherent therein is the concept that a feeling of well-being or some level of fitness enhances life. Maybe it is an outgrowth of

Americans' search for the fountain of youth, but seemingly fitness is valued, or at least the appearance of fitness.

Not a fad, this commitment of fitness has become an integral part of life for many. Executives may choose their companies based on the availability of exercise programs, or employers may hire employees only if they are healthy and fit. Families often focus vacations and leisure time around various recreational and sports activities. Thousands of people sign up for marathons, 10-kilometer road races, and fun runs. Walking has become popular for people of all ages. Sporting goods and sports clothing sales continue to gross millions of dollars. Sports facilities, such as health clubs, aerobics centers, tennis courts, swimming pools, and golf courses, increasingly attract people who take both their health and sports seriously.

A number of factors in contemporary life have reemphasized the importance of physical activity. The threat of cardiovascular disease has contributed to a realization of the need to exercise the heart muscle. Poor nutritional habits have adversely affected the health of thousands. Longer life expectancies have raised the consciousness levels of many who not only want to live longer, but who also want to enjoy their later years. Technological advances have reduced the amount of exercise inherent in our daily lives while simultaneously providing greater amounts of leisure time and discretionary income. Stress proliferates as a frequent by-product of technology and a highly competitive business world. In each case, exercise, along with a knowledge of how the body functions in response to activity, can enhance fitness and the overall quality of life.

Millions of people in the United States, however, do not participate in any physical activity because of lack of motivation, time, money, skills, or knowledge. To encourage participation is the role of physical educators. Are you willing to accept responsibility for changing attitudes and developing programs to get the inactive involved? Teachers, can you sell your students on the value of activity? Sports leaders, can you get participants to adhere to, rather than drop out of, their sports programs? How do you activate the lethargic? The future is unlimited for sport educators and physical educators because less than 50% of our population exercises regularly. Many of the inactive are either older adults or children; others are poorly skilled and economically disadvantaged.

Aerobic activities are important for all ages and both genders. (Photo courtesy Lisa Sense.)

The contribution of physical education and sport to the quality of life can be enhanced by balancing participation in team sports and individual sports. Schools, recreation departments, and large corporations offer league competitions in baseball, volleyball, basketball, football, soccer, and softball. Within these settings, team members learn and demonstrate teamwork, cooperation, communication skills, and the ability both to lead and to follow. Team camaraderie may lead to lifelong friendships and the willingness to place the team's benefit above individual goals. Nevertheless, although some of these sports can become ageless pursuits, many individuals discontinue participation because of the lack of sufficient players or because of the physical demands of the sport.

Individual sports are often called lifetime sports because of the greater likelihood of continued participation throughout life. Most of these sports can be engaged in by an individual either alone or with only one other person. Aerobics, bowling, fishing, golf, hiking, jogging, racquetball, swimming, tennis, walking, and weight lifting are the most popular of these sports and activities. They can be engaged in recreationally, or participants can become competitive through leagues, tournaments, and organized events. Individual sports, like team sports, can teach fair play, self-confidence, how to win, and how to lose, as well as specific sports skills.

Typically, school athletic teams and city or business recreational leagues attract skilled participants or those at least moderately comfortable with their skills. Those lacking skills, however, are often relegated to spectator roles or to their easy chairs in front of their televisions, video games, or computers. More instructional programs and beginning level leagues and teams are needed for individuals of all ages. Unfortunately, there is frequently an overlap between the lower skilled and the economically disadvantaged. Because of the cost of tennis, golf, and swimming, for example, these have often been categorized as upper-class sports. Therefore, tax-supported recreation departments need to provide opportunities for these and other activities for all individuals.

Moderate activity often meets both the social and the recreational needs of senior citizens.

An intramural flag football game may include exercise, play, recreation, and sport components. (Photo courtesy Lisa Sense.)

Senior citizens, an increasingly large percentage of the population of the United States, also have recreational needs. For example, exercise has been found to reduce osteoporosis, a breakdown of the calcium in the bones, especially for women in their postmenopausal years. This group needs activities tailored to its capabilities. On the other end of the spectrum, children have many needs for physical activity that remain unanswered. Daily physical education from kindergarten through the twelfth grade would greatly enhance children's movement skills and fitness capacities. Nonschool sport programs also can provide opportunities for fun. For each of these groups, increased fun-filled opportunities for physical activities will contribute to the development of a healthy lifestyle. You, as a coach, recreation leader, personal trainer, or teacher hold the key to unlocking this door of opportunity for them.

WHAT IS PHYSICAL EDUCATION? WHAT IS SPORT?

Physical education and **sport** are allied activities that can overlap, merge, and even disassociate. Are they synonymous with exercise, play, games, leisure, recreation, or athletics? Before physical education can be defined, each of these terms needs to be understood. **Exercise** means to practice, to strengthen, or to condition through physical activity. **Play** refers to amusements engaged in freely, for fun, and devoid of constraints. **Games,** usually implying winners and losers, can range from simple diversions to cooperative activities to competitions with significant outcomes governed by rules. Freedom from work or responsibilities describes **leisure,** which may or may not include physical activity. Similarly, **recreation** refreshes or renews one's strength and spirit after toil, again with or without activity. **Athletics** are organized, highly structured, competitive activities in which skilled individuals participate. The physical activity matrix shown in Figure 1-1 helps differentiate among these similar terms.

Definitions

Sports may be played both for exercise and as a game. Sports participants may use their leisure time to play games recreationally. Some describe bridge and

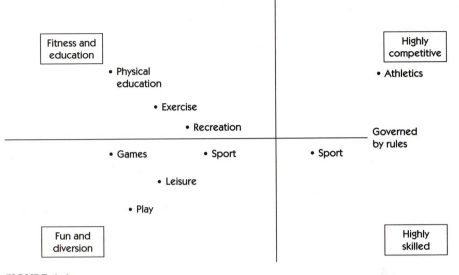

FIGURE 1-1

This matrix shows how various types of physical activity relate to each other and the specified areas of emphasis.

chess games as sports, while others claim that rock climbing, fly fishing, and sky-diving are sports. When the rules governing a sport, who participates, their requisite skill levels, and the significance placed on the outcome are rigidly structured, sport becomes athletics. Usually, sport refers to contests in which the outcome is viewed as important by the players, who will emerge as either winners or losers. Broadly defined, sports are physical activities governed by formal or informal rules that involve competition against an opponent or oneself and are engaged in for fun, recreation, or reward.

Traditionally, the definition of physical education has been restricted to formal instruction in a school or college. Yet, instruction in physical activities also can occur in an aerobics center, a sports club, a corporate fitness program, and a recreational league. In these settings, people learn skills, develop fitness, and commit to enhancing their physical well-being. The National Association for Sport and Physical Education defines the physically educated person as one who (1) has learned skills necessary to perform a variety of physical activities, (2) is physically fit, (3) does participate regularly in physical activity, (4) knows the implications of and the benefits from involvement in physical activities, and (5) values physical activity and its contributions to a healthful lifestyle. To encompass the various outcomes experienced by all people in diverse programs, physical education is defined here as a process through which an individual obtains optimal physical, mental, and social skills and fitness through physical activity. In recent years, many colleges have chosen to rename their departments to use the term kinesiology instead of physical education. **Kinesiology,** the scientific study of human motion, focuses on the art and science of how the body moves. This term encompasses the scientific analysis, teaching, and description of human movement for all ages and skill levels. Researchers are exploring how to maximize the potential of human movement through physiological, biomechanical, and psychological studies. Practitioners are applying these findings to improving the quality of life for all who incorporate physical activity into their lives. Thus, the term *kinesiology* rather than physical education may more broadly define what people know and do relative to human movement.

PURPOSE OF PHYSICAL EDUCATION AND SPORT

What exactly do physical education and sport programs seek to accomplish? A purpose is a stated intention, aim, or goal. Used interchangeably, these terms describe desired long-range achievements that will only occur after many hours of effort and incremental progress. Working to make the dean's list this semester, earning a grant-in-aid based on performance as a walk-on athlete, getting invited into an academic honorary society, and saving money from a part-time job to purchase a car are all examples of goals. As Figure 1-2 illustrates, whether called an aim, a goal, or a purpose, each is achieved by meeting several objectives, such as spending long hours studying or perfecting athletic skills.

Historically, physical educators have been challenged to significantly improve the quality of life of each person taught. Physical education and sport experiences, inside and outside of educational institutions, provide opportunities to teach motor and sports skills and to dynamically affect the physical, psychological, and emotional well-being of others. Physical education and sport programs aim to increase every individual's physical, mental, and social benefits from physical activities and to develop healthy lifestyle skills and attitudes. To help each person make these attitudinal and behavioral changes, the purpose of physical education and sport programs is to optimize quality of life through a long-term commitment to enjoyable physical activity and sport experiences that will meet varied needs in a changing world.

A purpose provides the answer to the question why. Physical education and sport programs must add value to the lives of participants, or they cannot be

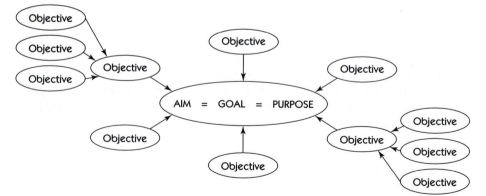

FIGURE 1-2

Relationship among aims, goals, purposes, and objectives. Long-range *aims, goals,* or *purposes* (interchangeable terms) are achieved by attaining short-term and incremental *objectives*. Each objective may be achieved through small steps or sub-objectives as illustrated.

Tennis skills learned at a young age can be used throughout life. (Photo courtesy Lisa Sense.)

justified. A "roll out the ball" physical education class that results in no development of physical fitness or motor skills should be eliminated. A school sports program that fails to teach fair play, cooperation, and self-control cannot be defended. A corporate or community fitness or sport program that is poorly organized, results in injuries and attrition because it is not based on sound physiological principles, and is not fun for the participants is doomed to failure. Conversely, the purpose of physical education and sport programs is to ensure that each person benefits physically, mentally, socially, and emotionally. People who enjoy, for myriad reasons, being active is the reason why these opportunities exist. An improvement in the quality of their lives will be the desired and valued outcome that we can help them achieve.

Physical activity, physical fitness, health, and wellness are components essential to the achievement of the purpose of physical education and sport. **Physical activity** includes all movements that can contribute to improved health. **Physical fitness** is developed through endurance and resistive exercises of sufficient frequency, duration, and intensity to enhance heart and other bodiy functions. **Health** refers to the well-being of body and mind. It also encompasses the absence of disease and illness, such as coronary heart disease, high blood pressure, and depression. **Wellness** includes the mental, emotional, spiritual, nutritional, and physical factors that lead to healthy behaviors. Each of these is vital to everyone's quality of life.

OBJECTIVES OF PHYSICAL EDUCATION AND SPORT PROGRAMS

The objectives of physical education and sport programs are often stated more specifically than the purpose because they consist of particular learning outcomes. Professional colleagues and the general public often learn about physical education's worth through an examination of its objectives and their fulfillment.

Through the years, physical education and sport objectives have increasingly focused on the whole person. Dudley Sargent, a recognized leader in physical education for college students in the late 1800s and early 1900s, suggested that physical education achieved hygienic, educative, recreative, and remedial objectives. Outcomes that he noted in his programs included improved health, fun, reduction of illness and injury, and enhanced knowledge about how the body moved and learned. Clark Hetherington, one of the "new physical educators," helped lead in the transition from exercising methodically to developing the entire person. In 1910, he recommended that physical education programs seek organic, psychomotor, character, and intellectual objectives.

In 1934, the American Physical Education Association's (today's American Alliance for Health, Physical Education, Recreation and Dance) Committee on Objectives listed physical fitness, mental health and efficiency, social-moral character, emotional expression and control, and appreciation as the desired objectives. In 1950, these were restated: to develop and to maintain maximum physical efficiency, to develop useful skills, to conduct oneself in socially useful ways, and to enjoy wholesome recreation. In 1965, the American Association for Health, Physical Education and Recreation stated five major objectives (*This is physical education,* 1965):

1. To help children move in a skillful and effective manner in all the selected activities in which they engage, in the physical education program, and also in those situations that they will experience during their lifetime.
2. To develop an understanding and appreciation of movement in children and youth so that their lives will become more meaningful, purposive, and productive.
3. To develop an understanding and appreciation of certain scientific principles concerned with movement that relate to such factors as time, space, force, and mass-energy relationships.
4. To develop through the medium of games and sports better interpersonal relationships.
5. To develop the various organic systems of the body so they will respond in a healthful way to the increased demands placed on them.

Before examining physical education's objectives in greater detail, it is essential to understand how they relate to those of education.

In 1918, the Educational Policies Commission stated seven objectives of education: health, command of fundamental processes, worthy home membership, vocation, citizenship, worthy use of leisure time, and ethical character. In 1938, these were consolidated into self-realization, human relationship, economic efficiency, and civic responsibility. Through all of these objectives, educational leaders sought to develop the whole child. Justification for any educational program was based on what contributions it could make. Since the 1930s, physical education has verified its value as a school subject by demonstrating its alignment with Benjamin Bloom's domains of learning—cognitive, affective, and psychomotor objectives. Educators, physicians, legislators, and parents have affirmed that physical education and sport programs have helped achieve the educational objectives listed in the box on page 11. The domains of learning encompass mental, physical, and social and emotional components. Physical

EDUCATIONAL OBJECTIVES WHOSE ACHIEVEMENT IS ENHANCED THROUGH PHYSICAL EDUCATION AND SPORT PROGRAMS

Physical
- Reduces risk of coronary heart disease, diabetes, obesity, high blood pressure, and colon cancer
- Improves muscular strength and endurance, flexibility, and cardiovascular endurance
- Regulates weight, tones bodies, and improves body composition
- Promotes overall health and fitness
- Strengthens bones
- Develops movement skills

Mental
- Improves academic performance
- Increases interest in learning
- Improves judgment
- Promotes self-discipline
- Encourages goal setting and achieving these goals

Psychological and Social
- Improves self-confidence, self-esteem, and self-control
- Provides an outlet for stress
- Strengthens peer relationships
- Reduces the risk of depression
- Promotes healthier lifestyles

education and sport programs are unique because they contribute to the all-around person. The psychomotor objective focuses on the development of motor skills and physical fitness. Activities in these programs include an integration of cognitive abilities for optimal learning. Through participation in physical activities, individuals learn to value and appreciate themselves and others, as well as the experiences.

Cognitive Development

Cognitive objectives focus on the acquisition, comprehension, analysis, synthesis, application, and evaluation of knowledge. Minimal preparation in physical education course work includes studying the body's structure and function, health, first aid, history and philosophy, growth and development, organization and administration, motor learning, and exercise physiology. Regardless of the setting, content learned in such courses is essential for teachers to understand and disseminate information and for program participants to comprehend and apply what they have learned.

Increased cognitive involvement usually leads to better execution of a skill and to a better understanding of the activity. In meeting cognitive objectives, physical educators need to explain not only how but especially why the body's movements result in certain outcomes. For example, they can explain why hand position, release technique, and follow-through are critical to the success of throwing a ball. Teachers in all settings need to emphasize learning rules, strategies, skills, safety principles, and proper etiquette. An example of a measurable cognitive learning outcome would be—"a participant will demonstrate knowledge of the rules of tennis by answering at least 15 of 20 questions correctly."

Thus, physical activity often enhances cognitive development. Not only may performance in reading, math, language, and other subjects be enhanced through participation in certain physical activities, but the content of these areas can also be incorporated into activities. In addition, mental fatigue from studying or working can be reduced through exercise, so that a subsequent classroom session or job task is more productive. Stress can impede cognitive processes, but activity can reduce stress and enhance productivity.

Affective Development

Affective objectives emphasize the development of attitudes, appreciations, and values; this domain contains both social and emotional dimensions. In the social realm, both individual and group needs are met while positive characteristics are developed. Learning self-confidence, courtesy, fair play, sportsmanship, and how to make value judgments through cooperative activities benefits all students. In team sports, decision-making abilities, communication skills, and affiliation needs are enhanced, as long as the outcome of the event is not overem-

Jogging to develop and maintain cardiovascular endurance has become an important part of the lifestyle adopted by many Americans.

phasized. Individuals' values and attitudes toward involvement in physical activity are solidified, as are appreciations for participation and performance when the achievement of realistic personal goals is paramount. On the emotional side, self-discipline, fun, learning how to win and how to lose, tension release, self-control, and self-expression are enhanced through the give-and-take of challenging oneself and competing with and against others. An example of an affective learning outcome would be "students take turns tossing balls to classmates in such a way that the classmate can catch at least 8 out of 10."

Physical Fitness and Motor Skill Development

Movement undergirds all physical education and sport programs that seek to achieve the objectives of physical fitness and motor skill development. Although any person can learn the fundamental movement skills, children learn more easily because they do not have to break habitual inefficient motor patterns. Also, if the basic locomotor, manipulative, and perceptual-motor skills are learned early, they provide the foundation for lifelong enjoyment of physical activity.

Movement concepts include body awareness; spatial awareness including space, direction, level, and pathways; qualities of movement such as time, force, and flow; and relationships with objects and with people. Walking, running, jumping, leaping, and sliding are some of the basic locomotor movements; conversely, stretching, twisting, pushing, lifting, and swinging are nonlocomotor movements. Manipulative skills, involving propelling or absorbing force from an object, include throwing, catching, striking, and kicking.

Developing and improving fundamental movement skills and game skills are important objectives, since sport, aquatic, and dance skills begin with learning basic and efficient movement patterns. Children need to explore their bodies' capabilities as they learn to walk, run, or jump independently, in conjunction with others, or by using apparatus. Similar principles can apply as individuals

Physical education helps children develop fitness and psychomotor skills as they learn to enjoy activity. (Photo courtesy Gid Alston.)

experiment with solving other movement challenges. Manipulative skills are developed by exploring the potential of hoops, ropes, balls, rackets, bats, and other implements. Perceptual-motor skills, such as the eye-hand coordination needed to strike a ball with a racket or the reaction time needed to judge how quickly a partner's thrown ball will arrive, are also important skills. Once these abilities are mastered independently and in combination at each person's developmental level, then game skills, such as catching, throwing, and batting, can be incorporated into lead-up games and sport situations. An example of a motor skill development learning outcome would be—"the participant will use the proper technique in successfully executing at least 7 out of 10 dominant-hand basketball lay-ups."

Physical fitness includes cardiovascular endurance, muscular strength and endurance, flexibility, and body composition. The ability to sustain physical activity that requires oxygen for exertion indicates cardiovascular endurance, the most essential component of physical fitness. Similarly, the ability to exert and sustain maximal force against a resistance constitutes muscular strength and endurance. Flexibility gained by statically stretching the muscles improves the range of

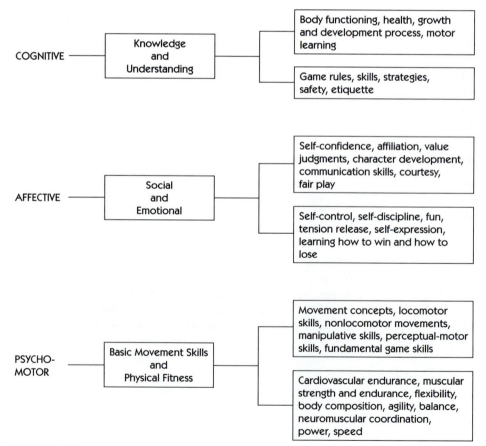

FIGURE 1-3

Objectives of physical education and sport.

motion in the joints. Body composition relative to physical fitness refers to the percentage of fat in the body. Caloric expenditure through exercise helps regulate body fat. Agility, balance, neuromuscular coordination, speed, and power also contribute to physical fitness. Agility permits quick changes in direction during activity. A person's balance, or state of equilibrium, stabilizes the body in preparation for future movements or actions. Neuromuscular coordination, including reaction time, integrates the senses with motor function. Speed permits rapid execution of a movement, while power combines speed with muscular strength.

Figure 1-3 summarizes the objectives of physical education and sport. It is essential to recognize that these objectives interrelate rather than exist in isolation. For example, while learning to hit a tennis ball, people not only enhance their eye-hand coordination but also learn proper body position for a level swing and cooperation with those with whom they take turns tossing the ball. The box on p. 16 provides several examples of how the objectives of physical education and sport are achieved and interrelated.

FIELDS ALLIED WITH PHYSICAL EDUCATION AND SPORT

Health, recreation, and dance traditionally have been allied in purpose with physical education and sport, although their programs differ somewhat in emphasis. Coaching, another allied field, often is a combined career with teaching physical education in the schools. Today, personal trainers, athletic trainers, sport managers, sport psychologists, exercise physiologists, and others help achieve the purpose and objectives of physical education and sport programs.

Health

Many of the early school and college physical education programs in the 1800s emphasized health benefits as their primary justifications. For example, at Amherst College, beginning in the 1860s, the president supported a physical education program to help students become and stay healthy. As was the case with many other institutions, the person charged with directing this program was a physician. In the twentieth century, the dual role of the health-physical educator divided as colleges prepared physical education teachers for jobs that focused on teaching physical activities, especially in alignment with educational objectives rather than health objectives. In 1937, health was added to the title of today's American Alliance for Health, Physical Education, Recreation and Dance, to emphasize the importance of health within the educational system. Since then, health has struggled for its own identity as a field of study. Because health and physical education programs share the goal of good health, and because school health classes are often assigned to physical educators (who at best have minimal academic preparation in this field), acceptance of health as a separate discipline has been gradual.

Although the disciplines of health and physical education share some content and objectives, each also seeks to achieve unique outcomes. Physical activity and sports participation contribute to fitness and overall well-being. Health, in

EXAMPLES OF PHYSICAL EDUCATION AND SPORT OBJECTIVES

Cognitive Development

- The participant will explain the principles for playing zone defense in basketball.
- The participant will analyze the technique for executing a flat tennis serve.
- The participant, using the entire stroke (whole teaching method), will synthesize the principles of learning the crawl stroke in swimming.
- The participant will apply knowledge of cardiovascular functioning in establishing a personal exercise program.
- The participant will evaluate another person's weight-lifting technique and provide corrective feedback.

Affective Development

- The participant will express appreciation for the excellence of an opponent's high-level performance.
- The participant will enjoy playing hard and doing his or her best, regardless of the outcome of the contest.
- The participant will cooperate and take turns with others.
- The participant will demonstrate fair play in unsupervised activities.
- The participant will value the rights of others and the regulations governing the situation.

Physical Fitness and Motor Skill Development

- The participant will improve eye-hand coordination by weekly practicing racquetball forehand and backhand shots.
- The participant will explore ways to manipulate a ball without using the hands.
- The participant will design and perform a one-minute dance that includes use of two locomotor movements and two objects.
- The participant will demonstrate the proper technique for executing a volleyball spike.
- The participant will execute four exercises designed to improve flexibility of the shoulders.

addition to being the traditional absence of disease, also encompasses soundness of body, mind, and spirit. School health curricula include the study of nutrition, mental and emotional health, avoidance of the abuses of tobacco, alcohol, and other drugs, and human sexuality. Community and corporate health programs focus on disease prevention, smoking cessation, safety and first aid, child care, weight loss and control, and stress management.

Knowledge of health and a personal application of its concepts may determine whether life's goals can be successfully achieved. Most of America's children and their parents do not exercise regularly. However, the popularity of the healthy-looking figure or physique has led some to join fitness clubs, to dress in active wear accenting fitness, and to enjoy the social atmosphere of a health club or road race. While more upper-class adults have joined health clubs and changed their inactive lifestyles, the economically disadvantaged lack the money and leisure time for club memberships and sports equipment. Corporations have

Soccer helps develop many of the components of physical fitness. (Photo courtesy Lisa Sense.)

encouraged their employees to exercise regularly by providing equipment, trained personnel, and incentives, often to try to contain escalating health care costs.

Hypokinetic disease refers to those diseases and health problems associated with physical inactivity and a sedentary lifestyle. Coronary heart disease, high blood pressure, stress, ulcers, obesity, and low back pain often affect individuals who fail to engage in regular exercise. When school, work, and family place few physical demands on our bodies, these degenerative diseases may develop. Health education and physical activity can help alter or deter the disease process.

In 1992, the American Heart Association identified physical inactivity (along with high blood pressure and high cholesterol) as a primary risk factor for coronary heart disease. Maybe now thousands more will realize that participating in regular physical activity and exercise is essential.

Recreation

Recreation, a diversion that occurs during leisure hours, renews and refreshes one's strength and spirits after work. In 1938, recreation was included in the title and structure of the national professional organization, joining physical education and health. This change reflected the important role of recreational activities for people of all ages. Schools, businesses, communities, and families have increasingly offered activities for fitness and pleasure as each of these groups accepts some responsibility for educating for leisure. Businesses provide work-site fitness centers, sponsor sports teams, and offer a variety of fitness activities for employees and their families. The popularity of home fitness programs and equipment illustrates how some adults have decided to use personal resources to develop and maintain fitness.

The recreation services industry is growing rapidly in the United States because of increased leisure time and larger discretionary incomes. Also, as the American population ages, more and more retired persons are seeking appropriate recreational outlets. No longer can municipal recreation departments fulfill their missions simply by sponsoring youth leagues in the traditional team sports. Americans also want adult competitive leagues, instructional clinics, open facilities for family outings, organized trips and moderate exercise programs for seniors, and child care so that a parent can recreate. Environmental concerns have led many people to expect resource management by state and national authorities so that the beauty of nature and access to it will not be impaired for outdoor recreators. Schools and colleges have expanded their curricula to include the lifetime activities of backpacking, canoeing, rock climbing, and downhill skiing. Thus, a

Rafting has become a popular recreational activity. (Photo courtesy Terry Dash.)

Lifetime recreational activities such as rock climbing are now part of some school/college curricula. (Photo courtesy Aram Attarian.)

similarity of outcomes of physical education, sport, and recreation programs is evident.

Dance

Bodily movements of a rhythmical and patterned succession usually executed to the accompaniment of music constitute **dance.** Both as physical activity and as performing art, dance varieties include aerobic, ballet, ballroom, folk, clogging, jazz, modern, square, and tap. Dance can provide participants opportunities for aesthetic expression whether in a beginner's class or on stage. People of all ages can dance for fitness and for fun. Although dance was for many years a vital component of school and college programs, it was not until 1979 that dance officially became a part of the title of the American Alliance for Health, Physical Education, Recreation and Dance. Some schools and most colleges have dance specialists, yet many dance classes are taught by physical educators who sometimes have had minimal preparation in this field.

IMPORTANCE OF PHYSICAL ACTIVITY

In 1985, only 12% of people 18 and older engaged in enough vigorous physical activity to promote cardiovascular fitness. In the mid-1980s, only 36% of school children participated in daily physical education. Nearly a quarter of American adults in 1985 engaged in no leisure-time physical activity; many of these live in families whose annual family income is less than $20,000, and some are individuals with disabilities. Approximately 30% of adult American women and 25% of adult American men are overweight. By age 18, most students will have spent more hours watching television than they will have been in classes.

Daily physical education leads to skill development so that individuals can play at high skill levels as adults. (Photo courtesy Lisa Sense.)

HEALTHY PEOPLE 2000

Objective 1.1
Reduce coronary heart disease to more than 100 per 100,000 people.
> Baseline in 1987: 135 per 100,000

Objective 1.2
Reduce overweight condition to a prevalence of no more than 20% among people aged 20 and older and no more than 15% among adolescents aged 12–19.
> Baseline in 1976: 26% for people 20–74; 15% for adolescents 12–19

Objective 1.3
Increase to at least 30% the proportion of people 6 and older who engage regularly, preferably daily, in light to moderate physical activity for at least 30 minutes per day.
> Baseline in 1985: 22% of people 18 and older were active for at least 30 minutes 5 or more times per week.

Objective 1.4
Increase to at least 20% the proportion of people 18 and older and to at least 75% the proportion of children and adolescents 6–17 who engage in vigorous physical activity that promotes the development and maintenance of cardiorespiratory fitness 3 or more days per week for 20 or more minutes per occasion.
> Baseline in 1985: 12% for people 18 and older; 1984: 66% for youth 10–17

Objective 1.5
Reduce to no more than 15% the proportion of people 6 and older who engage in no leisure-time physical activity.
> Baseline in 1985: 24% for people 18 and older

Objective 1.6
Increase to at least 40% the proportion of people 6 and older who regularly perform physical activities that enhance and maintain muscular strength, muscular endurance, and flexibility.
> No baseline data

Objective 1.7
Increase to at least 50% the proportion of overweight people 12 and older who have adopted sound dietary practices combined with regular physical activity to attain an appropriate body weight. Baseline in 1985: 30% of females and 25% of males 18 and older are overweight.

Healthy People 2000: The National Health Promotion and Disease Prevention Objectives, published by the federal government in 1990, reports these disturbing statistics and proposes a national plan to improve the health of all Americans. One of its three principal goals is to increase the span of healthy lives of Americans, and seven of its objectives specifically address physical activity and fitness.

HEALTHY PEOPLE 2000 (CONTINUED)

Objective 1.8

Increase to at least 50% the proportion of children and adolescents in grades 1–12 who participate in daily school physical education.

Baseline in 1984–86: 36%

Objective 1.9

Increase to at least 50% the proportion of school physical education class time that students spend being physically active, preferably engaged in lifetime physical activities.

Baseline in 1983: estimated 27% of class time being physically active

Objective 1.10

Increase the proportion of work sites offering employer-sponsored physical activity and fitness programs:

target for 50–99 employees is 20%	Baseline in 1985:14%
target for 100–249 employees is 35%	Baseline in 1985: 23%
target for 250–749 employees is 50%	Baseline in 1985: 32%
target for 750 employees is 80%	Baseline in 1985: 54%

Objective 1.11

Increase community availability and accessibility of physical activity and fitness facilities: 1 per 10,000 for hiking, biking, and fitness trail miles; 1 per 25,000 for public swimming pools; 4 per 1,000 people for acres of park and recreation open space.

Baseline in 1986:   1 per 71,000 people for trails
1 per 53,000 people for pools
1.8 per 1,000 people for open space

Objective 1.12

Increase to at least 50% the proportion of primary care providers who routinely assess and counsel their patients regarding the frequency, duration, type, and intensity of each patient's physical activity practices.

Baseline in 1988: Physicians provided exercise counseling for about 30% of sedentary patients.

Healthy People 2000: The National Health Promotion and Disease Prevention Objectives, Washington, D.C., 1990, U.S. Government.

In particular, the *Healthy People 2000* goals listed in the box on pages 20–21 are important guidelines which physical educators and sports leaders can help achieve. By teaching, coaching, conducting research, and helping individuals develop personal exercise programs, people in our field can improve the health and well-being of millions.

In 1996, the first ever *Surgeon General's Report on Physical Activity and Health* emphasized that Americans can substantially improve their health and the quality of their lives by participating in regular physical activity. Despite the *Healthy People 2000* goals, the patterns and trends in physical activity reported in the *Surgeon General's Report* indicate little progress and even some decreases in activity. A few of these low participation levels include:

1. Approximately 15% of adults and about 50% of individuals 12–21 years old in this country engage in vigorous physical activity at least three times a week for at least 20 minutes.
2. Approximately 22% of adults in this country engage in sustained physical activity at least five times a week for at least 30 minutes.
3. About 25% of adults and 25% of individuals 12–21 years old in this country engage in no physical activity.
4. Daily attendance in high school physical education classes between 1991 and 1995 declined from approximately 42% to 25%.

These data verify the significant challenge facing physical educators and leaders in sport.

As the *Surgeon General's Report on Physical Activity and Health* concludes, people of all ages and both genders can benefit from regular physical activity. Significant health benefits can be obtained by including a moderate amount of physical activity. Significant health benefits can be obtained by including a moderate amount of physical activity on most, if not all, days of the week. Regular physical activity improves health by reducing the risk of dying prematurely, dying from heart disease, developing diabetes, developing high blood pressure, and developing colon cancer. Daily, moderate physical activity helps reduce blood pressure in people who already have high blood pressure, reduces feelings of depression and anxiety, helps control weight, helps older adults become stronger and better able to move about without falling, and promotes psychological well-being.

Physical activity has numerous beneficial physiologic effects on the cardiovascular and musculoskeletal systems, but also benefits the metabolic, endocrine,

Individuals of all ages are seeking to achieve the healthy benefits of physical activity. (Photo courtesy Lisa Sense.)

and immune systems. Maintaining normal muscle strength, joint structure, and joint function only occurs when activity is sustained. Many of the beneficial effects of endurance and resistance activities diminish within two weeks if physical activity is substantially reduced, and effects disappear within two to eight months if physical activity is not resumed. Thus, the health benefits can only be enjoyed if physical activity becomes a regular part of a person's life.

SUMMARY

Physical education and sport programs exist to improve the quality of life and the physical well-being of participants. People of all ages enjoy playing games, engaging in recreational activities, and exercising to maintain good health. Competitive, rule-bound sports provide opportunities to test one's skills against opponents. Through all of these, the all-around development of the individual is enhanced during activity. The purpose of these programs is to optimize quality of life through enjoyable physical activity and sport experiences. Educational objectives through cognitive, affective, and physical fitness and motor skill development are sought and achieved. Several of these objectives are shared with the allied fields of health, recreation, and dance. A significant challenge facing physical education and sport professionals is to help all Americans participate in regular physical activity so they can enjoy the associated health benefits.

CAREER PERSPECTIVES

RICH CENDALI
Physical Education Specialist
Boulder Valley Public Schools
Boulder, Colorado

EDUCATION
A.A., Recreation Administration, San Diego City College
B.S., Physical Education, University of Colorado
M.S., Physical Education and Administration, University of Colorado

JOB RESPONSIBILITIES AND HOURS

Rich teaches physical education to children in kindergarten through the fifth grade. He also teaches first aid classes throughout the district and serves on his school's academic accountability committee. Typical hours for him are 8:00 A.M. to 4:00 P.M. daily.

SPECIALIZED COURSE WORK, DEGREES, AND WORK EXPERIENCES NEEDED FOR THIS CAREER

The collegiate courses most valuable to Rich in his career have been movement education, methods of teaching, and curriculum development, which included new motivational ideas in physical education. Colorado, like other states, requires that all teachers have a state teaching certificate. Colorado also mandates that teachers take a state history course and complete student teaching, if a teaching certificate has been earned in another state. Rich believes that prior experiences in athletics and sports demonstrate a love of various physical activities that is helpful for anyone in this field.

SATISFYING ASPECTS

Rich states that working with kids and having the opportunity to make a difference in children's lives is the reason he chose to become a physical education specialist.

JOB POTENTIAL

Career advancement opportunities within the schools are somewhat limited. But, the experienced teacher can earn steady salary increases. In his district, teachers begin at $24,500 with a baccalaureate degree and can progress beyond $50,000 if they earn a doctorate.

SUGGESTIONS FOR STUDENTS

Rich stresses that if you love working with kids, you truly enjoy teaching. However, if you do not like kids, stay out of teaching.

REVIEW QUESTIONS

1. How can physical education and sport contribute to the improvement of one's quality of life?
2. How do physical education and sport relate to athletics, leisure, and play?
3. What is the relationship and difference between sport and physical education?
4. How do physical education and sport objectives relate to general educational objectives?
5. What types of knowledge are important within the cognitive domain of physical education and sport? Give examples of each.
6. How are the social and emotional outcomes of the affective objective achieved in physical education and sport programs?
7. What are the nine components of physical fitness?
8. What is hypokinetic disease, and how can it be prevented or reduced?
9. How do health, recreation, and dance relate to physical education?
10. What is the primary conclusion of the *Surgeon General's Report on Physical Activity and Health?*

STUDENT ACTIVITIES

1. Interview three individuals of differing ages (for example, below 18, in their 30s, and over 60) to determine what role physical activity plays in their lives.
2. Ask at least two friends who are not majors in your field what they think physical education and sport are.
3. Write a one- or two-page description of how you would incorporate three movement concepts or skills into a youth soccer program.

4. Write a one-page summary of how the three domains of physical education and sport objectives have influenced your life and career choice.
5. In groups of three to five students, develop several strategies that would effectively change the physical activity patterns of children, teenagers, and adults. Present two-minute reports to the class.

REFERENCES

This is physical education, Washington, D.C., 1965, American Association for Health, Physical Education and Recreation.

Healthy people 2000: the national health promotion and disease prevention objectives, Washington, D.C., 1990, U.S. Government.

The Surgeon General's report on physical activity and health, Washington, D.C., 1996, U.S. Government.

SUGGESTED READINGS

Allensworth D: Cardiovascular objectives for youth in *Healthy people 2000: update on the status of risk factors, J of Health Ed* 27, Supplement: S-17, 1996. This article provides the latest data on the health status or risk reduction objectives for children and youth. Of the fourteen objectives reported on, only one has been met.

Corbin CB, Pangrazi RP: How much physical activity is enough?, *JOPERD* 67(4):33, 1996. It is recommended that the inactive need some physical activity; beginners need to start slowly and then progress; adults need at least 30 minutes of moderate intensity physical activity most days; some vigorous activity is recommended; implementing the FIT formula (frequency, intensity, and time) helps to achieve and maintain high levels of physical fitness and weight control; and, some weekly activity designed to build muscular strength and endurance and flexibility is encouraged.

Fernandez-Balboa J-M, Barrett K, Solomon M, Silverman S: Perspectives on content knowledge in physical education, *JOPERD* 67(9):54, 1996. The authors described the pragmatic, cognitive, constructivist, and critical perspective on content knowledge in physical education.

Foret CM, Clemens JM: The elderly's need for physical activity, *JOPERD* 67(4):57, 1996. Based on their entry-level health status, seniors need to participate in properly administered exercise programs that help them improve their functional capacity.

Gill DL (ed.): Quality of life: through movement, health, and fitness, *Quest* 48:245, 1996. This issue contains 14 papers presented at the 1995 meeting of the American Academy of Kinesiology and Physical Education. All of these papers focused on quality of life through movement, health, and fitness.

Haskell WL: Physical activity, sport, and health: toward the next century, *Res Q* 67 Supplement to No. 3: S-37, 1996. The need to promote a physically-active lifestyle has become more critical because of the impact of new technology on work and leisure time and the general aging of the population. The author recommends seven strategies for enhancing health.

Kimiecik JC (ed): A practitioner's guide to exercise motivation, *JOPERD* 62(7):33, 1991. Three articles, on children, adults, and older adults, stress how to encourage all ages to increase and persist in their physical activity.

Newell KM: Kinesiology: the label for the study of physical activity in higher education, *Quest* 42:269, 1990. The author defines kinesiology as the study of movement or physical activity. It is argued that this term should be acceptable to those favoring the disciplinary, professional, and activity dimensions of this field.

Pangrazi RP, Corbin CB, Welk GJ: Physical activity for children and youth, *JOPERD* 67(4):38, 1996. Children should be encouraged to participate in sporadic, high volume, moderate-intensity physical activities. These should be individualized and enjoyable so that youth learn behavioral skills that lead to lifetime activity.

Physical Activity, Health, and Well-Being—An International Scientific Consensus Conference, *Res Q* 66:268, 1995. This special issue published the papers of the eight scientists who were invited to review the current specialist knowledge in their fields at this 1995 conference.

CHAPTER 2

Philosophy and Physical Education and Sport

KEY CONCEPTS

- Philosophy is the pursuit of truth and the resultant knowledge and values.
- Idealism, realism, pragmatism, naturalism, and existentialism have influenced the growth of physical education.
- Ethics is a branch of philosophy that deals with moral values.
- The practical application of philosophical theories will help you develop a personal philosophy of physical education and sport.
- Philosophy, though often misunderstood and neglected, can provide focus, a communication bond, a clarity of vision and direction, and an opportunity to analyze the present to expand one's horizons for the future.

The pursuit of truth is as pervasive today as it was during the development of diverse philosophies in the past. This chapter examines the importance of philosophy by focusing on five of the traditional philosophies, with emphasis on how they have influenced physical education and sport. Other philosophies are discussed because of their impact on today's programs. Based on the knowledge gained from this study, you are encouraged to develop a personal philosophy of physical education and sport.

WHY STUDY PHILOSOPHY?

Philosophy can be defined as a love of wisdom or more broadly as the pursuit of truth. Philosophy is both the developmental process and the resultant factors, theories, and values. Philosophy is an attempt to understand the meaning of life by analyzing and synthesizing why; simply having a purpose and objectives, as discussed in Chapter 1, is not sufficient. You must know why these are of value both to you and to others, and you need to be able to articulate their importance.

What is the worth of physical education to a school child? What is the value of learning a lifetime sport? What constitutes a healthy lifestyle? What is the role of play? These are just a few of the questions that your philosophy can help answer.

Developing a personal philosophy can improve teaching effectiveness, influence your behavior, provide direction in program development, contribute to society's awareness of the value of physical activity, and encourage a feeling of commonality among co-workers. How, you might ask, could a personal philosophy help accomplish all these? When you determine what goals you want your students or those with whom you work to attain, it will influence what you include in your curriculum or program and how you proceed. For example, if you value the development of physical fitness for your students, you will emphasize content and activities that can contribute to improving their fitness levels. Conversely, if you prioritize the development of movement and sport skills, then you will focus on instructing and having students practice these skills. Another example of how a personal philosophy influences what is accomplished would be to consider whether you will emphasize fair play as a coach. If you believe in playing by the rules and living ethically, you can serve as a positive role model for your students, athletes, and co-workers.

The discussion of the traditional philosophies that follows will challenge your thinking as you decide what you value and how to formulate your personal philosophy. By articulating what you believe in and what is important, you are laying the foundation for your personal philosophy.

FIVE TRADITIONAL PHILOSOPHIES

Idealism, realism, pragmatism, naturalism, and existentialism provide the foundation for educational philosophy, including that of physical education. These five traditional philosophies are defined in the box on page 31 A brief overview of the basic tenets of each philosophy and their application to physical education is provided. Table 2-1 generally delineates these five philosophies, and Table 2-2 applies the tenets of these philosophies to physical education and sport. The box on page 37 further clarifies specific characteristics of each philosophy. To assess your understanding of the five traditional philosophies, after you have studied them, take the philosophy quiz in the box on page 38.

Idealism

Idealism centers on the mind as critical to understanding, since only through reasoning and mental processes can truth emerge. Never-changing ideals, not things, constitute the ultimate reality. Idealists since the Greek philosopher Plato have stressed that only the reflective and intuitive individual can arrive at truth.

Ideals, virtues, and truths are universal and external and remain the same regardless of how individual interpretations may vary. As people develop and exercise their free will, they make choices through their intellectual powers. These decisions, whether right or wrong, do not alter the values important to the idealist.

TABLE 2-1

FIVE TRADITIONAL PHILOSOPHIES

	Idealism	Realism	Pragmatism	Naturalism	Existentialism
Source of Truth	Ideas	Scientific reality	Human experiences	Nature	Human existence
Most Important	People	Physical world	Society	Individual	Individual
How to Arrive at Truth	Reasoning and intuition	Scientific method	Experiencing changes	Laws of nature	Individual determination
Importance of the Mind	Emphasized	Reasoning powers and scientific method used	Learning by inquiring, observing, and participating	Physical and mental balance for whole person	The individual's determination of the subject matter and the learning method
Importance of the Body	Simultaneous development with mind	Emphasis on the whole individual	Variety of activities for effective functioning in society	Physical activity essential for optimal learning	Freedom to choose activity and to be creative
Curriculum Focus	Teacher centered through examples for students; qualitative	Subject centered; quantitative	Student centered; based on individual differences	Individual readiness to learn	Individual centered; based on self-realization
Importance of the Teacher	A model and example	Orderly presentation of facts; drills and scientific method used	Motivator, especially through problem solving	Guide and helper	Stimulator and counselor
Importance of the Personality	Moral and spiritual values stressed	Learn for life adjustment	Development of social skills and meeting one's needs	Development of social skills important	Learning self-responsibility and knowing oneself
Education	Self-development	To meet realities of life	For social efficiency	Natural process	Teaching acceptance of individual responsibility

TABLE 2-2
APPLICATION OF FIVE PHILOSOPHIES TO PHYSICAL EDUCATION AND SPORT

	Idealism	Realism	Pragmatism	Naturalism	Existentialism
Objectives	Development of personality and mind	Training students to meet realities of life	Helping students to become better-functioning members of society	Development of whole person	Assisting students to become self-actualizing, independent beings
Subject Matter	Utmost importance	Required; the focus of learning	Experiences in a wide variety of activities	Play; self-directed individual activity	Wide selection of alternatives, especially individual activities
Methodology	Lecture; question-answer; discussions	Use of real world; drills, lectures, and projects	Problem solving	Informal; problem solving	Questions raised, thoughts provoked, and freedom of action encouraged by the teacher
Teacher's Role	More important than process	Selects knowledge to learn	Guide	Guide; nature teaches	Guide
Student's Role	Development of total person	Emphasizes the whole individual	Focus of the program to learn about moral self	Individualized rate of learning	Focus of the program for self-realization
Evaluation	Subjective; qualitative	Quantitative; use of scientific means	Subjective and self-evaluation	Based on attainment of individual goals	Unimportant in the traditional sense
Weaknesses	Resistance to change; development of the physical secondary to the mind	Too narrow a view; everything must conform to natural laws or it is wrong	Lack of fixed aims to give students stability and direction	Too simple an education for the complex world	Overemphasis on individuality precludes preparation for social life

FIVE TRADITIONAL PHILOSOPHIES THAT HAVE INFLUENCED THE DEVELOPMENT OF PHYSICAL EDUCATION AND SPORT

Idealism—A philosophical theory advocating that reality depends on the mind for existence and that truth is universal and absolute.

Realism—The philosophical system stressing that the laws and order of the world as revealed by science are independent from human experience.

Pragmatism—An American movement in philosophy emphasizing reality as the sum total of each individual's experiences through practical experimentation.

Naturalism—A belief that the scientific laws of nature govern life and that individual goals are more important than societal goals.

Existentialism—A twentieth-century philosophy that centers on individual existence and advocates that truth and values are arrived at by each person's experiences.

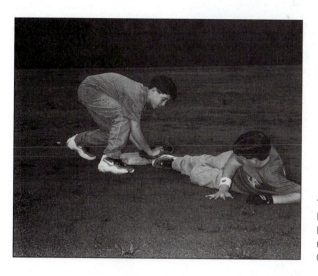

The mental side of sports, such as knowing when and how to slide or how to apply the tag to a sliding runner, is valued by the idealist. (Photo courtesy Bob Hilliard.)

The development of the total person is the objective of idealism as applied to physical education. The individual is important and should be nurtured through an emphasis on the mind and its thought processes. Because reality is mental rather than physical, sometimes physical activity is relegated to a secondary status, even though the mind and the body are supposed to be developed simultaneously.

Since the curriculum focuses on ideas, teachers, who are more important than the process, are free to use any methods that would help students achieve their optimal levels of personality and character development. Outcomes of the affective domain, such as creativity and fair play, are also values upon which idealism places emphasis.

Relative to physical education and sport, the idealist emphasizes that students, athletes, and others engaged in physical activity learn how and why any skill or movement is important and how it is executed. The idealist stresses that while there is one correct way to perform an overhead shot in tennis or to putt a

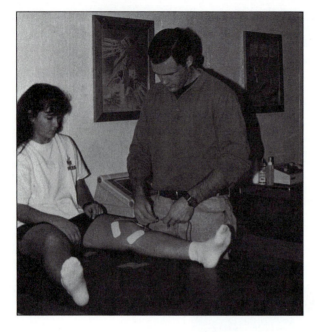

Realism advocates using the scientific method such as through the use of electrical stimulation for the rehabilitation of injuries. (Photo courtesy Bob Hilliard.)

golf ball, it is important that the participant understands why this is the proper technique. The teacher will model how to execute a specific movement and through questions and answers ensure that the person being taught conceptualizes how to complete the skill.

Realism

As a revolt against some of the tenets of idealism, the Greek philosopher Aristotle and today's advocates of realism state that the laws of nature, rather than existing truths, are in control. The scientific method provides the realist with the process for acquiring and applying truth (i.e., the knowledge that originates in the physical world but emerges through experimentation). Scientific investigation examines the material things of the world when seeking truth.

The role of education, according to the realist, is to train the student to discover and to interpret the real things in life (i.e., things that can be shown by the scientific method) to ensure adjustment of the individual in the real world. Since the emphasis is on the whole individual, physical education, including the traditional objectives of organic fitness, neuromuscular development, intellectual ability, and social and emotional development, has a vital contribution to make.

Inductive reasoning (see box on page 33), an orderly progression in learning, extensive use of drills, and objective evaluation are important methodologies used by the realist teacher. Learning is subject centered, rather than teacher centered, as is true for the idealist. The curriculum includes activities and experiences that enable students to understand the laws of the physical world.

Relative to physical education and sport, the realist does not assume that physical fitness is developed just because this is a curricular focus. Rather, the realist administers fitness tests to verify that an increase in fitness parameters such

INDUCTIVE AND DEDUCTIVE REASONING

Inductive reasoning derives general principles from particular facts. For example, it is a fact that individuals can throw a ball farther with the foot on the opposite side as the throwing hand in front of the body. It is a fact that individuals can throw a ball farther when they transfer most of their weight onto the forward foot. Thus, opposition and weight transfer are important principles of proper throwing technique. Conversely, deductive reasoning infers a conclusion by moving from the general to the specific. For example, if a tennis player repeatedly hits the ball into the net due to a closed racket face or beyond the baseline due to an open racket face, through deductive reasoning it can be concluded that the angle of the racket head at the point of contact with the ball contributes to the place to which the ball is hit.

as cardiovascular endurance or flexibility has occurred. The realist presents factual information, such as how to execute a forearm pass in volleyball, uses a variety of drills so that all students can progress naturally in learning how to do this skill, and administers an objective test to assess skill development.

Pragmatism

Pragmatism states that experiences, not ideals and realities, provide the key to seeking truth. Ultimate reality must be experienced and is not absolute. Circumstances and situations constantly vary from person to person; thus, pragmatism is characterized as dynamic and ever changing.

In seeking knowledge, the pragmatist looks for truth that works in a given situation. If it does, then it is true at that moment. Truth is a function of the consequences of the time and even the social context and is considered good if successful. Values are also relative and result from judgments about one's experiences as long as they are evaluated in terms of the good of the group, not selfishly. Pragmatists emphasize social responsibilities, since it is essential that every individual functions within and contributes to society.

The overall objective of a pragmatic education is the development of social efficiency in students, according to the most famous American pragmatist, John Dewey. That is, students need to have opportunities to experience solving the problems of life and to learn how to become better-functioning members of society. Through the use of problem solving, the teacher focuses on the needs and interests of the students. This student-centered curriculum encourages students to apply the scientific method and to experience a wide variety of activities. Team sports stress cooperation and the development of interpersonal skills, and movement activities provide opportunities for exploring numerous solutions to problems.

Relative to physical education and sport, the pragmatist loves to play sports and experience physical activities, especially with others. Pragmatists enjoy developing their social skills through sports and activities because these interpersonal skills can help them in other situations in life. Self-pacing and self-evaluation activities, such as developing and implementing a personal weight training program, lead to achieving the pragmatic goal of improved health and fitness.

Participation in a variety of activities, such as a combination of roller skating and frisbee, can help individuals function more effectively in society, according to pragmatists. (Photo courtesy Pamela G. Royal.)

A natural setting provides an excellent learning environment for developing social, intellectual, and physical skills. (Photo courtesy Aram Attarian.)

Naturalism

The naturalist believes in things that exist within the physical realm of nature, which is itself the source of value. Since naturalism emphasizes the individual more than society, education focuses on meeting each student's needs.

Stressing "everything according to nature," eighteenth-century philosopher Jean-Jacques Rousseau led in espousing this oldest known philosophy of the Western world. He advocated that education must use the physical world as the classroom and that teachers by example should guide students through inductive reasoning to draw their own conclusions. The laws of nature dictate to the teacher and to the student the logical pattern of growth, development, and learning. Rousseau also encouraged education of the mind and body simultaneously. Physical well-being should then enhance a readiness to learn mental, moral, and social skills.

Naturalism also declares the importance of individualized learning through self-education and self-activity. Exploration of one's capabilities and interests leads directly to greater skills and adjustments to nature. Noncompetitive team, individual, and outdoor activities provide play opportunities that benefit students physically, psychologically, and, especially, socially. Through physical activities, the individual develops in an all-around way.

Relative to physical education and sport, the naturalist prefers to use nature as the teacher, such as learning about preserving the environment while backpacking and learning about marine biology while scuba diving. The naturalist encourages students to explore how to execute a locomotor movement like jumping or to discover through trial and error the most effective technique for catching a ball. Through problem solving, individuals progress at their own rates to learn how to do a forward roll or to hit a ball tossed to them. The naturalist in physical education uses the principles of movement education and individualized instruction.

Existentialism

According to existentialism, human experiences determine reality. Emerging in the 1900s as a reaction against societal conformity, this philosophy subjugated everything to the individual as long as acceptance of responsibility for oneself was recognized. Leaders of existential thought include Jean Paul Sartre and Karl Jaspers.

Reality for the existentialist is composed of the experiences of humans and is determined by the choices they make. One's experiences and free choices result in truth and are uniquely personal. An individual's value system, while totally controlled by choice, must be tempered by an understanding of social responsibility. No values are imposed by society; instead, each person is free to think and to act as personal desires dictate.

The self-actualizing person is the desired educational outcome, as each student is given freedom to choose. However, students must accept the consequences of their actions. In the curriculum, students are presented with a wide variety of activities, especially individual ones, through which to develop creativity,

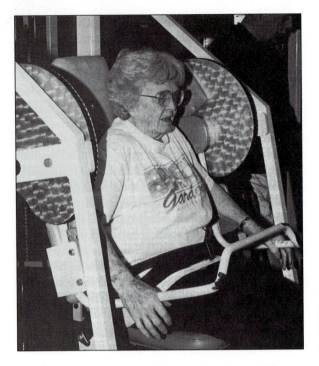

The existentialist teaches acceptance of individual responsibility, such as self-motivation in designing and implementing a personal fitness program. (Photo courtesy Bob Hilliard.)

self-awareness, self-responsibility, and realization of individual essence. The teacher raises questions and provokes reflective thinking but leaves students free to choose their own courses of action.

Relative to physical education and sport, the existentialist emphasizes individuality so the curriculum will focus on individual activities. The existentialist will allow students choices, such as in-line skating, aerobic dance, and self-challenging or adventure activities so that they can enjoy their experiences and will persist in their participation. The individual is given tremendous self-responsibility for learning by the existentialist, such as through self-paced instruction and contract grading.

Other Philosophies

Although less of an influence on overall educational programs, other philosophies merit mention because of their impact on physical education and sport. Asceticism is usually associated with the spread of Christianity and the increase in monasteries. The body was believed to be evil, and thus it had to be subordinated to the spirit. Radical ascetics even tortured their bodies to demonstrate the body's inferiority. Meditation, not physical activity, was praised. Another philosophy entitled scholasticism focused on the development of one's intellect with an accompanying deemphasis on the physical.

The Renaissance spawned the development of humanism. This cultural and intellectual movement valued peoples' achievements and stressed each individual's worth and ability. Vittorino da Feltra and Francois Rabelais were two humanists who stressed the importance of combining physical and mental education.

COMPARISONS OF THE FIVE TRADITIONAL PHILOSOPHIES RELATIVE TO PHYSICAL EDUCATION AND SPORT

Curriculum

- The idealist will select the curriculum without student input.
- The realist will allow students to select activities from various options.
- The pragmatist will pace each curricular offering based on students' individual differences.
- The naturalist will offer those activities that students indicate a readiness to learn.
- The existentialist will focus on each child's progress regardless of the activity.

Teaching fitness and sports skills

- The idealist and the realist focus on content.
- The pragmatist and the existentialist emphasize experiencing a wide variety of activities.
- The naturalist advocates play and self-directed activity for students.

Teaching methodology

- The idealist controls learning through lectures and some interactions with students.
- The realist maintains control using drills.
- The pragmatist and the naturalist encourage problem solving with the teacher as a guide.
- The existentialist guides by using questions and challenges.

Evaluation

- The idealist's qualitative assessments always subjugate the physical to the mental.
- The realist overemphasizes testing using scientific means for quantitative results.
- The pragmatist advocates subjective self-evaluation that, in the absence of specific goals, often leaves students without any sense of accomplishment.
- The naturalist focuses singularly on the attainment of individual goals.
- The existentialist views evaluation as nonessential because only self-realization is important.

Progressivism is a theory that applies pragmatism to education by focusing on the individual child rather than on the subject matter. Progressives, led by John Dewey, opposed the formalism of traditional education, its strict discipline, and its passive learning. This philosophy that children learn by doing is highly valued within physical education, although many have criticized experiential learning, especially when resources are limited.

ETHICS

You be the judge:

- A high school defensive tackle sharpens the edges of the fasteners that hold his chin guard to his helmet. After he plays a few downs, several of the opposing players have been cut and are bleeding. Is this action ethical? Is suspending this player from the team and school ethical?

PHILOSOPHY QUIZ

Fill in the blanks with one of the following: *existentialist, idealist, naturalist, pragmatist,* or *realist.* (Answers are at the end of the chapter.)

1.   The _____ advocates that students must indicate their readiness to attempt to learn a cartwheel.

2.   The _____ models or provides demonstrations of exactly how to serve a volleyball.

3.   The _____ encourages students to use their reasoning powers to decide how to align defensive players to stop an opposing team that fast breaks.

4.   Since a curriculum based on this philosophy focuses on the individual, the _____ focuses on teaching the acceptance of responsibility for self-discipline, cooperation, and fair play.

5.   The _____ emphasizes learning team sports through which social skills are developed.

6.   A physical education and sport researcher often is called a/an _____ because he or she utilizes the scientific method of inquiry.

7.   The _____ encourages students to select their own movement activities and to be creative, such as through designing a new cooperative game or exploring playground apparatus.

8.   The wholeness rather than duality (mind versus body) of people is stressed by the _____ and the _____ by their seeking to achieve psychomotor, cognitive, and affective outcomes in all classes.

9.   Since to the _____ experience is critical for learning, students are encouraged to experiment with their own techniques in executing body movements.

- An elementary student in a physical education class records that she walked one mile each day to help her team win the special field trip to the zoo, even though she did not do all of this exercise. Is this action ethical? Is suspending this student from school ethical?

- An athletic trainer gives a track athlete amphetamines to help boost his energy level. Is this action ethical? Is this athletic trainer violating the National Athletic Trainers' Association Code of Ethics on p. 42?

These scenarios deal with **ethics**, which is the study of moral values. It deals with good and bad, right and wrong, obligation and choice, and principles of conduct. From the time of the ancient Greeks until today, educators have been held responsible for the nurturance and enhancement of ethical behavior. Character development, for example, has traditionally been a vital concern of educators, including physical educators, coaches, and other sports leaders. Drawing from the fields of religion, philosophy, and psychology, values serve as the foundation of a way of life; people are expected to conduct themselves in accordance with certain values.

Ethical dilemmas are often associated with whether behaviors are within the spirit of the rules. (Photo courtesy Lisa Sense.)

Moral reasoning consists of determining what is the right thing to do. In this moral reasoning process, a person has to assess what he or she knows and values about a particular moral issue before acting on what is decided. Kohlberg (1981) suggested that all people learn and develop morally in a six-stage sequence, organized into three levels:

Preconventional

- Stage One focuses on actions done to avoid punishment.
- Stage Two emphasizes following rules for self-interest.

Conventional

- Stage Three suggests that people react to the expectations of parents, peers, and authority figures.
- Stage Four assumes that people conform to the social system and social order.

Postconventional

- Stage Five expects people to fulfill contract and individual rights.
- Stage Six posits universal ethical principles as the basis for all actions.

Kohlberg stated that the higher stages require more complex moral reasoning, however, moral development could remain at any stage.

A moral reasoning strategy begins with what a person believes. These beliefs lead to the development of values about ourselves, society, and others. Values are the answer to the question of what is most important or what has relative worth? Moral values can be described as the relative worth associated with something virtuous and good. Examples of these moral values include justice, honesty, responsibility, and beneficence.

Most ethical theories are based on teleology, deontology, or a combination of the two. *Teleological* theories focus on the end results or consequences of processes or occurrences. For the most prominent of these theories, John Stuart

EXAMPLES OF CATEGORICAL IMPERATIVES IN SPORT

- Fair play means playing within the letter and spirit of the rules.
- Seeking to win within the letter and spirit of the rules is acceptable while winning "at-all-costs" is unacceptable.
- An opponent should be treated with respect and exactly as everyone would wish to be treated.
- Games are to be played as a mutual quest for excellence with intimidation inappropriate.
- Retribution for a violent or unfair action done by an opponent or an official is never acceptable.

ETHICAL CHOICES IN SPORTS

1. Should every child play in every contest in youth sports programs?
2. Should extrinsic awards (such as trophies, plaques, or money) be given to sports champions?
3. Should alumni be allowed to give money or tangible gifts to prospective college athletes during their recruitment?
4. Should athletes be allowed to befriend their opponents before or after a competition?
5. Should a coach be allowed to verbally abuse officials?
6. Should strikes for more benefits or rights by professional athletes be allowed?
7. Should males and females receive identical treatment in school and college sports?
8. Should all college students be required to pay athletic fees?
9. Should a coach have the right to require that an athlete (at any age) compete in only one sport (that is, specialize)?
10. Should an athlete be allowed to use drugs (such as amphetamines or anabolic steroids) to enhance performance?
11. Should sports competitions be open to players of both sexes?
12. Should an athlete be required to pass all school subjects in order to play on an interscholastic team?
13. Should a coach teach athletes how to circumvent sports rules to their advantage?
14. Should college coaches who violate recruiting regulations be banned from coaching?
15. Should fans be protected from the misbehavior of other fans?
16. Should a coach have the right to verbally or physically abuse an athlete?
17. Should an athlete ever be allowed or required to play when injured?
18. Should children ever be cut when trying out for a youth sports team?
19. Should high school or college alumni be able to influence the hiring and firing of coaches?
20. Should every child get an opportunity to play all positions in youth sports programs?
21. Should sports gambling be legalized?
22. Should fans have to pay to view the major sporting events on television?
23. Should colleges be allowed to generate millions of dollars of revenues from their football and basketball programs, while the athletes who help generate these revenues receive only grants-in-aid?
24. Should a television network be allowed to dictate the date and time of a college or professional competition?
25. Should athletes be punished for breaking team rules during the season?

Mill's *utilitarianism,* the goal is the creation of the greatest good for the largest number of people. Since the benefit of the group or society as a whole is the goal, actions are judged to ensure that the good effects outweigh the bad. The utilitarian, however, lacks concern for how the results are produced and may have difficulty determining what society values most highly.

Immanuel Kant helped formulate the theory of moral obligation known as *deontology.* According to this ethical theory, actions must conform to absolute rules of moral behavior, which are characterized by universality, respect for the individual, and acceptability to rational beings. That is, deontology argues that regardless of the particular situation, moral action should make sense to each person and lead to the same behavior. Kant's *categorical imperative* stated that moral duties are prescriptive and independent of consequences. The box on p. 40 provides examples of how categorical imperatives relate to sport.

How to teach ethical standards most effectively has been a dilemma for physical educators and coaches for a long time. Since fair play is not an inherent characteristic of physical activities, how does it occur? When play, games, sports, and other physical pursuits are engaged in for their inherent pleasure, ethical problems seldom emerge. When the outcome becomes so highly significant that some

Sport participants often face ethical choices, such as whether to acknowledge touching the net during a volleyball match.

NATIONAL ATHLETIC TRAINERS' ASSOCIATION CODE OF PROFESSIONAL PRACTICE

Ethical Principles

1. Athletic trainers should neither practice nor condone discrimination on the basis of race, color, sex, age, religion, or national origin.
2. Athletic trainers should not condone, engage in, or defend unsportsmanlike conduct or practices.
3. Athletic trainers should provide care on the basis of the needs of the individual athlete. They should not discriminate on the basis of athletic ability.
4. Athletic trainers should strive to achieve the highest level of competence. They should use only those techniques and preparations which they are qualified and authorized to administer.
5. Athletic trainers should recognize the need for continuing education to remain proficient in their practice. They should be willing to consider new procedures within guidelines that assure safety.
6. Athletic trainers should recognize that personal problems and conflicts may occur which may interfere with professional effectiveness. Accordingly, they should refrain from undertaking any activity in which their personal problems are likely to lead to inadequate performance or harm to an athlete or colleague.
7. Athletic trainers should use care to be truthful and not misleading when stating their education, training, and experience.

or all of the participants employ whatever means possible to achieve success, then questionable behavior is readily evident, to the detriment of values. A person's moral values do not preclude seeking to perform to the best of one's ability. But, doing so at the risk of impinging on what is good, on one's obligation to others, or on principles of proper conduct violates these values.

Can physical education and sport teach ethics? In spite of our materialistic and pragmatic world, physical education and sport has an obligation to teach and to perpetuate moral and ethical principles that are basic to society. Among these principles are sensitivity to individual needs and differences, responsibility for our personal conduct, concern for others, and devotion to honesty, integrity, and fair play. Physical educators and sport leaders in all settings should exemplify ethical behavior and treat everyone fairly, so that others are positively influenced. We must constantly be aware that our actions will teach character louder than our statements.

The ethical choices on p. 40 challenge you with several ethical choices. These can be discussed in class or with others. Each question may have multiple alternatives or you may believe there is only one response. Your answer is a direct reflection of the ethical values that are uniquely yours. You also should realize that your attitudes toward and reactions to these and similar situations will influence those with whom you work in a physical education and sport career. The box above illustrates how the National Athletic Trainers' Association emphasizes the importance of ethical conduct through its code of professional practices.

DEVELOPING A PERSONAL PHILOSOPHY OF PHYSICAL EDUCATION AND SPORT

Everyone who plans a career in physical education and sport needs to develop a personal philosophy as a guide to future actions. For example, if fair play is essential to your philosophy, you will stress this in your own behavior, your instruction of others, and the programs you lead. A personal philosophy forces you to think logically and analytically and to explain the worth and the value of physical education and sport. This developmental process will help you relate physical education and sport to general education and will enhance your professional growth. Too frequently, physical educators have failed to develop definite personal philosophies, resulting in the loss of career direction and purpose. Therefore, it is essential that you formulate principles, guidelines, and directions for your career. If you do not know where you are going, it is unlikely that you will end up where you want to be (wherever that is!)

Some of the tenets of the philosophies discussed in this chapter differ significantly. For example, pragmatists advocate helping students become better-functioning members of society, while existentialists focus on students becoming self-actualizing, independent beings. In light of this potential disagreement in values and knowledge, you must proceed logically and specifically.

Many educators and philosophers have adopted an eclectic approach rather than accepting all aspects of one particular philosophy. *Eclecticism* is a combination of theories and doctrines from several philosophies into a consistent and compatible set of beliefs. For example, you may believe that the teacher should model correct skill performance, like the idealist would, yet encourage problem solving as the pragmatist and naturalist advocate. You may design your program to focus on individualized learning (naturalism) and to allow for individuality (existentialism), yet also emphasize developing social skills valued by pragmatists. You may choose to evaluate your students using subjective (idealist) and quantitative (realist) measures. Based on your experiences and established values, an eclectic philosophy may emerge as the foundation for your personal philosophy. Again, the key is to realize the importance of examining what you believe, why you believe it, and what your values mean.

Before developing your personal philosophy and to show how your attitudes, beliefs, and values influence your moral reasoning process, read the following situations and give your responses. A composite of your opinions should help you better understand your values and knowledge and how they provide the foundation for your personal philosophy.

- Situation 1—During a basketball game, player 44 (team A) and player 12 (team B) both attempt to control a loose ball, but it goes out of bounds. As the official, you blow your whistle and award the ball to team A. Player 44 acknowledges touching the ball last. Do you change your call? If you were the player, would you have acknowledged causing the ball to go out of bounds?

- Situation 2—During a recreation league softball game, you as the field supervisor learn that one of the teams is playing an individual not on the team roster. That team is in last place in the league standings. What action, if any, do you take? Would your response differ if this team was in first place?

- Situation 3—All funds for physical education at your school have been transferred to the athletic budget. As a teacher (not in physical education) and a coach, do you approve or disapprove, and why?

- Situation 4—As a collegiate football player you are told by the coach to take anabolic steroids to help build muscle bulk. Do you take the drugs? Is this cheating or gaining a competitive edge?

- Situation 5—Your soccer team of 9- and 10-year-olds is in the last game of the season. If your team wins, it will capture the league championship. Your best player twists an ankle just as the first half ends. The player is in pain, but there is seemingly no fracture and only slight swelling. Do you allow that player to participate in the second half? Should the player be forced to play?

Outside of the competitive sports realm, people also face situations that challenge their philosophies and their value systems. Your responses to each of the following real dilemmas will assist you in understanding yourself better.

- Situation 1—In applying for a position as an athletic trainer with a rehabilitation clinic, you are told that a preemployment drug test and annual random drug testing are required. Does this violate any of your beliefs or constitutional rights? Would you continue to seek this job?

- Situation 2—The health club at which you just took a position depends on enrolling at least 20 new members monthly to meet its expenses. In your first staff meeting, you are trained how to sell memberships without explaining the required annual fee that is assessed after the first month. You are also told that selling memberships is more important than customer service. Does this contradict any of your values? Is this pragmatic approach offensive to you? Will you assist members less while working more diligently to convince guests to join the club?

- Situation 3—For the recreation department where you serve as special events director, you are planning to conduct a family fun run, walk, and road race. A local hardware store that has pledged $1000 to fund this event calls one week before the event to notify you that it will not be able to donate the money. You are distraught. Just then you receive a call from the new beer distributor in town offering to provide financial support ($1000) for recreational activities in exchange for advertising. Do you accept this offer even though young people are participating in this event? Should the recreation department have a policy regarding the companies from which support can be received? Is it better to cancel the event or to accept the beer company's offer?

- Situation 4—As you assess the fitness of an employee at a corporate fitness facility, you are told by that person that several employees have been padding their expense accounts to pay for golf outings and sports tickets. Are you bound by any rules of confidentiality in this situation? Should you tell your supervisor? Is this action justified because everyone is doing it, or is it embezzlement?

- Situation 5—As a local sportswriter you are given the facts about a 14-year-old who just transferred to a public magnet school because of promised financial benefits. This student happens to be an outstanding athlete. Do you write this story?

Your responses to these real-life situations should help you understand the importance of developing a personal philosophy. Your answers to the following questions can assist you in this developmental process.

- What is the basis for my ethical judgments personally, interpersonally, and programmatically?
  - Is the action honest, fair, responsible, and beneficent?
  - Will the action benefit me?
  - Will the action harm others?
  - Will the action violate a societal tradition, law, or expectation?
  - Will the action violate my personal values?
- Who and what are most important to me in my program?
  - Students
  - Participants
  - Employers
  - Parents
  - Taxpayers
  - Co-workers
  - Athletes
  - Fans
  - Teaching
  - Learning
  - Participation
  - Adherence to the program
  - Fun
  - Skill development
  - Fitness
  - Winning
  - Developing social skills
  - Fair play
  - Classroom management
  - Stress reduction
  - Safety
  - Critical thinking
- How do I determine what the program content should include?
  - Required state curriculum
  - National organization standards
  - Interests of participants
  - Traditional offerings

- Latest published research findings
- Popularity of new innovations
- Something learned at a recent workshop or conference
- Whatever helps win

- What instructional and operational approaches will I use?
  - Lecture
  - Problem-solving
  - Guided discovery
  - Self-pacing
  - Mentor
  - Guide
  - Role model
  - Motivator
  - Counselor
  - Leader
  - Facilitator
  - Autocrat
  - Friend
  - Boss

- How will I know if program objectives and personal goals have been achieved?
  - Skilled are learned.
  - Participants persist in lifetime activity.
  - Winning occurs.
  - Everyone, including me, has fun.
  - Fitness is developed and maintained.
  - Career advancement occurs.
  - Evaluations are positive.
  - Job security exists.

Hopefully, responding to these questions can start you on the way to developing a personal philosophy that will help guide you into a career that matches what you value. A personal philosophy, though, is an evolving and changing perspective on how a person views those things of most value and the role each will serve in his or her life.

SUMMARY

As you progress in your education and enter your career, your philosophy may change. You may borrow concepts from idealism, realism, pragmatism, naturalism, or existentialism, or you may adopt an eclectic approach. You will face ethical decisions often. Regardless of the values chosen, having a philosophy is essential: it is your personal commitment to what you want to do and become. You can use your philosophy to help you think critically, to examine yourself, to resolve personal and professional issues, and to understand your career better.

CAREER PERSPECTIVES

RICHARD J. CAREY, ATC/L
Health Educator/Athletic Trainer
Lyons Township High School
Western Springs/LaGrange, Illinois

EDUCATION
A.A., Pre-Physical Therapy, Grays Harbor Junior College (WA)
B.A., Health Education, University of Washington
M.S., Health Education, Pennsylvania State University

JOB RESPONSIBILITIES AND HOURS

As the head athletic trainer, Rich is responsible for 22 girls' and boys' teams at two campuses. He covers all home and away football games and home events for all other sports. He prepares athletes for practices and competitions, plans and administers conditioning and rehabilitation programs, and maintains athletes' treatment records, coordinates two training rooms, and supervises 24 student trainers. He also teaches three classes of health education to sophomores and two classes of sports medicine to juniors and seniors. Monday through Friday, Rich works from 7:30 A.M. to 7:00 P.M. and on Saturday, from 7:30 A.M. to 5:00 P.M. These are typical hours for an athletic trainer who also teaches. Additionally, he works longer hours when back-to-back sports competitions occur.

SPECIALIZED COURSE WORK, DEGREES, AND WORK EXPERIENCES NEEDED FOR THIS CAREER

Certification by the National Athletic Trainers' Association and a college degree in education with the appropriate teaching certification are required. Some states also require regulation (Illinois requires licensure) in athletic training. Rich recommends obtaining emergency medical technician training as well as instructor certification in cardiopulmonary resuscitation. He emphasizes the importance of attending sports medicine workshops and symposia whenever possible. Many of these sessions build on one's undergraduate and graduate education and provide the opportunity to obtain required continuing education units.

SATISFYING ASPECTS

Rich enjoys helping others recover from an injury or illness. He likes serving as a counselor for teens during their injury recovery period with its emotional ups and downs. Keeping up-to-date to teach his health education class is a pleasant challenge for him. The two months off in the summer help compensate for the long hours worked during the school year.

JOB POTENTIAL

At Rich's school, one's salary increases with educational hours and years of continuous service in sports. The salary range is $33,000 to $78,000 for teaching, with a $3000 to $20,000 stipend for athletic training. Professional time is available for speaking and publishing, with the school paying part of the associated expenses.

SUGGESTIONS FOR STUDENTS

Rich recommends accumulating the highest educational degrees possible. You must be willing to relocate from your home in securing a position. Certification in a teaching field other than health and physical education when coupled with athletic training certification may enhance your employment options. Personally, he stresses that one's physical and mental health must be high, with sufficient stamina to work long hours. As an athletic trainer, you must be able to deal with all kinds of people and demonstrate a great sense of humor. You also must show a genuine understanding and supportive attitude during an athlete's convalescence period. In the classroom, you need to use diversified strategies to teach health knowledge and decision-making skills. Rich suggests teaching with, not at, your students. He adds that if you work hard and remain dedicated, you can attain any goal you desire as a teacher-athletic trainer.

REVIEW QUESTIONS

1. What does philosophy mean?
2. Using the philosophy of idealism, contrast the role of the teacher with the role of the student.
3. How do realists seek truth?
4. Which philosophy seeks to help students become better-functioning members of society, and how is this accomplished?
5. Which philosophy focuses on self-realization for each student?
6. Which philosophies stress using a problem-solving approach?
7. How would naturalism emphasize attaining individual goals?
8. How can physical education teach ethics?
9. Why is a personal philosophy of physical education and sport important?
10. What is an eclectic philosophy?

STUDENT ACTIVITIES

1. Select one of the five traditional philosophies discussed in this chapter and write a two-page paper explaining how it applies to your physical education and sport experiences as a student.
2. Divide the class into five groups with each group adopting one of the five traditional philosophies. Ask each group to prepare and present a five-minute defense, based on their assigned philosophy, of the inclusion of required physical education classes in the schools.
3. Respond to each of the 10 situations listed on pages 43–45 and be prepared to discuss them in class. Be ready to justify your opinions.
4. Write your personal philosophy of physical education and sport.
5. Ask a person in a physical education or sport career to explain to you his or her personal philosophy.

REFERENCE

Kohlberg L: *The philosophy of moral development: moral stages and the idea of justice,* New York, 1981, Harper & Row.

SUGGESTED READINGS

Bartlett L, Luck G: Good conduct rules for high school athletes—are they effective, *JOPERD* 65(3):62, 1994. This article reports on a study of whether states and schools have good conduct rules for high school athletes. While many believe that the existence of these good conduct rules positively impacts students, little research exists to substantiate this perception.

Boudreau F, Konzak B: Ben Johnson and the use of steroids in sport: sociological and ethical considerations, *CAN J Sp Sci* 16:88, 1991. The conflict between the search for sports excellence and the extrinsic rewards for winning relative to steroid usage is examined from an ethical and a sociological perspective.

Fraleigh WP: Different educational purposes: different sport values, *Quest* 42:77, 1990. Using Jewett and Bain's five curriculum value orientations, the author establishes five different educational purposes: disciplinary mastery, social reconstruction, learning process, self-actualization, and ecological validity. Then, sport values relevant to each are identified.

Gibbons SI, Ebbeck V, Weiss MR: *Fair play for kids*: effects on the moral development for children in physical education, *Res Q* 66:247, 1995. This study reported on the effect of participation in educational activities selected from *Fair play for kids* on the moral judgment, reason, intention, and prosocial behavior of children. The results validated the *Fair play for kids* curriculum for effecting change in the moral development of elementary school students.

Lumpkin A: Living ethically, *J of Interdis Res in PE* 1:15, 1996. An erosion in moral responsibility has led to unethical behavior in research, business, sport, and society. Conversely, living ethically includes three principles: do not break societal laws and traditions, do not harm another person physically or emotionally, and do not violate personal values.

Lumpkin A, Stoll SK, Beller JM: *Sport ethics—applications for fair play,* St. Louis, 1995, Mosby-Year Book, Inc. This book describes moral reasoning and fair play behavior as a foundation for chapters on elimination, eligibility, intimidation and violence, ergogenic aids, commercialization, racial equity, gender equity, and morality.

Malloy DC, Zakus DH: Ethical decision making in sport administration: a theoretical inquiry into substance and form, *J of Sp Mgmt* 9:36, 1995. A synthesis of four philosophical approaches to ethics and two psychological approaches to moral reasoning are presented as ways to understand the decision-making behavior of sport managers.

Mangers BC, Ingersoll CD: Approaches to ethical decision making in athletic training, *J of NATA* 25:340, 1990. The authors suggest different ethical problem-solving approaches and use a hypothetical case to illustrate the application of these alternative approaches.

McLean DD, Russell RV: Future visions for public park and recreation agencies, *J Park & Rec Adm* 10(1):46, 1992. Due to the shifting of values in our culture, an ethical-decision-making model is proposed. Park and recreation professionals are challenged to provide ethical responses consistent with these values.

Meier KV: Philosophical anorexia, *Quest* 43:55, 1991. The author argues that physical education and sport lacks philosophical understanding, synthesis, and direction.

Answers to the Philosophy Quiz on page 38: 1. naturalist; 2. idealist; 3. realist; 4. existentialist; 5. pragmatist; 6. realist; 7. existentialist; 8. realist and naturalist; 9. pragmatist

CHAPTER 3

Physical Education and Sport as an Academic Discipline

KEY CONCEPTS

- An academic discipline includes a body of knowledge that is scholarly and theoretical and seeks to gain greater insights.
- The identity of physical education and sport as an academic discipline has conflicted with its traditional identity as a profession.
- Twelve applied sciences contribute to the body of knowledge known as physical education and sport.
- As a multidisciplinary field, physical education and sport shares content knowledge with the sciences, nutrition, computer technology, and the humanities.

A critical issue in the field of physical education and sport is whether it can be considered an academic discipline. The major question debated in the 1960s was whether physical education possessed a body of knowledge that was formally organized and merited scholarly study. An emphasis on the theoretical and scholarly content of physical education rather than on its practical aspects resulted in attempts starting in the 1980s to rename this field the art and science of human movement or to use some more scholarly description. This chapter gives an overview of the contributions of 12 applied sciences and a few related fields to determine whether physical education and sport deserves such a categorization.

WHAT IS AN ACADEMIC DISCIPLINE?

An **academic discipline** is a formal body of knowledge discovered, developed, and disseminated through scholarly research and inquiry. The components of an academic discipline include:

1. A body of knowledge
2. A conceptual framework
3. Scholarly procedures and methods of inquiry
4. Both the process of discovery and the end result

If physical education and sport merits the distinction of being called an academic discipline, these criteria must be met.

A body of knowledge refers to an area of study that seeks to find answers to important questions. Participants in a field seek to gain information and to contribute to the knowledge available to others. Have physical educators discovered and reported information that is of value to researchers and practitioners in other fields? Examples of their contributions include studies about the effects of drugs on physical performance, the importance of feedback to learning, and the role of sports in developing cultures. In these and many other studies, the physical educator examines the physiological, psychological, historical, or sociological impact of physical activity on people.

Similarly, research studies in an academic discipline must be guided by a conceptual framework. Proper hypotheses and experimental designs, strict controls, absence of bias, accurate reporting of findings, and interpretive analyses should characterize each attempt to gain new knowledge. This process requires stringent adherence to protocol to give credibility to the results.

Scholarly procedures and methods of inquiry are built upon this conceptual framework. For example, the sport historian must not rely on secondary, and often inaccurate, sources in examining changes or significant events. Motor development specialists must evaluate the role of genetics and the environment in assessing readiness to learn. The exercise physiologist must control extraneous variables when analyzing the effect of a treatment, such as a diet or a drug, on a training regimen.

In seeking knowledge, the process of discovery and the end result are equally important. How the researcher collects the data influences the findings; therefore, accuracy in reporting and interpretation is vital. Also, replication studies should verify the results consistently.

Other characteristics of an academic discipline include a substantial history and tradition, a broad scope that is unique in comparison with other fields, and a specific language. Thus for physical education and sport to qualify as an academic discipline, it must contribute to the body of knowledge by using a conceptual framework, scholarly procedures and methods of inquiry, theoretical processes of discovery, and analysis of the end results.

THE DISCIPLINE-PROFESSION DEBATE

Since the 1960s, a debate has raged within physical education at the college level concerning whether it should be classified as a discipline or a profession. Academicians in recent decades claim that the only way that their research can be accepted as meritorious, and thereby their status within academe enhanced, is to disassociate from their historical roots. Conversely, advocates of physical education as a profession stress that our only justifiable uniqueness is "educating the physical." Let us examine this debate more fully.

Physical educators have long viewed themselves primarily as practitioners who taught knowledge, skills, and values. Although many early physical educators in the colleges held medical degrees, most physical educators in the schools and colleges received degrees from teacher training institutions. They studied the scientific foundations, but emphasized the application of this knowledge for the development of movement and sports skills. Physical education starting in the 1930s aligned itself closely with educational goals while specifying that it made a unique contribution to the education of the whole child. Teachers in the schools, who were often the coaches, too, enthusiastically supported the belief that theirs was a practical field.

In contrast, the acquisition of knowledge for its own sake, rather than for any applied purpose, was the rallying cry of the academicians. They focused on researching, conceptualizing, and theorizing. Those who emphasized that physical education must defend itself through scholarly writings and publications seemed worlds apart from the practitioners in the gymnasium. As this chasm widened in the 1970s, the academicians established numerous specialized organizations that provided outlets for their research in scholarly journals and through presentations at annual conferences.

The debate continued as those involved in disciplinary research sought knowledge for its own sake, while the teacher desired ways to help improve instruction. As society increasingly became more specialized in all areas and the quality of the scholarship produced by the academicians improved, this disciplinary approach began to influence students' selection of majors. Simultaneously, many school physical education programs experienced cuts that resulted in a reduced demand for teachers. Students selecting nontraditional career options in physical education and sport, such as in athletic training, exercise science, fitness, and sport management, quickly exceeded the number choosing teacher education. The physical education generalist who could teach, coach, and work in a recreation program or a camp gave way to the specialist.

An alternative to this debate is to define physical education as field. Some physical educators are professionals while others may more accurately be called academicians. Others prefer to use terms such as athletic trainer, exercise physiologist, sport manager, or recreation director that they identify with more closely. Using the term field, instead of profession or academic discipline, suggests that we should commit to common goals, different roles, and a cross-disciplinary body of knowledge.

Returning to the discipline-profession debate, there has been a widespread emergence of new subdisciplines. As these developed, many interested in psychology, sociology, and other areas adopted "sport" as an identifying label because of some resistance to physical education as a teaching field and because of the tremendous popularity of and research interest in sports. At the same time, colleagues within university departments such as those of psychology, sociology, and history, began to assert that they were the best qualified to teach sport applications. Today, most sport psychologists, sport sociologists, and others researching sport are housed within exercise science, kinesiology, human performance, or similarly renamed departments.

THE SCIENTIFIC FOUNDATION OF PHYSICAL EDUCATION AND SPORT

Before describing the **applied sciences** that constitute physical education and sport, it is important to realize that our scientific foundation is multidisciplinary. Numerous academic fields of study provide many of the principles and methods of scientific inquiry used by researchers and practitioners in physical education and sport. One cornerstone is biology, the study of life and life processes. Upon these biological facts and information are built anatomy, physiology, chemistry, and physics.

Anatomy and physiology are the studies of the structure and function, respectively, of the human body. Chemistry is the study of the composition, properties, and reactions of matter. The specialization of biochemistry focuses on biological substances and processes, such as how the body's cells use food to obtain energy through respiration. The study of physics examines interactions between matter and energy including various types of motion and forces. These and other sciences rely on applied mathematical concepts and computations.

History, philosophy, psychology, and sociology are often called social sciences because they seek knowledge in more experiential ways than do the "hard" sciences described above. The historian seeks to record and analyze past events. In the pursuit of wisdom through intellectual and logical means, the philosopher investigates the causes and laws underlying reality. The psychologist examines mental processes and behaviors. The sociologist studies human behavior in society. After the 12 applied sciences are discussed, refer to Table 3-1 (p. 67) to examine the relationships between these scientific foundations and the applied sciences of physical education and sport.

THE APPLIED SCIENCES OF PHYSICAL EDUCATION AND SPORT

Adapted Physical Education

Adapted physical education prepares teachers to provide specialized programs for individuals with diverse abilities and limitations. Based on federal protection of individuals' rights and changing societal attitudes, increasingly school children are being placed in regular classes, including physical education. *Inclusion* is the placement of students with physical, mental, or emotional disabilities or limitations into regular classes with their peers. The inclusion of students who may have hearing limitations, are wheelchair-bound, have attention deficit disorders, suffer from cerebral palsy, or who are autistic presents significant challenges to the physical educator who must help these and all other students achieve cognitive, affective, and motor skills and physical fitness goals.

Individualized programs or modified activities are needed to help all students have successful learning experiences. To make this approach effective, differently-sized and weighted pieces of equipment, choices in task dimensions and goals, and variety in evaluation measures should be used. Peer tutors, collaborative teaching, and cooperative learning activities have proven effective in inclusion classes.

Adapted physical educators can work with "regular" physical educators to reap the benefits of inclusion classrooms. Students gain respect for those who may be different, greater social acceptance is demonstrated, attitudes are changed, and equal status is recognized. The collaboration among students as well as among the teachers who design the curriculum positively impacts learning. Inclusion implies that special resources, personnel, and curricular adaptations

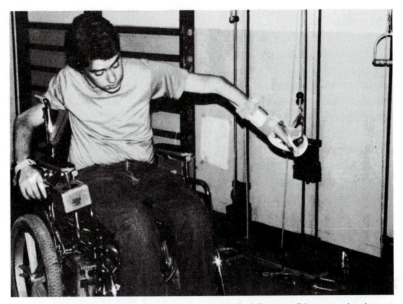

Through adapted physical education, persons with disabling conditions can develop physically by achieving their individual goals. (Photo courtesy Boyd Newman.)

make it possible to educate all children with disabilities, mild to severe, in regular classrooms.

Physical educators are increasingly sharing their expertise with and borrowing from the various therapeutic fields. The value of exercise in retarding osteoporosis and other degenerative diseases carries broad implications for recreational activities for senior citizens. Physical therapists and athletic trainers are seeking the best programs for injury rehabilitation. Exercise physiologists are working with physicians in the prescription of exercises for individuals who have suffered heart attacks. Recreational therapists and adapted physical educators together may provide appropriate activities for disabled employees and school children. In each of these cases, the medium of exercise is involved and, through consultation, the best activities are prescribed.

Exercise Physiology

The study of bodily functions under the stress of muscular activity is called **exercise physiology.** The anatomic bases for human movement include the 206 bones in the human skeleton; the joint structure, which includes cartilage, ligaments, and muscular attachments; the muscular system; the nervous system; and the circulatory and respiratory systems. More than 400 muscles, through a system of levers in conjunction with the skeletal system, provide the physiological key and guide to human movement. This potential for motion is released through the initiation of the nervous system and the biochemical reactions that supply muscles with energy. Exercise physiology also draws vital information from nutrition, psychology, and biochemistry.

Exercise physiologists measure the metabolic responses of the body to exercise and training through various endurance, flexibility, and strength programs. In

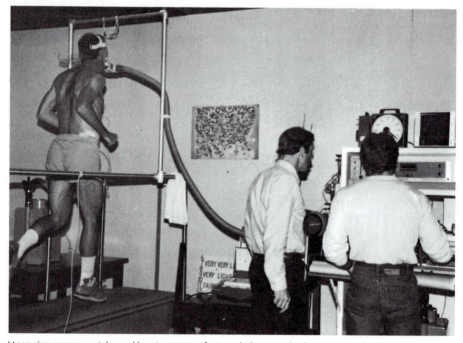

Measuring oxygen uptake and heart response factors during exercise is one example of exercise physiology research. (Photo courtesy Bob McMurray.)

these projects, they may examine changes in the cardiovascular system, stroke volume, pulse rate, blood composition, and other physiological parameters. Others study how the body utilizes carbohydrates, fats, and proteins during exercise; the effects of diet, smoking, and temperature on performance; and differences between trained and untrained individuals based on a variable such as sleep, diet, and gender.

Exercise physiologists, because of their expertise in understanding bodily functions under the stress of muscular activity, often are consulted about or given the responsibility for prescribing and monitoring exercise programs for cardiac patients. Specialists in cardiac rehabilitation monitor exercise paradigms for individuals who have experienced cardiovascular trauma or prescribe preventive programs for people demonstrating coronary disease risk factors. Biomechanists and exercise physiologists often work together to design the most appropriate training programs for elite athletes, such as those at the United States Olympic Training Center in Colorado Springs.

Researchers in exercise physiology often prescribe workouts on treadmills to monitor oxygen uptake and expired carbon dioxide, to take heart rate and function measurements, and to analyze the chemical activities of the body. Using computers to interface some of these measurements with one another has furnished accurate and immediate results. Exercise physiologists also conduct joint research projects with athletic trainers concerning the prevention and rehabilitation of injuries and with physicians in the areas of muscle biopsies and blood lactate analyses.

Motor Development

Motor development is the maturation of the neuromuscular mechanism permitting progressive performance in motor skills. Motor development frequently is associated with children because movement and skill performance are constrained by heredity. Yet, since motor development continues throughout life, research studies frequently measure skill learning over time. These longitudinal studies are important because of the genetic limitations on each individual's body type, posture, and body mechanics. Age and experiences correlate with a person's developmental readiness, as do height, weight, and other growth indexes. Motor development depends on the interactions of all of these factors.

Developmentally-appropriate activities for elementary-age children and people with physical, mental, or emotional disabilities comprise part of the motor development knowledge base. The adaptive physical education specialist uses motor development principles to teach basic movement patterns. The problem-solving and guided-discovery approaches used in movement education are grounded in understanding the stages of motor development.

Motor Learning

Motor learning is the study of the cognitive processes underlying motor acts associated with skill acquisition through practice and experience. This field also can be defined as an area of psychology dealing with human performance and behavior. Information processing, which is essential to motor learning, includes input of information from various sources, decision making, output by the respondent, and the feedback received. Various types of feedback in activity settings, such as intrinsic, extrinsic, terminal, concurrent, visual, verbal, constant, and interval, may enhance or impede performance.

As people attempt to learn movement and sport skills, they must receive feedback in order to improve. Motor learning research confirms that just practicing a skill is insufficient to correct performance errors. Since each person's learning style differs, the most effective type of feedback varies. One person may respond most positively to immediate, specific, verbal corrections. Others may

Motor learning knowledge, such as use of various types of feedback, can enhance an archer's performance. (Photo courtesy Lisa Sense.)

need to visualize mistakes in their technique, such as by viewing a videotape, in order to improve. Another person may be a kinesthetic learner who can be guided through touch into proper skill execution.

The learning curve, knowledge of results, overlearning, and perceptual interpretation of stimuli combine to influence the concept of learning progressions. Methods of practice and skill-development situations affect learning progression as well as motor control. The method of practice, such as speed or accuracy, whole or part, massed or distributed, and physical or mental, helps determine the degree of learning that occurs. The study of motor learning also examines the degree of transfer of training, or specificity versus generality of tasks, from activity to activity.

Motor learning research has concluded that no one method of practice is most effective, because people learn skills differently and because it depends on the complexity of the skills being learned. Some skills, such as a volleyball set, should be learned at a slow, progressive pace before speeding up the execution. Simple skills, like jumping, can be learned as one whole skill, while complex skills, like heading a soccer ball, must be learned in parts followed by a combination of the parts into one skill. Some people need to focus large blocks of massed practice time on learning a skill, while others benefit from incremental skill practice over longer periods of time. Some skills, such as free throws in basketball, can be perfected through mental practice once the physical technique is learned. These are just a few examples of how motor learning has impacted physical education and sport.

Sport Biomechanics

Sport biomechanics is the study of the effects of natural laws and forces on the body through the science and mechanics of movement. Biomechanists study the musculoskeletal system, the principles of mechanics, and activity analyses. They examine the force of muscular contractions; flexion, extension, pronation, and supination of the muscles during activity; the composition of muscle fibers; equilibrium, center of gravity, and base of support; transfer of momentum; and projection of the body or an object. Their findings have contributed to improved athletic performance and have been used to prevent injuries, which is of special interest to physical therapists and athletic trainers. For example, through biomechanical analysis, minor flaws in throwing technique for the discus or stride length for sprinting can be isolated and corrected to enhance distance or to reduce time. Scientific answers can be provided to questions such as what kind of shoe support is needed for individuals participating regularly in aerobics, what weight of bat is optimal for hitting home runs, what type of weight training is appropriate for judo or volleyball players, and what type of exercise program is best for increasing joint flexibility for seniors.

Biomechanists explain movement in relation to acceleration, energy, mass, power, torque, and velocity. Mechanical principles focused on are force application and absorption, leverage, and stability. Use of cinematography (motion-picture photography) has become common among coaches and teachers for the analysis of performance. Electromyography is the measurement of electrical discharges from a muscle to study the action potential and the sequence of muscular activity. An analysis of the position and movements of joints is possible with

Biomechanical analyses are used to enhance sports performances. (Photo courtesy John R. Stevenson.)

electrogoniometry. Biomechanists also measure muscular forces using a force platform, determine speeds or frequencies using stroboscopy, and record movements and electrical responses, such as the heart rate, using telemetry. Computer-assisted analyses have helped them isolate components of physical skills that then can be corrected or changed to improve efficiency.

Sport History

Sport history is the descriptive and analytical examination of the significant people, events, organizations, and trends that shaped the past within the social context of the time. Sport historians investigate the past seeking to explain how, what, when, where, and why things occurred. Descriptive history explains events, individuals' contributions, and pivotal happenings using primary sources such as archeological artifacts, original writings, and eyewitness accounts. Such firsthand information is judged to be reliable and accurate, especially when confirmed by other primary sources. When no original information is available, sometimes secondary sources must be used to document history. History reported in secondary sources, however, must be verified meticulously to ensure accuracy. The narrative approach is often used in descriptive history to chronicle events, individuals, and developments.

More difficult, but vital to an understanding of why events happened as they did, is the interpretive or analytical perspective. This analysis attempts to explain the significance of each historical event while comparing it with contextual happenings. Thus, the sport historian must interpret findings in the context of the time and society in which they occurred. Sport historians examine changes and progress as they record biographies, examine organizations and their activities, describe trends and movements, and analyze how and why societal events occurred when they did.

So, of what value is knowing the past? Sport historians reveal that Greek athletes competed in the nude because that society revered the body as a work of art dedicated to the gods. When the reason disappeared, so did the practice. Sport historians report that the National Collegiate Athletic Association was established to reform football to prevent widespread injuries and deaths. Sport historians analyze the role that sport has played in racial integration and how this process positively influenced societal attitudes. These are just a few examples of how sport historians help us interpret our past as it informs how to better understand events today.

Sport Management

Sport management is the study of the management of personnel, programs, budgets, and facilities in various sports settings. It includes the management functions of planning, organizing, directing, and evaluating as well as the business components of marketing, accounting, economics, finance, and law. This field encompasses the spectator sport and fitness industries, sporting goods sales, and recreational and educational sport programs.

The sport industry, as broadly defined, involves sport products and services, all of which need sport managers. Career options exist in professional sports, intercollegiate athletics, high school sports, recreation programs, the leisure and travel industry, private and public health and sports clubs, and sporting goods businesses.

Sport managers need to learn applied competencies to qualify for these careers. These include communication skills, facility and event management abilities, sport marketing skills, financial management skills, and personnel management abilities.

Sports Medicine

Athletic training, or **sports medicine** as it is often called, includes the prevention, treatment, and rehabilitation of sports injuries. Sports medicine involves physicians, who may be general practitioners, orthopedic surgeons, or other specialists. Physicians must both initially and after an injury clear athletes for practice and competition as well as attend to the needs of athletes in events in which the risks of injury are high. Athletic trainers are involved almost daily. They are consulted about and often help design appropriate sport conditioning during the preseason, the postseason, and the off-season; they tape, preventively as well as protectively, athletes before activity; they are responsible for assessing injuries at the time they occur, for providing immediate and appropriate first aid, and for supervising the rehabilitation process upon the recommendation of a physician.

Extensive knowledge of anatomy and physiology of the body and skill in applying this knowledge to injury situations in order to fulfill their responsibilities are essential traits for athletic trainers. Sometimes, they need to be able to console injured athletes and to keep them from trying to return too quickly. At other times, athletic trainers may need to encourage athletes to work more diligently during their rehabilitation.

Athletic trainers, who may also be educated as physical therapists, are expected to use various treatments, such as ultrasound, whirlpool, ice massage, or heat. These professionals constantly help athletes play despite minor injuries by using the above treatments or various taping techniques.

Sport Pedagogy

The goal of teaching is learning. **Sport pedagogy** studies how to enhance instructional content, the learning process, and the achievement of learning outcomes. The school or college physical educator, the club pro, the youth sport or high school coach, and the personal trainer teach.

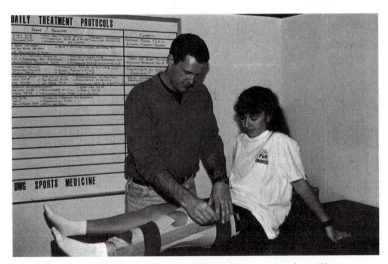

Athletic trainers apply splints to immobilize injured areas such as legs. (Photo courtesy Bob Hilliard.)

The pedagogist, or teacher, must provide an effective learning environment that focuses on successful practice opportunities. Each student or participant should spend most practice time "on task," rather than being subjected to management or organizational distractions such as waiting to use the equipment. Each individual needs to be sequentially challenged by the movement experience or sports skill to achieve success while being motivated to pursue additional progress. These components of quality teaching are so critical that each will be explained in greater depth.

The first objective is to use class or practice time effectively. Each teacher must plan extensively to ensure that all equipment is readily accessible, that handouts explaining the day's lesson are prepared for distribution, and that instructional learning cues appropriate for students with heterogeneous abilities are ready for use. The good teacher is also prepared to handle management tasks, such as calling roll and passing out equipment, and discipline problems with minimal loss of instructional and practice time. Each day's lesson is sequentially structured to provide maximal opportunities to practice each new skill.

The second essential criterion of quality teaching focuses on helping students or participants achieve success and challenge themselves to higher levels of skill development. Specific, corrective feedback and positive reinforcing comments about proper execution of a skill or movement must be provided by the teacher. Only when participants, within individual limitations, enjoy learning will they want to continue. A feeling of success is the key to this enjoyment.

The primary reason that people choose a career in teaching is the pleasure and reinforcement they receive when their students learn, enjoy the learning process, and continue to participate and to develop their skills. Teaching is personally, more than financially, rewarding. This feeling of success occurs when

An essential component of practice time is receiving specific, positive feedback from teachers. (Photo courtesy Bob Hilliard.)

teachers plan and implement innovative curricula, continually improve student-to-student and teacher-student interactions, and assess students' performance in order to ensure that learning is occurring.

Researchers within sport pedagogy seek to improve the instructional process through observation, analysis, and evaluation. By examining the amount of academic learning, direct instruction, and management time, sport pedagogists determine how teachers' and students' behaviors influence learning. Research studies also look at teachers' expectations for students, the classroom learning climate, and the type and amount of feedback, all critical to student learning.

Sport Philosophy

Sport philosophy is the search for truth and values and the interpretation of these, thus being both the process and the product. Every person has a philosophy, although it may be unstated. Philosophy dictates thought patterns, behaviors, and aspirations. Sport philosophers analyze concepts, make normative statements that guide practical activity, and speculate or extrapolate beyond the limits of scientific knowledge. Within the schools, sport philosophers examine how physical education contributes to both educational objectives and social values by explaining the nature, import, and reason for programs. Meeting peoples' needs, relating physical activity to human performance of all kinds, and enhancing the quality of life are the roles of sport philosophy outside the schools.

Most individuals in physical education and sport use philosophy to analyze issues of today. For example, what are the moral values depicted in films like *Chariots of Fire, Hoosiers,* and *Rudy?* Why do the problems such as gambling, sports agents, and a lack of sportsmanship plague intercollegiate athletic programs today? Why do so many athletes, even at the high school level, use anabolic steroids? What lesson is learned by youth soccer players when the congratulatory hand-slap at the end of the game is eliminated when members of one team spit on their hands and then slap their opponents' hands? Sport philosophy

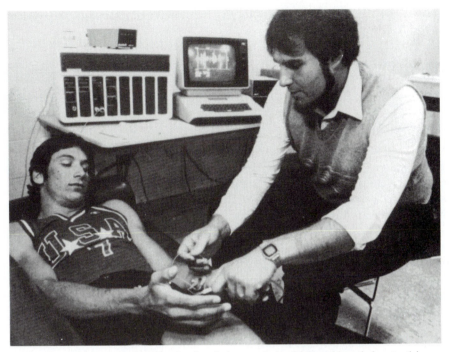

Sports psychologists often use biofeedback techniques to help athletes achieve their potential. (Photo courtesy John Silva.)

seeks to know and understand why such things exist as a reflection of what is valued.

Sport Psychology

Sport psychology is the study of human behavior in sports, including an understanding of the mental processes that impact motor skill performance. Theories and laws of learning, the importance of reinforcement, and the linking of perceptual abilities with motor performance contribute to this body of knowledge. Sport psychologists utilize this information when studying topics such as achievement motivation, arousal, attribution, and personality development. Achievement motivation research examines how to fulfill the higher needs of esteem and self-actualization. Excitement and relaxation, as well as tension reduction, are among the parameters of arousal studies. The study of causal attribution weighs the importance placed on ability, effort, luck, and task difficulty relative to contest outcome. Aggression, competitiveness, anxiety, independence, extroversion, and self-confidence are among the personality traits researched. Sport psychologists also examine the influence of group dynamics, exercise addiction, and enhanced body image on people who are physically active.

Applied sport psychology focuses on understanding psychological theories and techniques so that they can help athletes improve their performance. This area has grown in popularity as coaches and athletes seek a competitive edge. Specific strategies assist athletes in managing stress, concentrating more effectively, and maintaining confidence. Sport psychologists help athletes achieve their physical potential by improving their mental state.

The clinical interventions used by sport psychologists include relaxation training, biofeedback, breath control, desensitization, and mental imaging. Through these, athletes are aided in coping with the stressors and pressures of competition.

Sport Sociology

Sport sociology is the study of social units and processes within the sport context. This discipline examines the role of sports in human society by seeking to determine why people play and how participation in various physical activities influences them. The sport sociologist examines play, games, sports, recreational activities, and leisure-time pursuits in analyzing the expected outcomes of fun, relaxation, self-expression, wish fulfillment, and social interaction. The dynamics of socialization may reveal examples of racial and gender integration, exclusion, affiliation, competition, cooperation, conflict, rivalry, teamwork, and fair play.

Sport sociologists investigate sport as a game and as an institution. They examine the concepts of social mobility, class and gender stratification, status, racial and ethnic discrimination, team dynamics, and social consciousness and values. Understanding the sociology of sport requires dealing with the relationship between sports and social institutions.

Sport is woven into the daily and seasonal fabric of American society. The sport sociologist helps explain the following:

- Why did a mother purchase a death contract on the girl who beat out her daughter for a spot on the high school cheerleading squad?
- Why did a sophomore in high school commit suicide after leading his team to the state football championship?
- Why is a Major League baseball player paid $55 million over 5 years?
- Why do some college athletic administrators refuse to equitably fund women's athletics?
- Why are so few African Americans hired to coach professional and college teams?
- Why do approximately half of all children drop out of sports by age 12?
- Why do 25% of teenage and adult Americans participate in no regular physical activity?
- Why has television been allowed to dictate rule changes in sports?
- Why do youths kill other youths in order to take their shoes or jackets?

Sport sociologists may not have all the answers, but they can provide insights into the pervasiveness of sport that has led to these and other real-life situations.

As shown in Figure 3-1, these applied sciences are important spokes in the well-rounded discipline of physical education and sport. Take the Applied Sciences Quiz on page 65 to review the key areas of emphasis for each of these. All of the applied sciences contribute to the greater whole. Rather than being mutually exclusive, they interact with each other.

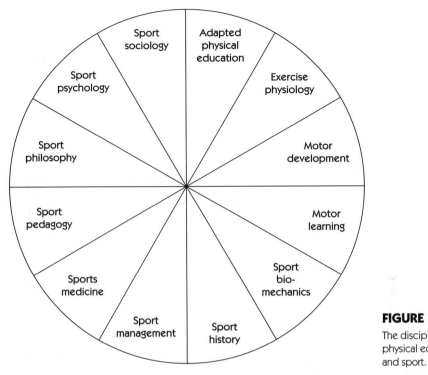

FIGURE 3-1

The discipline of physical education and sport.

APPLIED SCIENCES QUIZ

1. Which of the applied sciences studies oxygen utilization during cardiovascular exercise and metabolic responses to exercise and training?
2. Which of the applied sciences describes and analyzes the past?
3. Which of the applied sciences studies how people learn skills, especially through practice and feedback?
4. Which of the applied sciences studies how sport impacts social units, processes, and institutions?
5. Which of the applied sciences examines instructional planning, teacher-student interactions, and assessment of performance and learning?
6. Which of the applied sciences analyzing the impact of motion, force, and energy on sport performance?
7. Which of the applied sciences focuses on analyzes the developmental patterns associated with movement and skill performance?
8. Which of the applied sciences focuses on meeting the needs of every student regardless of ability level?
9. Which of the applied sciences uses extensive knowledge of the body to help athletes stay injury free and return to competition safely?
10. Which of the applied sciences seeks to understand why people act as they do based on their values?
11. Which of the applied sciences involves providing sports products and managing sporting events?
12. Which of the applied sciences uses various mental coping strategies to aid sports performance?

(Answers are at the end of the chapter.)

CROSS-DISCIPLINARY KNOWLEDGE FROM OTHER FIELDS

Physical education and sport is cross-disciplinary. As described earlier in this chapter, several sciences contribute to its knowledge base. Research in each of the specialty areas of the academic discipline of physical education and sport can draw upon the scientific method of inquiry and results of studies within each discipline upon which it depends. For example, results from medical physiologists' examinations of the effects of asthma on respiration may help exercise physiologists develop training programs for athletes who experience exercise-induced asthma. Application of research findings to physical education and sport settings is enhanced by specialists and those working in cross-disciplinary areas. For example, physicists and biomechanists working with equipment manufacturers help improve the design, effectiveness, and safety of poles used in vaulting. Collaborative efforts such as these to benefit physical education and sport appear limitless.

Other fields contribute vital knowledge to physical education and sport. *Nutrition,* often studied by exercise physiologists, encompasses the understanding of how the body utilizes its food intake relative to energy output. Numerous factors, such as sleep, drugs, work, and stress, influence how the body reacts to a specific diet or an exercise paradigm. Biochemical and physiological tests isolate those nutritional factors that most dramatically affect performance. Studies include the effects of marathon training on nutritional needs, the risks or benefits of vitamin supplementation, and the effects of caffeine on various heart parameters. Nutritional information is also vital for the athlete in training who maintains a specific weight, for the physically disabled individual who is minimally active, and for the senior citizen whose metabolic rate has slowed.

Computer technology in physical education and sport programs is vital, and it is important that those considering careers in one of the applied sciences understand the basics of computer systems. Most individuals today are familiar with hardware such as personal computers, keyboards, video display terminals or monitors, floppy and hard disk drives, and printers. Less familiar are disk operating systems, such as the common MS-DOS, that control the general operation of computers, modems that allow communications between computers using telephone lines, and CD-ROMs (compact discs that store large amounts of information on read-only-memory). Computer software allows the user to execute word processing, database management, spreadsheets, statistical analyses, graphics, to send electronic mail, and to surf the Internet.

To illustrate a few of the capabilities of computers relative to physical education and sport, a few examples will be provided. Computers have been used to help individuals regain partial use of dysfunctional limbs through electrical stimulation. Biomechanists use computers to analyze position and movement of joints to improve the techniques and performances of elite athletes. By using specialized software to analyze the measurement of oxygen uptake and expired carbon dioxide, heart rate functioning, and chemical reactions, exercise physiologists obtain immediate and valid data for exercise prescription. Sport psychologists using biofeedback techniques need computers to monitor arousal levels. In sports medicine, computers using database management allow athletic trainers to monitor training, injuries, and rehabilitation programs of hundreds of athletes.

TABLE 3-1

RELATIONSHIPS AMONG DISCIPLINES

Influencing Discipline	Applied Science	Interacts with Applied Sciences
Physical therapy	Adapted physical education	Motor development Sport pedagogy
Anatomy Biology Chemistry Physiology	Exercise physiology	Motor learning Sport biomechanics Sports medicine Sport psychology
Physiology Psychology	Motor development	Adapted physical education Motor learning
Anatomy Physiology Psychology	Motor learning	Exercise physiology Motor development Sport biomechanics Sport pedagogy
Mathematics	Sport biomechanics	Exercise physiology Motor learning Sport medicine
History Philosophy Sociology	Sport history	Sport philosophy Sport sociology
Accounting Finance Law Management Marketing	Sport management	Sport sociology
Anatomy Physical therapy Physiology Psychology	Sports medicine	Exercise physiology Sport biomechanics Sport psychology
Psychology	Sport pedagogy	Adapted physical education Motor learning
History Philosophy	Sport philosophy	Sport history
Physiology Psychology Sociology	Sport psychology	Exercise physiology Sports medicine Sport sociology

Sport managers use spreadsheets for budget control, databases for ticket sales, and statistical programs to compile team and individual statistics.

Humanities, encompassing the areas of art, literature, and music, are noteworthy from both historical and current perspectives. Archaeological discoveries from early civilizations verify the significance attached to physical activity for survival, group affiliation, religious worship, and enjoyment. From Myron's

R. Tait McKenzie's *The Joy of Effort* won the King's Medal at the 1912 Stockholm Olympic Games. (Courtesy the University of Tennessee Press.)

"Disco-bolus" during the Greek zenith to R. Tait McKenzie's "The Joy of Effort" (which received the King's Medal in the Fine Arts Competition at the 1912 Stockholm Olympic Games) to a wall fresco of the first women's Olympic marathon champion Joan Benoit, art has vividly shown the beauty of human movement. The Sport Art Academy of the National Association for Sport and Physical Education encourages continued expression, through displays of paintings, photographs, sculptures, and other works, of the efforts and pleasures inherent in physical education and sport.

Homer's *Iliad* and *Odyssey* verify the importance of athletics in Greek times. According to several presenters at conferences of the North American Society for Sport History, some literature in the United States today, as well as that of earlier times, affirms the socialization role expected of sports.

Music provides the rhythm for movement experiences for all ages. The Greeks exercised to the music of the lyre; music became a vital component of German school gymnastics in the 1800s. Children in elementary physical education today frequently experiment with and explore movement to the accompaniment of their favorite songs. In the 1980s, the addition of music to exercise routines helped popularize aerobics. Athletic team practice sessions, weight training workouts, and daily jogs often include music. Art, literature, and music can help focus on the development of a fit body, the socializing nature of sport, and the free experimentation of movement, thereby facilitating the application of physical education and sport's body of knowledge.

SUMMARY

An academic discipline includes a body of knowledge, a conceptual framework, scholarly procedures and methods of inquiry, and both a process of discovery and an end result. Based on its heritage as a teaching profession, physical education and sport has expanded to seek acceptance as a multidisciplinary field of academic merit. Our body of knowledge relies heavily on a foundation of both the "hard" and social sciences. Twelve applied sciences have developed into specializations within physical education and sport. While individuals in each applied science seek through scholarly inquiry to expand the body of knowledge, many have developed applications for school, competitive sport, and recreational settings. Related fields, such as nutrition, computer technology, and the humanities, also contribute to the academic discipline of physical education and sport.

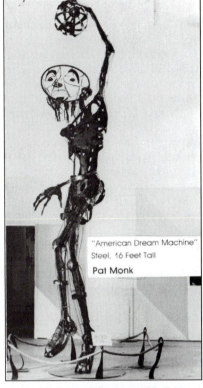

"American Dream Machine"
Steel, 16 Feet Tall

Pat Monk

Pat Monk's *American Dream Machine* in an unusual, yet lifelike, manner depicts one type of sport. (Photo courtesy Pat Monk.)

CAREER PERSPECTIVES

DORIS R. CORBETT

Sport Sociologist
ICHPER.SD President 1991–1999
AAHPERD President 1990–1991
NAGWS President 1980–1981
EDA-AAHPERD President 1987–1988
DCAHPERD President 1976–1978

EDUCATION

B.S., Health and Physical Education, North Carolina College
M.S., Physical Education, North Carolina Central University
Ph.D., Sociology of Sport, Sociology, University of Maryland

JOB RESPONSIBILITIES AND HOURS

As a Howard University professor, Doris' primary duties include teaching, research, and public service related to the profession. She teaches courses in Sociology of Sport, Ethics and Moral Reasoning in Sport, and History and Philosophy of Physical Education and Sport. Doris, as the ICHPER.SD President, works diligently throughout the world to improve the quality of health, physical education, recreation, sport and dance programs internationally. She serves on the International Olympic Committee (IOC) Sports For All Commission, as thesis advisor to several international students, and as curriculum advisor to Ministries of Sport and Culture in several countries. Doris dedicates many hours of her work internationally by traveling to more than four countries annually to speak on topics related to ethics and morality in sport, women in sport, leadership, and politics in sport. Doris' hours are 6.00 A.M. to 7.00 P.M. on most days of a typical work week, but her hours may be longer depending on departmental, research, and international initiatives.

SPECIALIZED COURSE WORK, DEGREES, AND WORK EXPERIENCES NEEDED FOR THIS CAREER

A doctoral degree in one of the applied sciences, such as Sport Sociology, is required for university professional rank. The ability to listen to people and to *hear* what the needs are of the various constituencies she serves is vitally important. To prepare for an academic professorship, take courses in the sociology of sport, women in sport, psychology of sport, sport management, history and philosophy of sport, comparative and international physical education and sport, cultural diversity, Olympism, human relations, research, and statistics.

SATISFYING ASPECTS

Doris values the national and international connection to colleagues throughout the continental USA and abroad and the opportunity to share information and to gain new knowledge and skills from a community of professionals globally.

JOB POTENTIAL

If a professional attains a doctor's degree and engages in scholarly activity, then earning a tenured faculty position is realistic. A salary range of $45,000 or more can be achieved by an experienced, tenured professor in one of the applied sciences. Becoming a department chairperson, dean, or program director is a possibility for interested and competent professionals.

SUGGESTIONS FOR STUDENTS

One must be academically prepared. One must be willing to spend long hours in meetings and travel, be open to learning new information, be flexible, be disciplined, purposeful and responsible, be honest with self and others, be a good listener, and not be afraid to let others know when you need help.

REVIEW QUESTIONS

1. What are the characteristics of an academic discipline?
2. What is the basis for the conflict between the professional approach to physical education and the academic discipline approach?

3. What is the scientific foundation for physical education and sport?
4. What is biomechanics?
5. What is the difference between motor development and motor learning?
6. Within which applied science would research studies on mental practice to improve performance be conducted?
7. Describe how any three of the applied sciences in physical education and sport interrelate in their research interests.
8. What applied science in physical education and sport conducts research studies in conjunction with nutritionists?
9. Describe how computers are used extensively in physical education and sport.
10. What relationship exists between physical education and sport and the humanities?

STUDENT ACTIVITIES

1. Select one of the 12 applied sciences and describe how it contributes to physical education and sport's body of knowledge.
2. Volunteer to help a faculty member or a graduate student conduct a research project specific to one of the 12 applied sciences.
3. Read two research articles that contribute to the body of knowledge of physical education and sport. Summarize their conceptual framework, scholarly procedures and methods of inquiry, and the process and end result of each study.
4. Develop a five-minute defense of physical education and sport as an academic discipline. Be prepared to present your defense in class.
5. Invite a specialist in each of the applied sciences to present an overview of this subdiscipline and to explain the interaction among this and other subdisciplines.
6. Divide the applied sciences into the following groups (adapted physical education, motor learning, motor development, and sport pedagogy; exercise physiology, sport biomechanics, and sports medicine; sport history, sport philosophy, and sport sociology; sport management and sport psychology). Divide the class into four groups and assign one to each of the applied science groups. Conduct a debate about the significance of the contributions of each of the groups to the achievement of the purpose and objectives of physical education and sport.

SUGGESTED READINGS

Blinda EM: Teaching sociology of sport: an active learning approach, *Teach Soc* 23(3):264, 1995. Four learning activities designed to help students understand the pervasiveness and significance of sport as a social institution are discussed.

Boyce BA: Making the case for the case-method approach in physical education pedagogy classes, *JOPERD* 63(6):17, 1992. This article focuses on the use of the case-method approach for helping undergraduate teacher education students learn to apply content knowledge in real situations.

Christina RW, Eckert HM, eds: Enhancing human performance, *The Academy Papers* 25, 1992. This volume of *The Academy Papers* describes new concepts and developments for enhancing sport performance. It includes discussions about biomechanics, sport psychology, exercise physiology, and other applied sciences.

Corbin CB: The field of physical education—common goals, not common roles, *JOPERD* 64(1):79, 1993. Based on historical developments characterized by professional and disciplinary influences and conflicts, the author advocates that physical education should be a field encompassing both.

Craft DH (ed): Inclusion: physical education for all, *JOPERD* 65(1):23, 1994. This nine-article feature describes how physical educators must meet the challenge of teaching children with disabilities in regular physical education.

Lawson HA: Sport pedagogy research: from information-gathering to useful knowledge, *J of Teach in PE* 10(1):1, 1990. Research is yielding increasing amounts of information about how to improve school- and agency-based physical education programs and about adjustments in organizing, communicating, and applying research findings.

Lehnus DL, Miller GA: The status of athletic marketing in division 1A universities, *Sp Mkt Q* 5(3):31, 1996. Data from questionnaires returned by university presidents, athletics directors, and marketing personnel revealed that the two most important problems facing college athletics in the next decade will be gender equity and inadequate finances. Marketing professionals can help with generating new revenues but indicate a need for greater understanding by others about the function or concepts of sport marketing.

Park RJ, Eckert, HM, eds: New possibilities, new paradigms?, *The Academy Papers* 24, 1991. The papers in volume 24 of *The Academy Papers* examine a reconceptualization of physical education with a look toward a multi-disciplinary study of human movement.

Pinheiro VED, Simon HA: An operational model of motor skill diagnosis, *J of Teach in PE* 11(3):288, 1992. Processes critical in motor skill diagnosis are discussed along with an operational model of motor skill development.

Silverman S: Communication and motor skill learning: what we learn from research in the gymnasium, *Quest* 46(3):345, 1994. After discussing the design for research in physical education settings, it is concluded that teachers are important in structuring and communicating expectations to students as they learn motor skills.

Answers to the Applied Sciences Quiz (p. 65):

1. exercise physiology; 2. sport history; 3. motor learning; 4. sport sociology; 5. sport pedagogy; 6. sport biomechanics; 7. motor development; 8. adapted physical education; 9. sports medicine; 10. sport philosophy; 11. sport management; 12. sport psychology

CHAPTER 4

The Profession of Physical Education and Sport

KEY CONCEPTS

- Physical education and sport and its many diverse careers are characterized by the four components of a profession.
- The American Alliance fulfills its objectives through the programs of its associations and through conventions, publications, and other activities that benefit its membership and the people it serves.
- Many professional organizations promote the study of and involvement in sports, leisure activities, fitness programs, and other related pursuits.
- Physical education and sport specializations in athletic training, coaching, fitness, sport management, exercise and sport sciences, and therapeutic fields, prepare students for diverse careers following the completion of specialized course work.
- A teaching option prepares students through academic, professional, and pedagogical course work for state certification.

Physical education has long been recognized as a part of the teaching profession, evidenced by its affiliation with the National Education Association since 1937. Even earlier, in 1885, a group of teachers and other interested individuals formed the Association for the Advancement of Physical Education to encourage the exchange of program and instructional ideas. Today, the American Alliance for Health, Physical Education, Recreation and Dance along with a multiplicity of affiliated organizations, promotes a broad discipline that encompasses physical education, health, sports, dance, leisure, and fitness. This chapter describes many of these associations along with their purposes, publications, and services. To understand physical education and sport as a profession, it is important to know the requisite educational background needed to enter many physical education and sport careers; therefore, the teaching option and some nontraditional specializations are described.

IS PHYSICAL EDUCATION A PROFESSION?

Before looking specifically at physical education as a profession, we need to define what a profession is. A **profession** is a learned occupation that requires training in a specialized field of study. The characteristics of a profession include:

- Is based on a complex, systematic body of theoretical knowledge
- Accepts individuals who have attained extensive knowledge and experience through a formal educational process
- Requires standards and competencies for entry, often through a certification process
- Provides mechanisms and opportunities for growth and development within the field to ensure adherence to established standards and competencies
- Serves a socially valuable function that has received societal recognition and status
- Is governed by a code of ethics to protect those served

Physical educators usually have at least a bachelor's degree and frequently have advanced study and training in an extensive body of knowledge that takes considerable time and effort to learn. Colleagues in related careers share research findings and new ideas while serving people in all aspects of society.

While the above describes physical education as a profession, Chapter 3 presented it as an academic discipline. Are these contradictory or complementary perspectives? Physical education includes the 12 applied sciences, any of which may be a career emphasis. As individuals continue to specialize, most often they take on the identity of exercise physiologists or sport managers, even though their areas of work are founded on physical activity. Historically, physical education has been one of the teaching professions. It has retained the characteristics of a profession even though it has expanded into teaching in various nonschool settings or into nonteaching, activity-related careers. Thus, physical education has evolved into both or either an academic discipline and a profession. Some prefer to combine these two and call physical education a field.

NATIONAL ORGANIZATION AND SERVICES

The American Alliance for Health, Physical Education, Recreation and Dance (AAHPERD, or the Alliance) has grown from 49 to more than 40,000 members and served these members for over a century. One reason for the widespread influence of AAHPERD is that many professional groups have merged into its structure. In 1937, as a department of the National Education Association, the former American Physical Education Association became the American Association for Health and Physical Education. (It became an alliance in 1974.) Recreation was added to its title in 1938, and dance was added in 1979.

The American Alliance for Health, Physical Education, Recreation and Dance is an educational organization designed to facilitate and promote the purposes and activities of its members, associations, and affiliated groups. The Alliance, comprised of six associations (see box below), seeks to:

- Encourage, guide, and support professional growth and development in health, leisure, and movement-related programs based on individual needs, interests, and capabilities
- Communicate the importance of health, leisure, and movement-related activities as they contribute to human well-being
- Encourage and facilitate research which will enrich health, leisure, and movement-related activities and to disseminate the findings to professionals and the public
- Develop and evaluate standards and guidelines for personnel and programs in health, leisure, and movement-related activities
- Coordinate and administer a planned program of professional, public, and government relations that will improve education in areas of health, leisure, and movement-related activities
- Conduct other activities for the public benefit

It is headquartered at 1900 Association Drive, Reston, VA 22091-1599. For more information about the Alliance, call 1-800-213-7193. The services provided by the Alliance include holding an annual national convention; publishing brochures, research abstracts, conference proceedings, and other information pertinent to its fields of interest; positively influencing public opinion and legislation; and providing consultant services.

Four periodicals are published by the Alliance. The *Journal of Physical Education, Recreation and Dance* includes articles of a broad and practical nature, while the *Research Quarterly for Exercise and Sport* reports research findings. *Strategies* publishes practical articles for physical educators and coaches. The *Journal of Health Education* features research-based and practical information. *Update,* in newspaper format, keeps the membership apprised of current events and legislation. Issues of *Update* include notices of job vacancies and information about graduate assistantships.

AMERICAN ALLIANCE FOR HEALTH, PHYSICAL EDUCATION, RECREATION AND DANCE (AAHPERD)

The Alliance comprises six associations. These are:

- American Association for Active Lifestyles and Fitness (AAALF)
- American Association for Health Education (AAHE)
- American Association for Leisure and Recreation (AALR)
- National Association for Girls and Women in Sport (NAGWS)
- National Association for Sport and Physical Education (NASPE)
- National Dance Association (NDA)

The American Association for Active Lifestyles and Fitness (AAALF) represents numerous special interest groups that fill special niches to help achieve its purposes as well as those of the Alliance. These councils and societies conduct conferences, publish position papers, and collaborate in promotional initiatives in areas such as aging, aquatics, adapted physical activity, administration, facilities, international relations, measurement, physical fitness, and safety.

The American Association for Health Education (AAHE) promotes health education in schools, public and community health agencies, business and industry, and colleges. Among the health issues vigorously addressed by AAHE are drug use prevention, HIV prevention and AIDS education, cultural awareness and sensitivity. AAHE offers continuing education credits for health education professionals through a credentialing process using the *Journal of Health Education*.

The American Association for Leisure and Recreation (AALR) seeks to enhance the quality of American life through the awareness and promotion of leisure and recreational experiences. In addition to helping integrate the concepts of positive leisure attitudes and values into education, AALR professionals formulate and disseminate leisure knowledge, trends, and delivery methods. This organization's commitment to uplifting the human spirit results in efforts to conserve cultural and natural resources so individuals can enjoy life-enriching experiences. The "Leisure Today" feature in the *Journal of Physical Education, Recreation and Dance* focuses on the provision of leisure and recreational programs for all populations including older individuals and those with special needs. In collaboration with the National Recreation and Park Association, the AALR accredits programs and has developed standards for evaluating services delivered by community, park, and recreation agencies.

The National Association for Girls and Women in Sport (NAGWS) seeks to improve and expand sport opportunities for girls and women in all levels of competition. It advocates for the initiation and enhancement of opportunities for sports participation and leadership for females. NAGWS helps coordinate the

The National Association for Sport and Physical Education, of the American Alliance for Health, Physical Education, Recreation and Dance, serves over 25,000 members through various projects and programs. (Photo courtesy Mary Ellen Saville.)

annual celebration of National Girls and Women in Sports Day. Through collaborative work with other associations, NAGWS is an advocate for equity in sport.

The largest of the Alliance associations, the National Association for Sport and Physical Education (NASPE) supports quality physical activity programs for children and adults. NASPE crusades for quality, daily physical education for each school student through conferences, print ads, public service announcements, and observance of the National Physical Education and Sport Week (May 1–7). Specialized councils (see box below) serve NASPE members through conferences and workshops, convention programs, and the establishment of guidelines and position statements, such as "Developmentally Appropriate Physical Education Practices for Children."

The National Dance Association (NDA) advocates for standards and assessments in dance, theater, the visual arts, and music through the America 2000 Arts Partnership. It promotes dance through conferences, workshops, publications, research, and liaisons with numerous groups, such as the Kennedy Center for the

---

NATIONAL ASSOCIATION FOR SPORT AND PHYSICAL EDUCATION

K–12 Physical Education Councils
- Council of Physical Education for Children (COPEC)
- Middle and Secondary Physical Education Council (MASSPEC)
- Council of School Leadership in Physical Education

Research/Professional Development
- Biomechanics
- Curriculum and Instruction
- Exercise Physiology
- Motor Development
- Sport Art
- Sport History
- Sport Philosophy
- Sport Psychology
- Sport Sociology
- Applied Exercise Science Council
- College and University Physical Education Council (CUPEC)
- Council on Professional Preparation in Physical Education (COPPPE)
- Sport Management

Sport Councils
- Coaches Council
- National Council of Athletic Training (NCAT)
- National Council of Secondary School Athletic Directors (NCSSAD)
- National Intramural Sports Council (NISC)
- Youth Sports Coalition (YSC)

Performing Arts' education program. The NDA cooperates with Dance USA to promote National Dance Week.

The Student Action Council serves student members in each of the associations and works with collegiate majors' clubs. Because the future of the profession and its organizations depends on today's students, it is essential that students become actively involved in professional activities. (You should start now by joining the Alliance; a sample membership form is provided for you in Figure 4-1. To obtain a form, call 1-800-213-7193) The objectives of the Student Action Council include improving local, state, district, and national student programs, providing opportunities for student leadership experiences, supporting and promoting youth services projects, and serving as an advocate for maximum involvement of students in all Alliance associations. This group also promotes the active involvement of students in local physical education majors' clubs as avenues for leadership and enhanced professional preparation.

The Alliance is divided into these six district associations that share the goals and activities of the Alliance while providing leadership opportunities and services within each region. (See Figure 4-2.) Membership in the Alliance and in a district is combined, thus enabling professionals to attend their district conventions and the Alliance's annual conventions. During these conventions, the Alliance provides a job placement service where graduates can learn about vacancies and interview for jobs. Nonconvention workshops, clinics, and seminars provide Alliance members with the latest research findings, innovative activities, and teaching approaches as well as opportunities for personal enrichment and growth. One example of this leadership in research and education is the Southern District's position paper on physical education (see box on p. 81).

Similarly, state HPERD associations provide professionals the opportunity to learn different coaching techniques, acquire new skills, and interact and exchange information with other members at their annual conventions. Students, especially you, should take advantage of state conventions, because not only will you learn from these experiences but you also may make contacts with many individuals who later may hire you or help you to get a job.

Thus, physical education provides enrichment opportunities to its members as they prepare themselves to serve others. They are joined in their efforts by related groups who seek to share knowledge for the benefit of all.

AFFILIATED ORGANIZATIONS

Although AAHPERD is the largest organization associated with physical education and its related fields, it shares its interests with numerous other groups. The discussion that follows briefly describes some of these organizations.

Higher Education

In 1978, the National Association for Physical Education in Higher Education (NAPEHE) was formed by a merger of the National Association for Physical Education of College Women and the National College Physical Education Association for Men. Since the merger, NAPEHE has continued the publication of *Quest* and its conference proceedings.

Join AAHPERD

❶ Yes, I want to join AAHPERD.

Name (Mr.) (Mrs.) (Ms.) _____

Address _____

City _____   State _____   Zip _____

Telephone: (H) _____   (W) _____

Fax (____) _____   Internet _____

❷ *As an AAHPERD member, you are entitled to join either one or two of the following associations. If you choose to join two, circle your first and second choice. If you prefer only one, you may select one association twice. Students receive one association choice. (Each association that you select receives a portion of your dues.)*

1 2 American Association for Active
         Lifestyles and Fitness (AAALF)
1 2 American Association for Health
         Education (AAHE)
1 2 American Association for Leisure
         and Recreation (AALR)
1 2 National Association for Girls and
         Women in Sport (NAGWS)

1 2 National Association for Sport
         and Physical Education (NASPE)
1 2 National Dance Association (NDA)

☐ Research Consortium, for those
     interested in research. (A check
     here does not affect your association
     affiliation.)

❸ *In addition to your choice of association membership, you have a choice of periodical options and membership options. You may choose to subscribe to as many publications as you wish; your membership rates are based on the number of periodicals you choose. Fill out the information on the other half of this card.*

Periodicals Options
✓ *Update* (the AAHPERD newsletter,
     an automatic benefit of membership)

*JOPERD—The Journal of Physical
Education, Recreation & Dance*

Journal of Health Education

Research Quarterly for Exercise and Sport

*Strategies: A Journal for Sport and Physical
Educators*

*(Add $8 for each periodical mailed outside
the U.S. or Canada)*

Membership Options
Select a membership option based on your status in the profession and choice of periodicals. Check the appropriate category, then circle the option you desire. *(Of your dues, $4 are allocated to* Update; *$25 for each selected periodical.)*

Professional	1-year	2-year	3-year
One periodical	$100.00	$180.00	$240.00
Two periodicals	125.00	230.00	315.00
Three periodicals	150.00	280.00	390.00
Four periodicals	175.00	330.00	465.00

☐ Student *(applies to full-time graduate
and undergraduate students)*

One periodical	$ 30.00
Two periodicals	55.00
Three periodicals	80.00
Four periodicals	105.00

Life membership
$2,000 (payable in four installments)

(Prices subject to change without notice.)

Payment of Dues
I am remitting my dues by:
☐ enclosed check, payable to AAHPERD
☐ VISA   ☐ MasterCard
☐ American Express

Card number _____

Expiration date _____

Fill in amount enclosed here: $ _____

Signature _____

Office Use Only	Dt:_____
Ck:_____	Amt:_____

101

FIGURE 4-1

AAHPERD application.

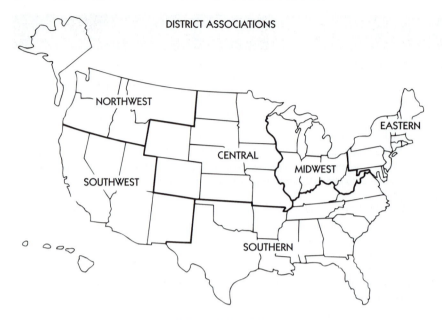

DISTRICT ASSOCIATIONS

STATE ASSOCIATIONS

NORTHWEST DISTRICT
Alaska
Idaho
Montana
Oregon
Washington

CENTRAL DISTRICT
Colorado
Iowa
Kansas
Minnesota
Missouri
Nebraska
North Dakota
South Dakota
Wyoming

SOUTHWEST DISTRICT
Arizona
California
Guam
Hawaii
Nevada
New Mexico
Utah

SOUTHERN DISTRICT
Alabama
Arkansas
Florida
Georgia
Kentucky
Louisiana
Mississippi
North Carolina
South Carolina
Oklahoma
Tennessee
Texas
Virginia

MIDWEST DISTRICT
Illinois
Indiana
Michigan
Ohio
West Virginia
Wisconsin

EASTERN DISTRICT
Connecticut
Delaware
Washington, D.C.
Maine
Maryland
Massachusetts
New Hampshire
New Jersey
New York
Pennsylvania
Puerto Rico
Rhode Island
U.S. Virgin Islands
Vermont

FIGURE 4-2

District and state associations.

Since 1930, the American Academy of Kinesiology and Physical Education has been the highest honorary group in health, physical education, and recreation. Its more than 125 active members have contributed scholarship and professional service, especially in colleges and universities. Some research studies are published annually in *The Academy Papers*.

SOUTHERN DISTRICT AAHPERD POSITION PAPER ON PHYSICAL EDUCATION

Physical education contributes to the growth, development, motor skill acquisition, and fitness of students through physical activity/movement and health-related activities. Participation in physical education can contribute to awareness and positive attitudes that regular vigorous activity is essential throughout life to maintain health and to enrich the quality of life. Because of its unique and essential contribution to the total education program, daily quality physical education should be required in grades K–12.

In grades K–5, classes should be a minimum of 30 minutes each for a minimum total of 150 minutes per week. In grades 6–12, classes should be the length of a regular class period for a minimum total of 250–300 minutes per week. Class size should be consistent with other subjects in the school curriculum.

Classes should be scheduled by grade level and, whenever possible, by ability and physical maturation level. Classes should be designed to accommodate differences in ability among all students including those with identified special needs. Students with identified special needs should be placed in special classes only when it is demonstrated that there is not a reasonable opportunity for success in regular classes through the use of appropriate modifications and accommodations.

No substitutions should be permitted for participants in marching band, interscholastic sports, ROTC, and other extracurricular activities.

Both indoor and outdoor physical education facilities should be provided and should be maintained to meet safety standards. Quality equipment and supplies should be provided in sufficient quantity to meet the needs of all students. Appropriate clothing designed for free and safe movement should be worn in all physical education classes.

Physical fitness, including concepts, should be emphasized as a vital component of the curriculum at all levels. The elementary school curriculum should emphasize the development of basic movement awareness, fundamental motor skills, and fitness, as applied to educational games, educational dance, and educational gymnastic contexts. The middle school/junior high school curriculum should emphasize gymnastics, stunts, and tumbling, aquatics, dance, individual, dual, and team activities/games, recreation, and outdoor education. The secondary/senior high school curriculum should emphasize progressive lifetime-leisure activities and individualized fitness-related theory and exercise programs.

Elementary classes should be taught by instructors certified in physical education with an elementary physical education emphasis. Secondary physical education should be taught by instructors certified in physical education with a secondary physical education emphasis.

(Courtesy the Southern District of the American Alliance for Health, Physical Education, Recreation and Dance.)

Health

Since 1926, the American School Health Association (ASHA) has sought to improve health instruction, healthful living, and health services in the schools. Although originally only for physicians, membership is now open to anyone engaged in school health work. This association publishes the *Journal of School Health*.

Recreation

The National Recreation and Park Association (NRPA) is dedicated to improving the human condition through improved park, recreation, and leisure opportunities and to developing and expanding programs and services and addressing environmental concerns. It facilitates the training of personnel who conduct community recreation programs. The *Journal of Leisure Research, Legal Issues in Research Administration, Therapeutic Recreation,* and *Parks and Recreation* are NRPA publications.

The National Intramural-Recreational Sports Association (NIRSA) was begun in 1950 to provide an opportunity for college intramural directors to meet annually to exchange ideas and information. With the expansion of college programs into recreational services of all kinds, the Association assumed its present name in 1975. Sharing innovative program ideas, reporting research, and discussing policy and procedures highlight its annual convention and the *NIRSA Journal.*

Sports Medicine

The need to establish professional standards and to disseminate information led to the establishment, in 1950, of the National Athletic Trainers' Association (NATA), which publishes the *Journal of Athletic Training* for its over 21,000 members drawn from athletic trainers at all levels of sport. The NATA accredits all approved undergraduate and graduate athletic training programs.

The American College of Sports Medicine (ACSM) was founded in 1954 by individuals drawn from medicine, physiology, and physical education. Among its objectives are advancing scientific research dealing with the effects of physical activities on health and well-being; encouraging cooperation and professional exchange among physicians, scientists, and educators; initiating, promoting, and applying research in sports medicine and exercise science; and maintaining a sports medicine library. The ACSM encourages research publications in injury

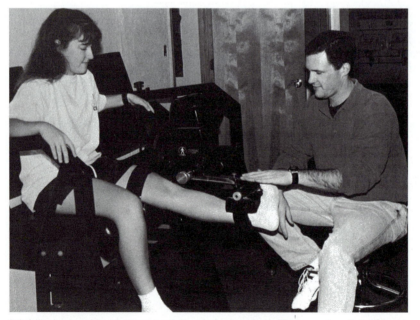

Rehabilitation is an important responsibility of athletic trainers. (Photo courtesy Bob Hilliard.)

prevention and rehabilitation and in environmental effects of exercise, nutrition, and other factors through its *Medicine and Science in Sports and Exercise.*

Psychology, History, and Management

Psychologists, psychiatrists, and physical educators founded the North American Society for the Psychology of Sport and Physical Activity (NASPSPA) in 1967 to promote this increasingly popular field of study. Since 1973, the North American Society for Sport History (NASSH) has encouraged scholarly research in all aspects of this discipline of sport, conducted an annual conference, and published the *Journal of Sport History.* The North American Society for Sport Management (NASSM), established in 1985, focuses on the professional development of practitioners and researchers in this specialization. Articles in the *Journal of Sport Management* encompass both the theory and application of management to sport settings. The Association for the Advancement of Applied Sport Psychology (AAASP), founded in 1986, promotes research and intervention strategies in sport psychology. It publishes the *Journal of Applied Sport Psychology.*

Fitness

The National Strength and Conditioning Association, founded in 1978, is comprised of athletic trainers, physical therapists, sports medicine physicians, and sport science researchers. It promotes the total conditioning of athletes for optimal performance. It publishes the *Journal of Strength and Conditioning Research* and *Strength and Conditioning.*

Aerobics instructors can choose from several organizations for certification. The National Dance-Exercise Instructor's Training Association (NDEITA) (established in 1980) provides standardized training and certification for its 40,000 members. The Aerobics and Fitness Association of America (AFAA), started in 1983, has over 100,000 members. The American Council on Exercise (ACE), established in 1985, certifies aerobics instructors and personal trainers. Appendix B lists several organizations should you seek to obtain certification to teach aerobics or aqua aerobics.

Athletics

In the realm of college athletics, the regulatory bodies include the National Collegiate Athletic Association (NCAA; founded in 1906), the National Association of Intercollegiate Athletics (NAIA; founded in 1940), and the National Junior College Athletic Association (NJCAA; founded in 1938). The NCAA, with over 1000 member institutions and conferences promotes competition through championships for women and men. The *NCAA News,* in newspaper format, provides updates on issues and events for its members along with numerous job announcements. Athletes in small colleges that hold membership in the NAIA compete in 24 women's and men's championships. The NJCAA, representing over 500 institutions, conducts championships in the major sports for women and men. Other athletic organizations that encourage the exchange of ideas include the College Sports Information Directors of America, the College Athletic Business Management Association, and the National Association of Collegiate Directors of Athletics.

The Amateur Athletic Union (AAU) was founded in 1888 to promote amateur sports and to check the spread of the problems associated with professional sports. Its over 3,000,000 members participate in and conduct local, regional, and national sports events for athletes ages 3 to 19.

The National Federation of State High School Associations (NFSHSA; founded in 1920) and the 50 state and associated high school athletic and activities associations work to protect the activity and athletic interests of high schools, to promote the growth of educational interscholastic athletics, and to protect high school students from exploitation. It publishes *Interscholastic Athletic Administration*.

Many states also have coaches' associations that either are specific to one sport or have coaches from all sports in their memberships. These groups usually sponsor statewide or regional workshops or clinics about specific coaching techniques or strategies, rule changes, values and ethics in school athletics, and sport psychology. The National High School Athletic Coaches Association (NHSACA) (founded in 1965) and the National Federation Interscholastic Coaches Association (NFICA) (founded in 1981) combined have nearly 100,000 members. Many volunteer coaches join the National Youth Sports Coaches Association (NYSCA).

•   •   •   •

The value and importance of joining and participating in a professional organization is multifaceted. First, membership entitles each person to receive journals, newsletters, directories, and other materials. If read, these keep the practitioner up-to-date with the latest techniques, research, methodology, and applications. Second, many of these organizations sponsor conferences and workshops, which provide additional opportunities to stay current through timely updates and to interact with and learn from colleagues in similar careers. Third, organizational affiliation may lead to service on committees and leadership positions, where you can contribute to the promotion of standards and share your expertise with others. Fourth, job announcements in newsletters and placement centers at conferences may lead to career advancement. Thus, professional involvement enlivens your career.

The basic objectives of all professional groups are to exchange information, to learn, and to serve. To enhance both your knowledge about and commitment to your chosen career, you should seek opportunities through these organizations to grow professionally. By exchanging program ideas and instructional and motivational techniques, members can improve their abilities to serve others and to learn how to communicate their goals and activities to colleagues and to the general public. Through the sharing of experiences and research, many ideas for further study are generated. Therefore, as a young professional, you are encouraged to join your college, state, and national associations and one or more of the organizations in your interest area. You also should begin to read physical education and sport periodicals, as listed in the box on p. 85 to help you more fully understand your profession.

SELECTED ACADEMIC AND PROFESSIONAL JOURNALS*

Adapted Physical Activity Quarterly
Dance Magazine
Journal of Athletic Training
Journal of Health Education
Journal of Leisure Research
Journal of Physical Education, Recreation and Dance
Journal of Sport and Exercise Psychology
Journal of Sport Management
Journal of Teaching in Physical Education
NIRSA Journal
Parks and Recreation
The Physical Educator
The Physician and Sportsmedicine
Research Quarterly for Exercise and Sport
Scholastic Coach
Sociology of Sport Journal
Strategies: A Journal for Sport and Physical Educators
Strength and Conditioning

*See Appendix A for mailing addresses for ordering these and other academic and professional journals.

UNDERGRADUATE SPECIALIZATIONS

Assuming that you are considering a career in physical education and sport, the following section of this chapter introduces you to the various options or specializations that exist in many colleges and universities. This discussion will prepare you for Chapter 5, which describes many careers related to physical education and sport, and Chapter 6, which explains many specific programs and certifications.

Professional preparation programs in physical education traditionally have been oriented toward teacher education, although most colleges offer nonteaching specializations. As the demand for teachers decreased dramatically in the late 1970s, colleges and universities revised their curricula to include the increasingly popular sport and fitness-related specializations. This expansion in the fields of fitness, leisure, recreation, athletics, and sport resulted in diverse career opportunities for students specializing in athletic training, exercise science, and sport management.

Athletic Training

Many students opt to specialize in athletic training, which deals with the prevention, treatment, and rehabilitation of sports injuries. Athletic trainers work with coaches to develop conditioning programs to optimally prepare athletes for participation and competition. Trainers also provide supportive taping to help ensure

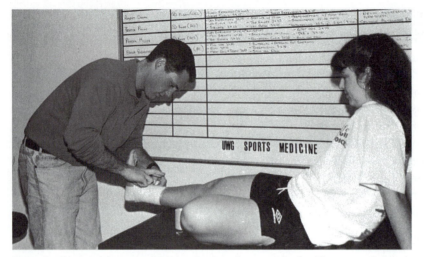

Careers in athletic training are available in schools, colleges, professional leagues, and clinical settings. (Photo courtesy Bob Hilliard.)

safe participation. When injuries occur, athletic trainers are the primary care-givers; they simultaneously conduct on-site assessments about the severity of injuries. If these injuries are minor, first aid measures and the administration of ice, whirlpool, ultrasound, and other treatments fall within their purview. Under a physician's supervision, athletic trainers rehabilitate athletes suffering from more serious conditions, such as loss of mobility due to a broken bone or surgery. In addition, athletic trainers often counsel athletes to help them deal with injuries and rehabilitation.

Most states do not require certification as a prerequisite for athletic trainers in the schools. This situation, however, places the trainers, athletes, and schools at risk when proper care is not given. Almost all colleges, professional teams, and sports medicine clinics stipulate that applicants must hold certifications from the National Athletic Trainers' Association (NATA) for employment (see box on p. 87).

In the schools, athletic trainers can expect to teach at least a partial load of classes, if they hold a teaching certification, because these positions are seldom full-time training. Salaries are determined by the local school district's salary schedule and are based on years of experience and educational degrees. Additional stipends for extracurricular work are possible. Salaries could range from $30,000 to $70,000.

College athletic trainers, depending on the size of the institution and the number of trainers, may be full- or part-time. They may teach in a NATA-approved program or in some other field. They may serve one team, like football, or be responsible for all of the intercollegiate sports teams. Depending on the job description, salaries can vary widely, such as $30,000 to $80,000.

Another popular career choice for athletic trainers is in a clinical setting. These jobs may be affiliated with a hospital, with a rehabilitative focus, or in a private clinic that serves the public. Individuals helped by athletic trainers may have suffered sports-related injuries or need assistance in returning to activity after inactivity or some nonsports-related injury.

SPECIALIZATION IN ATHLETIC TRAINING

Five Domains of Athletic Training

- Prevention of athletic injuries
- Recognition, evaluation, and immediate care of athletic injuries
- Rehabilitation and reconditioning of athletic injuries
- Health care administration
- Professional development and responsibility

Certification Requirements

- At least 1500 hours (documented) over 2–5 years of athletic training experience under the supervision of a NATA-certified athletic trainer
- Completion of courses in health, human anatomy, human physiology, physiology of exercise, kinesiology, basic athletic training, and advanced athletic training, OR
- Completion of a NATA-approved athletic training curriculum or one accredited by the Commission on Accreditation of Allied Health Education Programs in no less than 2 years with a minimum of 800 hours of athletic training experience under the supervision of a NATA-certified athletic trainer, AND
- Pass three-part (written, practical/oral, and written simulation) national certification examination

Employment Opportunities

- Secondary school interscholastic athletic programs
- Intercollegiate athletic programs
- Professional athletic teams
- Corporate health programs
- Sports medicine clinics
- Health clubs
- Clinical and industrial health care programs
- Athletic training curriculum programs

Coaching

Coaching specializations or minors are popular choices for undergraduates who want to continue their involvement with sports. Interscholastic and youth programs need individuals who want to coach young athletes. The demand for coaches of school teams exceeds the supply because of increased numbers of girls' teams, the hiring of fewer new teachers, and the resignation of tenured physical educators from coaching, but not from teaching. The millions of children competing on youth sport teams deserve coaches who know how to teach fundamental skills while making sports fun.

Almost all youth league coaches are volunteers. Regardless of the type of employment of these volunteers, they need a basic knowledge in first aid, coaching concepts, human growth and development, and sport sciences. Although a

Coaching and teaching are often combined into one career in schools and colleges.

few independent programs offer educational programs and certifications for these coaches, most volunteers demonstrate minimal competence.

Few individuals only coach in the schools; the dual role of teacher-coach characterizes most. Whereas states require subject matter certifications for teachers, only a few specify that coaches show competencies or complete certain courses. Coaching curricula typically include courses in first aid, care and prevention of athletic injuries, anatomy, physiology, exercise physiology, coaching theory, coaching techniques in specific sports, human growth and development, sport management, sport psychology, and sport pedagogy.

Fitness

A specialization in fitness prepares students to enter myriad careers in this growing field. One appealing feature is the opportunity to help others attain and maintain healthy lifestyles. Another is the pleasure of associating with people who value fitness. Although fitness specialists avoid most of the discipline problems and management minutiae in the schools, they typically work during the leisure hours of others.

Regardless of the setting, the fitness specialist must have a strong scientific background, such as in biomechanics and exercise physiology, especially if any activity programs are being designed and prescribed. A knowledge of business and management not only helps in entry-level positions but is essential for career advancement. Fitness specialists typically find jobs in corporate and industrial fitness settings, commercial aerobics, health, fitness, or sports clubs, or recreation departments. However, there are also openings on cruise ships, in resorts, or as personal trainers.

Sport Management

The burgeoning sports industry attracts graduates who seek to apply business and management knowledge to sports settings. The best academic preparation encompasses the triad of management foundations, sports applications, and an internship, or work experience, within the field. It is imperative that students understand that careers in this area are "bottom-line," or profit-oriented. Therefore, courses in accounting, economics, finance, organizational behavior, and law are important. Built on these should be applications courses such as sport management, sport law, facility management, sport ethics, and personnel management. The culminating experience that links this knowledge and application is the internship.

Exercise and Sport Science

The academic preparation of the exercise and sport science student focuses on the sciences. Usually courses are completed in biology or zoology, anatomy, physiology, chemistry, exercise physiology, biomechanics, and possibly biochemistry. Also beneficial is the development of strong statistical and computer technology skills along with background in nutrition. This strong scientific foundation also helps prepare a student to pursue advanced degrees for a college professorship. On the practical side, exercise prescription skills are necessary to qualify for many positions, such as those in corporate fitness programs, clinical settings, or cardiac rehabilitation centers. Experiences gained through an internship or part-time work are decided advantages when entering this specialization.

Physical Therapy, Adapted Physical Education, and Therapeutic Recreation

The therapeutic field encompasses physical therapy, adapted physical education, and therapeutic recreation. Whether in the schools or in clinics, specialists in these fields help individuals with disabling conditions. Majors in physical therapy prepare for the licensing exam through course work based on the sciences and extensive clinical experiences. The adapted physical educator may instruct one-on-one, in a special school, or in inclusion classrooms. Activities outside of schools are used by the therapeutic recreation professional to enhance mobility, self-confidence, and independence. Internships or experiences working with people with different disabling conditions facilitate the application of therapeutic knowledge and skills.

Teaching Option

Teacher certification following graduation from an accredited four-year institution is the goal of graduates choosing a teaching option. Teacher preparation courses may be taken throughout the undergraduate years or may be concentrated in just two years following the completion of general education courses taken at a junior or community college or at a four-year institution. Certifications for physical education may include those for pre-kindergarten (P) through grade 6, grades 5 through 8, grades 7 through 12, P through grade 12, health education, and dance.

The National Council for Accreditation of Teacher Education (NCATE) allows learned societies, such as the National Association for Sport and Physical Education, to recommend guidelines for the professional studies component of its standards. These guidelines, containing all the attitudes, knowledge, and skills required of a physical education teacher, have been subdivided into three

Teachers need expertise to instruct in nontraditional activities.

elements: academic, professional, and pedagogical. Aquatics, dance, exercise, games, sports, and other leisure pursuits are components of the unique academic content of physical education. The applied sciences of motor development, sport management, sport pedagogy, motor learning, sport philosophy, sport biomechanics, adapted physical education, exercise physiology, sport history, sport psychology, sport sociology, and sports medicine, as discussed in Chapter 3, provide the intellectual and theoretical bases for studies in physical education. The professional aspect of the undergraduate program develops an awareness of and commitment to the various educational, research, and service activities of physical education. These include studies of curriculum models, organizational structures, diagnostic and evaluative procedures, and problem-solving techniques. Knowledge about teaching and learning physical skills constitutes the pedagogical element. Abilities to plan, implement, and evaluate learning are observed in a supervised student teaching experience.

•   •   •   •

These specializations, while not the only ones available, illustrate the variety of alternative career choices in physical education and sport. Chapter 5, Selecting a Career, will assist in your career choice and career development process.

SUMMARY

This chapter focuses on being a professional, not on joining a profession. Physical education is characterized by extensive training in a disciplinary body of knowledge and service; therefore, communication among colleagues is essential.

The services provided by the Alliance will enhance development of each of the component parts of the profession. The Alliance's six national associations are composed of professionals in leisure and recreation, health, fitness, sport, physical education, dance, and related fields. Numerous other professional associations provide avenues for collaboration and individual career development. Journals and conferences are the two most noteworthy services provided by these organizations. Become involved while you are a student. Participate in conferences, attend workshops, and read publications of physical education-related organizations to prepare for your chosen career.

Undergraduate specializations in physical education and sport include athletic training, coaching, fitness, exercise and sport science, and teaching. Various career options await graduates with specialized knowledge and skills in one of these fields.

As a young professional, you can make a significant contribution to the quality of life of those you serve as a teacher, a researcher, or a program leader. You have the opportunity to become a role model by planning and implementing effective programs that meet the activity needs of diverse groups. Rather than reacting, you can become proactive by promoting the values of physical education and sport and by implementing beneficial programs.

CAREER PERSPECTIVE

MICHAEL DELONG
Head Football Coach
Springfield College
Springfield, Massachusetts

EDUCATION
B.S., Physical Education, Springfield College
M.A., Physical Education, University of North Carolina at Chapel Hill

JOB RESPONSIBILITIES AND HOURS

The responsibilities of college and university coaches vary tremendously, depending on the emphasis placed on the institution's program and the sport. Mike organizes and administers an NCAA Division III football program, including directing a staff of two full-time assistant coaches and 12 graduate assistants, recruiting student athletes, planning games and practices, working directly with admissions and financial aid officers, fund-raising, developing community support, and carrying out on- and off-field coaching duties. He also teaches four semester hours in-season and six to eight semester hours out-of-season and advises Physical Education majors a typical work load at a smaller institution. Like most coaches' Mike's weekly hours, which vary from 85 in-season to 70 off-season to 30 during the summer, are demanding. Salaries are based on each coach's experience and won-lost record, the institution and its reputation, and the sport. At the NCAA Division III level, the salary range is $28,000 to $70,000 for head coaches and $18,000 to $30,000 for assistant coaches.

SPECIALIZED COURSE WORK, DEGREES, AND WORK EXPERIENCES NEEDED FOR THIS CAREER

Although college or university coaching does not require a master's degree, teaching at smaller institutions may require attaining this degree. Physical education is the most common major for coaches at both the undergraduate and graduate levels, although many coaches have degrees in other disciplines. Opportunities to become head coaches usually follow years of coaching high school teams, serving as effective graduate assistants or full-time assistant coaches, or completing successful college or professional playing careers. Volunteering to coach a youth, school, or club team may provide an entry into this career. Mike recommends that prospective coaches emphasize exercise physiology, oral and written communication skills, problem-solving techniques, organizational skills, motivational strategies, and theory and technique courses. He encourages prospective coaches as well as those already in positions to visit successful programs and to learn from others.

SATISFYING ASPECTS

People may choose this career because they love a particular sport, want to continue associating with it, enjoy teaching its skills and strategies, like to help athletes develop their talents to their optimal levels, or for a combination of reasons. Mike especially enjoys player-coach relationships, coach-coach interactions, and the feeling of accomplishment as the team improves. Coaching can be tremendously satisfying, not only in terms of wins and losses, but in watching teams and players grow and mature. For Mike, helping individuals reach their goals is the most rewarding part of coaching.

JOB POTENTIAL

Mike states that to be secure in a college or university coaching position, winning is essential. If you perform within the rules, he says, you will be secure; if you do not perform, you can expect to be relieved of your duties. Promotion is also based on performance. Coaches who are proven workers have a good chance for advancement in the profession. Politics also plays a role, so it helps to know people. Since getting your foot in the door is difficult and highly competitive, a major part of the initial hiring process is knowing someone who can help you secure a full-time position. Once you have proven your abilities and made connections with people, things generally go a little easier. The job market is extremely competitive, especially for the best jobs. Patience and perseverance are two essential characteristics necessary for success.

SUGGESTIONS FOR STUDENTS

Mike states that coaching is a great career because of the fun and excitement. Coaches are surrounded by great people who like to work and play hard. The rewards of developing players and a team to perform to their fullest potentials are tremendous. Mike advises that prior to becoming a coach you make sure you are ready to make a full commitment, because the players you will coach deserve your best effort. Your family also must be aware of the sacrifices that they will have to make because of the time demands of this career. He adds that you need to be flexible and to be ready to overcome obstacles and setbacks; there are both extreme highs and extreme lows with which you must cope. The rewards of coaching are directly proportional to the effort you put into the team. If you give your best, in the long run, coaching is well worth the effort.

REVIEW QUESTIONS

1. What are the characteristics of a profession?
2. How can you justify that physical education is a profession?
3. How has the American Alliance for Health, Physical Education, Recreation and Dance sought to achieve any one of its objectives?
4. What types of services are provided by the National Association for Sport and Physical Education?
5. What is the Student Action Council, and what are its objectives?
6. What are the purposes of the American College of Sports Medicine?
7. What one national association has led in the expansion of aerobics programs?
8. According to the National Council for Accreditation of Teacher Education, in what three elements of physical education must a prospective teacher gain knowledge?
9. What is required for certification as an athletic trainer?
10. What are several career possibilities for individuals specializing in exercise and sport science?

STUDENT ACTIVITIES

1. Join the American Alliance for Health, Physical Education, Recreation and Dance (1900 Association Drive, Reston, VA 22091), using the membership form provided.
2. Write to one physical education and sport organization that interests you (other than the AAHPERD) and request information about possible careers.
3. Read at least one article from any two of the periodicals listed in the box on page 85. Describe its key points.
4. Write a one-page statement defending the proposition that physical education is a profession.
5. Attend at least one professional workshop or clinic during this school year.
6. In small groups, prepare a five-minute defense for the importance and advantages of joining a professional organization.
7. Interview one person in each of the undergraduate specializations to learn more information about their careers. Write a one-page report about each or share this information in a two-minute class presentation.
8. Select one of the professional organizations and give a two-minute presentation about its unique programs and services.
9. Read one position paper or publication of one of the six Alliance organizations and write a one-page report about it.
10. The following problem-solving exercise will help solidify the knowledge learned from Chapters 1–4: The Board of Trustees of Midwest College has directed the President to cut programs on campus due to the current financial crisis. The President has decided that physical education, intramurals, and athletics are expendable because they contribute little to achieving the mission of the college. The President has formed three task forces, one composed of student physical education and sport majors,

another of physical education faculty, and another of Athletic Department personnel. Each is charged with justifying why these programs should NOT be eliminated. (The city has offered to buy the existing physical education and athletic facilities, thereby eliminating this financial burden.) Form three groups representing these task forces and prepare responses. The task forces may proceed in any way they choose to collect pertinent data and information to justify the importance of these programs. Each task force should also prepare and present alternative strategies for the President to consider. Each task force will be chaired by a person responsible for delivering a five-minute defense during class.

REFERENCE

American Alliance for Health, Physical Education, Recreation and Dance: Bylaws, Article III, Reston, VA, 1996, the Alliance.

SUGGESTED READINGS

Anderson MK: Women in athletic training, *JOPERD* 63(3):42, 1992. This article describes some of the early experiences of, barriers confronted by, and progress made by women in athletic training.

Brunner R, Hill D: Using learning style research in coaching, *JOPERD* 63(4):26, 1992. After discussing the learning style approach in coaching, where coaching methods are matched to athletes' learning preferences, the authors describe how this approach helped one high school wrestling coach develop a winning team.

Bunker LK: Virtual reality: movement's centrality, *Quest* 46(4):456, 1994. Human movement should be the central focus of physical education as a profession. To facilitate this transformation, the author suggests several key principles—uniqueness, communication, accountability, diversity, teamwork, ethics, change, and the production of theoretical and practical knowledge.

Clark DE: A new code of ethics for NRPA, *Parks and Rec* 30(8):38, 1995. The National Recreation and Parks Association has addressed concerns about ethical violations of public trust and how to educate its members about the value of ethical behavior.

Corbin CB, Eckert HM, (eds): The evolving undergraduate major, Champaign, 1990, Human Kinetics Publishers, *The Academy Papers* 23. Physical education as a discipline and as a profession is described and contrasted. The name and image crisis issue is also examined.

Dustin DL: Leisure today: equity issues in leisure services, *JOPERD* 61(8):25, 1990. Articles in this feature examine equity issues of conservation, resource allocation in wildland recreation, opportunities for people of color and people with disabilities, meeting needs of all children, women's programs, and public sector resources.

Grunbaum JA, et al: A comprehensive approach to school health program needs assessment, *J of Sch Health* 65(2):54, 1995. This article describes one approach using surveys, interviews, and observation for assessing whether school health programs are effectively addressing topics such as violence, smoking, substance abuse, sexual behavior, nutrition, and physical activity.

Hester D, Dunaway D (eds): NAGWS: paths to advocacy, recruitment, and enhancement, *JOPERD* 62(3):29, 1991. Nine articles explain how the National Association for Girls and Women in Sport has achieved its three goals: advocacy for women's full participation in physical activity and sports leadership; recruitment, development and promotion of female leadership positions; and advocacy for initiating and enhancing quality sport and physical activity programs for all females.

Lambrecht KW: A study of curricular preparation needs for sport club managers, *J of Sp Mgmt* 5:47, 1991. Based on responses to a national questionnaire, sport club managers, regardless of the number of members served, identified the eight leading curricular preparation needs. These included marketing, business management, sales communications, public relations, budgeting, communication (speaking) skills, internship in club management, and facility and equipment management.

Stroot SA (ed): Socialization into physical education, *J of Teach in PE* 12(4):337, 1993. This issue focuses on the socialization of preservice and beginning teachers. Among the topics are teachers' perspectives, beliefs about teaching during preservice training, induction of physical educators, faculty consensus concerning teacher education, and perspectives on socialization research.

CHAPTER 5

Selecting a Career

KEY CONCEPTS

- Self-assessment inventories help identify individuals' characteristics and desired lifestyles that influence career choices.
- Traditional and nontraditional settings foster the teaching-learning process yet differ in clientele, work hours, and related responsibilities.
- Programs for the development of fitness offer careers for those interested in helping others incorporate healthful habits and practices into their lives.
- Schools, colleges, nonschool agencies, and professional leagues expect coaches, administrators, trainers, officials, and other personnel to direct and to provide quality athletic programs.
- Many schools and public and private organizations need individuals with sport management knowledge to direct their programs.
- Sport marketing has grown to be a multimillion-dollar business as it capitalizes on the nation's enthusiasm for fitness.

Career choices today are more complex decisions than they were formerly because of the obsolescence of some jobs, the burgeoning of technology, the demographic shifts in population, the acceptance of women and minorities in more jobs in the work force, and economic necessity. People seldom continue with their initial career choices; they change jobs several times during their working years.

The preceding chapters described the broad spectrum of physical education and sport, laying the foundation for the career options presented in this chapter. You should now be prepared to assess objectively your future in a physical education or sport career. This assessment is not a one-time event, but rather an ongoing process. Your initial career choice is not necessarily a lifetime commitment but one that should be reevaluated periodically. As you read this chapter and assess your interests, abilities, and goals, remember that you are choosing a career pathway, not necessarily a single job.

Before embarking on this process, identify your attitudes and expectations. Your attitude toward a career greatly influences whether you will be successful

FACTORS INFLUENCING CAREER CHOICES

Using the scale below, indicate how you value each of the following in relation to your selection of a career:

5	4	3	2	1
Most highly valued	Strong influencing factor	Average consideration	Weak influencing factor	Not valued at all

_____ Influence of your family and significant others

_____ Identification with role model(s)

_____ Knowledgeable about many aspects of this career

_____ Would personally enjoy this career

_____ Enjoy working with people

_____ Desire to serve others

_____ Ease of entrance into this career

_____ Monetary and other benefits from this career

_____ Time compatibility (work hours versus leisure time) meets your desires

_____ Job security available in this career

_____ Job location close to family and friends

From the list above, select the five that you think are most important to you in your career choice and write them (in descending order of importance) in the spaces below.

1. _____

2. _____

3. _____

4. _____

5. _____

Other factors influencing your career choice:

_____

_____

and happy. A major factor is your self-concept. How do you evaluate your abilities? Are you willing to listen to the advice of teachers, coaches, parents, and others? Can you objectively assess your personal strengths and weaknesses? Are you people oriented? Are you motivated to do your best?

Before considering available careers, analyze the relative importance of some personal and job-related factors. Two self-assessment inventories are provided in the boxes on pages 97–98. Your responses to both of these will help you determine which physical education and sport career best meets your needs and aspirations.

FACTORS INFLUENCING CAREER CHOICES

Family influences regarding a career choice can be positive, negative, or both. Parents may overtly or subtly persuade you to pursue a career on which they place a high value. Many times parents have forbidden their children to major in

LIFESTYLE PREFERENCE ASSESSMENT

1. Where would you prefer to live (state or region)? _____

2. Would you prefer an urban, small town, or rural work environment? _____

3. Do you prefer to work for yourself or for others? _____

4. Do you prefer a large or small work environment? _____

5. What ages of people (if any) would you prefer to interact with daily? _____
_____

6. Do you prefer an outdoor or indoor work environment? _____

7. Do you prefer a sedentary or an active job? _____

8. How much travel (if any) would you want as a regular part of your work? _____
_____

9. What days of the week would you prefer to work? _____

10. What hours of the day would you prefer to work? _____

11. What salary would you need now? _____ in 10 years? _____

12. How much vacation time would you want each year? _____

13. What fringe benefits would you want as part of your job? _____
_____
_____

14. How important to you is career advancement? _____

15. What other job characteristics do you think would be important to your job satisfaction? _____
_____
_____

physical education because they viewed it as frivolous, nonacademic, or not prestigious enough. On the other hand, parents may push their children into a physical education-related career because of their own rewarding past experiences. Regardless of the situation, remember that your family will not be going to work for you each day or fulfilling the responsibilities of your chosen career. Parents, siblings, and significant others, although they can express their opinions and share their experiences, should not decide for you.

Whether consciously or not, many people select a career because they respect and admire someone who is in a particular position, a role model whom they wish to emulate. This may be a parent, sibling, coach, teacher, or friend who has demonstrated enjoyment of and dedication to a career that you wish to share. One precautionary note is that you may not be able to find the same type of position or may not possess the same abilities. Remember, you need to develop your own niche rather than trying to mimic another person.

The skills, knowledge, abilities, and experiences that you bring to your career will influence whether you are successful. This is not to imply that all career preparation precedes employment; certainly there is considerable learning while you are on the job. Your confidence in accepting an initial position is based on two factors, only one of which is prior formal preparation. Always remember the importance of the second factor of gaining experiences, including voluntary or internship experiences, that may enhance your chances of career advancement or change.

An important criterion for continuation in a job is the level of personal fulfillment and satisfaction. If you dread going to work, hate the day-to-day routine,

Career satisfaction often comes when your athletes achieve their goals, which may include participation in a sport as well as winning medals. (Photo courtesy Barry Pennell.)

and think the negative aspects far outweigh the positive gains, then it may be time for a change. It is not disastrous to sacrifice job security and material benefits in order to start a career that enhances self-worth and pleasure. One way to make a career change less traumatic is to prepare yourself for a broad physical education and sport career pathway that can offer you numerous alternatives.

Some people prefer a solitary setting; others need to interact frequently with people. If you are people oriented, you need to identify the ages of those with whom you find the greatest enjoyment and seek a career that includes these opportunities. It is also important for you to identify which aspects of working with people you enjoy the most. Do you prefer to work with large groups, small groups, or one-on-one? Do you prefer constant or periodic interactions? Can you make decisions with others and about them?

Sometimes interaction with others is so highly valued that your personal needs become secondary to those of others. This characteristic is known as altruism. Teachers in traditional and nontraditional settings focus on helping their students develop healthy lifestyles, even though their own material benefits seem small compared with the hours spent in instruction.

Career opportunities in physical education and sport are expanding. Your expertise is needed because of increased leisure time, higher standards of living, and the emphasis on fitness. However, your ideal job in the exact location you wish and with the dreamed-for salary may not be available. After realizing that jobs are available for those who actively seek them, you must be willing to accept the probability of starting at the bottom. As a young professional, you can expect to work hard, to volunteer for extra duties, to learn new ideas, to gain experiences, and to accept less desirable responsibilities as a test of commitment to your field. If you do so successfully, you will advance.

You must determine the importance you place on monetary and other material benefits as you choose a career. Your response on the Lifestyle Preference

CAREER OPPORTUNITIES IN PHYSICAL EDUCATION AND SPORT

Teaching

Traditional
- Elementary school (K–6)
- Middle school (5–8)
- Secondary school (7–12)
- Junior/community college
- College/university
- Adapted physical education

Nontraditional
- Sport club
- Health club
- Sport camp or school
- Recreation department
- Corporate or industry fitness
- Senior citizens' program
- Military
- Dance studio
- Resort
- Cruise ship

Fitness

Development
- Private sport club
- Recreation department
- Dance studio
- Corporate or industry fitness
- Protective services (police and fire)

Rehabilitative
- Therapeutic recreation
- Cardiac rehabilitation
- Sports medicine clinic
- Weight control center
- Stress management clinic
- Massage clinic
- Fitness and nutrition counseling

Athletics

School
- Coaching
- Athletic administration
- Athletic training
- Sport officiating

College and University
- Coaching
- Athletic administration
- Athletic training
- Business management
- Facility management

Assessment indicates the value that a certain salary has for you and how it relates to other aspects of your life, such as family, status, location, and travel. The importance that salary has for you is also shown in the hours and days that you prefer to work as well as your desired vacation time. Money, however, is only one type of remuneration. Other benefits, including health insurance, retirement benefits, an expense account, travel, club memberships, and prestige, may offset a lower salary. Only you can decide the importance of money and other benefits, but you must do so honestly, since they frequently are pivotal factors in career selection.

A five-day, 8-to-5 work week is unlikely in most physical education and sport careers. Your career choice could result in working any number of hours a week, nights, holidays, and weekends, and anywhere from 9 to 12 months a year. Only you can weigh your personal preferences versus each job's characteristics.

CAREER OPPORTUNITIES IN PHYSICAL EDUCATION AND SPORT (CONT'D)

Sports information
Sports marketing
Academic counseling
Sport officiating
Ticket sales
Strength and conditioning coach
Sport psychology

Sport Management

Business and Industry
    Sport club
    Health club
    Sport camp and school
    Corporate or industry fitness
    Theme park and resort
    Sport hall of fame and museum
    Public fitness and recreation
    Facility management

School
    Program/department head
    Intramurals/campus recreation
    Research

Sport Marketing
    Clothing sales
    Equipment sales
    Club membership sales
    Book sales

Sport Communication
    Sport broadcasting
    Sport journalism
    Spot photography

Begrudging time spent working often results in negative feelings toward that task. How important is the amount and scheduling of leisure time for you? How do work hours relate to monetary benefits in importance?

Job security varies dramatically in physical education and sport careers. Competent fulfillment of job responsibilities in some careers results in retention of positions based on merit; careers in education require earned tenure for job security. Some careers carry no guarantee of future employment other than the demand for your services. Associated with the concept of job security is the potential for advancement. Relocation is often necessary for advancement because the position you qualify for or seek may not be available in the same city or with the same employer. Challenge and stimulation are important to many people for continuation in a career, as are recognition for a job well done and increased material benefits.

As you decide on a career, review and weigh all these factors. Take advantage of your institution's career services office, which can assist you in evaluating various career options. Only after evaluating the most influential considerations and your own personal preferences can you objectively select a career pathway. Regardless of your choice, the key is your commitment and motivation.

The box on pages 100–101 provides a broad overview of career opportunities. The rest of the chapter describes these broad categories and some of the options, presenting educational requirements, job availability, and positive and negative aspects. After you have finished this chapter, refer to Figure 5-1 on pages 118–119 for sample questions to ask of professionals in any careers you are considering.

TEACHING

Schools and Colleges

Employment for college graduates with majors in physical education has traditionally been in public and private schools. Teaching remains a viable choice for both beginning and lifelong careers. Teachers' salaries are determined by each state's salary schedule and local school district supplements. Additional stipends for extra responsibilities like coaching are possible. Base salaries for beginning teachers with baccalaureate degrees will be at least $25,000. To find jobs, graduates may have to move to smaller communities, urban settings, or different states. In the latter situation, a reciprocal agreement may exist between the certifying state and the new state, or additional course work may be required before full certification is granted.

Many states require *The Praxis Series: Professional Assessments for Beginning Teachers* for certification. This is a three-part series which: (a) tests reading, writing, and mathematics skills needed by all teachers, (b) measures prospective teachers' knowledge of their major fields of study, and (c) judges actual teaching skill through the use of trained assessors.

Junior high and senior high physical educators in their first years sometimes teach classes outside their major fields. Preparing to teach in a second subject area through taking courses and obtaining certification will enhance the likelihood of securing a teaching position. Willingness to accept these teaching assignments may lead to full-time physical education positions in subsequent years. The physical educator, although perhaps not prepared to teach or interested in teaching health, frequently is assigned classes in this area, too. Some schools hire certified health educators, and others have health consultants, but because of budget constraints many health classes are taught by physical educators in the secondary schools. Physical education teachers work a minimum of seven hours at school, which usually includes one planning period and at least five classes. In addition, the teacher is expected to plan classes; grade papers; monitor the halls, lunchroom, and buses; and complete administrative reports. Some secondary teachers are faced with discipline problems, apathetic students, drug abuse, inadequate facilities and equipment, lack of administrative and community support, and sometimes even violent behaviors. On the other hand, professional involvement and educational enrichment are encouraged by supportive administrators. Low salaries deter some good candidates, while opportunities to positively influence students' lives, retirement and health benefits, summer vacations, and job security are attractive job characteristics.

Adapted physical education specialists are hired most frequently by large systems and state departments of education so that many schools may share the expertise of one individual. This specialist helps classroom teachers and physical educators meet the needs of disabled students who have been included in regular classes, or they may individualize instruction for students with special needs. Educational background and experience emphasizing adapted physical education is essential for this career. Hours and salaries correspond with those of other teachers.

In some states, elementary school physical educators are in demand; in others, jobs are scarce. Their responsibilities vary from teaching daily classes for children at one school to conducting ten 30-minute classes at a different school each day of the week. The intrinsic satisfaction of helping children learn and develop is the reward cited most often by these teachers. The benefits of positively influencing children's attitudes toward movement skills and encouraging healthy lifestyles outweigh problems like inadequate facilities and equipment and limited administrative support.

Teaching physical education in junior or community colleges or in four-year colleges and universities requires education beyond the bachelor's degree. In smaller institutions, faculty with master's degrees are expected to teach pre-major or major courses. Most institutions also require sports and activity instructors to have master's degrees. Since university activity instructors and small-college teachers spend more time teaching than researching, job security or tenure is based primarily on teaching and service rather than on scholarly productivity. (These same teachers often are expected to advise students and to serve on departmental and university committees.) Beginning salaries range widely according to location and status of the institution, with benefits including health insurance, retirement programs, and summer vacations. In their activity and theory classes, these teachers

Teaching fundamental skills to children may lead to their continued participation in physical activity throughout life. (Photo courtesy Bob Hilliard.)

Teachers must be knowledgeable, organized, good communicators, enthusiastic, and respectful of others, as well as possess interpersonal skills and demonstrate professional integrity. (Photo courtesy Bob Hilliard.)

Golf instruction is popular in schools and colleges as well as in private and public clubs.

enjoy helping adult students learn healthy lifestyles and relish the generalist approach to teaching physical education three to six hours per day and four to five days a week.

In larger institutions, physical educators with doctorates specializing in biomechanics, exercise physiology, sport psychology, or other applied sciences teach undergraduate and graduate courses in addition to conducting research. Research productivity, teaching effectiveness, and professional service are required for tenure, which is granted in five to seven years. For university professors, conducting research, writing articles for professional journals, and giving scholarly presentations are prerequisites for job security. Lack of time for research and class preparation is cited frequently by university teachers as a problem. Although their hours are somewhat flexible, committee meetings, student advising, and other departmental responsibilities besides teaching, research, and service extend the work week well beyond 40 hours.

Noneducational Settings

Opportunities abound for those who want to teach fitness and sports skills outside a school environment. Dance studios provide instruction in aerobic, jazz, ballet, tap, and modern dance for children and adults. Individuals with dance majors or specialized dance course work teach various dance forms to customers for fees (ranging from $5 per hour for group lessons to $25 per hour for private lessons) at these studios. Classes may be scheduled throughout the day and evening as well as on weekends.

Sport clubs focus on individual sports, such as tennis, aquatics, or racquetball, and need instructors for private and group lessons. Other clubs, which usually have expensive membership fees, may cater to several sports, such as country clubs that offer swimming, golf, and tennis. Vacation resorts are increasingly providing sports instruction for their guests. Health clubs usually offer fitness programs in aerobic conditioning and weight training, sports instruction, such as in racquetball, and possibly classes in stress management and weight control. Because of the tremendous variety in clubs, salaries depend on location, clientele, instructional expertise, and assigned responsibilities. Salaries for instructors may start at $8 to $10 an hour and increase as responsibilities grow.

Sport camps have become booming businesses related to commercial recreation. Both children and adults attend these highly successful ventures in the summer or on weekends and holidays. For young physical educators, sport camps provide excellent opportunities for gaining teaching experience and for making valuable contacts that may lead to permanent positions. For school teachers looking for summer employment related to physical education and sport, opportunities abound in sport camps. Expertise in teaching one or more activities is important for employment, as is a desire to work with various age and skill levels. Responsibilities, such as those of an instructor or program director, determine salaries, which may vary widely. Day camp instructors may earn $25 to $50 per day, while residence camp instructors can expect salaries at about twice this level.

Concomitant with increasing life spans in the United States is the critical need for professionals trained to provide recreational and leisure activities for senior citizens. By the year 2000, approximately 20% of the population of the United States will be 65 years of age or older. Federal programs, as well as private agencies, increasingly must provide health, physical education, recreation, and dance services in retirement homes, day care centers, and senior citizens' apartment complexes. The job potential for individuals trained to prescribe and to direct activities for this clientele will expand rapidly in the years ahead.

Opportunities to teach in and lead sport and fitness programs in the military abound because fitness training is highly valued by the various branches of the armed services. Instructional assignments in physical development programs are available to enlistees. Frequently, though, civilians instruct at the service academies, on military installations, and at special training facilities. Programs for the military vary widely—from basic conditioning drills for men and women to broad-based fitness and sport opportunities for career personnel to family-oriented recreational offerings. Highly competitive leagues in a variety of sports are commonplace on most military bases, since skilled, fit servicemen and servicewomen are valued. As an employee of the federal government, your pay would depend on classification, but benefits are excellent.

FITNESS, EXERCISE, AND SPORT SCIENCE

Many large industries and corporations provide fitness centers for their executives. Concerns about work efficiency and loss of time and money from absenteeism have resulted in elaborate facilities for daily aerobic, strength, and flexibility workouts. The directors of these corporate fitness centers are usually individuals trained in exercise physiology. Occasionally a bachelor's degree with an emphasis in exercise and sport science may qualify you; however, because of the attractiveness of these jobs and the in-depth knowledge needed, holders of master's degrees in exercise physiology usually are hired. Minimally, each individual should hold a certification in exercise testing (such as that given by the American College of Sports Medicine), if not one as an exercise leader. Directors of corporate fitness centers are responsible for designing individually prescribed programs for executives that include exercise sessions, nutritional changes, stress management hints, and other recommended lifestyle alterations. Close monitoring is required because for many, these programs dramatically alter their previous habits. Also, because

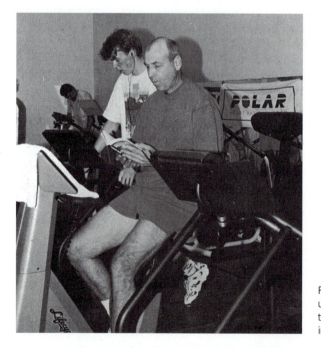

Fitness program participants often use a variety of exercise equipment to enhance their aerobic conditioning. (Photo courtesy Bob Hilliard.)

lack of adherence is the primary reason goals are not achieved, these exercise physiologists, along with their instructional staffs, who often are holders of physical education or recreation degrees, must constantly encourage and help motivate participants in their prescribed programs. In addition, personnel and program management skills are critical in these corporate settings.

Many companies have extended their fitness programs and recreational services to include all of their employees. Although these programs are not as elaborate as those for executives, management has realized the interrelationship of exercise and work efficiency; thus physical educators are needed to provide the supervision and instruction for these programs. Working with people in a non-structured setting appeals to many people in spite of the hours, which are frequently scheduled during workers' leisure time.

Many corporations have chosen to subcontract their fitness programs. In this arrangement, the business provides the site, but all daily administration and staff are provided by an outside supplier. This management firm hires fitness specialists to teach classes and to instruct one-on-one. Instructors can expect starting salaries of over $20,000, with significant variance depending on the location, number of clients served, and experience.

Related to both industry and job-site fitness is the need for professionals to design and to implement training programs for workers in the protective services (public safety officers). Physical educators, especially those with training in exercise physiology, are being hired to test the fitness levels of these workers and to prescribe exercise programs to meet their individual needs and to prepare them to meet the demands of their jobs. Satisfaction in observing positive lifestyle changes is rewarding; frustration may result when public safety officers fail to achieve their goals.

The fitness mania pervading the United States has led to a proliferation of public facilities and programs promoting lifestyle changes for all groups. Directors and program coordinators organize and implement fitness programs, sport teams, and various social activities. Job security is good, yet few advancement opportunities exist unless management skills learned in this setting are transferred to a related career. The minimal wages earned in many part-time positions in public recreation are offset by the invaluable experiences gained.

Cardiac rehabilitation programs have grown out of the need to help heart attack and heart disease victims regain their health and develop fit lifestyles. Programs in universities, community centers, hospitals, private clinics, and many other settings provide the exercises and activities prescribed by physicians and implemented by individuals with degrees in physical education or fitness, exercise, and sport science.

LEISURE SERVICES

Programming and Instruction

Recreation and leisure services are allied fields with physical education and sport. Recreation and leisure services professionals provide activities and programs for individuals of all ages and ability levels. The private sector provides millions of jobs in commercial recreation. Many physical education and recreation graduates obtain their first jobs in the following:

1. **Lodging**—management, operation, and programming for housing services, such as resorts, cruise ships, and camps
2. **Recreation**—planning, management, and operation of recreational programs, facilities, and areas for agencies such as commercial/private, governmental, volunteer, industrial, outdoor, and therapeutic institutions
3. **Entertainment services**—management, operation, and programming for such organizations as theme parks, racetracks, and toy and game manufacturers
4. **Culture services**—management, operation, and programming for institutions that deal with the fine arts, such as museums and historical sites
5. **Sports**—management, operation, and programming for athletic areas and facilities, such as racquetball and tennis complexes, health and fitness clubs, and professional athletic organizations

Although numerous opportunities exist in these areas, probably the sports sub-cluster appeals to most individuals in physical education, with instruction and program planning being the major types of jobs available. Racquetball, tennis, golf, and swimming are among the popular types of specific sports clubs; multi-sport complexes also exist. Health and fitness clubs are examples of these general and specific types of leisure-service organizations.

The thrill of activities like rock climbing attracts many enthusiasts to careers in recreation. (Photo courtesy Aram Attarian.)

All of these activity-related clubs or businesses require membership, thereby excluding a segment of the population. Most individuals who work for these organizations are encouraged, if not required, to sell memberships as one of their responsibilities. Hours vary by club but are usually in the afternoons, in the evening, and on weekends, since these are the leisure hours of those who join. Job security varies with each person's expertise, yet potential for advancement into management and even ownership is good. Benefits include working with people and seeing their improvement as well as having the opportunity to maintain your own healthy lifestyle in these settings. Social skills, sales ability, and sports expertise are more important than a college degree, although being knowledgeable about the components of physical fitness and having expertise in skill analysis are quite helpful. Attaining a national certification in exercise testing can increase career options and lead to a higher salary.

The lodging subcluster includes resorts, condominium complexes, and camps that are increasingly hiring specialists in golf, tennis, swimming, and other sports to organize and to instruct groups and individuals. For these recreation directors, hours vary to meet the needs of the guests, but the pleasant work environment may compensate for a typical schedules.

City and county recreation departments offer a broad spectrum of activities, from instructional classes to league play to trips and nontraditional events. In early mornings, afternoons, and evenings especially, but also throughout the day, teachers are needed for recreational classes offered in water aerobics, rock climbing, massage, cross-country skiing, karate, arts and crafts, mother and child aerobics, various types of dance, and racquetball. During the summers and evening hours, competitive and recreational leagues abound in basketball, baseball, football, volleyball, softball, soccer, tennis, and other popular sports.

Sponsored trips to museums, art events, state parks, zoos, and other attractions especially appeal to retirees and families. Fun runs, road races, and triathlons attract serious competitors as well as weekend athletes. The availability of facilities for a private swim, weight training session, or workout on a stationery bike or for a pickup basketball game also falls under the responsibility of recreation departments. Therefore, program supervisors and administrators have major responsibilities in the provision and scheduling of facilities to ensure that events operate smoothly. Increasingly in the future, recreation departments will be charged with the preservation of green space in cities to ensure that park areas are available for use during leisure hours. Recreation professionals who teach can anticipate starting salaries around $20,000. These salaries will grow as management responsibilities increase.

Rehabilitative

An outgrowth of the desire for a healthy lifestyle is the proliferation of specialized clinics and counseling centers, including those for weight control, massage, nutrition, and stress management. Weight-control centers sometimes promote a particular diet or system, and usually provide information about nutrition and encourage safe exercise. In massage, a method of tension release and relaxation, one manipulates the body with various stroking, kneading, rubbing, or tapping motions. Wellness programs emphasize the development of nutritional, exercise, and attitudinal lifestyle changes through counseling and participatory sessions. The pro-liferation of stress management classes, clinics, seminars, workshops, and counsel-ing centers indicates the demand for information and for preventive and corrective strategies. Since these are fee-based businesses, salaries vary dramatically.

In sports medicine clinics on college campuses and in hospitals, physicians, physical therapists, and athletic trainers treat and rehabilitate sports-related injuries. Team physicians for professional, college, school, and community teams must have earned medical degrees before specializing in this field. Physical ther-apists must be certified.

ATHLETICS

Schools and Colleges

A second career aspiration of many secondary school and some elementary school physical educators is coaching the numerous teams for boys and girls. Many schools have coaching vacancies but no teaching positions in physical edu-cation, because of the resignations of some physical educators from coaching but not from teaching, and because of the increased number of girls' teams. If certi-fied in and willing to teach in a second subject area, the physical educator/coach is automatically more marketable. Coaching positions in the more visible sports of basketball and football are not as easy to obtain as those in other sports, and more openings exist for coaches of girls' sports than for boys'.

In many schools, coaches are expected to work with more than one team and may sometimes have to work with as many as three teams. Some states allow nonteachers or substitute teachers to coach; in others, only employees of the school system can be hired. Monetary supplements (ranging from $500 to $5000) are minimal when compared with the long hours and the innumerable demands on coaches. Job security for football and basketball coaches in some high schools does not exist unless winning teams are consistently produced. Victories are not as critical to job retention for coaches of other sports.

Other athletic opportunities within the schools include athletic training, sport officiating, and administration. High school sport officials normally work at other jobs, including those related to physical education, and only umpire or referee as a hobby or as a second job. A former coach or current coach usually serves as the school's athletic director. This individual coordinates team schedules, budgets, and facilities, and supervises the overall athletic program.

Athletic programs vary dramatically depending on the size of a college. In junior or community colleges and small four-year colleges and universities, many coaches teach in physical education or in other departments, with coaching remaining a secondary responsibility. These individuals receive coaching supple-ments to their salaries and/or reduced teaching loads. Most sports at these institutions are nonrevenue-producing, although for some teams recruiting is expected, since athletic grants-in-aid are awarded. At larger universities, coaches of nonrevenue-producing sports may hold full-time positions in athletics by coach-ing more than one sport or team or by carrying out additional administrative responsibilities. Other coaches at larger institutions teach or coach only part-time.

The teacher-coach, administrator-coach, part-time coach, or full-time coach frequently works day and night because of the increasing competitiveness of intercollegiate athletics (and the rewards that accrue to the victorious). Seldom is there an off-season or free time. While most college coaches have earned master's degrees, this is not a prerequisite, and the major field does not have to be physical education, although it often is. Ways of gaining entrance into college coaching vary. For example, you may volunteer to serve as an assistant or to serve as a graduate student assistant coach, you may earn an assistant coach's position after a successful high school coaching career, or you may win a job because of outstanding collegiate or professional play. In most cases, future head coaches, even those at small institutions and for nonrevenue-producing sports, must get experience serving as successful assistant coaches.

Once jobs are obtained, most coaches, although not guaranteed tenure, retain them as long as they abide by the rules, keep their athletes happy, maintain their own desire to coach, and develop successful programs. In larger institutions, most football and basketball coaches have job security only when they win and show that they can handle the pressures of the job without violating institutional, NCAA, or other rules. For these coaches, the long hours and pressures are compensated for by the material benefits and the prestige. Most coaches take satisfaction in helping their athletes improve their skills and in seeing them mature as individuals.

Coaches' salaries are dependent on the sport, the competitive divisions in which their teams play, whether their sport is revenue-producing or not, their years of experience, their past won-lost records, and additional benefits such as sport camp revenues, shoe contracts, and radio and television shows. Assistant coaches may receive no salaries, only tuition and fee waivers as graduate students, or may receive starting salaries around $30,000. Part-time coaches, who teach or hold other jobs, can expect stipends ranging from $1000 to $10,000 depending on the factors listed above. Full-time, head coaches' salaries can range from $20,000 to over $100,000. Entire salary packages for a few coaches with winning records at large universities can exceed a million dollars.

In small colleges, coaches are often the directors of athletics. As larger universities' athletic programs grew, however, they entered the entertainment business and required administrators to direct them. Athletic directors, associate and assistant directors, fund-raisers, and ticket managers often have earned master's degrees in sport management to prepare them for these careers. Money and people management skills are crucial, as is expertise in public relations, since skyrocketing budgets have made fund-raising vital. When skillfully achieved, all of these factors mesh into a successful athletic program that brings prestige and lucrative benefits to their directors. Security is based on the institution's overall program rather than on one team's performance, although the successes of the revenue-producing sports are certainly most important.

Associated with intercollegiate athletics and vital to their programs are numerous career options. Assistant and associate athletic directors assume responsibility for facility management, NCAA compliance, grants-in-aid, business affairs, fund-raising, and coordination of nonrevenue-producing sports. These positions may be filled by coaches, former athletes, or people trained in sport management. Job security is not guaranteed: continuation is based on successful completion of assigned duties. A major benefit is the association with a successful athletic program and its reflected glamour. Individuals in these management positions earn from $30,000 to over $100,000 depending on level of responsibility, experience, and the institution served.

For individuals who wish to combine writing skills with athletics, sports information is an applicable career choice. This vital component of the athletic program is responsible for compiling statistics and personal information about the players and teams to publicize upcoming events and to provide post-game data. Press releases and team brochures further publicize the intercollegiate program. A degree in journalism or sport communication would be appropriate, but volunteer experience and the willingness to start at the lowest level and work upward may be necessary to gain entrance into this athletic career. Travel, personal contacts with players and coaches, and contributing to the success of a program are among the benefits.

Sports promotions specialists are responsible for filling the stadium and the coliseum through advertising and various promotional strategies. At a small college, one person may handle both sports information and sports promotions, or each coach may have to accept these additional responsibilities. Large institutions have promotions specialists who frequently share in activities to raise funds for grants-in-aid and facilities. Public relations skills are usually more important than a particular educational degree. These persons' primary efforts are directed toward bringing money into the athletic department through gifts and donations. Salaries for these individuals are directly linked with their abilities to market their teams, thus selling tickets and raising money.

Strength and conditioning coaches design and implement training programs for all athletes. Frequently, these positions are filled by physical educators with strong exercise physiology and biomechanics backgrounds and those who hold certifications from the National Strength and Conditioning Association. Helping athletes reach their athletic potentials is the greatest reward for these individuals.

Many professional teams and a few colleges hire sport psychologists to work individually with athletes. Because the athletic skills of all elite athletes are superior, many believe that the key to athletes achieving optimal performances is

Sports promotions specialists work to attract fans to intercollegiate competitions. (Photo courtesy Lisa Sense.)

mental. Sport psychologists use biofeedback, relaxation, imagery, and various coping mechanisms to help athletes handle the pressures of competition, achieve their potential, and enjoy their experiences.

Nonschool

More than 20 million children participate on youth sports teams sponsored by recreation departments, private clubs, community service organizations, national sport associations, and churches. In most cases, the coaches are volunteers; the officials and the league, program, and association directors are usually paid. Many of these same groups also provide athletic competition for adults, such as softball and basketball leagues, master's swimming events, and road races. Experience gained as a volunteer coach, program administrator or assistant, or official may lead to a full-time job in a recreation-related career.

Professional

Prior playing experience in college and as a professional is an asset for coaches of professional teams, although not necessarily a prerequisite. Coaches are hired on the basis of demonstrated success with high school, college, or professional teams and are fired for not producing winning teams. Lucrative salaries, some in excess of a million dollars, help compensate for the pressures to win and constant media bombardment.

Professional sports require hundreds of people working behind the scenes to ensure that events take place as scheduled. A commonality of many of these positions is the need for experience in business and marketing. Responsibilities of the ticket sales staff include season ticket packaging, selling tickets for individual

The hours of practice and competition necessary for highly skilled athletes to develop and refine their talents may help qualify them for coaching careers later in life. (Photo courtesy UNC Sports Information Office.)

events, and arranging for complimentary seating. Correspondence and direct contacts with fans are extensive, with the greatest challenge always remaining that of trying to satisfy as many fans as possible. Customer satisfaction is essential. No formal educational background is required, but a sport management degree is highly desirable.

Business managers are responsible for planning budgets and administering the expenditures of all monies for the program. Although accountants and secretaries may actually handle the daily transactions, business managers oversee multimillion-dollar budgets and the many personnel who work in this area. A business background is helpful, but on-the-job training in a small program or as an intern may be equally valuable in obtaining this job.

Marketing directors serve various functions, depending on the situation. With teams struggling to gain fan support, their primary responsibility focuses on public relations efforts to increase ticket sales. Radio or television commercials, newspaper advertisements, exciting upcoming events or opponents, or winning records may be used to generate greater spectator interest. Season ticket sales are the next promotional effort, since these stabilize income and indicate increased and consistent fan support. Marketing directors also may help promote team emblems or merchandise. These marketing specialists are hired for their proven abilities to fulfill job responsibilities rather than for any educational degree.

Professional sport officiating provides many part-time and some full-time (mostly in baseball and basketball) careers. No specific educational background is required, but years of experience are necessary. As early as possible, such as in recreational youth leagues, anyone interested in officiating should start learning the rules and the techniques while gaining experience and expertise. There may be some reflective glamour and prestige, but officials often are the villains and are only begrudgingly accepted as vital to professional games. After years of success in the high school and college ranks and completion of training programs, the best-qualified officials may get opportunities to officiate for the pros. Most officials, however, hold other jobs and officiate as a hobby or as a second career. Unusual hours and travel are inherent characteristics, although salaries for professional officials are quite good.

SPORT MANAGEMENT

Business and Industry

Golf courses, bowling lanes, gymnastics schools, tennis camps, swimming centers, racquetball clubs, and health spas all require managers who have administrative skills in addition to knowledge about physical skills. Directors in each of these settings must possess budgetary skills, personnel management abilities, planning knowledge, and supervisory capabilities. Although these organizations are primarily interested in producing profits and thus maintaining high enrollments or large attendance, they must hire qualified instructional staff. These sport managers may earn $30,000 to $50,000.

Corporate fitness programs also demand management, motivational, and supervisory skills. Exercise and sport science and fitness specialists who possess knowledge in public relations and marketing can advance more easily into management positions within corporate fitness programs. Since employers want the dollars spent for fitness programs to result in enhanced worker productivity, the goals are to motivate workers to adhere to fitness programs and to increase participation.

Theme parks and resorts have become multimillion-dollar ventures providing leisure for people of all ages. Recreation administration and sport management backgrounds are essential for handling the massive budgetary, facility management, and personnel aspects of these businesses.

More than 150 sport halls of fame and museums each year host millions of people who examine sports memorabilia and photographs and recall stars of the past. These tourist attractions highlight the achievements of former heroes and heroines and periodically elect new enshrinees; some host events to promote their respective sports. Sport historians and administrative curators are needed for these careers.

Facility managers are associated with arenas and stadiums at universities, in communities, and with professional teams. To be cost-efficient, large facilities must be multipurpose because audiences must be attracted to several different sporting events as well as to concerts, speeches, and conventions. There are some specialized facilities, such as aquatic or ice arenas, that are limited to competitive and recreational uses. Facility managers must have planning and organizational abilities foremost, but also must possess personnel management skills as well. Facility managers either work for a university, private corporation, or a professional team and then schedule events around the major team(s) or work for a municipality that rents time to teams. Depending on the size of the facility and the number of scheduled events, the individuals administering them may earn salaries of $40,000 to $80,000.

Schools and Colleges

Administration is another career possibility for physical educators in the schools. This position may be as a department head who accepts management responsibilities, resulting in a reduced teaching load, or as a principal, headmaster, or superintendent. Advancement into this career can result from successful service to the school, advanced education, or interest in and demonstrated competence for these positions. In these jobs, increased salaries parallel longer hours and greater responsibilities.

Colleges and universities have many administrative positions, ranging from program director to department head to college dean. These careers are open to individuals with doctoral degrees, years of experience, expertise in working with people, and management skills. Competition for these positions is strong. Administrative hassles, such as personnel problems, tight budgets, and day-to-day operational demands are offset by opportunities to effect program change, to lead faculty in the attainment of professional goals, and to positively impact students' education.

Intramural-recreational sports and campus recreation programs are popular components of collegiate life. Directors, assistant directors, facility supervisors, and program coordinators constitute the staff. Job responsibilities vary from publicity to facility management and from personnel to programming. These intramural and recreational programs are administered through either the physical education department or the office of student affairs. In the first context the staff may also teach; in the second, they seldom do. Most intramural-recreational sports or campus recreation professionals have earned at least master's degrees in physical education or recreation. Increasingly, the trend is to make these positions non-faculty, with job security based solely on fulfillment of assigned responsibilities. Rather than the usual school-day hours, these programs operate in the afternoons, evenings, and weekends, the leisure hours of the students they serve. Student interactions in nonacademic activities and the opportunities to administer fun-filled programs attract people to these positions. Entry-level program coordinators may earn $20,000 to $25,000; assistant directors' salaries range from $30,000 to $50,000; directors are paid between $50,000 and $70,000.

SPORT MARKETING

Sporting attire is popular for all, whether the wearer is exercising, going out on the town, or working. From cross-training shoes to designer warm-up suits to team logo jackets, everybody is wearing sports clothing. Billions of dollars of athletic and sports clothing and shoes are sold annually. Regardless of skill level, seemingly only oversized tennis rackets, custom-made golf clubs, and auto-

Sporting goods sales provide numerous career opportunities for individuals interested in combining business skills with knowledge about sports equipment and clothing.

graphed baseball gloves are good enough for aspiring athletes. Therefore, jobs are and will continue to be plentiful in the sales and marketing of sporting goods. Expertise in sports is an advantage for people in sales, marketing, and management. Individuals choosing sales may enjoy flexible hours, travel, rapid advancement, and job security if they are good at what they do.

Most administrators and many instructors in health clubs and sport clubs are expected to sell memberships. Those who are especially adept at this task frequently advance into management positions with increased marketing responsibilities, such as initiating special promotions.

The design of new equipment and improved facilities requires a great deal of research. Safety and improved performance motivate these efforts to produce the best ball or surface. Inventors or innovative designers may reap financial benefits, if their products gain the same kind of wide acceptance that the makers of over-sized tennis rackets, for example, have seen.

SPORT COMMUNICATION

The interdependence of the media and sports has created numerous opportunities in the glamour careers of sport broadcasting, sport journalism, and sport photography. Broadcasting opportunities vary from prime-time, national telecasts to special events coverage to sports reporting for a local network. On-the-air experience, expertise in play-by-play announcing, an aptitude for interviewing, and a smooth delivery in reading sports news overshadow an educational degree. Willingness to start in small markets is a key to advancement. Cable networks provide another avenue for aspiring sport broadcasters.

Since sports sell newspapers and magazines and increase television ratings, thereby selling commercial time, professional and college teams are especially sensitive to the media. The sportswriting field attracts a large number of people, although the percentage who succeed in it is small. Many sportswriters have earned college degrees in journalism, but some secure newspaper or magazine jobs because of their past experiences in college sports information offices, their own sports careers, or their background in physical education. A sportswriter must possess an inquiring mind, a desire to talk with people, the ability to listen, and the willingness to work unusual hours while under the pressures of deadlines and space limitations.

A sport photographer may start by taking pictures for a college newspaper or yearbook and then progress to assignments with a major publication. A thorough understanding of the intricacies of various sports provides a photographer with the insight necessary to capture the essence and meaning of sports as well as the outcome of a particular event. Generally, long hours, low compensation, and little glamour may eventually be rewarded with extensive travel for a national publication.

OTHER RELATED CAREERS

In addition to the aforementioned broad categories of jobs open to physical education and sport majors, several other specific careers are available. Many of these, however, require specialized education, training, or certification. For the

INTERVIEW OUTLINE

Name: _____

Title: _____

Company or Institution: _____

JOB RESPONSIBILITIES AND HOURS

What are your primary job responsibilities?

_____

_____

_____

_____

_____

_____

What are your normal work hours? Are these typical?

_____

Is overtime or extra work required? If so, how often and for how long?

_____

What is the salary range for people in your career?

_____

SPECIALIZED COURSE WORK, DEGREES, AND WORK EXPERIENCES NEEDED FOR THIS CAREER

What specialized experiences were necessary as a prerequisite to being qualified for this career?

_____

_____

What academic degrees, certifications, or licenses are required to do your job?

_____

_____

_____

_____

What course work that you completed is most useful in fulfilling your job responsibilities?

_____

_____

_____

(Continued)

SATISTYING ASPECTS OF YOUR CAREER

What are the most satisfying aspects of your career?

_____
_____
_____
_____
_____

Are there any aspects of your career that you dislike?

_____
_____
_____
_____
_____

JOB POTENTIAL

What are the opportunities for advancement (salary, responsibility, and promotion) in this career?

_____
_____
_____
_____
_____

SUGGESTIONS FOR STUDENTS

What suggestions and advice can you give students considering a career like yours?

_____
_____
_____
_____
_____

FIGURE 5-1

Interview Outline–Sample questions about potential careers.

medical doctor with an interest in sports, there are specializations in exercise physiology, orthopedic surgery, and sports podiatry as well as the option to serve as a team physician. Sport nutrition and sport psychology are growing fields for both private practice and consultation with college and professional athletes. Lawyers may choose to emphasize the ever-expanding area of sport law.

Dance careers include not only those of performing artists with national and regional companies but also those of artistic directors, managing directors, development officers, public relations agents, booking agents, dance journalists,

JOB OPPORTUNITIES MATCHED WITH PREREQUISITE BACKGROUNDS

Undergraduate Degree and Certification in Physical Education Required
Public school teacher, K–12

Public school coach (some states only)

Undergraduate Degree in Physical Education or Recreation Preferred
Sports instructor in a private club, camp, resort, or military installation

Recreation department programmer

Leader in a corporate or industry fitness program

Specialized Course Work, Internship, or Certification Required
Athletic trainer

Corporate or commercial fitness exercise specialist

Health or fitness clinic leader

Sport official

Strength and conditioning coach

Master's or Doctor's Degree Required
College or university professor

Intramural/campus recreation director or staff

Sport psychologist

Sport Management Course Work Preferred
Athletic director or athletic administrator

Corporate fitness director

Facility manager

Recreation department director

Experience or Internship at a Lower Level
College coach

Sport broadcaster

Sports information director

Sport journalist

Sport marketer

and dance photographers. Many of these positions are held by former dancers who understand the world of dance and can better market it as an art form. Limited jobs and long hours, though, deter some people from pursuing careers as dancers or in dance-related jobs. No educational degree is required for these positions or for those of studio teachers, yet all who pursue them have spent years developing their expertise.

Rather than viewing the sky as falling, a young professional should view the sky as the limit. The box above provides an overview of some potential careers

Teachers in all settings should serve as role models for healthy lifestyles.

and lists the necessary preparation. Knowing these alternatives should help you focus on one or more broad areas of interest as you choose a career pathway.

Individuals choosing to enter a career in physical education and sport have the additional challenge of serving as positive role models for fitness and healthy lifestyles. The overweight, unfit person, who also may smoke, use other tobacco products, or abuse alcohol or other drugs, is a poor representative of the principles valued by those in physical education and sport careers. Rather, teachers, coaches,

INFORMATION ON CAREERS IN PHYSICAL EDUCATION AND SPORT

See *The Guide to Careers in Sports,* by Len Karlin, 1995 for information on:

- Professional leagues
- Sport facilities management
- Sport marketing and management industry
- College sport management
- Golf industry
- Turf management
- Tennis industry
- Sport broadcasting
- Athletic trainers
- Recreational management

Contact the American Alliance for Health, Physical Education, Recreation and Dance at 1-800-213-7193 for information about careers in these and related areas. Colleges and universities, school counselors, and state departments of education also have information about careers in these areas.

Contact the certifying organizations listed in Appendix B for information about careers in exercise physiology, fitness, and sport medicine.

fitness specialists, recreation directors, exercise and sport science professionals, athletic trainers, and sport managers should participate in sports and activities to maintain their fitness lifestyles.

See the box on page 121 for suggestions about how to locate more information about careers.

SUMMARY

In this rapidly changing, technological world, career changes as often as every 10 years may become the norm rather than the exception. Instead of looking at one specialty, you need to become a multispecialist who can make different applications of your knowledge. Young people entering the work force need to bring creativity and imaginative reasoning to their jobs as well as an adventuresome willingness to accept risks and failures while bouncing back to try again. Your first challenge is to assess your preferences and interests. Factors that influence your career choice(s) include family, role models, knowledge about career alternatives, opportunities to work with certain age groups, ease of entry, salary range, career advancement, time compatibility, job security, and location. Career opportunities abound in physical education and sport in teaching, inside and outside educational institutions, in developmental and rehabilitative fitness, in school and college athletics, and in sport management, marketing, and communication. After matching your aspirations and abilities with career characteristics, you can select one or more as the focus for your college preparation and life's work.

CAREER PERSPECTIVES

PATRICIA ANN HIELSCHER

President
P.H. Enterprises of Apex, Inc., Apex, North Carolina

EDUCATION

B.S., Physical Education, University of North Carolina at Greensboro
M.S., Physical Education, University of North Carolina at Greensboro

JOB RESPONSIBILITIES AND HOURS

Developing your own sports business permits absolute freedom to design it in any way. Based on her interests and expertise, Pat's business initially offered five related, yet different, services and products. While developing her business, Pat conducted volleyball camps and clinics, marketed and sold volleyball uniforms and equipment, exhibited at professional conferences, contracted for screen printing of T-shirts sold to various groups, and offered a consignment program for summer sport camps. Once the business grew sufficiently to become self-sustaining, she discontinued the volleyball camps and clinics to focus on sales. Ordering, billing, selling, and stocking her product lines are vital parts of her responsibilities. Generally Pat works from 8:00 A.M. to 5:00 P.M. and some evenings, typical hours for this career. The amount of time worked determines the salary or income. Pat has chosen to stay a one-person business because she wants to be able to guarantee quality to her customers, most of whom she knows; getting rich is not her goal.

SPECIALIZED COURSE WORK, DEGREES, AND WORK EXPERIENCES NEEDED FOR THIS CAREER

Pat recommends that students interested in forming their own sports products and services businesses take physical education courses with a coaching emphasis, psychology, and business courses, such as marketing and accounting. Although no degree is absolutely necessary, based on her experiences, a bachelor's degree in physical education combined with a business minor and coaching experience would be ideal. Pat has found her background in coaching, including administrative duties such as managing a team, ordering equipment, and fundraising, and her master's degree in physical education most helpful. Coaching, developing personal contacts with people in athletics, having a general background in sales, and having some work in business are important experiences to help prepare for this career.

SATISFYING ASPECTS

The popularity of sports and leisure activities provides a bountiful market for services and products that anyone may wish to furnish as a career. Satisfaction comes both from helping others select the equipment, shoes, and clothing that will enhance their pleasure in sports participation and from teaching skills that can motivate people to start or to continue participating in a sport. Pat designed her business so she could enjoy a continued association with female athletes and coaches and could maintain involvement with the promotion of women's sports.

JOB POTENTIAL

There are many jobs for men and women in athletic sales and services throughout the country, especially in urban areas. These opportunities include running one's own business or working for others. For Pat specifically, as owner of her own business, there is no security except that which comes from her belief in herself. While working for others may lead to greater job security, self-employment guarantees maximal freedom to design a custom-made career. Pat adds that her business is successful because 75% of it is with people she knows, her products are good quality and priced fairly, and she maintains a pleasant, trusting relationship with her customers.

SUGGESTIONS FOR STUDENTS

First, Pat suggests talking with people in this career and considering their advice. Second, she advocates working for someone else before starting a business, to get vital training and experience, especially in marketing, sales, and accounting. Third, she recommends getting experience in athletics as a player, coach, and official to learn the needs and preferences of future customers as well as to learn to communicate with them. Last, she cautions not to become discouraged by people who say that women's sports or a particular sport cannot provide a viable career.

REVIEW QUESTIONS

1. What are several factors that may influence one's career choice?
2. What factors may outweigh the importance of one's salary?
3. What are several noneducational careers that involve teaching?
4. What are several careers in professional sports?
5. What are the responsibilities of the sport marketing specialist?
6. What are three careers related to the media and sports?
7. What is the job potential for careers in recreational services for senior citizens?
8. What are several types of careers in which a sport management background would be beneficial?
9. What are typical entry-level positions in coaching that may lead to becoming a college coach?
10. What are the major differences between the responsibilities of athletic directors at small colleges and large universities?

STUDENT ACTIVITIES

1. Complete the self-assessment inventories in the boxes on pages 97–98.
2. Write a three- to five-page essay describing your professional and personal career goals.
3. Compile a list of the abilities and characteristics needed for success in your prospective career.
4. Talk with one person in each of the following careers: (a) one that you think you definitely would like to pursue; (b) one that you think you might like to pursue; (c) one that you know little or nothing about.
5. Read any two of the suggested readings, and relate each article's concepts to your career choice.
6. Using the outline of Figure 5-1 on pages 118-119, conduct a formal interview of a person in a career that you are considering entering.
7. Using the Internet, find and describe briefly five career options discussed in this chapter or identify five newly-emerging physical education and sport careers.

SUGGESTED READINGS

Aldana SG, Stone WJ: Report to fitness professionals—changing physical activity preferences of American adults, *JOPERD* 62(4):67, 1991. According to this survey of Arizona adults, more engage in regular, vigorous physical activity than in the past two decades. Walking surpassed jogging/running, aerobics, swimming, weight lifting, dance, basketball, and calisthenics in popularity for males and females of all age groups.

Anderson SC, (ed): Therapeutic recreation—meeting the challenge of new demands, *JOPERD* 62(4):25, 1991. This nine-article "Leisure Today" feature suggests alternative approaches to meeting the needs of Americans with disabilities. These approaches include integration into community-based programs, social skills training, use of computers to link providers, enhanced professional preparation programs, creative play environments, a model for improving clients' self-esteem, use of volunteers, and music therapy.

Claxton DB, Lacy AC: Pedagogy: the missing link in aerobic dance, *JOPERD* 62(6):49, 1991. Aerobic dance instructors must know not only their subject matter but also possess sound pedagogical skills and knowledge in the content areas. Recommendations are provided to help aerobic dance teachers become more effective.

Francis LL: Improving aerobic dance programs: the key role of colleges and universities, *JOPERD* 62(7):59, 1991. The author suggests the course content for aerobic dance instructor training. Goal setting, health and fitness assessment, safety, exercise intensity, choreography, and grading are also discussed.

Green K: Leading the fit life: jobs in health clubs, *Occup Outlook* 39(2):14, 1995. This article describes the various types of positions available in health clubs and provides information about how to acquire credentials in this field.

Hofacre S, et al: Demographic changes in the U.S. Into the twenty-first century: their impact on sport, *Sp Mkt Q* 1(1):31, 1992. Sport marketers must identify changing demographics, such as an older and more ethnically diverse population and a society characterized by changes in family makeup, in order to properly target their potential customers in sports.

Mathes SA, McGivern AT, Schneider CM: The influence of participation and gender on employee's motives for involvement in a corporate exercise program, *J of Sp Mgmt* 6:1, 1992. In one selected corporate fitness program, males and females were surveyed to determine their reasons for their participation. Enhancing fitness, reducing stress, and learning to relax were most important as was having structured programs.

Mustain WC: Are you the best teacher you can be? *JOPERD* 61(2):69, 1990. The author suggests eight components that contribute to teaching effectiveness: goals and objectives, planning, lesson presentation, student engagement, management, student activity, feedback, and teacher assessment.

Rowe PJ, Miller LK: Treating high school sports injuries—are coaches/trainers competent? *JOPERD,* 62(1):49, 1991. Due to the large number of injuries experienced by high school athletes, the question is raised about the quality of care they receive. The risk of negligent first aid and the associated legal ramifications indicate the importance of employing a certified athletic trainer in each school.

Smith DS, Smith SH: Investigating the meaning of play and recreation for families, *J of Rec & Leisure* 13(1):1, 1993. The most important human institution, the family, can use play and recreation to improve relationships, sense of being connected, and enjoyment.

CHAPTER 6

Preparation for a Career

KEY CONCEPTS

- Establishing short-term and long-term goals directs career development.
- Course work required for a liberal arts education with a physical education major varies by institution and career choice.
- Extracurricular activities and volunteer work and internships in physical education and sport jobs offer important learning experiences and preparation for careers.
- Certifications in athletic officiating, aquatics, first aid, exercise testing, coaching, and other areas improve professional credentials for employment.
- Graduate programs provide opportunities for advanced study in specialized areas.

Professionalism is based on knowledge. Thus far, you have learned about the objectives, disciplinary content, and professional structure of physical education and sport. You have begun to learn more about various careers through the career perspectives in each chapter. Now, with a career targeted, you are getting ready to learn more about your work. The information in this chapter should help you get the most out of your college years. As you grow in knowledge about physical education and sport, experience various activities in the field, and obtain certifications, you are not just joining a profession; you are becoming a professional. This professionalism will demonstrate itself by your commitment to learning and your desire to develop your capabilities to the fullest.

While this chapter introduces you to various alternative careers, at this point you will want to focus on learning more about each one and the most about those of greatest interest to you. At the conclusion of your college studies, you will be provided information about writing application letters, developing a resumé, and preparing for interviews.

THE CHALLENGE

Everyone's existence depends on self-worth. All of us have varying degrees of this basic need that relate directly to our personal levels of happiness. Self-worth is developed by participating and achieving success in different activities. This may include feeling confident with one's sports skills as well as how a person has enhanced his or her leadership skills as a volunteer youth coach, a camp counselor, or an intern in a health and fitness club. Self-worth comes from taking on and completing competently responsible roles like team manager, lab assistant, Special Olympics or Senior Games volunteer, and sports reporter for a school newspaper. Most people want to feel satisfied with and successful in their lives. Each person, though, defines these concepts uniquely. Many factors contribute to our life's satisfaction because of the value we place on each. Below are listed some characteristics that people value personally. Select any of these that can help you establish a sense of direction for the personal, social, and professional goals that you will be setting. It may help if you can identify one or more individuals who you think personify those traits that you wish to emulate.

Analytical	Patient	Serious
Assertive	Persevering	Sincere
Benevolent	Poised	Sociable
Cautious	Polite	Spontaneous
Considerate	Practical	Stable
Creative	Progressive	Tactful
Determined	Prudent	Tenacious
Energetic	Quiet	Thorough
Friendly	Rational	Tolerant
Fun	Reflective	Trustworthy
Helpful	Reliable	Understanding
Mannerly	Resourceful	Versatile
Organized	Responsible	Warm
Outgoing	Sensitive	Witty

Once you have observed some of these traits in others, you are encouraged to learn how you can adopt these characteristics. Others who have been praised for being good role models usually are willing to share how they developed these abilities. These same individuals are often eager to share strategies that have worked to make them more successful.

Goal setting helps us assess abilities and interests and establish immediate and future expectations. Goal setting helps individuals establish their personal philosophies as described in Chapter 2. Short-term goals are accomplishments that can occur within a day, week, month, or other not-too-distant time period. Such goals could include attending a weekend workshop, starting a personal exercise program, or joining a professional association. It is important that short-term goals be readily achievable, positively reinforcing, and related to or

PERSONAL AND PERFORMANCE GOAL SETTING

Personal

1. What is your personal long-term career goal or dream?
2. Is it possible to achieve this goal if you work hard and push yourself the next few years?
3. What intermediate goals are necessary for you to fulfill as you progress toward your dream in the next few months?
4. What are immediate (today/this week) goals that you can accomplish that will move you toward your long-term career goal?

Performance

5. What is one academic goal that you can achieve this semester?
6. How can you improve your academic performance during the following semester?
7. If you fail to meet this academic performance goal, how will you feel about yourself?
8. What is one athletic or fitness goal that you can achieve this semester?
9. How can you improve your athletic or fitness performance during the following semester?
10. If you fail to meet this athletic or fitness performance goal, how will you feel about yourself?
11. What is one leadership goal that you can achieve this semester?
12. How can you improve your leadership performance during the following semester?

leading to the attainment of long-term goals. Long-term goals are larger in scope and often are comprised of short-term goals. Continual self-assessment and the reestablishment of goals are essential as interests and aspirations change. Before establishing some professional goals, it might be easier to start with personal and performance goals. To facilitate this process, respond to the questions in the box above.

Associated with developing positive character traits and goal setting is the skill of networking. As you decide what you want to do and determine the type of person you want to be, you can be helped by others who have experienced the same process through which you are progressing. Associating yourself with others who can serve as your mentors and who can introduce you to others in your chosen career can be valuable. These individuals can help you obtain internship experiences and possibly get an entry-level job. They are tremendous resources for information, guidance, and personal development.

EDUCATIONAL BACKGROUND

Academic success in college can greatly facilitate the achievement of your goals. Try to benefit as much as possible from these opportunities to learn and develop your skills and abilities. That does not mean that all you need to do is to study, although studying certainly is vital.

Everyone needs to develop basic academic competencies in reading, writing, speaking, listening, mathematics, reasoning, studying, and computer literacy. Basic academic competencies and general education course work constitute most liberal arts programs through which institutions provide students the broad knowledge base for their lives and careers. Advocates of a liberal arts education think that all students should be educated to function effectively in a culturally diverse and global world regardless of their career choices. Such an education potentially helps the research scientist interact with the practitioner, assists the coach in understanding family backgrounds and pressures on their athletes, provides insights about other people and their languages in our multicultural society, and develops appreciation for the arts, history, and philosophy.

Some students may fulfill these core requirements by taking a conglomeration of courses without much thought or direction. Whether general education courses are taken during the first two years at a junior or community college or throughout a four-year college program, however, you should seriously consider your selection and sequence of course work to maximize career preparation. Your major or specialized studies normally hold greater interest, because they seem to relate more directly to your chosen career. Nevertheless, you still need to make a serious commitment to learning the most that you can from each class.

Internships and fieldwork are valuable for career preparation. Some majors' programs require students to observe in the schools each week, to complete an internship, to design practicum experiences for their career choices through independent study courses, or to take a laboratory course that offers practical experiences. Usually, education courses for the prospective teacher require observation and mini-teaching experiences, some as early as the first year in college.

Several curricula allow students to earn college credit for paying jobs, such as recreation leader for a community, camp counselor, or sport club instructor, that provide learning experiences. An independent study option allows students to earn college credit for developing research projects or for work experiences specific to their areas of interest. Other curricula have experiential courses as a part of their requirements. Each of these options allows students opportunities to gain valuable experiences while they are selecting and preparing for their careers.

RELATED EXPERIENCES

Some people suggest that during the college years more learning occurs outside the classroom than inside. It is certainly true that experiential learning is important. For example, by serving as a team manager, sport official, or event coordinator in intramural-recreational sports, you can learn about personnel management, scheduling, and rules. Working with a club sport, like karate or rugby, you may get an opportunity to coach and to manage the club's financial affairs. Of course, you can learn many things just by participating in various college activities or as a varsity athlete.

Officiating

Officiating opportunities abound in intramurals, within recreation leagues, and in the junior high schools; some colleges offer classes in officiating. These learning experiences may result in advancement into the high school, college, and professional ranks. The National Federation of State High School Associations,

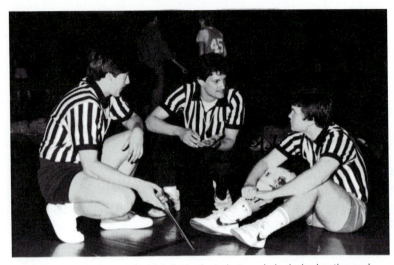

Officiating is a popular part-time job for both students and physical education and sport professionals.

through its state associations, requires clinic attendance and written and practical examinations for certification of prospective officials in various sports. Following successful completion of these requirements, individuals earn ratings that qualify them to officiate high school athletic contests. The most proficient officials receive the top rankings, earn the honor of working in championships, and may get an opportunity to advance to the next competitive level. The Affiliated Boards of Officials of the National Association for Girls and Women in Sport conduct clinics and rate officials for some high school and college sports. Several single-sport organizations, such as the United States Volleyball Association, also train and certify officials for their sports.

Volunteer Activities and Intern Opportunities

While the knowledge learned in college courses introduces content and provides the foundation for a career choice, experiences and practical applications solidify learning. Volunteer activities, while a student, offer valuable opportunities to gain experience. If athletic training interests you, volunteer to serve as a student trainer. Initially you will do a great deal of observing and maybe perform menial tasks. But, if you are an eager learner, soon you will be trusted to provide care and treatment to injured athletes. As your skills improve and increase, you may be given responsibility for a team. Remember, to qualify for the NATA certification examination, you must have worked a minimum of 1500 hours (usually all as a volunteer) under the supervision of a NATA-certified athletic trainer.

If a career in fitness appeals to you, you may start by attending aerobics classes or joining a health club before volunteering to assist instructors in these classes or clubs. You may progress in your skills to become an intern working with an aerobics leader or becoming an instructor yourself. Other volunteer possibilities in this field include conducting fitness classes for children in after-school programs, senior citizens at retirement centers, or students in your residence halls.

Volunteer assistance with a track meet may provide valuable experience in learning how to manage sporting events. (Photo courtesy Barry Pennell.)

Through volunteer officiating you can gain experience and help prepare for certification. (Photo courtesy Maggie McGlynn.)

Once you have developed your skills and expertise, you may be able to arrange paid internships to provide these services.

Exercise and sport science majors often choose to volunteer or complete internships in commercial or corporate fitness programs or a clinic setting. You will help exercise physiologists, fitness leaders, and physicians assess the fitness levels of clients, prescribe exercise programs, and monitor progress. You will observe and learn how to measure various fitness parameters and help participants adhere to their prescribed programs.

Volunteering to work with children in an after-school program can help develop teaching skills. (Photo courtesy Bob Hilliard.)

Exercise and sport science students who aspire to achieve graduate degrees should volunteer to serve as subjects in research studies or become laboratory assistants. Working with your professors, you can gain tremendous experience using exercise physiology, biomechanical, and other scientific instrumentation. You will quickly learn whether the research process—hypothesis, design, data collection, statistical analysis, and interpretation—appeals to you.

The sport management major can seek out volunteer and internship activities both on- and off-campus. Your college's intramural-recreational sports program needs students to serve as team managers for the residence units, club sports officers, and facility and activity supervisors. Also, opportunities may be available to organize special events such as fun runs, orientation sessions, or all-night activities. Volunteers and interns provide valuable assistance working with the Special Olympics, family recreational activities, Senior Games, church sports leagues, and State Games. After successfully completing minor tasks, you may qualify for the responsibility of coordinating sports competitions during these events. Volunteer coaches and paid officials are needed in youth sport leagues and recreation programs. Experiences gained in these settings may lead to opportunities to serve as an assistant coach or official in a junior or senior high school.

These experiences associated with your potential career choice may help confirm your interests or indicate that another field might be preferable. In each case as a volunteer or intern, you will help others while developing your abilities. Each time you participate in one of these activities, add this to a list of your extracurricular experiences. Later, when you apply for a job, you can include these activities on your resume. Volunteer and intern experiences help differentiate you from the other applicants.

BEGINNING YOUR CAREER INVOLVEMENT

While a student, get involved in career-related activities. Most colleges and universities have a Physical Education Majors' Club or a similar group. Majors often sponsor faculty-student colloquia, invite leaders in the profession to give presentations, and interact academically and socially. These organizations also frequently organize trips to state, district, and national conferences or workshops, where students learn about the profession, hear about current developments, and listen to research reports. Service projects, such as working with Special Olympics, holding Jump Rope for Heart programs, and officiating at sporting events to raise money for charities, are also popular ways for young professionals to help others by sharing their expertise; at the same time, they gain valuable experience.

Certifications

An important aspect of professional growth is obtaining one or more certifications. (See Appendix B for addresses of certifying organizations.) For those who choose a career in athletic training, certification by the National Athletic Trainers' Association (NATA) is strongly recommended, if not required. (Chapter 4 describes these requirements.)

The American Red Cross offers certifications for lifeguards and instructors in water safety, first aid, and cardiopulmonary resuscitation. The YMCA of the USA also certifies lifeguards and swimming instructors. These certifications allow for employment as pool and beach lifeguards and as swimming teachers.

The American College of Sports Medicine offers seven types of certifications. The clinic track for professionals working with individuals with cardiovascular, pulmonary, and metabolic disease includes certification for the exercise test technologist, the exercise specialist, and the program director. (The box on pages 134–136 presents information about these and other certifications). The health and fitness track, targeted to professionals working in corporate fitness centers, fitness clubs, and similar programs, includes certification for the exercise leader, health/fitness instructor, health/fitness director, and advanced personal trainer. Some colleges and universities also offer certifications in fitness, as shown in the box on page 137.

The American Sport Education Program offers educational and certification courses for coaches, youth sport directors, and parents. Its volunteer level is designed for volunteers who work with youth sports. The Rookie Coaches three-hour clinic teaches prospective youth sport coaches the responsibilities of coaching, effective methods for teaching skills, and how to conduct a safe program. The Coaching Young Athletes course, a five-hour clinic, introduces the basics of coaching philosophy, sport psychology, teaching sport skills, sport physiology, sports medicine, and parent management. The volunteer level also includes a one-hour parent education clinic. The leader level, entitled the National Federation Interscholastic Coaching Education Program, is required or recommended by most state interscholastic organizations and is the coaching education program of the National Federation of State High School Associations. It includes courses in coaching principles, sport first aid, and drugs and sport. The Sport Director series, designed for high school athletic directors, includes courses in facility and equipment management, promotion, event management, program evaluation,

CERTIFICATIONS

American College of Sports Medicine (ACSM)

Certification	Prerequisites
Exercise Test Technologist	Knowledge and ability to administer graded exercise testing procedures consistent with age and health status; ability to implement appropriate emergency procedures; designed for individuals evaluating diseased individuals
Exercise Specialist	Ability to execute individualized prescription of activities for patients referred to clinical exercise programs; ability to educate and counsel patients regarding activity and lifestyle issues; designed for individuals counseling patients, prescribing exercise, evaluating special populations, and testing maximal level
Program Director	Experience in a position of administrative authority within a clinical exercise program; ability to organize and administer preventive and rehabilitative exercise programs; designed for health care managers in the clinical setting working with special populations
Exercise Leader	High level of knowledge and experience in safely applying the principles of exercise and training to fitness programs; ability to interact and communicate with others; designed for leaders of aerobics and other exercise programs
Health/Fitness Instructor	Demonstration of knowledge of and skills in risk factor identification, fitness appraisal, and exercise prescription, experience in lifestyle behavior modification counseling skills, exercise leadership; designed for personal trainers, strength trainers, or health/fitness professionals testing on the submaximal level
Health/Fitness Director	Demonstration of knowledge of and skills in organizing and administering health and fitness programs; minimal of three years experience as a manager in a health club or wellness center
Advanced Personal Trainer	Knowledge enhancement in nutrition, exercise programming, diagnostics and program management, and techniques for working with special populations; designed for fitness instructors, rehabilitation specialists, and personal trainers

The Cooper Institute for Aerobics Research

Physical Fitness Specialist (Personal Trainer)	Five days of instruction in screening options, fitness assessment and goal setting, exercise prescriptions, nutritional programs, motivational techniques, feedback methods, safety programming, and scientific foundations; designed for individuals who are personal trainers or work in health and fitness centers, clubs, and clinics
Group Exercise Leadership	Three-day course designed to develop basic level leadership and technical skills for conducting group exercise programs; designed for exercise and aerobics instructors who are already teaching or for individuals entering the profession

CERTIFICATIONS (CONTINUED)

Advanced Physical Fitness	Four days of instruction built on knowledge learned during a previous certification program; includes in-depth, research-based information for implementing safe, effective, and motivational fitness programs; designed for health and fitness professionals
Health Promotion Director	Week-long course designed to provide training in starting or revitalizing a health promotion program, leadership, supervision and administrative skills using case studies and the implementation of activities that enhance and support healthful behavior changes, designed for experienced health promotion professionals
Specialty Certification for Aquatics	Two-day course comprised of lecture and activity sessions on aquatic exercise, safety, special populations, equipment, prototype lessons, and deep water walking; designed for aerobic instructors, personal trainers, and other health and fitness professionals who work with people who exercise in the water

American Council on Exercise (ACE)

Group Fitness Instructor	Knowledge on basic anatomy, kinesiology, and exercise physiology, nutrition, injury prevention, and emergency procedures, motivational and communication skills, and professional responsibilities
Personal Trainer	Knowledge in basic exercise sciences, nutrition, fitness assessment, exercise programming, and instructional and spotting techniques
Lifestyle and Weight Management Consultant	Knowledge about fitness assessment, exercise programming, and professional responsibilities to clients

Aerobics and Fitness Association of America

Fitness Practitioner	Advanced knowledge in assessment, nutrition, one-on-one training, and counseling for fitness management for life
Personal Trainer/Fitness Counselor	Designed for fitness professionals who work one-on-one in individualized fitness assessment and program design
Step	Knowledge and practical skills necessary to teach safe, effective step aerobics classes
Weight Room/Resistance Training	Designed for personal trainers or exercise science program graduates; includes information about lifting, spotting techniques, safety issues, and program design

National Dance-Exercise Instructor's Training Association

Aerobic Instructor	Knowledge about the basics of exercise sciences, cueing/choreography and music skills, and safe exercise evaluation
Personal Trainer	Knowledge about exercise sciences, health and fitness assessments, communication and leadership skills, and exercise programming for healthy adults

Continued

CERTIFICATIONS (CONTINUED)

YMCA of the USA
Selected Certifications

"Working with" series including

Working with Children up to Age 5
Working with 5- to 9-Year-Olds
Working with 10- to 14-Year-Olds
Working with 15- to 18-Year-Olds
Working with Program Volunteers
Working with People with Disabilities
Working with the Military

"Active Older Adults" series including
Working with Active Older Adults (AOA)
AOA Program Director
AOA Land/Water Exercise Leader

Aquatics
Principles of Aquatic Leadership
Y Skippers Swimming Instructor
Y Progressive Swimming Instructor
Lifeguard Crossover
New Lifeguard Recertification
Y's Way to Water Exercise Instructor
Aquatics for Special Populations Instructor
Swim Coach
Advanced Swim Coach

Camping
Day Camp Director

Health and Fitness
Principles of Y Health and Fitness
Exercise Instructor
Advanced Exercise Instructor
Nutrition and Exercise for Weight Management
Circuit Training
Movement for the Inactive
Resistance Training in Aerobics
Flexibility Training
Fitness Specialist
Strength Training Instructor
Youth Fitness Instructor
Healthy Back Land/Water Instructor

Sports
Gymnastics Instructor
Youth Sports Director
Youth Volleyball Instructor
Youth Racquetball Instructor
Triathlon Director

risk management, finance, and personnel management. The master level offers advanced courses in sport physiology, sport psychology, sports injuries, sports rehabilitation, nutrition and weight control, teaching sport skills, time management, sport law, and sport administration.

Coaching minors focus on course work taken in a particular area in addition to the major. For prospective school teachers, this may be in math, science, or history, thus improving their credentials for obtaining a job.

For the nontraditional teacher, minors may include course work in exercise and sport science, nutrition, coaching, or business. Often, minors can help prepare students for advanced study; for example, a student might complete a major in physical education with a minor in business, prior to seeking a master's degree in sport management.

PUBLIC/PRIVATE FITNESS CERTIFICATE

The Public/Private Fitness Certificate combines basic knowledge of business and management with scientific and clinical knowledge. Graduates work in a wide range of enterprises, including public, private, and corporate fitness programs and various wellness and rehabilitation programs.

Biochemistry

Computer applications

Directed internship

Electrocardiographic principles and interpretation

Leisure programming

Lifestyle management

Nutrition for fitness and sport

Organic chemistry

Personnel management

Principles of management

Test and exercise prescription for fitness specialists

GRADUATE EDUCATION

Your career objective may require advanced study in physical education or one of its applied sciences at an accredited institution. Master's degree programs usually take one to two years to complete; doctoral degree programs require two to four years beyond the master's degree. Master of Science (M.S.), Master of Arts (M.A.), Master of Physical Education (M.P.E.), Master of Education (M.Ed.), and Master of Arts in Teaching (M.A.T.) are the typical offerings. They normally require 30 to 36 semester hours for completion, although the actual course work taken varies from institution to institution. The M.S., M.A., and M.P.E. degrees generally emphasize more discipline-oriented study and may allow for specialization in athletic training, exercise and sport science, sport management, or sport psychology, as shown in the box on page 138. Completion of these degrees usually requires a thesis, an original research project, or an internship in addition to a comprehensive examination. Oriented toward education and teaching, the M.Ed. and the M.A.T. degrees lead to advanced certification for individuals working in the schools and usually require a practicum experience (see the box on page 139). Many institutions offer certifications in advanced study beyond the master's degree in special education, supervision, counseling, and administration as well as education specialist degrees.

The highest academic degrees are the Doctor of Philosophy (Ph.D.), the Doctor of Education (Ed.D.), and the Doctor of Physical Education (D.P.E.). The Ph.D. is oriented toward research in a specialty such as exercise physiology, sport history, sport management, pedagogy, sport psychology, and adapted physical education. The focus of most Ed.D. programs is advanced study in education, with physical education or exercise and sport science comprising one portion of the program. General course work in physical education and sport, combined with an area of specialized research, is the focus of the D.P.E.

EXAMPLES OF MASTER'S DEGREE SPECIALIZATIONS

Athletic Training

Clinical methods in athletic training

Exercise physiology

Human anatomy for athletic trainers

Management and rehabilitation of athletic injuries

Internship in athletic training

Research

Therapeutic analyses and modalities

Sport Management

Financial accounting

Internship in sport management

Organizational behavior

Personnel management

Research

Social issues in sport

Sport law

Sport marketing

Exercise and Sport Science

Cardiac rehabilitation

Nutrition for exercise and sport

Physiological functions in exercise

Internship in exercise physiology

Research

Seminar or independent study in
  exercise physiology

Statistics

Sport Psychology

Advanced sport psychology

Applied sport psychology

Motor learning

Research

Seminar or independent study in sport
  psychology

Social issues in sport

Statistics

Before deciding whether to enroll in a prospective graduate program, determine whether advanced education is needed in your career. If so, then you may want to find out which accredited universities offer the type of program that meets your needs. For example, only a few institutions offer a specialization in athletic training at the master's degree level. Although some institutions require an area of specialization for a master's degree, others offer a general physical education program.

Most admission requirements include an undergraduate degree in physical education or related applied science emphasis, a minimum of a 3.0 (on a 4.0 scale) grade point average, and a better-than-average score on the Graduate Record Examination (GRE) or the Miller Analogies Test (MAT). Since institutions are free to set their own admissions standards, review the institutions that offer the program desired. Libraries house catalogs of most leading institutions, or you may write for information. Applications should be completed during the middle of the senior year or at least six months prior to the expected entrance date. Required admissions materials include college transcript(s), letters of recommendation, application forms, and test scores, such as GRE or MAT results.

For careers that do not require advanced degrees, additional and ongoing education is beneficial. Employers sometimes provide this on the job; otherwise, employees need to attend workshops, conferences, or continuing education classes. Keep current with and stimulated by career changes and developments. These often result in greater job productivity and can lead to career advancement. Career development is a lifelong process.

TYPICAL COURSE WORK FOR MASTER'S DEGREE EMPHASIZING EDUCATION

Curriculum

Educational psychology

Educational research

Educational statistics

Issues and trends in physical education and sport

Legal issues in education

Motor learning in physical education and sport

Internship or field work experience

School and program management

Scientific foundations of physical education and sport

GAINING EXPERIENCE

While you are still a first- or second-year college student, it is important to investigate the job market by talking with older students, faculty members, or individuals in the career(s) you are considering, maybe by asking them the questions listed in the box on p. 140. Reflect on their responses as you continue to narrow or to broaden your career possibilities and make the most of your education. By carefully selecting your elective courses, you may be able to obtain a minor, or a double major, or be able to specialize in some area, such as adapted physical education or business. Through certain courses you may qualify for an internship, a summer field work experience, or a part-time job, or you may have an oppor-

One important component of graduate education is participation in research projects.

tunity to gain valuable experience as a volunteer in sports information, athletic training, or athletics.

Be sure during your college years to take advantage of your institution's resources. Most college libraries have materials on market trends, career guidance, and opportunities for advanced education. Counseling or guidance personnel offer career aptitude testing, assistance in resume writing, and hints for interviews. You should visit your college's placement center to learn about the services offered so you can take advantage of them to get a summer job as well as to help you get your first job after graduation.

It has been said that "it's not what you can do, but who you know," since many good jobs are obtained because of personal contacts. Why not let this happen to you? Notify friends, relatives, former employers, and other people whom you have met that you are looking for a part-time or summer job or an internship. Follow up on all leads, because it also is said that sometimes getting a good job results from "being in the right place at the right time." Initiate contact with anyone you think can help you. Networking is vitally important. You begin to establish a network of acquaintances in physical education and sport careers through your extracurricular activities, volunteer and internship experiences, summer jobs, and attending workshops and conferences. The people whom you meet, interact with, and impress can help you get your initial or subsequent job. Networking includes expanding your number of friends in the field and building positive relationships with them.

POSSIBLE QUESTIONS TO ASK ABOUT YOUR PROSPECTIVE CAREER

1. What is the educational background required?
2. How much prior experience is needed?
3. What are the typical hours?
4. What is the daily routine and the average time spent on each part of it?
5. What is the salary range?
6. How much vacation time is provided?
7. What are the fringe benefits?
8. To what extent will this job affect my personal life?
9. What are the requisite skills and knowledge for this job?
10. What personal characteristics, such as creativity, problem-solving ability, or enthusiasm, are necessary for this job?
11. What is the potential for employment in this career?
12. In what regions or states is this job available?
13. What is the potential for advancement in this career?
14. Is on-the-job training or advanced education required to maintain employment or to advance in this career?
15. What are the specific work responsibilities of this type of job? How much time is spent doing each?
16. How and on what criteria is job performance evaluated?
17. What are the most satisfying or advantageous aspects of this job?
18. What are the most frustrating or disadvantageous aspects of this job?
19. What has been your biggest disillusionment?
20. What has been your most rewarding or enjoyable experience?

SUMMARY

As you prepare for your career, you need to begin to set short-term and long-term goals. These will help you make incremental progress toward the achievement of your career aspirations. As an undergraduate, your choices of courses to fulfill requirements, your selection of a major, and your use of electives will determine the quality of your education and career preparation. The quantity and diversity of your extracurricular activities will enrich your college years and possibly assist in your career choice. Volunteer and internship activities, especially those that enable you to gain invaluable experiences related to your interest area, are important additions to your undergraduate years. Obtain certifications prior to seeking your first job, since many positions require these for employment. In addition, completing advanced degrees in an area of specialization will enhance your marketability and content knowledge. The process of getting a job starts while you take courses, gain experiences, and demonstrate your abilities as a young professional. Build upon this base of knowledge and experience by examining various career options, developing a resume, writing application letters, and interviewing, even for a part-time or summer job.

REVIEW QUESTIONS

1. What are the values of establishing long-term and short-term goals?
2. Why is an internship important?
3. What is the process for getting certified to officiate a high school sport?
4. What are four examples of volunteer and internship experiences that can enhance your undergraduate years and make you more marketable in your job search later?
5. What are the various types of graduate degree programs, and what is the emphasis of each?
6. What are five important questions that you should ask about your prospective career?

CAREER PERSPECTIVES

SUSAN B. JOHNSON
Director of the Division of Continuing Education
Cooper Institute for Aerobics Research
Dallas, Texas

EDUCATION
B.S., Physical Education, Memphis State University
M.Ed., Physical Education, Memphis State University
Ed.D., Teacher Behavior in Physical Education, University of North Carolina at Greensboro

JOB RESPONSIBILITIES AND HOURS

Susan and her staff develop and conduct certification workshops for exercise instructors, law enforcement agencies, and a variety of other health and fitness professionals such as physicians, fitness specialists, and personal trainers. She also authors articles, initiates research, develops new materials, teaches workshops, and consults with agencies, businesses, and organizations in regard to physical fitness programs. Susan works from 7:00 A.M. to 5:00 P.M. Monday through Friday and 10:00 P.M. to 2:00 P.M. most Saturdays, typical hours for this career.

SPECIALIZED COURSE WORK, DEGREES, AND WORK EXPERIENCES NEEDED FOR THIS CAREER

Management is a major function of this job, so administrative courses are important. Also, teaching is a primary responsibility, so education courses are critical. It is highly recommended that individuals wishing to pursue this career possess specialized knowledge in health promotion, exercise physiology, psychology, kinesiology, nutrition, and sociology. Susan states that her doctorate has provided a vital background for her specific responsibilities, although other corporate fitness careers may require only master's degrees. In addition, a medical background and a knowledge of statistics, computer applications, and research methodology complement this work. Other abilities needed include competence in speaking before groups, writing skills, leadership abilities, and administrative skills. Jobs that involve teaching and research will best prepare students. Also, administrative jobs could help students acquire necessary organizational and management skills.

SATISFYING ASPECTS

One reason for the need for health and fitness professionals is the growth in corporate fitness programs. Leaders in business and industry are realizing that taking care of their number one asset, their employees, is cost-efficient as well as an excellent fringe benefit for the participants. Many physical educators are attracted to working with adults in the fitness field, where the major challenges are developing motivational and adherence strategies. Susan especially enjoys training fitness leaders to implement safe, effective, and enjoyable programs. She also takes pleasure in seeing individuals make lifestyle changes that lead to healthier and happier lives.

JOB POTENTIAL

Susan predicts that the fitness boom will continue to expand and will affect all phases of life—work, home, school, business, and church. As the twenty-first century approaches, the availability of jobs in training health and fitness professionals will expand dramatically. Businesses and industries will continue to provide fitness programs for executives, and they will offer more programs for blue-collar workers, too. Urban areas where larger companies are located will have more jobs, although businesses in small cities may jointly offer programs for their employees. Occupational groups, such as police officers, will begin to set health and fitness standards for their members, and the general public will seek out qualified professionals to help them regain and maintain health. The salary range is $50,000 to $80,000 for this type of fitness management position.

SUGGESTIONS FOR STUDENTS

Susan suggests that students study the field and all its related subdisciplines and acquire as much knowledge as possible from current leaders in the field and from their writings. Students should become involved in professional organizations and develop professional networks and contacts. On an emotional level, she recommends that students find a special area of interest or study that appeals to their sense of commitment. In the field of physical fitness, Susan stresses the importance of functioning as a role model. Credibility is lost if fitness leaders smoke, are overweight, use drugs, or practice unhealthy habits. Susan believes that working as a team player and being willing to do a variety of tasks to reach an ultimate goal are important. She also recommends that physical educators learn to think futuristically and to act progressively and productively to make valid plans come to life.

STUDENT ACTIVITIES

1. Talk with other students who have done volunteer work and had internships in intramurals, in athletics, with a community group, in a corporate fitness program, or with a sports business. Ask them about the positive and negative aspects of their experiences.
2. Get involved in one professionally related extracurricular activity for at least one semester. Evaluate your experiences to determine what you learned and how they could help you in the future.
3. Find out about your institution's Physical Education Majors' Club and become actively involved with it.
4. Select a certification, such as one in officiating, coaching, or first aid, and set short-term and long-term goals for achieving it.
5. Interview individuals in a career that interests you. Ask their advice about how best to prepare to enter that career.
6. Write a letter of application for a position in your chosen career. In one paragraph, highlight your most significant qualities.
7. Using the Internet or library resources find out information about three graduate programs that you might be interested in attending.
8. Conduct a debate in class about the pros and cons of doing volunteer activities.
9. Find three articles about the value of either networking, volunteering, or internships. Write a one-page paper reporting on each.

SUGGESTED READINGS

Barretta R: Criteria for aquatic personnel, *JOPERD* 61(5):44, 1990. This article briefly describes the recommended certifications for lifeguards, aquatic instructional specialists, aquatic administrators, and coaches.

Campbell K, Kovar SK: Fitness/exercise science internships: how to ensure success, *JOPERD* 65(2):69, 1994. The authors identify four potential areas associated with internship—academic preparation, intern accountability, supervisors' skills, and appropriateness of the internship site. They suggest possible solutions.

Cuneen J, Sidwell MJ: Sport management interns—selection qualifications, *JOPERD* 64(1):91, 1993. This article examines and rates the qualities and qualifications that sport managers are looking for in candidates for internships.

Field N: Your A to Z guide to sports careers, *Women's Sp & Fit* (no volume or issue number):48, September 1994. Various sports careers are described along with brief job descriptions, salary ranges, employment outlooks, and suggested contact people.

For the love of coaching, *Palaestra* 6(3):26, 1990 (Special Issue). The keys to Special Olympics are the volunteers who give of their time and energy so that individuals with mental retardation can participate in sport and recreational activities.

Helitzer M: *The dream job $port$—publicity, promotion and marketing,* ed 2, Athens, OH, 1996, University Sports Press. This easily-read book describes effective strategies for marketing, publicizing, and promoting college and professional sports.

Parks JB: Directory of fitness certifications, *JOPERD* 61(1):71, 1990. After describing the aerobic dance industry, seven examples of fitness certifications (taken from the NASPE Directory of Fitness Certifications) are listed. This listing includes the certifying organizations' addresses, requirements, procedures, renewal procedures, publications, and conferences.

Pollock ML: Exercise prescription for physical fitness, *Quest* 47(3):320, 1995. The current guidelines for physical fitness are described along with the differences between these and the guidelines for physical activity for health.

Sessoms HD: Anatomy of the leisure service professional certification exam, *Parks & Rec* 26(12):54, 1991. The National Recreation and Park Association initially offered its Certified Leisure Professional examination in 1990. This article outlines how the test was developed and its content.

Stumbo NJ: Overview of state credentialing concerns: a focus on licensure, *Ther Rec J* 24(2):40, 1990. Licensure, a form of credentialing, is governed by state regulations and a testing program. After presenting some of the issues surrounding initiating and administering such a program, comparisons are made between various configurations of state regulatory agencies and several states' therapeutic recreation credentialing plans.

UNIT TWO

History and Development of Physical Education and Sport Programs

European Heritage

KEY CONCEPTS

- Early civilizations, including the Greeks, valued physical development to varying degrees.
- The Greek Ideal stressed the unity of the "man of action" with "the man of wisdom."
- Knightly training was the primary source of physical development valued during the Middle Ages.
- A search for knowledge and an emphasis on "a sound mind in a sound body" emerged during the Renaissance.
- Naturalism focused on teaching children when they were ready to learn and on meeting their individual needs.
- European gymnastics programs developed to train soldiers for nationalistic purposes and later influenced school curricula.
- The English popularized and spread their love of sports and games.

Throughout history, people have participated in various physical activities. In early civilizations, integral to the survival tasks of seeking food, clothing, shelter, and protection were the utilitarian skills of running, jumping, throwing, wrestling, climbing, and swimming. Before formal educational programs, tribal leaders and parents mandated that children learn and practice survival skills through imitation. Communal requirements stressed physical prowess for both aggressive and defensive reasons.

Modern programs of physical education in the United States borrowed primarily from the philosophies, activities, and developments of Europeans from prehistoric times through the 1800s. The Greeks revered optimal physical prowess, and Greek athletics laid the foundation for subsequent physical education and sport programs. Military training in many countries served utilitarian purposes and replaced aesthetic or religious ideals. After social conditions stabilized,

146

the philosophy of naturalism stressed development of the body to help educate the whole child. Gymnastics that stressed nationalistic goals borrowed the apparatus and activities of the earlier naturalistic programs. Sports and games in England offered an alternative to these formalized gymnastics systems.

EARLY CULTURES

The Egyptians (2000 to 30 B.C.) have been recognized for their scientific, agricultural, and engineering prowess and their alphabet rather than for their educational achievements. Although the Egyptians did not have health objectives related to physical activity, they showed interest in physical development if it served to achieve a vocational, recreational, or religious objective. The warrior class trained physically in hunting, charioteering, using weapons, and wrestling. For recreation, the people of all classes swam, hunted, and played ball games. Dancing, like wrestling, was used for entertainment; dancing was also important in religious ritual.

The Chinese, between 2500 B.C. and A.D. 1200, adhered to an entrenched social system based on reverence for the aged scholar. Although in earlier eras physical training was somewhat valued, the religions of Taoism, Buddhism, and Confucianism emphasized the contemplative life. The defense-minded Chinese maintained a military class, who participated in archery, boxing, chariot racing, football, and wrestling, but these activities were never popularized for everyone. Other Chinese flew kites, played chess, practiced light exercises called Cong Fu, and hunted and fished. For the Chinese, literary studies and moral and religious training were valued most.

In India (2500 B.C. to A.D. 500), the Hindu religion imposed an unchanging social caste system upon the people. This dogma renounced pleasure and individualism and advocated asceticism in preparation for the next life. Spiritual well-being led to healthful practices and to participation in physical exercises such as yoga, a system of meditation and regulated breathing. Buddhism sought to reform the excesses of the Indian caste system, yet it too deemphasized physical activities.

For various reasons, the Egyptians, Chinese, and Indians engaged minimally in physical activities. Not until the Greeks did a civilization openly stress physical prowess and prescribe organized methods for its development.

Greece, regarded as the birthplace of Western civilization, produced a rich heritage of art, drama, history, mathematics, oratory, philosophy, poetry, science, and sculpture as well as the earliest recorded athletic or sports activities. This dynamic, progressive society, which recognized the importance of educating the whole individual, evolved through four models: (1) the Homeric model from prehistoric times until the first recorded Olympic victory, in 776 B.C., (2) the model of the totalitarian city-state of Sparta, in the period from 776 B.C. to 371 B.C., (3) the early Athenian model emphasizing democracy and individual freedom, in the period from 776 B.C. to the end of the Persian Wars, in 480 B.C., and (4) the later Athenian model, in the period from 480 B.C. until 338 B.C., resulting from heightened intellectual curiosity (Van Dalen and Bennett, 1971).

THE HOMERIC GREEKS (BEFORE 776 B.C.)

The Homeric era was named for the Greek poet Homer, who is credited with writing the *Iliad* and the *Odyssey,* which included the earliest records of athletic competitions. Book XXIII of the *Iliad* described the funeral games held in honor of Patroclus, Achilles' friend who had been killed in the Trojan War. The contests included a chariot race, boxing, wrestling, a footrace, a duel with spears, a discus throw, archery, and a javelin throw. Athletes of the period competing in individual activities fought fiercely to win. In the *Odyssey,* Homer chronicled the wanderings and return of Odysseus from the Trojan War. Illustrative of these adventures was one episode in Book VIII in which Odysseus, taunted by the Phaeacians, responded by throwing the discus beyond the distances achieved by their athletes.

The predominant philosophy that developed during the Homeric era became known as the **Greek Ideal,** which stressed the unity of the "man of action" with the "man of wisdom." This all-around mental, moral, and physical excellence was called **arete** and was personified by the Greek gods. Revered as part deity and part human, the 12 major gods of the Olympic Council were worshipped as the personifications of the Greek Ideal, with superior intellectual and physical capacities, such as strength, endurance, agility, and bravery. In funeral games held in honor of both respected soldiers killed in battle and the gods, Greek warrior-athletes competed to prove their arete; but, success was valued more highly than prizes. Prior to competing, many sought the favor of the gods.

THE SPARTANS (776 B.C. to 371 B.C.)

The Greeks organized themselves into small governmental units known as city-states. The two dominant, though dramatically contrasting, city-states were Sparta and Athens. By the eighth century B.C., Sparta had begun its military conquests. As Sparta conquered land and took captives, a strict code of discipline, not adherence to the Greek Ideal, was imposed on its people. The **agoge,** an educational system that ensured the singular goal of serving the state, evolved. Mandating complete submission, the Spartan civilization became static because everything, including education, was controlled exclusively by the government.

At birth a child was examined by a council of elders. If healthy and strong, the child was spared. Weak or sickly children were exposed to the elements to die. The mothers' roles in raising children resembled those of state nurses; they had to suppress all tender and maternalistic feelings. While sons were taught to value their roles as obedient soldiers, daughters learned about their responsibility to bear healthy children.

To prepare themselves physically for this duty, girls participated in state-prescribed gymnastics in addition to wrestling, swimming, and horseback riding. Dancing was also important in the education of girls and boys as a means of physical conditioning and of honoring the gods.

The boys' educational system, the agoge, was highly structured and formalized. Boys were conscripted by the state at seven years of age and remained in military service until death. Spartan boys began their military training with running and jumping for conditioning. They progressed to swimming, hunting, wrestling, boxing, playing ball, riding horses bareback, throwing the discus and the javelin, and competing in the **pancratium,** a combination activity of wrestling and boxing skills. They were trained to endure hardships and pain. Discipline reigned supreme; youths who failed to develop valor, devotion to the state, and military skill were punished.

Beginning at 20 years of age, youths engaged in intensive military maneuvers and actual warfare. These Spartan soldiers, who had been conditioned to fight until death, repeatedly demonstrated their superiority over neighboring city-states and other foes. Not only did the Spartans dominate militarily during this time, but they also won more Olympic victories than athletes from any other city-state. Spartan men, at the age of 30 years, qualified for citizenship and were expected to marry; however, their obligation to the state continued as they trained youth in the public barracks. The Spartan military machine, with its singular focus on physical prowess and disregard for intellectual development, contributed to its inability to rule its innumerable captives and lands. Although they made excellent soldiers, the people were not trained to think for themselves, but rather to perform on command. Also, the Spartans were few in number because of their strict practices. Combined, these factors led to the end of their domination as a city-state in 371 B.C.

THE EARLY ATHENIANS (776 B.C. to 480 B.C.)

Athens differed sharply from Sparta. The Greek Ideal became the Athenian Ideal as this city-state sought to provide an educational system that encouraged boys to develop their physical and mental abilities. Within this framework of democracy, liberalism, and the popularization of various philosophies, physical prowess flourished as an integral part of the preparation of boys for war and as a means through which beauty and harmony could be depicted.

Girls remained at home under the care of their mothers and received little or no education. Once married, they lived secluded lives. Unlike the physically trained women in Sparta, the Athenian women's social role, quite typical for that time, was very different from the men's role. Boys in the lower classes, though, were as uneducated as girls.

The Athenian educational system, which valued the all-around citizen, dominated the life of upper-class boys who, under the guidance of their fathers, learned about their future responsibilities. Usually beginning at seven years of age and lasting until 14 to 18 years of age, formal education occurred at privately owned schools. The time when each boy started, the length of time he attended, and the time when he ended this phase of his education were determined solely by the father, since no governmental regulations existed. Not all boys could attend these schools, since fathers had to pay for their sons' education.

The importance attached to the all-around development ideal was evident in each boy's attendance at two schools. A music school provided instruction in arithmetic, literature, and music, while at a **palaestra,** or wrestling school, the boys trained physically. Both schools were equally valued, as the unity concept

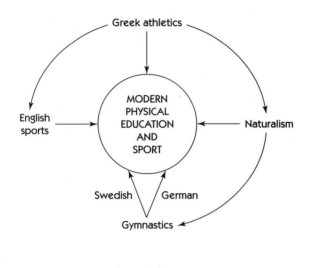

FIGURE 7-1

European contributions to modern physical education and sport.

prevailed. Palaestras, owned and directed by **paidotribes,** the first physical education teachers, were not elaborate athletic facilities but varied from simple rooms to separate buildings. There the boys practiced wrestling, boxing, jumping, and dancing. Some palaestras also included playing fields and a place for swimming.

At the age of 18 years, Athenian boys became eligible for citizenship. For two years thereafter they were subject to military service, if the state needed them, although no mandatory conscription existed. From 20 years of age throughout their lives, upper-class Athenian men did not work but instead spent their days at government-furnished **gymnasiums.** There they practiced athletics to maintain their readiness as warriors in case they were needed by the state. Intellectual discussions, governmental decisions, and social interactions were equally important occurrences at the gymnasium.

Greek dancing provided one means of honoring the gods as part of religious worship and also enhanced physical conditioning and demonstrated the symmetry and beauty adored by the Athenians. Athletics played a similar role, as festivals honoring the gods gave Greek men the opportunity to display their physical prowess and aesthetically pleasing bodies. The importance of honoring the gods eventually led to a proliferation of festivals throughout Greece. Figure 7-1 depicts how Greek athletics and subsequent European contributions resulted in modern physical education and sport.

THE LATE ATHENIANS (480 b.c. to 338 b.c.)

The Athenian-led victory over the Persians in 480 b.c. set the stage for several cultural changes. Economic expansion, self-confidence, increased leisure time, intellectual curiosity, and expansion of political franchise combined to shift the educational goals away from devotion to the state and toward a heightened pursuit of individual happiness. This rampant individualism led to a deemphasis on the physical aspects of education, because, as members of the dominant city-state, citizens no longer saw the need to train as soldiers. The Athenian warrior-athletes were replaced by mercenaries and professional athletes.

The gymnasiums became more like pleasure resorts than exercise areas and provided sites for philosophical discussions and the training of professional athletes. The Golden Age of Athens (443 B.C. to 429 B.C.) was highlighted by a flowering of democracy and intellectual curiosity led by the Sophists, a class of teachers of rhetoric, philosophy, and the art of successful living, and by philosophers such as Plato. Warning cries from some philosophers about the undermining of the Athenian society went largely unheeded. As a result, the Athenians were militarily unprepared and fell to the Macedonians in 338 B.C.

THE OLYMPICS (776 B.C. to A.D. 400)

Festivals honoring the gods during the Homeric period led to the establishment of regular celebrations, which expanded dramatically in the fifth century B.C. The warrior-athletes, who were expected to perfect their skills for warfare, used these religious festivals to demonstrate their physical prowess, especially because this proved their allegiance to the Greek Ideal as personified by the gods. Some of these Panhellenic (meaning for all Greeks) festivals also included choral and musical events and aquatic displays. Although the festivals were predominantly for men, at least one, the Heraean Games, was staged for maiden women competing in a footrace.

The Olympics, unmatched in prestige among these festivals, was held every four years at Olympia in honor of Zeus, the chief Greek god. It began at least by 776 B.C. (the date of the earliest existing artifact of an Olympic victory), but probably started much earlier. The sacrifices to Zeus, feasting, and athletic contests lasted five days in August and attained such prestige that the perennially warring city-states would guarantee safe passage to travelers to the games. The box on page 152 lists when each event became a part of the Olympics and provides an outline of how events were organized during the five days. This sequence of events reinforced the link between religious service and athletic competition.

To be eligible for the Olympics, prospective athletes had to be Greek-born and had to train for 10 months before the contests, the last month at Olympia under the guidance of the judges. Although the games were open to men from all social classes, the training requirement precluded participation by most poor Greeks, who had to work. Athletes were required to take an oath of fair play. Victors received a simple wreath of olive branches to symbolize their highly respected victory. Accorded a hero's welcome when returning home, a victor reveled in triumphal processions and banquets, special privileges, and monetary rewards. Initially, Olympia provided no accommodations for either spectators or athletes, as neither a stadium nor a site for the contests existed. The games were scheduled in open spaces with spectators sitting wherever they could. Later, construction of a stadium for footraces and the hippodrome for horse and chariot races provided space for about 40,000 spectators.

ANCIENT OLYMPIC GAMES

Chronology

776 B.C.	Stade race
724 B.C.	Added the two-stade race
720 B.C.	Added the long distance race
708 B.C.	Added pentathlon and wrestling
688 B.C.	Added boxing
680 B.C.	Added chariot race
648 B.C.	Added pancratium and horse race
632 B.C.	Added boys' events
580 B.C.	Added the race in armor
472 B.C.	Festival set as a five-day event and the sequence of events set as follows:

First Day

Oath-taking ceremony

Contests for heralds and trumpeters

Contests for boys

Sacrifices, prayers, singing of hymns, and other religious observances

Second Day

Chariot race

Horse race

Pentathlon (discus, javelin, long jump, stade race, and wrestling)

Third Day

Main sacrifice to Zeus

Footraces

Fourth Day

Wrestling

Boxing

Pancratium

Race in armor

Fifth Day

Prize-giving ceremony

Service of thanksgiving to Zeus

Banquet

The pentathlon consisted of five events: the stade race, javelin, long jump, throwing the discus, and wrestling.

The stade race, so named because it was a footrace the length of the stadium (about 200 meters), was probably the only event in the first Olympic Games. A two-stade race (about 400 meters), a long race of about 4800 meters (12 laps), and a race in armor were later added to this phase of the athletic contests. Marble slabs may have served as starting blocks, and a trumpet blast started these events. In the 400-meter and 4800-meter races, the athletes rounded a post at the opposite end of the stadium.

Remains of the stadium at Olympia.

Hand-to-hand combat events included boxing, wrestling, and the pancratium. Since no weight categories existed, boxing pitted two athletes of any size against each other, until one raised a hand to admit defeat. No gloves were worn; the boxers' hands were wrapped with pieces of leather. Blows were confined to the head, often resulting in severe injuries. Wrestling, one of the most popular events because its competitors displayed agility, gracefulness, and strength, was done standing. The objective was to throw the opponent to the ground three times. The pancratium borrowed from boxing and wrestling to become an "almost anything goes" combat. Except for biting and gouging, an athlete employed any maneuver, such as tripping, breaking fingers, and strangle holds, to force an opponent's admission of defeat.

Chariots, two-wheeled vehicles pulled by four horses, raced, as did horses, at the hippodrome, a narrow field about 500 meters long. These races were limited to the wealthy who could afford to maintain the horses and to hire the charioteers. The victors were the owners, not the charioteers or jockeys. The chariot race consisted of 12 laps; the horse race covered two to six laps.

The winner of the **pentathlon** was recognized as the best all-around athlete. Although the order of events and the method of determining the victor have been lost in antiquity, the discus throw, the javelin throw, the long jump, the stade race, and wrestling constituted the pentathlon. Like the long jump and the javelin throw, the discus throw existed only as a pentathlon event. A circular piece of stone or bronze about one foot in diameter and weighing four to five pounds was hurled by the athlete. In the long jump, probably similar to today's triple jump, one athlete recorded a distance of more than 55 feet. Jumpers were aided by handheld weights, called *halteres,* which were swung to enhance their performances. The javelin was thrown for both distance and form as a test of skill and strength. A leather thong was wrapped around the 8- to 10-foot javelin, giving it a rotary motion upon release, thereby increasing accuracy. The stade race and then the wrestling match probably climaxed the pentathlon, although they may not have been held if one athlete had already won the first three events.

The ancient stadium at Delphi, site of the Pythian Games.

Pancratium.

Two developments ushered in a change in attitude toward the Olympic Games and the other Panhellenic festivals. Beginning in Athens, intellectual curiosity and a search for knowledge replaced the Greek Ideal and hence lessened interest in physical development. Within the games themselves, lucrative prizes increasingly overshadowed the earlier motive of honoring the gods through displays of athletic prowess (see box, p. 157). Professional athletes who trained under coaches at the gymnasiums and who specialized in certain events became prominent in the contests. Expensive prizes led to cheating, corruption, and bribery. Although officially ended by Roman decree around A.D. 400, the Olympics had much earlier lost association with their former values.

PANHELLENIC FESTIVALS

Name	Frequency	Honoring	Location	Wreath for victor
Olympic Games	Every four years	Zeus	Olympia	Olive leaves
Pythian Games	Every four years (third year of each Olympiad)	Apollo	Delphi	Bay leaves
Isthmian Games	Every two years (second and fourth years of each Olympiad)	Poseidon	Corinth	Dry parsley leaves or pine
Nemean Games	Every two years	Zeus	Argolis	Fresh parsley
Panathenaean Games	Most prominent local festival	Athena	Athens	None

THE ROMAN REPUBLIC (500 B.C. to 27 B.C.)

The Roman civilization began as a small tribal community near the Tiber River during the height of the Greek civilization. By extending its rule over neighboring tribes, the Roman nobles, who were landowners, succeeded in establishing a republic around 500 B.C. Soon the common people, who had been given land for their military service, demanded and received greater voice in the government. Thus many Romans, through this democratization process, attained a higher degree of political and economic freedom.

Roman life during this era focused singularly on serving the state, even though the home provided education for youths without government involvement. Fathers and mothers taught their sons to become citizen-soldiers, including in their education a mental and physical readiness for war, respect for the law, and reverence for the gods. Accompanying their fathers to the Campus Martius or other military camps, boys learned through imitation military skills, such as archery, fencing, javelin throwing, marching, riding, running, swimming, and wrestling, and they developed bodily strength, courage, and obedience to commands as they trained. Conscripted into the military at 17 years of age, men were available for active duty, if needed, until the age of 47. During these 30 years, men were expected to fulfill their business and political duties as well.

Daughters were educated to assume a vital role in raising children and were expected to instill in their sons the importance of fighting for and even dying for the state. Roman women were more highly respected and socially active than Athenian women.

Religious festivals honoring the gods held as prominent a place in the Roman society as they had during Greek times, yet the Romans did not participate in athletic contests or dance. Rather, they offered sacrifices to their gods and then watched horse and chariot races or gladiatorial contests. These festivals provided leisure-time relief from strenuous training but served no educational purposes.

THE ROMAN EMPIRE (27 B.C. to A.D. 476)

The economic and political freedoms gained by citizens during the Republic were rapidly undermined during the century before the Empire was established in 27 B.C. under Augustus Caesar. The hardy peasants, who had received land in exchange for military service, were ravaged by years of war and debts and mortgages. Powerful landowners seized this opportunity to expand their estates and to gain greater political influence. The poorer citizens who were forced off their land migrated to Rome, where they lived off the public dole. Replaced by a professional army and denied political freedoms and personal dignity, the common people spent their days attending the festivals and games sponsored by corrupt, upper-class senators or the emperors. Gambling on the outcomes of these contests became a favorite pastime.

TABLE 7-1

COMPARISON OF ATHLETIC PROGRAMS

Early Athens	Late Athens	Roman Republic	Roman Empire
Participants			
Aristocratic citizens	Professional athletes	Citizen-soldiers	Professional gladiators and charioteers
Motivation			
All-around development	Profit	Preparation for war	Profit
Training			
Gymnasiums and palaestras	Gymnasiums under trainers	Military camps and fathers	Specialized schools
Events			
Archery, boxing, chariot races, discus, footraces, javelin, and wrestling	Boxing, chariot races, footraces, horse races, pancratium, pentathlon, and wrestling	Archery, fencing, javelin, marching, riding, running, swimming, and wrestling	Chariot races and gladiatorial contests
Organization			
Festivals	Scheduled games and festivals	Festivals	Frequent, organized festivals
Number of Stadiums or Arenas			
Few	Many	Few	Many
Number of Spectators			
Limited	Thousands	Limited	Thousands
Professionals or Amateurs			
Amateurs	Professionals	Amateurs	Professionals
Awards			
Some, but not most important	Lucrative benefits	Limited awards	Lucrative prizes

At least 200 days per year were public holidays and provided opportunities for festivals. Up to 260,000 spectators watched chariot races at the Circus Maximus, attesting to the popularity of these contests. Professional charioteers hired by the teams (the blues, the greens, the reds, and the whites) raced their low, light chariots drawn by four horses in seven-lap races around a *spina,* for a distance of about three miles. The Colosseum became the favorite site for the gladiatorial contests, where, to the pleasure of as many as 90,000 spectators, animal fights featured elephants, bulls, tigers, lions, panthers, and bears. Condemned criminals, social undesirables, and Christians were forced to combat lions, tigers, and panthers. Massive sea battles in the Colosseum provided additional bloody, gory entertainment. Gladiators armed with shield and sword, buckle and dagger, or net and spear, fought each other for freedom or for money.

Gladiators and charioteers trained physically, but most other Romans lost interest in developing their own bodies because they were no longer expected to serve as soldiers. Instead, **thermae,** or baths, provided sites for contrast baths of varying water temperatures for both men and women, with separate hours reserved for the women. At the numerous thermae, Roman men participated in health gymnastics or ball play to overcome indolent lifestyles that featured gluttonous feasts and drinking bouts.

Thus the moral fabric and physical abilities of a once-strong people dissipated rapidly during an era characterized by governmental upheavals, power struggles, and an apathetic and dependent populace. In A.D. 476, with the deposition of the last emperor by the Visigoths under Odoacer, the domination of the Roman Empire came to an ignoble end. As was true of the demise of the Athenians, a lack of emphasis on physical development contributed to the decline of a once-powerful civilization. (Table 7-1 compares Greek and Roman athletic programs.)

MEDIEVAL EUROPE (500 to 1500)

The years following the fall of the Roman Empire represented a low point physically and intellectually. Many church leaders during the Middle Ages, such as St. Augustine, spoke against dancing because it had degenerated from its earlier status for religious expression. They also opposed frivolous activities that might detract from piety, proper commitment to worship, and godly living. The Catholic church, in seeking a higher level of morality than displayed by most Romans, regarded the body and anything that benefitted it as sinful. Asceticism, a doctrine that renounces the comforts of society and espouses austere self-discipline, especially as an act of religious devotion, was practiced by many monks during medieval times.

The only schools that existed during this time were at the monasteries, thus restricting intellectual education to those who served the church. Survival rather than education highlighted this era, although the monks preserved the Greek philosophies until a time when they would again be studied and valued.

European society in the eleventh to the sixteenth centuries was feudalistic. The economic, political, and social aspects of life centered around ownership of land and the military power to maintain or expand territory. The monarch, at least theoretically, owned the land. Unable to rule diverse properties successfully, the king divided the territory among nobles who, in turn, promised military service. As vassals to the king, they similarly divided their holdings among lesser vassals,

Medieval knights prepared for battle.

with the same reciprocal protection guarantees. At the bottom of this pyramidal structure were the serfs, or peasants, who toiled in the fields. Their labors were meagerly rewarded with protection provided by those they served.

The vassal landowners, who were knights, were the only ones in the feudal society to value physical training, although the peasants engaged in various recreational pursuits. At seven years of age, the sons of nobles left their homes to go to the manors of other knights. Under the guidance of the ladies of the castles for the next seven years, the pages were educated through stories about chivalry and its code of moral and social duties of knighthood. Squires, beginning at 14 years of age, learned the arts of archery, climbing, dancing, fencing, jousting, riding, swimming, tourneying, and wrestling. As a valet for a knight, the squire served meals, cleaned armor, cared for the knight's horse, played chess and backgammon, and accompanied the knight into battle. Following seven years of extensive training as a squire, the youth became eligible for knighthood. Once knighted, these nobles engaged in hunting and hawking and continued their training for battle.

In the isolation of the manorial system of the Middle Ages, few opportunities existed for social interaction and entertainment, so tournaments grew in popularity to fill this void. Although festive occasions, these tournaments focused on combats between knights, who divided into two teams and fought under conditions similar to war in the *grand tourney*, or *melee*. Although strict rules and blunt weapons supposedly limited the injuries, fatalities frequently occurred in the melee, leading to its demise. Another event at the tournaments was *jousting*, which pitted two mounted knights armed with lances in a head-on attempt to unseat each other. Since weapons were blunt and the objective was not to kill the opponent, the joust gradually became the primary event of the tournaments.

Because war served as an adventurous solution to boredom and because service to God was required of the knights, many willingly volunteered for the eight Crusades between 1096 and 1270. Instigated by the church, these military expeditions attempted to expel the Moslems and the Turks from the Holy Land and to establish papal control in that region. The knights profited from the captured spoils of war, and some took part mainly for this reason.

Interaction with people from other civilizations through the Crusades contrasted markedly with the isolated lifestyle of the feudalistic period, which peaked between 1250 and 1350. While the importance of the knights lessened because of the invention of gunpowder, towns were being established as trade centers. The emergence of a strong merchant class in these towns started the transition to a period of intellectual, cultural, and social reawakening.

THE RENAISSANCE AND THE REFORMATION (1450 to 1650)

A renewed appreciation for classical culture grew out of the centuries of intellectual void of the Middle Ages. Intellectual curiosity and creativity were encouraged rather than stymied as education came to be highly valued by people of all social classes. During the Middle Ages, several allied, yet diverse, philosophies developed; these blossomed during the **Renaissance** period. They directly influenced attitudes toward physical education, although most often the mind and the body were viewed as two separate entities. Scholasticism, based on the authority of church leaders and the writings of the Greek philosopher Aristotle, placed intellectual development in a revered position to the detriment of the body.

Humanistic education in Italy stressed the harmonious development of humans and embraced the Greek Ideal of unity. "A sound mind in a sound body" described this philosophy, which implemented the principles of humanism and emphasized the physical as well as the intellectual development of students. Humanists stressed the importance of a healthy body as preparatory to intellectual endeavors rather than stressing a dichotomous relationship between mind and body.

Realism, which grew out of humanism, emphasized the importance of understanding the Greek classics and of educating for life. The development of health through exercise and play and scientific thinking became critical educational outcomes for the realists.

Educational moralism developed during the Protestant Reformation of the 1500s and 1600s as religious fervor combined with nationalism. Although initially desirous only of purifying the Catholic church, reformers such as Martin Luther and John Calvin led this era of intense religious change. Their doctrines stressed personal salvation, moral responsibilities, and state duties. Most of the Protestant sects deemphasized physical development as a distraction from these objectives. One religious group, the Puritans, was especially vehement in its opposition to frivolous activities and tried to enforce its strict doctrines on others in the American colonies. While humanism and realism furthered the Renaissance theme of "a sound mind in a sound body," moralism hindered its acceptance as an educational goal.

Throughout the Renaissance, the 1700s, and most of the 1800s, education was valued for boys, especially from the upper class, who attended boarding schools or were taught privately by tutors. Seldom was education provided for girls.

THE AGE OF ENLIGHTENMENT (1700s)

The Renaissance set the stage for the Age of Enlightenment, during which two additional philosophies influencing physical education developed. Englishman John Locke wrote about educational disciplinarianism. He said that character, especially valued for upper-class boys and requiring "a sound mind in a sound body," developed best through moral and physical discipline. Jean-Jacques Rousseau, a French philosopher, led the rebellion against the devaluation of the individual. In *Emile,* a description of the ideal way to educate a boy, Rousseau stressed **naturalism,** or "everything according to nature." That is, each child possessed a unique readiness to learn in a natural developmental process that should dictate when a child was exposed to various types of knowledge. The child, free to explore nature while recreating, would thus prepare physically for later intellectual pursuits and would, therefore, learn optimally. The Age of Enlightenment provided additional insights into how to educate a child, thereby laying the foundation for European gymnastics programs. Before examining these programs, however, it is important to frame the 1400s to 1800s into an educational context by describing some of the leaders in education.

EDUCATIONAL PROTAGONISTS (1400s to 1800s)

Vittorino da Feltre (1379–1446) has been acclaimed for his greatness as a teacher and for leading the way in educational theory, which began with humanism during the Renaissance. As a teacher in the Italian "court," or private, schools supported by wealthy patrons, he stressed the importance of intellectual, moral, and physical development. In elevating physical education to a place of prominence in the curriculum, he used archery, fencing, riding, and martial exercises to help create the complete citizen.

François Rabelais (1490–1553) helped provide a bridge between Renaissance humanists and seventeenth-century realists. He emphasized that physical education should focus on teaching skills to prepare young gentlemen for war. Especially valuable were the knightly exercises of the medieval days.

Michel de Montaigne (1533–1592) advocated that the body and soul were equal and inseparable. Thus, the mind and body were to be educated simultaneously, as the Greek philosopher Plato had stated centuries earlier. Montaigne's plan of education stressed thinking, learning by doing, developing the whole person, and preparing students for life.

John Comenius (1592–1670) in *The Great Didactic* set forth a comprehensive methodology for teaching. A body-mind dualist, like John Locke, he regarded play as essential for children's development, especially for ensuring healthy, vigorous bodies.

John Locke (1632–1704) despite his preoccupation with the education of gentlemen, valued physical exercise for its health benefits. His phrase "a sound mind in a sound body" taken from *Some Thoughts Concerning Education* (1693) became the motto for physical educators who supported his belief in the development of the healthy body as a primary function of education.

Jean-Jacques Rousseau (1712–1788) in *Emile* (1762) described an ideal education that continues throughout life. Physical activity within a natural setting should occur as the child is ready to learn.

EDUCATIONAL PROTAGONISTS

Individual	Philosophy	Focus	Program/Setting
Vittorino da Feltre	Humanism	Physically sound youth with alert intellect	Ball games; riding; running; fencing; dancing
François Rabelais	Verbal realism	Prepare gentlemen for war	Horsemanship; swordsmanship; swimming
Michel de Montaigne	Social humanism	Shape aristocratic youth for integrated life as a gentleman	Running; wrestling; dancing; hunting; riding
John Comenius	Sense realism	Play is essential to the natural educational process	Children's games; play with toys
John Locke	Educational disciplinarianism	A sound mind in a sound body	Swimming; dancing; riding; fencing
Jean-Jacques Rousseau	Educational naturalism	Everything in education according to nature	Jumping; leaping; climbing; ball play
Johann Pestalozzi	Educational developmentalism	Children learn progressively and in harmony with the body and mind	Games; gymnastics; outdoor activities
Friedrich Froebel	Educational developmentalism	Connect interest in learning with pleasure	Games in the open air; play

Johann Pestalozzi's (1746–1827) ideas, as expressed in *Leonard and Gertrude,* established the foundation of modern educational theory. He advocated sense impression so children could learn to observe accurately, progression of learning from the simple to the complex, developmental readiness to learn, and use of children's interest as an indicator of ability to understand. Daily physical exercise aided his students in achieving full unity and harmony between the body and intellect.

Friedrich Froebel (1782–1852) believed in play as the highest phase of child development. The efficacy of play could bring children to a realization of the internal and external unity of the world.

These educational protagonists are compared in the box above.

NATURALISM (1770 to 1830)

Although the French were not receptive to Rousseau's educational theories, Johann Basedow, a German teacher, was. In establishing a school for boys called the Philanthropinum in 1774, Basedow sought to implement naturalistic principles that focused on meeting individual needs, and he stressed the principle of a readiness to learn. At this school he allotted three hours each day to instructional and recreational activities, such as gymnastics, sports, and games, and two hours to manual labor. While Basedow advocated dancing, fencing, riding, and vaulting, the teacher hired to direct the program, Johann Simon, introduced Greek gymnastics, consisting of jumping, running, throwing, and wrestling. Simon utilized natural settings to provide the apparatus, such as balance beams, high-jumping poles, jumping ditches, and tree swings. Johann Du Toit, Simon's successor, added archery, skating, swimming, marching, gardening, and woodworking to Basedow's original scheme.

In 1785, Christian Salzmann patterned the program at Schnepfenthal Educational Institute after Basedow's naturalistic lessons in games and gymnastics. Johann GutsMuths, who taught at Schnepfenthal for 50 years, was strongly influenced by Basedow's writings and provided similar activities and pieces of apparatus. GutsMuths' three- to four-hour daily program consisted of natural activities, such as jumping and running; Greek gymnastics, such as throwing and wrestling; military exercises, such as fencing and marching; knightly activities, such as climbing and vaulting; and manual labor, such as gardening and woodworking. GutsMuths influenced many people with two significant books: *Gymnastics for the Young* (1793), which not only described Schnepfenthal's program but also laid the theoretical foundation for modern programs, and *Games for Exercise and Recreation of the Body and Spirit* (1796), which described the skills developed in 105 games or activities and illustrated apparatus, such as climbing masts, hanging ladders, rope ladders, and wooden horses.

NATIONALISM (1800s)

Friedrich Jahn, a German educator and an ardent patriot, visited the Schnepfenthal Educational Institute and borrowed many aspects of GutsMuths' program. Jahn's purpose in promoting physical development was nationalistic, rather than naturalistic, because he sought to develop fitness and strength in German youth for the eventual unification of all German people. After encouraging his students to climb trees, jump over ditches, run, and throw stones on half-holiday excursions from classes, he established, in 1811, the first *turnplatz* near Berlin. A turnplatz was an outdoor exercise area where the boys, who became known as *turners,* trained using balance beams, ropes and ladders for climbing, high-jumping standards, horizontal bars, parallel bars, pole-vaulting standards, broad-jumping pits, vaulting horses, a figure eight-shaped track, and a wrestling ring. Jahn also promoted **nationalism** through patriotic speeches and stories and group singing of patriotic songs. First boys and then, as this turner system of gymnastics expanded, males of all ages and social classes participated in the increasingly popular gymnastic exercises. Jahn explained his program, in 1816, in his book *German Gymnastics.*

German gymnastics on the horse.

The turners vigorously advocated a unified Germany, and many local turn-platz sites initially received government subsidization. After the Congress of Vienna in 1815 realigned Germany into a confederation of 38 independent states, the turners' single-minded goal of a unified nation was viewed as threatening. Finally, in 1819, government leaders succeeded in banning turner gymnastics. Not until 1840 was it again legal to participate in turner gymnastics, although underground programs thrived during these years. Turner gymnastics never gained widespread popularity in other nations because of the nationalistic appeal and emphasis on strength.

Adolph Spiess borrowed from his training in turner gymnastics to devise a system of German school gymnastics in the 1840s. Approval of his program in the increasing number of public schools hinged on his defense of gymnastics as a subject equal to all others, one that had progressions for various ages, for boys and girls, and for all ability levels, and one that required trained teachers and equipped indoor and outdoor facilities. Although influenced somewhat by Jahn's and GutsMuths' programs, Spiess devised a school system that stressed discipline and obedience and included diverse activities, such as marching, free exercises, and gymnastics with musical accompaniment.

Nationalism dominated Danish gymnastics in the early 1800s, too. Fitness, strength, and military competence emerged as goals of Franz Nachtegall. In 1799, he established a private gymnasium in Copenhagen, the first of its kind. Nachte-gall's curriculum, which borrowed extensively from the apparatus and exercises of GutsMuths, gained popularity and helped Denmark initiate the first European school program in physical education for boys, in 1809. His *Manual of Gymnastics,* published in 1828, provided the curriculum for the schools. Teachers for the schools were initially educated alongside military men at the Military Gymnastic Institute, founded in 1804 by the king of Denmark, with Nachtegall as its director.

Class of women students at the Royal Gymnastics Central Institute.

Danish gymnastics in the military and in the schools was based totally on command-response exercises, with the rigid, mass drills associated with the nationalistic theme.

Patriotism raged in Sweden in the later 1700s and in the 1800s, because of the loss of much of Sweden's territory to Russian foes and Napoleonic forces. This nationalistic fervor initially influenced Per Henrik Ling to study and write about the Scandinavian heritage. While pursuing this objective in Denmark for five years, he learned gymnastics from Franz Nachtegall and engaged in fencing, through which he improved an arthritic arm. The personal therapeutic benefits that Ling experienced resulted in his emphasis on this contribution of gymnastics throughout his career. Returning to his homeland in 1804, Ling became a fencing master and an instructor of literature and history, while also teaching gymnastics.

Ling's theory that the knowledge of Norse literature and history combined with gymnastics training could coalesce Sweden into a stronger nation influenced the king. As a result, the Royal Gymnastics Central Institute was established in Stockholm in 1814, under Ling's direction. As a training program for military men, this program allowed Swedes to stress precise execution of movements on command, mass drills, specific exercises on specially designed pieces of apparatus, and posture-correcting movements. England, Denmark, Belgium, Greece, and other countries adopted Swedish gymnastics for military training. Ling initiated therapeutic, or medical, gymnastics to restore health through exercises. He also promoted gymnastics for pedagogical (educational) and aesthetic purposes. Swedish apparatus, such as stall bars, booms, vaulting boxes, and oblique ropes, as developed by Ling, were always subordinated to the exercises and to students' needs. (The box on p. 167 compares the three major gymnastics systems in Europe.)

When Hjalmar Ling, Per Henrik Ling's son, began teaching at the Royal Gymnastics Central Institute, he initiated the development of Swedish school

COMPARISON OF EUROPEAN GYMNASTICS SYSTEMS

System	Theme(s)	Participants	Program	Apparatus
German	National regeneration; physical education used to develop strong, sturdy fearless youth	Working and lower-middle classes; first boys, then adults, too	Individualized under Jahn and *vorturners* (teachers)	Vaulting horses; parallel bars; ropes and ladders for climbing; balance beams; running track
Swedish	National prepared-ness; therapeutic healing; peda-gogical; aesthetics	Soldiers; teachers	Movement on command; posture cor-recting	Stall bars; vaulting boxes; climbing poles; oblique ropes; Swedish boom
Danish	Nationalism	Soldiers; teachers	Formalized exercises on command; no individual expression	Hanging lad-ders; rope ladders; masts and poles for climbing; balance beams; vaulting horses

Swedish school gymnastics.

gymnastics. Borrowing from his father's program the principles of progression and precise execution of movements on command, Hjalmar Ling devised the Day's Order, systematized daily exercises that progressed through the whole body from head to toe. These lessons were appropriately graded for the age, ability, and sex of each child and used apparatus designed for children. Mass drills under a teacher's direction remained paramount.

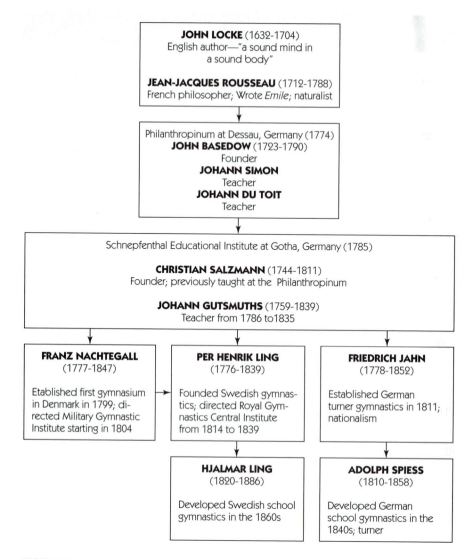

FIGURE 7-2
Origins of modern physical education.

The time line in the box on page 169 depicts for each era of time what activities people participated in and their purposes. Figure 7-2 illustrates how European philosophies and innovators influenced subsequent programs.

ENGLISH SPORTS (1800s)

The nationalistic fervor for European gymnastics never gained prominence in England, other than minimal usage of Ling's program by the British military. As the dominant world power, Great Britain had not faced territorial decimation as

	EUROPEAN HERITAGE TIME LINE		
Dates	*People*	*Popular Activities*	*Purpose*
Pre-776 B.C.	Homeric Greeks	Chariot racing; boxing; wrestling; footracing; throwing the discuss and javelin	Preparation for war; honoring the gods
776 B.C. to 371 B.C.	Spartans	Running; jumping; wrestling; boxing; horseback riding; throwing the discus and javelin; pancratium; hunting; swimming	Military supremacy
776 B.C. to 480 B.C.	Early Athenians	Wrestling; boxing; jumping; throwing the discus and javelin; dancing	Preparation for war; honoring the gods
500 B.C. to 27 B.C.	Romans during the Republic	Archery; fencing; throwing the javelin; marching; riding; running; swimming; wrestling	Preparation for war
A.D. 500 to 1500	European knights	Archery; climbing; dancing; fencing; jousting; riding; swimming; wrestling; hunting; hawking	Preparation for war
1450 to 1650	Educational protagonists	Archery; fencing; riding; games; play; gymnastics	Education of the whole child
1770 to 1830	Naturalists (Germans)	Dancing; fencing; riding; vaulting; jumping; running; throwing; wrestling; manual labor; gymnastics; games	Meeting individual needs
1800s	German turners	Climbing; vaulting; jumping; wrestling; running	National regeneration
1800s	Danish	Vaulting; climbing; jumping; gymnastics exercises	Nationalism
1800s	Swedish	Vaulting; climbing; gymnastics exercises	Nationalism; therapy

so many other nations had, so nationalism failed to undergird a gymnastics program in that country. Instead, the English legacy to both European and world-wide physical education has undoubtedly been its sports and games.

The Greek Ideal paralleled Englishman John Locke's "sound mind and sound body" concept. The Greek love for athletic supremacy, rather than lucrative benefits, during Panhellenic festivals is remarkably similar to the **British Amateur Sport Ideal** of "playing the game for the game's sake." The Greek Ideal as displayed by upper-class males in England dramatically influenced Frenchman Pierre de Coubertin, who founded the modern Olympic Games.

Sports and recreational pastimes have traditionally been divided along class or socioeconomic lines in England. Working-class males were especially attracted to pugilism (bare-knuckle boxing), blood sports, such as cockfighting, and varieties of football (soccer). These "poor man's sports" required little equipment, usually encouraged gambling, and were often banned by the church.

English upper-class sports, such as cricket and rugby, were popularized at private boys' boarding schools, called public schools, in the 1800s. Thomas Arnold, headmaster at Rugby School, praised the role of sport in the book *Tom Brown's Schooldays*. Regularly, Arnold advocated that through sports participation boys learned moral virtues, such as cooperation, leadership, loyalty, self-discipline, and sportsmanship. Sport within the public schools stressed participation in a variety of sports, rather than specialization in one; playing the game, rather than training in skills and fitness; and interhouse competition (between the boys in various residences). Public school boys often demonstrated greater learning through sport than in their scholastic efforts. Since graduates of these public schools were the future leaders of the nation, lessons learned in sports were acclaimed for preparing better citizens.

Cricket, rowing, association football (soccer), track and field athletics, rugby, and field hockey became the most popular sports at Oxford University and Cambridge University despite faculty disfavor. The British Amateur Sport Ideal of playing the game for the game's sake, rather than for remuneration, prevailed in these sports competitions.

The emergence of the philosophy of muscular Christianity, that is, the teaching of values through sport, impacted English sports and subsequently those in the United States. Most Protestants, and especially the Puritans, had viewed

The English popularized rugby in boys' boarding schools in the 1800s.

SELECTED SPORTS AND THEIR ORIGINS		
Wrestling	China	1788 B.C.
Boxing	China	850 B.C.
Track and Field	Greece	776 B.C.
Rugby	England	900
Golf	Scotland	1457
Cricket	England	1679
Gymnastics	Germany	1816
Baseball (Rounders)	England	1846
Soccer	England	1859
Badminton	India	1870
Tennis	England	1873
Water Polo	England	1885
Field Hockey	England	1886
Table Tennis	England	1889

participation in sports and games as sinful. However, when people refused to conform to rigid prohibitions, attitudes gradually softened to permit sporting diversions as long as moral values could be taught and reinforced. Religion and sport peacefully coexisted whenever ethical virtues remained foremost. Fair play, honorable victories, respect for the opponent, and sports for fun, not for winning at all costs, characterized British upper-class and schoolboy sports.

Many sports either started in England or were spread throughout the world during their years of colonization (see box above). Horse racing, tennis, golf, soccer, badminton, field hockey, and rugby are a few of the most prominent of these sports. Most American sports were introduced by and popularized by British colonists.

SUMMARY

The European legacy of athletics, gymnastics, and sports laid the foundation for physical education and sport programs in the United States. The Greeks provided a rich heritage of mind-body unity and glorified the aesthetically developed, all-around athlete. Varying dramatically from this ideal were the Spartan soldiers and the specialized, professional athletes of the later Greek era. The Romans, during the Republic but not the Empire, illustrated the utilitarian goal of a fit people. During the next thousand years, only the knights developed their bodies, but they did so primarily for military conquest rather than for any inherent value. Church leaders discouraged frivolous activities. Philosophers and educators, during the Renaissance, reemphasized physical development for overall education and grappled with whether the mind and body were educated separately or simultaneously. Naturalism and nationalism directly influenced the development of gymnastics systems in Germany, Denmark, and Sweden. English sports and games, with their associated emphasis on values, laid the foundation for physical education and sport programs in the United States.

CAREER PERSPECTIVES

JOHANN CHRISTOPH FRIEDRICH GUTSMUTHS
(1759–1839)

BACKGROUND

Johann GutsMuths taught gymnastics at the Schnepfenthal Educational Institute for 50 years. His program, based on naturalistic principles, provided the model for subsequent European and American programs, and his many writings added a philosophical framework and descriptions of his various activities. Historians have acclaimed him as the "grandfather of physical education" for his monumental contributions.

In 1786, GutsMuths ended his years as a private tutor to accept a teaching position at Schnepfenthal, where he continued the gymnastics program started by Christian Andre. Initially and throughout his tenure there, GutsMuths experimented with new exercises and apparatus as Christian Salzmann, the founder of Schnepfenthal, provided him with bountiful opportunities to offer activities for the students. Gymnastics was taught between 11:00 and 12:00 daily. After the noon meal and in the evening, time was set aside for recreation. Games and outdoor excursions filled Sunday afternoons under GutsMuths' guidance.

ACCOMPLISHMENTS

GutsMuths opposed the traditional European methods of education and thus eagerly practiced naturalistic principles. He stressed that health, strength, and overall physical development were essential. The influence of naturalism on the program at Schnepfenthal was readily evident. Andre instituted walking on the balance beam, jumping standards, pole-vaulting across a ditch, vaulting (jumping over a piece of apparatus), and other outdoor activities. GutsMuths introduced seesaws, rope ladders, vertical ropes for swinging, and climbing masts. In addition to activities using the above apparatus, the students engaged in leaping, jumping, running, throwing, wrestling, climbing, skipping, dancing, walking, swimming, and military exercises. GutsMuths' and Salzmann's belief that manual labor was important led to instruction in woodworking and gardening. GutsMuths' program thus included influence from naturalistic, Greek, knightly, and military exercises as well as manual labor. He divided his gymnastic exercises into three categories: for bodily improvement, for manual labor, and for social games.

CONTRIBUTIONS TO PHYSICAL EDUCATION

Although people throughout Europe visited Schnepfenthal and observed his program and teaching, GutsMuths' greatest impact resulted from his writings. His two greatest works were *Gymnastics for the Young* (1793) and *Games for Exercise and Recreation of the Body and Spirit* (1796). The first of these, 700 pages in length, was the first modern book about physical education. In exhaustive fashion, he explained exactly how and why physical education activities developed the body. Published in Denmark, England, the United States, Holland, Bavaria, France, Sweden, and Austria, *Gymnastics for the Young* went through several revisions. *Games for Exercise and Recreation of the Body and Spirit,* published in three editions, provided detailed descriptions of 105 games. GutsMuths classified these according to the function and the skills each should develop. GutsMuths also wrote *Small Manual of the Art of Swimming for Self-Teaching, Mechanical Avocations for Youths and Men, Book of Gymnastics for the Sons of the Fatherland,* and *Catechism of Gymnastics: A Manual for Teachers and Pupils.* Several of these also underwent revision.

Health and strength were the goals of GutsMuths' gymnastics program. Naturalism provided the methodology through which it could be achieved. His legacy to the programs that followed was a mammoth one, as physical educators then and later to varying degrees borrowed from his philosophy, his apparatus, or his exercises.

REVIEW QUESTIONS

1. What is the Greek Ideal, and why did it evolve?
2. How did the education of girls and boys in Sparta and in Athens differ?
3. What took place at an Athenian gymnasium during both the early and the later eras?
4. Why did the Olympic Games start, and how did they attain such a prestigious status?
5. Why were the Romans a nation of spectators?
6. How and why did the Renaissance serve as a transitional period between the Middle Ages and the Age of Enlightenment?
7. How did naturalism influence the early development of European gymnastics?
8. How did nationalism influence the development of European gymnastics?
9. What were the similarities and differences among the school gymnastics programs of Adolph Spiess in Germany, Franz Nachtegall in Denmark, and Hjalmar Ling in Sweden?
10. What outcomes were stressed to justify sports and games for boys in the public schools in England?

STUDENT ACTIVITIES

1. As a class project, reenact the ancient Olympic Games by having each student participate in an appropriate athletic contest. Each student will be expected to research the specifics about the assigned or selected event before "competing" against classmates.
2. Select one activity or area of training of a page or squire during medieval times. Prepare a five-minute oral report and demonstration of how the boys were taught and how they practiced the necessary skills.
3. Along with several classmates, prepare a demonstration of German, Swedish, or Danish gymnastics, and then lead the rest of the class in a five-minute lesson.
4. Write a five-page paper about the early history and development of any sport that originated in England.

5. Challenge yourself to find 16 people, ideas, or terms from the medieval era forward in the history puzzle below. Define or describe each one found.

```
E R H S I L B U F J A H N E H T M O R F N O I T N I R W G O R O E S I W N G R
T H A V S T E S W I N L E T A R P U Y O S B N Y L A O L A Z C X U D E S U E U
D H E T A R K A G E S E S D I C S O M S T Y P O L Q E N Z V B K S A J M U B G
S F E I R B S M E T I A I D E M H E G D E L W O N K T A N R H C E A Q O S L B
P R E R U T C E L D S A S P I R T I D N I F H L C R I C K E T U T I W O P L Y
I Z X C V T U R N V E R I E N S O L V J U Z X P R E W Z S D H I Y O P C V B U
E N M B V C X Z L K J H G F D S A B N A E W Q A T Y L R O U S S E A U O P U X
S F N A T U R A L I S M E S Y T E I R A L E W Q J I O P L M Y H N R F L S C U
S Q P O I U T R E W L K J H G F D S U I O R E W Q J I O P L M Y H N R Y S X C
Y U I O P T Y B A S E D O W Q W E R T Y I F Y O P L K J H G F D S A M M B V P
P C V X B N M J I K L A G Y T F D E S G U T S M U T H S L M H Y I A U P U R E
S Z G H S W C D C R U S A D E S S B G T N H M Y J U K I P O Z A G W S I Y I O
C B V X J I F O N O S D F G H J O Q O N A C H T E G A L L O L U P T R C O E B
O Z P X A O C I V U B Y N A T W E R E N A I S S A N C E O K L Y U G C S V B A
P E R H E N R I K L I N G A M S N A T I O N A L I S M C H X J Z L Q E J H R G
```

6. Conduct a class debate about the similarities and differences between early and later Athenians, the Roman Republic and Empire, and modern-day sporting activities and competitions.
7. Identify 20 contributions to or influences on American physical education as described in this chapter.

REFERENCE

Van Dalen DB, Bennett BL: *A world history of physical education,* ed 2, Englewood Cliffs, N.J., 1971, Prentice-Hall.

SUGGESTED READINGS

Broekhoff J: Physical education, sport, and the ideals of chivalry, in Bennett BL, editor: *History of physical education and sport,* Chicago, 1972, The Athletic Institute. During the Middle Ages, chevaliers learned about courtly love; the ideals of chivalry, and, especially, the knightly arts of riding, swimming, shooting, climbing, jousting and tourneying, wrestling, fencing and fighting; courtly manners and behavior; and playing board games.

Gerber EW: *Innovators and institutions in physical education,* Philadelphia, 1971, Lea & Febiger. Fifty outstanding leaders in European and American physical education along with 10 significant institutions are described in this comprehensive history.

Guttmann A: Recent work in European sport history, *J of Sp Hist* 10(spring):35, 1983. This article briefly analyzes the major works, including comprehensive histories, monographs, and interpretive histories, written about European sports history in the preceding decade.

Harris, HA: *Sport in Greece and Rome,* Ithaca, 1972, Cornell University Press. This classical scholar comprehensively examines athletics, ball games, and chariot racing in both Greece and Rome and helps the reader understand the role of each in life in these early civilizations.

Kyle DG: Winning and watching the Greek pentathlon, *J of Sp Hist* 17:291, 1990. The author suggests how the winner of the Greek pentathlon was determined based on a reexamination of the archaeological evidence. Some comments on Greek sport and spectating are offered.

Mangan JA: *Athleticism in the Victorian and Edwardian public school: the emergence and consolidation of an educational ideology,* Cambridge, 1981, Cambridge University Press. This book comprehensively examines the role played by sport in the English public schools during the latter half of the nineteenth century and the beginning of the twentieth century.

Polidoro JR, Simri U: The games of 676 B.C.—a visit to the centenary of the ancient Olympic Games, *JOPERD* 67(5):41, 1996. This article describes the site, program of events, athletes, officials, and spectators, and rewards of the 676 B.C. Ancient Olympic Games.

Spears B: A perspective of the history of women's sport in ancient Greece, *J of Sp Hist* 11(summer):32, 1984. Women's participation in sports in Greece between 800 B.C. and A.D. 400 was reflective of their place in society, one of insignificance when compared with that of men, although a few skilled women achieved athletic fame at the athletic festivals.

Struna NL: Gender and sporting practice in early America, 1750–1810, *J of Sp Hist* 18:10, 1991. This article describes the expansion of recreational activities and sport with particular emphasis on the role of gender.

Ueberhorst H: *Friedrich Ludwig Jahn,* Bonn-Bad Godesberg, 1978, InterNations. This biography of the controversial "father of gymnastics," Friedrich Ludwig Jahn, describes his achievements in promoting nationalism through turner gymnastics.

CHAPTER 8

Early American Physical Education and Sport

KEY CONCEPTS

- Native Americans' participation in sports was a valued part of their lives.
- Immigrants to the United States, especially those from England, brought with them a love for sports and games.
- Early physical education programs in the United States promoted calisthenics, light gymnastics, hygiene, and strength development.
- German gymnastics and Swedish gymnastics had many American advocates and provided alternatives in the Battle of the Systems.
- Teacher training institutes and a professional organization provided the educational foundation and a forum for the future development of physical education and sport programs.
- Play became recognized as a right of children.
- Amateur sports in clubs and on college campuses were organized and became competitive.

Immigrants to the New World found Native Americans playing sports. These mostly Europeans brought with them a love for sporting pastimes. Once survival was assured, time was spent bowling, racing horses, skating, wrestling, and playing various ball games. Formalized exercises comprising the German gymnastics and Swedish gymnastics systems appealed to a few, but neither won full acceptance as a unified, national approach to physical education appropriate for people in the United States. The English, through worldwide colonization, including North America, spread their love of sports and games. **Hygiene,** the science of preserving one's health, was the focus of many early school programs in the United States. These programs were often called physical culture or physical training because of the beneficial effects of exercise. Emphasizing health, strength, and bodily measurements, physical training programs in the 1800s were added to school and college curricula. Leaders established teacher training institutes that offered course work in the theoretical aspects of the emerging profession of physical education. Sports and play activities drawn from a European heritage continued to grow in popularity as college students and upper-class clubs sponsored contests. Many towns also provided playgrounds, further stimulating interest in physical education and sport.

Before examining the major programs and developments that contributed to early American physical education and sport, it is important to explain their significance. From Native Americans, European immigrants, and individuals born in this new country, physical training programs and sports were introduced, evolved, and expanded in influence. The emerging field of physical education was built upon a heritage of hygiene, medicine, strength development, formalized exercises, play, and sports. Physical education and sport developed organizations to govern its myriad activities. Many individuals contributed to the sound foundation laid prior to the twentieth century that led to subsequent developments in physical education and sport described more fully in Chapter 9.

PHYSICAL ACTIVITIES IN THE COLONIES

Sports, physical activities, and dance occupied a prominent role in the traditional life of most Native Americans during the colonial period. These events were associated with religious ceremonies, festive celebrations, and social relaxation. Yet, the great diversity among Native American cultures makes generalizations impossible. Differences in language, lifestyles, geographic regions, livelihoods, and overall cultures verify that one cohesive image did not exist. Most tribes' playful, nonserious outlook on life contributed to the popularity of their preferred sporting pastimes.

According to Oxendine (1988), some of the more important factors characterizing traditional Indian sports include the following: (a) a strong connection between sport and other social, spiritual, and economic aspects of daily life; (b) the serious preparation of mind, body, and spirit of both participants and the community as a whole prior to major competition; (c) the assumption that rigid adherence to standardized rules and technical precision was unimportant in sport; (d) strong allegiance to high standards of sportsmanship and fair play; (e) the prominence of both males and females in sport activity, but with different expectancies; (f) a special perspective on team membership and on interaction and leadership styles; (g) the role of gambling as a widespread and vital component in all sports; and (h) the importance of art as an expression of identity and aesthetics (pp. 3–4). The most popular Native American sport was *lacrosse,* also called *baggataway,* meaning ball game, or the game of ball. The competitors displayed grace, adroitness, and dexterity, often in honor of their gods. The courage, ruggedness, skill, speed, and endurance required to play this game certainly trained the males for war. The rules, size of the playing field, equipment, and clothing varied by tribe.

Native Americans, including many females, played *shinny,* a ball and stick game similar to modern field hockey. Women also actively participated in *double ball,* in which a stick was used to propel two balls attached by a string.

Footraces, especially among Native Americans, served as a source of motivation and pride. Besides children's play and ceremonial uses by adults, running skills benefitted tribes in war, pursuit of game animals, and delivery of messages. The sacred ball race combined kicking a ball along a prescribed 25-mile course and running after it each time.

Other sports of major interest to Native Americans included archery, swimming, fishing, canoeing, and snow snake, which involved sliding a pole a great distance across a frozen path. Ritualistic dances and games of chance were also popular.

The first colonists came to the New World in the late 1500s in search of a new life, adventure, and religious freedom. During that century, the prime motivator for physical activity was survival: men hunted, fished, and grew crops while women performed domestic chores. What little time existed for relaxation was frequently spent in work-related recreation, such as barn raisings, corn huskings, or quilting bees. Dancing and games were often a part of these gatherings, although some religions forbade dancing.

The European, and especially the English, sporting heritage became increasingly popular in the 1700s. In spite of Puritan-initiated laws forbidding gambling, card playing, and mixed dancing, New Englanders relaxed by bowling, fishing, fowling, or playing cricket, rugby fives (a game similar to handball), or marbles.

Led by the Dutch in New York, the settlers in the middle colonies, without many of the religious prohibitions imposed on their northern neighbors, eagerly engaged in merriments such as pulling the goose (snapping off the head of a greased goose while riding horseback or while standing in a moving boat); played games, such as skittles (in which a ball or flat disk is thrown down an alley at nine skittles, or pins); and participated in outdoor amusements, such as boating, fishing, hunting, horse racing, and sleighing. These activities were enthusiastically pursued by the upper class. Interestingly, when nine-pin bowling was prohibited by law because of its association with gambling, a tenth pin was added to allow bowlers, and hence gamblers, to participate legally in their favorite pastime. The Quakers of Pennsylvania favored fishing, hunting, and swimming as diversions.

Virginia, strongly influenced by the English, emerged as the leading Southern colony. Emulating the gentry across the ocean, the Southern plantation owners sought to acquire all the trappings befitting their aristocratic status, including sporting pastimes. Cockfighting, bowling, card playing, and horse racing were pursued vigorously at taverns, which initially were exclusively for men. Fox hunting, hawking, and watching boxing matches found many enthusiasts.

Participation in various physical activities increased throughout the 1770s, as an emerging nationalism placed emphasis on the development of health and strength. Benjamin Franklin, Noah Webster, and Thomas Jefferson were among those who supported physical activities for healthful benefits. At the same time, sports involvement continued to win new adherents because sports offered competition, freedom, and fun.

In the late 1700s, as the colonists prepared for a confrontation with the English, military days provided opportunities for marching and drilling with weapons, yet they also offered times for social interaction and game playing. The military training was utilitarian in purpose, though, and did not lead to an emphasis on physical readiness in the post-Revolutionary War years. This trend repeated itself throughout the history of the United States as each war signaled a need to have trained soldiers; other than during these emergencies, there was little emphasis by the military on physical education programs.

Many immigrants traveled to the colonies in search of religious freedom. Mostly Protestants, they exalted labor and education, as long as the latter contributed to the development of the highest type of Christian manhood. Latin grammar schools, and a few universities, educated the intellectually and financially elite. Dame schools offered mostly boys the basics of reading, writing, and arithmetic (the three Rs).

Following the War of 1812, nationalism burst into popularity, setting the stage for a gradual extension of democratic rights to more people and for the provision of education to more children. Free, public education for boys and girls, beginning in the 1800s, consisted primarily of the three Rs. These public schools initially showed little interest in physical education, although in 1853 Boston became the first city to require daily exercise for children. In private academies and schools in the early 1800s, though, an enjoyment of sports and the belief that physical activities contributed to health led to children's participation in these. Prior to the Civil War, few colleges provided for their students' physical development; yet academies and private schools for boys and occasionally for girls (such as Mt. Holyoke Female Seminary in 1837) included physical exercises in their curricula.

Early American physical education and sport can be characterized into four major topical areas.

- Battle of the Systems
- Normal schools and a national organization
- Play for children
- Amateur sports for men and women

Each of these contributed significantly to the content and structure of twentieth-century physical education and sport programs, which are an amalgamation of gymnastics, formalized educational curricula, play, and sports.

EARLY GERMAN GYMNASTICS IN THE UNITED STATES

The most significant of the private schools to the origin of physical education in the United States was the Round Hill School, founded in 1823 in Northampton, Massachusetts. The box on page 180 lists this school's establishment along with other highlights in the development of physical education in the nineteenth century. The founders of Round Hill School scheduled time each day for sports and games even before they employed Charles Beck, a German turner, to instruct the boys in the German system of gymnastics. Beck established an outdoor gymnasium, taught the first turner exercises on apparatus in this country, and translated Friedrich Jahn's treatise on gymnastics. In addition, some Harvard students, in 1826, and Bostonians, in the 1820s, also were taught turner gymnastics by German immigrants. The interest in turner gymnastics dissipated when these Germans ceased to teach and because this system's emphasis on strength-developing work on apparatus failed to appeal to sports-minded Americans.

SIGNIFICANT EVENTS IN EARLY AMERICAN PHYSICAL EDUCATION

1823	Round Hill School established with physical education in its curriculum
1824	Hartford Female Seminary, directed by Catharine Beecher, included calisthenics in its curriculum
1825	Charles Beck became an instructor of German gymnastics at Round Hill School
1825	New York City high schools offered gymnastics
1826	Charles Follen organized gymnastics classes for students at Harvard University
1831	John C. Warren's *The Importance of Physical Education* published
1832	Catharine Beecher's *Course of Calisthenics for Young Ladies* published
1837	Mount Holyoke Female Seminary opened, with calisthenics listed as part of its school program
1837	Western Female Institute founded by Catharine Beecher
1848	Friedrich Hecker organized the first American turnverein in Cincinnati
1851	First national turnfest held in Philadelphia
1853	Boston became the first city to require daily exercise for school children
1855	Cincinnati, Ohio, first offered physical education using German gymnastics in its public schools
1856	Catharine Beecher's *A Manual of Physiology and Calisthenics for Schools and Families* published
1859	A. Molineaux Hewlitt, an African-American, appointed gymnasium instructor at Harvard University
1861	Normal Institute for Physical Education founded by Dio Lewis
1861	Edward Hitchcock became director of physical education at Amherst College
1862	Dio Lewis's *New Gymnastics for Men, Women, and Children* published
1865	First women's physical education program started at Vassar College
1866	California passed the first state physical education law
1866	Normal School of the North American Gymnastic Union established
1869	First YMCA gymnasiums opened in New York City, San Francisco, and Washington, D.C.
1872	Brookline, Massachusetts, became the first community in America to vote public funds for a playground
1879	Harvard University's Hemenway Gymnasium opened under the direction of Dudley Sargent
1883	Hartvig Nissen started teaching Swedish gymnastics in Washington, D.C.
1885	Nils Posse started teaching Swedish gymnastics in Boston, Massachusetts
1885	Association for the Advancement of Physical Education founded in Brooklyn, New York
1885	YMCA Training School established in Springfield, Massachusetts
1886	Brooklyn Normal School established by William Anderson
1886	Chautauqua Summer School of Physical Education established
1887	Harvard Summer School established
1889	Boston Normal School of Gymnastics established
1889	Boston Conference on Physical Training held
1890	Posse Normal School founded
1890	Edward Hartwell became director of physical education for the Boston public schools
1892	Ohio became the second state to pass a physical education law
1893	Harvard became the first college to confer an academic degree in physical education
1896	American Association for the Advancement of Physical Education began publication of *American Physical Education Review*
1897	Society of College Gymnasium Directors founded

When a second wave of political refugees fled Germany in 1848, they, too, brought their love of gymnastics to the United States, where they established societies of turners beginning in 1848 in Cincinnati and turner festivals in 1851. These *turnfests* featured thousands of turners exhibiting their physical prowess on German apparatus. In 1866, they founded the Normal School of the North American Gymnastic Union in New York City to prepare teachers of German gymnastics. When most German immigrants migrated to the Midwest, they settled in isolated communities and maintained their national identity, including their gymnastics programs. Gradually, these turner societies broadened their programs to include social functions and exercises for the entire family. Later in the 1800s they introduced the turner system into several schools, although it was modified with Adolph Spiess' school gymnastics principles. The influence of German gymnastics on programs in the United States was limited because of its regional nature and because of the emphasis on strength development and nationalism. However, during the late 1800s and early 1900s, many schools and colleges incorporated exercises on German apparatus into their programs. Some of these apparatus, such as the parallel bars, rings, and balance beam, remain vital parts of gymnastics today.

EARLY AMERICANS WHO INFLUENCED PHYSICAL EDUCATION PROGRAMS

Catharine Beecher, the first American to design a program of exercises for American children, tried to get daily physical activity into the public schools. As director of the Hartford (Connecticut) Female Seminary beginning in 1824, and later, when she founded the Western Female Institute in Cincinnati in 1837, she introduced girls to **calisthenics.** At the latter school, she set aside 30 minutes per half day for her program of exercises, which was designed to promote health, beauty, and strength. Beecher's initial objective was to aid girls in improving their vitality so that they could better fulfill their missions in life as wives and mothers. She expanded her concepts from a *Course of Calisthenics for Young Ladies,* which she wrote in 1832 primarily for girls, to *A Manual of Physiology and Calisthenics for Schools and Families,* published in 1856. In this book, Beecher advocated the

German gymnastics in the United States in the late 1800s.

introduction of physical training in the American schools for all children. Borrowing from the therapeutic concepts of Swedish gymnastics as developed by Per Henrik Ling, Beecher, through her writings and school programs, emphasized exercises that could be executed at home without a teacher and with only diagrams from her books as guides.

Although Beecher's efforts did not achieve their desired results, she did influence another American. Dio Lewis took Beecher's calisthenics, added light pieces of apparatus, such as bean bags, dumbbells, Indian clubs, and wands, and changed the name to **light gymnastics.** His promotional efforts resulted in the adoption of his system in the elementary schools in Boston. In 1861 he founded the Normal Institute for Physical Education, the first of its kind. A **normal school** is a specialized institution for preparing students to become teachers. It may focus on one subject, as did Lewis', or offer many subjects.

The first college physical education program was begun, in 1860, at Amherst College because its president was concerned about the health of the students. As director of the Department of Hygiene and Physical Education, Edward Hitchcock, beginning in 1861 and continuing throughout his life, gave health lectures, served as college physician, and supervised the required physical exercises for all students. As was true of most of the early physical educators, Hitchcock's primary credential for the job was a medical degree. Borrowing from Lewis' light gymnastics, Hitchcock's program, led by squad captains, included class exercises to the accompaniment of music. A portion of the class, which met four days per week, could be used by the students to practice sports skills or to exercise on the horizontal bars, rings, ropes, and vaulting horses. Hitchcock also administered a battery of bodily, or anthropometric, measurements, such as height, weight, chest girth, and lung capacity, to evaluate the effects of the program on students and to compare their progress from year to year.

Lewis' light gymnastics.

Class exercises at Amherst College.

A second noteworthy college physical education program was developed by Dudley Sargent at Harvard University beginning in 1879, when he was hired to direct the newly opened Hemenway Gymnasium. Since no required physical education program existed at Harvard, Sargent used an individualized approach to encourage students to exercise. Based on numerous anthropometric measurements, Sargent prescribed a series of exercises to meet each student's physical needs, using chest expanders and developers, leg machines, rowing machines, and other apparatus that he had designed. Opposed to strict German gymnastics and to light gymnastics programs, Sargent encouraged students to participate in baseball, bowling, boxing, fencing, rowing, and running in addition to their individual conditioning programs.

A brief summary of the contributions of the early leaders in physical education in the United States is provided in the box on pages 184–185.

EARLY SWEDISH GYMNASTICS IN THE UNITED STATES

The first American introduction to Swedish gymnastics as a complete system occurred in 1883, when a Norwegian, Hartvig Nissen, opened a Swedish Health Institute in Washington, D.C. Two years later Nils Posse, a graduate of the Royal Gymnastics Central Institute in Stockholm, introduced Swedish gymnastics in Boston. Impressed by Posse's program, philanthropist Mary Hemenway volunteered to the Boston School Committee to furnish free training for teachers in Swedish gymnastics, if the schools would offer this program to children. This led Hemenway to finance the establishment of the Boston Normal School of Gymnastics in 1889. Hemenway selected Amy Morris Homans for its director; Nils Posse was the first instructor. The graduates of this school taught in the Boston

EARLY LEADERS IN PHYSICAL EDUCATION IN THE UNITED STATES

Charles Follen (1796–1840)
Established gymnasium in Boston (1826)
Taught German gymnastics to Harvard University students (1826–1828)

Charles Beck (1798–1866)
Hired as first physical education teacher in the United States (1825)
Taught at Round Hill School (1825–1830)

Francis Lieber (1800–1872)
Directed Boston gymnasium and opened swimming pool (1827)

Catharine Esther Beecher (1800–1878)
Taught at the Hartford Female Seminary (1824)
Started the Western Female Institute (1837)
Promoted calisthenics in American schools for boys and girls

Dioclesian Lewis (1823–1888)
Developed light gymnastics with handheld apparatus
Started the Normal Institute for Physical Education (1861)

Edward Hitchcock (1828–1911)
Elected professor of hygiene and physical education at Amherst College (1861–1911)
Served as first president of the Association for the Advancement of Physical Education (1885)
Led in development of anthropometric measurements

Amy Morris Homans (1848–1933)
Directed the Boston Normal School of Gymnastics (1889–1909)
Directed the Department of Hygiene and Physical Education at Wellesley College (1909–1918)
Founded the Association of Directors of Physical Education for Women (1915)

schools and nationally, especially in women's colleges, thus spreading Swedish gymnastics. Edward Hartwell, as Director of Physical Training for the Boston public schools beginning in 1890, was a strong supporter of Swedish gymnastics. Previously, he had directed the Johns Hopkins University gymnasium, where he experimented with many of the principles that Dudley Sargent advocated.

THE BATTLE OF THE SYSTEMS

Between 1885 and 1900, a leading topic for discussion among physical educators was which system of gymnastics could provide a unified, national program for the United States. This raging controversy became known as the **Battle of the Systems.** Although there was some overlap between programs, in general the

EARLY LEADERS IN PHYSICAL EDUCATION IN THE UNITED STATES (CONT'D)

Dudley Allen Sargent (1849–1924)
Directed the Hemenway Gymnasium at Harvard University (1879–1919)
Led in development of anthropometric measurements
Founded the Sargent Normal School (1881)
Founded the Harvard Summer School (1887)

Edward Mussey Hartwell (1850–1922)
Instructed (1882) and directed (1885–1890) the gymnasium at Johns Hopkins University
Directed physical training for the Boston public schools (1890–1897)

William Gilbert Anderson (1860–1947)
Initiated the meeting that led to the formation of the Association for the Advancement of
    Physical Education (1885)
Founded the Chautauqua Summer School of Physical Education (1886)
Founded the Brooklyn (Anderson) Normal School (1886)

Hartvig Nissen
Introduced Swedish gymnastics at the Swedish Health Institute in Washington, D.C. (1883)
Served as assistant director (1891–1897) and then director (1897–1900) of physical training for
    the Boston public schools
Taught at the Harvard Summer School and the Sargent Normal School and directed the Posse-
    Nissen School

Nils Posse (1862–1895)
Graduated from the Royal Gymnastics Central Institute
Led in instruction of Swedish gymnastics in the United States (1885–1895)
Taught at the Boston Normal School of Gymnastics (1889)
Started the Posse Normal School (1890)

Delphine Hanna (1854–1941)
Taught at Oberlin College (1885–1920)
Became the first woman professor of physical education (1903)
Initiated anthropometric measurements of women
Taught Luther Gulick, Thomas Wood, Jay Nash, and Jesse Williams

German, Swedish, and American systems developed and vied for supporters (see Figure 8-1 and the box on p. 188).

In an attempt to introduce Swedish gymnastics to the general public and to leaders in physical training and thus to gain its acceptance as the program for American schools, Mary Hemenway, in 1889, financed the Boston Conference on Physical Training. Under the capable direction of Amy Morris Homans, this conference was highly successful and was one of the most important conferences in physical education ever held in the United States. Its significance was attributed to the exposure given to the various programs existing at that time. German gymnastics, Swedish gymnastics, Hitchcock's program, Sargent's system, and others

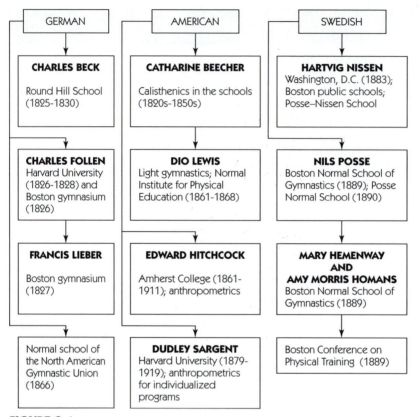

FIGURE 8-1

Leaders in early American physical education.

were explained and the merits of each discussed. Sargent, after explaining his program, proposed an answer to the search for an American system:

> What America most needs is the happy combination which the European nations are trying to effect: the strength-giving qualities of the German gymnasium, the active and energetic properties of the English sports, the grace and suppleness acquired from French calisthenics, and the beautiful poise and mechanical precision of the Swedish free movement, all regulated, systematized, and adapted to our peculiar needs and institutions. (Barrows, 1899, p. 76)

Although the leaders in physical education at this conference were exposed to the various systems, no one system was found to meet completely the needs of American programs because each seemed to have its weaknesses. Still, the Boston Conference provided an opportunity for leaders to learn about the various systems and to exchange ideas for the future promotion of American physical education.

Although German gymnastics in the Midwest and Swedish gymnastics in the Northeast were widely accepted, few states mandated physical education. California, in 1866, passed a law providing for twice-a-day exercises for a minimum of five minutes to promote health and bodily vigor, but it was short-lived. Ohio's 1892 law was the first lasting physical education law. Louisiana, in 1894,

Harvard University's Hemenway Gymnasium was equipped with exercise apparatus designed by Dudley Sargent.

Wisconsin, in 1897, North Dakota, in 1899, and Pennsylvania, in 1901, passed similar legislation. In the late 1800s most colleges included German and Swedish gymnastics in their physical education programs, but they also borrowed from Hitchcock's program and Sargent's principles and apparatus.

ESTABLISHMENT OF NORMAL SCHOOLS FOR PHYSICAL EDUCATION

One method through which the various programs were promoted was the development of normal, or teacher training, schools. The 1880s were especially noteworthy: six institutions were established to prepare physical education teachers either in a specific system or in an eclectic program that borrowed from several systems. In 1881, Dudley Sargent began teaching women from Harvard Annex and other women and men who were interested in his apparatus and methodology. At the resultant Sargent Normal School, he provided a general curriculum based on a theoretical, scientific foundation along with various activities of a practical nature.

Delphine Hanna took courses from Dio Lewis, Nils Posse, and Dudley Sargent, attending both the Sargent Normal School and the Harvard Summer School of Physical Education. The program she initiated at coeducational Oberlin College in 1885 closely resembled Sargent's. Besides using many of the pieces of apparatus that he designed, Hanna emphasized anthropometric measurements of female students to assess their individual development. The scope of her work included teaching a class to train men to instruct their fellow male students.

BATTLE OF THE SYSTEMS

System	Purpose	Advocates
German gymnastics	Developed individual abilities and healthy, strong youth for war or emergencies using apparatus	German turners including Carl Betz, C.G. Rathman, George Brosius, and William Stecher
Swedish gymnastics	Promoted health, correct expression, and beauty of performance using exact movement patterns	Hartvig Nissen; Nils Posse; Amy Morris Homans; Edward Hartwell; and women's colleges
Hitchcock's system	Emphasized hygiene through required exercises with light apparatus	Edward Hitchcock
Sargent's system	Advocated hygienic, educative, recreative, and remedial aims through individualized exercises on apparatus	Dudley Sargent; Delphine Hanna; women's colleges
Association gymnastics	Contributed to the development of the all-around man	YMCA directors
American system	Combined components and modifications of various programs into an eclectic system	William Anderson

A class at the Sargent Normal School performing an Indian club routine.

Among her first students were Thomas Wood and Luther Gulick, later luminaries in physical education.

The box on page 189 summarizes the early teacher training institutions in the United States and their curricula.

A unique normal school established in 1885 in Springfield, Massachusetts, was the Young Men's Christian Association (YMCA) Training School. The YMCA's

EARLY PROFESSIONAL PREPARATION INSTITUTIONS OR NORMAL SCHOOLS IN THE UNITED STATES

Years	Founder	Name	Program	Today
1861–1868	Dio Lewis	Normal Institute for Physical Education	Light gymnastics	Ceased to exist
1866–1951	Turners	Normal School of the North American Gymnastic Union	German gymnastics	Normal College of American Gymnastic Union of Indiana University
1881–1929	Dudley Sargent	Sargent Normal School	Theoretical and and practical curriculum	Boston University's Sargent College of Allied Health Professions
1885–today	Young Men's Christian Association	YMCA Training School	Association gymnastics	Division of Health, Physical Education, and Recreation, Springfield College
1886–1920s	William Anderson	Chautauqua Summer School of Physical Education	Advanced theoretical and practical curriculum	Ceased to exist
1886–1953	William Anderson	Brooklyn (Anderson) Normal School	Theoretical and practical curriculum	Amold College Division, University of Bridgeport
1887–1932	Dudley Sargent	Harvard Summer School of Physical Education	Advanced theoretical and practical curriculum	Ceased to exist
1889–1909	Mary Hemenway and Amy Morris Homans	Boston Normal School of Gymnastics	Swedish gymnastics	Department of Physical Education, Wellesley College
1890–1942	Nils Posse	Posse Normal School	Swedish gymnastics	Ceased to exist

goal, through its association gymnastics, was to develop the all-around man and to send him out as a physical director to the increasing number of YMCAs, both nationally and internationally. (The first YMCA gymnasiums had opened in 1869 in New York City, San Francisco, and Washington, D.C.)

In 1886, William Anderson led in the establishment of two additional institutions. While teaching in New York, he started the Brooklyn Normal School; later, when he became the director of the Yale University gymnasium, he moved this school to New Haven, Connecticut, and renamed it the Anderson Normal School. Anderson, along with Jay Seaver, also worked with leaders in the Chautauqua movement to set up the Chautauqua Summer School of Physical Education. The curricula at both schools focused on a generalized approach with theoretical and practical course work.

Dudley Sargent, in 1887, succeeded in gaining approval to open the Harvard Summer School of Physical Education that provided opportunities for teachers already in the field to start or to continue their professional training in physical education. The diversity and breadth of the offerings, along with its outstanding faculty, made attendance at the Harvard Summer School prestigious and a certificate from it highly respected.

Swedish gymnastics was taught initially at the Boston Normal School of Gymnastics in 1889 and continued to be taught following the school's affiliation with Wellesley College in 1909. Amy Morris Homans directed both programs. Nils Posse, in 1890, established the Posse Normal School, which also promoted Swedish gymnastics.

Beginning in the late 1800s, normal schools were replaced with teacher preparation programs that led to college degrees. At Oberlin College, in 1885, Delphine Hanna initiated a physical education teacher curriculum for women students; it became a four-year degree program in 1900. Only programs at Stanford University, the University of California, and the University of Nebraska preceded it.

FOUNDING OF THE NATIONAL ASSOCIATION

In the late 1800s, physical education programs offered a potpourri of activities reflecting the philosophies and interests of their leaders. As a young teacher, William Anderson recognized this diversity and the fact that few opportunities existed for the exchange of curricula and philosophical ideas among individuals interested in physical development. After seeking support from two recognized leaders in the field, Edward Hitchcock and Dudley Sargent, Anderson invited gymnastics teachers, ministers, journalists, school principals, college presidents, and others engaged in the promotion of physical training to meet at Adelphi Academy in Brooklyn, New York, on November 27, 1885, to discuss their various programs and to decide whether sufficient interest existed to regularly provide a forum for professional interchange. Of the 60 people who attended, 49 responded positively, resulting in the formation of the Association for the Advancement of Physical Education, today's American Alliance for Health, Physical Education, Recreation and Dance. (The box on page 191 traces its various name changes.)

Edward Hitchcock of Amherst College was elected the first president. Dudley Sargent, selected as vice president, later served as the third, fifth, and eighth

VARIOUS NAMES OF THE NATIONAL ORGANIZATION

1885	Association for the Advancement of Physical Education
1886	American Association for the Advancement of Physical Education
1903	American Physical Education Association
1937	American Association for Health and Physical Education
1938	American Association for Health, Physical Education and Recreation
1974	American Alliance for Health, Physical Education and Recreation
1979	American Alliance for Health, Physical Education, Recreation and Dance

president. William Anderson agreed to serve as the first secretary. Other recognized leaders in attendance included Dio Lewis; Henry Ward Beecher, clergyman and brother of Catharine Beecher; and William Blaikie, author of the acclaimed book *How to Get Strong and How to Stay So* and the second president of the Association. This organization's objectives, established in 1886, were "to disseminate knowledge concerning physical education, to improve the methods, and by meetings of the members to bring those interested in the subject into closer relation to each other" (Lee and Bennett, 1960, p. 27). Discussions in the early meetings focused on the strengths and attributes of the various gymnastics systems, methods of teaching, anthropometric measurements, military drills, athletics, and hygiene. To provide further for the sharing of professional knowledge and experiences, the *American Physical Education Review* was first published in 1896.

The American Association for the Advancement of Physical Education's (AAAPE) first contact with the National Education Association (NEA) occurred in 1893. The NEA asked Edward Hartwell, 1891–92 AAAPE President, to chair a departmental conference on physical education and hygiene at the International Congress on Education held in connection with the 1893 Chicago World's Fair. Two years later the NEA established a permanent Department of Physical Education; in 1924, this became the Department of School Health and Physical Education. The American Association for Health and Physical Education merged with this department when it became affiliated with the NEA in 1937.

PROMOTION OF PLAY FOR CHILDREN

While organized school programs were being established, the play movement outside the schools gained support and momentum. The industrialization of the United States directly influenced this development. The massive influx of Americans into urban areas, as well as immigration, resulted in overcrowded tenements. In an effort to provide suitable play space for children in this environment, sand piles were first erected in Boston in 1885. In 1888, New York passed the first state legislation that led to an organized play area for children. By 1899, the Massachusetts Emergency and Hygiene Association sponsored 21 playgrounds.

Boston constructed the Charlesbank outdoor gymnasium in 1889. Jane Addams' Hull House, a Chicago settlement house started in 1894, included a model playground. Religious leaders, school administrators, philanthropists, and

Play is a child's favorite activity. (Photo courtesy Bob Hilliard.)

social workers worked together or alone in the late 1800s to ensure that children were provided both places and opportunities to play. In part, these efforts demonstrated a genuine concern for the welfare of children and for society as a whole, and in part these playgrounds were used as a method of social control.

DEVELOPMENT OF AMATEUR SPORTS

Americans' love for sports began with the founding of the United States but really blossomed after the Civil War, as baseball became the national sport for men of all ages and for amateurs as well as professionals. Races between cyclists, horses, runners, and yachts, with associated gambling, were especially attractive to the upper class. Normally these races, as well as sports such as cricket, golf, and tennis, were staged by or played by members of elite social clubs. The New York Athletic Club, founded in 1868, led in the formation of the Amateur Athletic Union (AAU) in 1888. This organization sought to promote amateur sports while checking the evils of professional sports. In 1853, Scottish immigrants, through their Caledonian games, began to promote their native sports, such as hammer throwing, putting stones, and tossing the caber. The Czechoslovakian Sokols also promoted physical activities through mass displays in national festivals, such as that first held in 1879 in New York City. The box on page 193 lists many of the sports organizations that helped promote amateur sports during the late 1800s.

Frenchman Pierre de Coubertin, through persistent efforts, revived the Olympic Games and the spirit of amateurism that honored the integration of mind, body, and spirit. The classical restoration of the Panathenaic Stadium, in pure white marble, provided an awe-inspiring setting on April 5, 1896, for the opening of the Athens Olympic Games. Athletes (311) representing 13 countries competed. While track and field athletics occupied center stage, athletes competed

AMATEUR SPORTS ORGANIZATIONS

1871	National Rifle Association
1875	National Bowling League
1878	Cricketer's Association of the United States
1879	National Archery Association
1880	League of American Wheelmen (cycling)
1880	National Canoe Association
1881	United States National Lawn Tennis Association
1882	National Croquet Association
1884	United States Skating Association
1887	American Trotting Association
1888	Amateur Athletic Union
1892	United States Golf Association

Men's intercollegiate basketball was a slower-paced game years ago when a center jump followed each basket scored.

in eight other sports including cycling, fencing, gymnastics, lawn tennis, shooting, swimming, weight lifting, and wrestling.

Jim Connolly, one of the 13 athletes representing the United States, captured the first victory in the hop, step, and jump (triple jump) and was honored by the hoisting of an American flag while the national anthem played. Athletes from the United States dominated the track and field events, with silver first-place medals in the 100-meters, 400-meters, 110-meters, hurdles, broad jump, high jump, pole vault, shot put, and discus throw. Greek athletes had placed in swimming, cycling, fencing, gymnastics, shooting, and, won the marathon. Germans captured most gymnastics medals.

Two sports were developed in the YMCA and promoted by this association. In 1891, at the YMCA Training School, James Naismith developed the rules for and initiated the first game of basketball. This game was designed as an indoor sport to fill the void between football and baseball seasons. Five years later, William Morgan, at a YMCA in Holyoke, Massachusetts, originated volleyball as a less vigorous indoor game for businessmen. Both sports met a need and found more of their early adherents in the YMCAs than in the private clubs and colleges.

Gambling had been associated with sports since colonial times when owners and spectators bet on the outcome of horse races. Americans' propensity to gamble continued as they wagered on cockfights, wrestling bouts, boxing matches, walking contests, and baseball games throughout the 1800s. One of the evils the AAU sought to eliminate in its promotion of amateur athletics was gambling. Baseball promoters had to thwart the perception that all players and fans bet on the outcomes of professional games. Nevertheless, college students enthusiastically gambled on their sports competitions, especially football.

COLLEGIATE SPORTS FOR MEN

Sports on college campuses initially were organized as extracurricular activities because administrators and faculty viewed them as extraneous to the mission of higher education. The first intercollegiate event, in 1852, matched Harvard and Yale in rowing. The two early favorites in collegiate sports were baseball, which first matched Amherst against Williams in 1859, and football, which actually began as a soccer-like game between Princeton and Rutgers in 1869. Students founded organizations to standardize rules for competitions in rowing, baseball, football, and track.

College faculties paid little attention to sports until they began to infringe on students' academic work. Missed classes, decreased academic performance, injuries, gambling, property damage on campus and in nearby towns during victory celebrations, playing against professional teams, commercialization, and a general overemphasis on athletics compelled faculties to take action. In 1882, a group

The University of Virginia versus the University of North Carolina in baseball in 1895.
(Photo courtesy North Carolina Collection, UNC Library at Chapel Hill.)

of Harvard University faculty members recommended that a committee of three faculty members should oversee athletics. Three years later this committee was expanded to include two students and one alumni. In 1888, it again expanded to an equal representation of three faculty, three students, and three alumni. Representatives of nine eastern colleges met in 1883 as the Intercollegiate Athletic Conference and proposed that colleges should not compete against professional teams, no professional athletes should coach college teams, students should be permitted only four years of participation in athletics, contests should take place only on campuses, and faculties should control athletics. Because only three colleges ratified them, these regulations failed to take effect.

In 1895, the Intercollegiate Conference of Faculty Representatives (today's Big Ten Conference), made up of one faculty member from each of seven midwestern institutions, adopted rules that required enrollment of all players as students, enrollment of transfer students for six months at the institution prior to participation on a team, and maintenance of academic performance standards by

DEVELOPMENT OF COLLEGIATE SPORTS FOR MEN AND WOMEN

1843	First collegiate rowing club started by Yale
1844	Harvard forms a rowing club
1852	First intercollegiate sports competition in rowing occurs as Harvard defeats Yale by four lengths
1859	College Union Regatta Association established by Harvard, Yale, Brown, and Trinity
1864	Haverford beats Penn 89–60 in first intercollegiate cricket competition
1869	Rutgers outscores Princeton (6–4) in the first intercollegiate football game
1871	Rowing Association of American Colleges formed
1873	First intercollegiate track and field competition held in conjunction with the intercollegiate rowing regatta
1876	Intercollegiate Football Association established
1876	Intercollegiate Association of Amateur Athletes of America formed to govern track and field
1877	Harvard shoots 20 points better than Yale in the first intercollegiate rifle competition
1877	New York University defeats Manhattan (2–0) in the first intercollegiate lacrosse contest
1883	Intercollegiate Lawn Tennis Association founded
1883	Harvard's J. S. Clark wins the singles and the doubles (with P. E. Presbrey) events during the first intercollegiate tennis tournament
1883	Intercollegiate Athletic Conference established by Harvard, Princeton, and Cornell
1884	Penn defeats Wesleyan (16–10) in the first intercollegiate polo contest
1890	First intercollegiate cross country saw Penn beat Cornell
1894	Harvard outscores Columbia (5–4) in the first intercollegiate fencing meet
1895	Brown beats Harvard (4–2) in the first ice hockey intercollegiate game
1895	Intercollegiate Conference of Faculty Representatives formed by midwestern colleges
1896	Yale beats Columbia by 35 holes in the first intercollegiate golf event with six-man teams
1896	First intercollegiate swimming meet held with Penn defeating Columbia and Yale
1896	First intercollegiate sports competition for women in basketball occurs as Stanford defeats California (2–1)
1899	Penn surpasses Columbia (2–0) in the first intercollegiate water polo contest
1899	Intercollegiate Cross Country Association of Amateur Athletes of America established
1899	Yale's gymnastics team defeats competitors from 19 institutions in the first intercollegiate meet

athletes for eligibility to play. These few efforts, however, did not control the overwhelming growth of student-initiated and student-administered intercollegiate athletics in the late 1800s. The box on page 195 chronicles the initiation of collegiate sports organizations and competitions, primarily for men.

COLLEGIATE SPORTS FOR WOMEN

In the late 1800s, archery, croquet, and tennis were among the first sports to attract women as participants because these activities did not require revealing clothing and were nonvigorous. Males' and females' attitudes about proper feminine behavior and medical opinion that vigorous activity would irreparably harm women's reproductive capabilities combined to prevent women from engaging in aggressive and highly competitive sports. Bicycling introduced a radical change in attire with the bloomer costume, or divided skirt, which allowed freedom from the appropriate attire of the day that included voluminous skirts and petticoats and tightly laced corsets. Bloomers and middy blouses became the accepted costume for gymnastics and other physical activities, with students at the Sargent Normal School among the first to wear them.

Societal attitudes toward women in the 1800s closely paralleled the Victorian perception that females were weak, objects to be placed on pedestals for admiration, but not to be taken seriously, and incapable of mental achievements. Females who sought schooling, and especially college attendance, encountered ridicule and suspicions about their femininity. Their roles as wives and mothers were viewed as contradictory to the development of their minds.

Catharine Beecher's calisthenics and Swedish gymnastics with their therapeutic emphasis became acceptable because they complemented the feminine role. When college women enthusiastically participated in baseball, basketball, and rowing, many physicians and women strongly opposed such vigorous exertion. They argued that although mild activity such as walking, gardening, or moderate exercise could benefit women, an overexpenditure of energy might leave

Female archers in 1890s attire.

Senda Berenson, in the long skirt, with Smith College students in Northampton, Massachusetts, where women played in their first public basketball game on March 22, 1893. (Photo courtesy Basketball Hall of Fame.)

them infertile or hopelessly depleted of energy to survive childbirth or motherhood. Not until medical opinions gradually changed in the twentieth century did these restrictive opinions dissipate.

Women in the upper socioeconomic strata shared their husbands' and fathers' desires to engage in conspicuous consumption. The rich, in flaunting their wealth, popularized sports such as archery, golf, tennis, and yachting. In each case, these sports were participated in at private clubs or in settings where social interaction between the sexes usually was a desired outcome. Following the lead of men, upper-class women began to compete nationally in archery (1879), tennis (1887), and golf (1896). Because of societal expectations, they always dressed in the latest fashions, many of which severely limited their mobility and skill development.

Women eagerly adopted basketball and adapted and modified its rules to make the game less strenuous and not as rough. A Committee on Women's Basketball was established by the American Association for the Advancement of Physical Education to standardize these rules. In 1896 the first intercollegiate contest between women from the University of California and Stanford University occurred. In addition to basketball, field days for track events and a few other sports became popular in the women's colleges in the 1890s.

SUMMARY

Early physical education in the United States evolved from recreational sports and games into organized school and college programs that either emphasized one system of gymnastics or combined exercises from various systems. A Battle of the Systems raged as Swedish and German gymnastics had their advocates, but neither found widespread national acceptance. Health and strength were favored outcomes, but even these did not seem to satisfy fully Americans' needs. Prior to 1900, teachers of physical education had completed programs in normal schools, and a fledgling national association existed, but still a unified, national program had not emerged. With the popularization in the late 1800s of children's play and of sports in amateur clubs and on college campuses, the stage was set for the development in the 1900s of an American program based primarily on playing sports and games.

CAREER PERSPECTIVES

DUDLEY ALLEN SARGENT
(1849–1924)

EDUCATION
B.A., Bowdoin College
M.D., Yale Medical School

BACKGROUND

Dudley Sargent, one of the most influential leaders in physical education in the United States, contributed significantly in the areas of individualized programs, measurements of the dimensions and the capacities of the body, and teacher training. He also accepted leadership positions in professional organizations, wrote numerous papers, and made scholarly presentations.

After an early career as a professional acrobat, Sargent obtained a bachelor's degree from Bowdoin College and a medical degree from Yale Medical School. While a student at these institutions for nine years, he worked as Director of Gymnastics (at Bowdoin) and Director of the Gymnasium (at Yale). In 1879, he began his 40-year tenure at Harvard University after being named Director of the Hemenway Gymnasium and Assistant Professor of Physical Training.

ACCOMPLISHMENTS

Sargent immediately implemented an individualized program that focused on meeting the needs of the Harvard students who were physically underdeveloped. Sargent took a series of anthropometric measurements and, based on these, prescribed an individual exercise program for each student. Measurements of each student's progress were taken periodically and followed by changes in the prescribed program. Sargent opposed the heavy German apparatus as well as Dio Lewis' light apparatus and instead designed or improved devices adaptable to students' various abilities. In addition to chest weights and pulleys, he provided chest expanders and developers, leg machines, inclined planes, and hydraulic rowing machines— about 80 developing machines in all.

Athletes' abilities were also measured through various tests. Rather than opposing athletics, as some detractors have accused, Sargent encouraged students to engage in boxing, rowing, fencing, bowling, running, and baseball. Sargent's anthropometric measurement procedures and charts for athletes and all other students were widely used and contributed to physical education's entry into the scientific world.

Also a pioneer in the realm of teacher training, Sargent in 1881 opened the Sanatory Gymnasium to students at Harvard Annex and to women and men who wanted to become teachers of physical education. Although the resultant Sargent Normal School was coeducational between 1904 and 1914, few men enrolled. The high female enrollment made it the largest normal school in the United States as its more than 3000 graduates spread the Sargent system throughout the country. The school's eclectic curriculum consisted of theory courses emphasizing the sciences and practical exercises as varied as free movements, light gymnastics using dumbbells and Indian clubs, marching, sports, and heavy gymnastics.

The Harvard Summer School of Physical Education, established by Sargent in 1887, became the most significant source of professional education in the United States during physical education's early years. During a time when teachers had minimal or no training in physical education, Harvard Summer School met teachers' needs in an exemplary manner. An eminent faculty, often the recognized authorities in their subjects or activities, provided both theoretical and practical instruction, resulting in school administrators highly regarding a certificate from Harvard Summer School. Most of the students were teachers, but physicians, army officers, and other professionals attended, too. During its 46 summers, more than 5000 students attended.

REVIEW QUESTIONS

1. What types of physical activities were used as recreation by the colonists in the 1700s? How did these differ by region of the country?
2. Why did German gymnastics not gain wide acceptance in the United States in the 1820s and in the 1850s to 1880s?
3. What constituted the program of hygiene and physical education at Amherst College?
4. What were the basic principles of Dudley Sargent's program for Harvard University students?
5. Why was the Boston Conference on Physical Training in 1889 significant?
6. Why were normal schools for physical education established, especially in the 1880s?
7. Why was the Association for the Advancement of Physical Education founded?
8. What occurrences or developments started the playground movement?
9. Why did the faculty get involved in men's intercollegiate athletics?
10. What types of physical activities were considered appropriate for females and why?

STUDENT ACTIVITIES

1. As a class, reenact a portion of the Boston Conference on Physical Training (1889) by having each student report on one of the following systems: Swedish, German, Edward Hitchcock's, or Dudley Sargent's.
2. Read about the founding of the first professional organization in physical education (today's American Alliance for Health, Physical Education, Recreation and Dance), and report your findings orally to the class or in a three-page paper.
3. By examining histories of your state or region, find the most popular sport or recreational activity for one of the following groups:

   Native American adult males
   Native American adult females
   Native American children
   Early male settlers
   Early female settlers
   Children of early settlers
   Upper-class males in the 1800s
   Upper-class females in the 1800s
   Upper-class children in the 1800s
   Middle-class males in the 1800s
   Middle-class females in the 1800s
   Middle-class children in the 1800s
   Lower-class males in the 1800s
   Lower-class females in the 1800s
   Lower-class children in the 1800s

4. Find out the name(s) and the starting date(s) of the oldest normal school(s) for physical education for males and for females in your state.
5. Find out which college(s) in your state offered the first intercollegiate athletic competitions for men and for women. In which sports did these competitions occur?
6. Research any one of the individuals, events, or topics discussed in this chapter. Write a five-page paper about the major contributions of this individual, event, or topic to the history and growth of physical education and sport.

REFERENCES

Barrows IC: *Physical training,* Boston, 1899, George H. Ellis Press.

Lee M, Bennett BL: This is our heritage, *JOHPER* 31(4):27, 1960.

Oxendine JB: *American Indian sports heritage,* Champaign, Ill., 1988, Human Kinetics.

SUGGESTED READINGS

Bennett BL: Dudley Allen Sargent: the man and his philosophy, *JOPERD* 55(9):61, 1984. Harvard University students benefitted from Dudley Sargent's individualized exercise prescriptions for 40 years, while prospective teachers learned this and other systems at the Sargent Normal School and the Harvard Summer School of Physical Education.

Borish LJ: The sporting past in American history, *OAH Mag of Hist* 7(1):3, 1992. This article reviews the role of sports from the Puritans to today and suggests how primary sources and scholarly articles about sport can be integrated into history courses.

Davenport J (ed): The normal schools: exploring our heritage, *JOPERD* 65(3):25, 1994. This seven-part feature describes the contributions made by seven normal schools to the profession. Those described included Dio Lewis' Normal Institute for Physical Education, the Sargent School for Physical Education, William Anderson's Brooklyn Normal School, the Harvard Summer School of Physical Education, the Boston Normal School of Gymnastics, the Posse Gymnasium, and the H. Sophie Newcomb Memorial College.

Eyler MH: What the profession was once like: nineteenth century physical education, *The Academy Papers* 15:14, 1981. Drawing extensively from research written about this century, the author traces the significant themes and developments as physical education emerges as a unified field.

Lee M, Bennett B: Alliance centennial: 100 years of health, physical education, recreation and dance, *JOPERD* 56(4):17, 1985. This article reprints the "This Is Our Heritage" historical series in 15-year thematic sections that highlight significant occurrences related to the activities of today's American Alliance for Health, Physical Education, Recreation and Dance. It also chronicles the profession's major developments between 1960 and 1985.

Oxendine JB: *American Indian sports heritage,* Champaign, Ill., 1988, Human Kinetics. This book chronicles the sports and games in traditional Indian life with emphasis on ball games, footracing, children's play, and games of chance. The roles of leading Indian schools and the achievements of prominent Indian athletes are acclaimed.

Park RJ: Physiology and anatomy are destiny!?: brains, bodies and exercise in nineteenth century American thought, *J of Sp Hist* 18:31, 1991. Using the biomedical literature of that period, the author concluded that one's physiology and anatomy—that is, the body as icon for gender—dictated athletics for men and modest exercise for women.

Paul J: Centuries of change: movement's many faces, *Quest* 48:531, 1996. In this Amy Morris Homans lecture, Joan Paul provides a brief history of physical education in the United States.

Riess SA: The historiography of American sport, *OAH Mag of Hist* 7(1):10, 1992. The author provides a bibliography of sport history from 1850 to the present including primary sources, general histories, and works focusing on sport and the media, women, and minorities.

Spears B: *Leading the way: Amy Morris Homans and the beginnings of professional education for women,* Westport, Conn., 1986, Greenwood Press. Amy Morris Homans personified excellence in her leadership of the Boston Normal School of Gymnastics and of Wellesley College's Department of Hygiene and Physical Education. She demanded that her students attain and demonstrate the highest professional standards.

CHAPTER 9

Twentieth-Century Physical Education and Sport

KEY CONCEPTS

- The new physical education emphasized complete education, play, sport, and educational developmentalism.
- Programs developing from the play movement, the rise of teacher training, the growth of women's physical education, the education of the physical movement, the growing emphasis on fitness, the focus on human movement, and the principles of the scientific movement, educational developmentalism, and social education contributed to twentieth-century physical education and sport.
- Leadership from the national association and efforts to establish standards for teachers led to the recognition of physical education as a profession.
- Men's intercollegiate sports expanded from their intramural origins into commercialized businesses.
- Women's intercollegiate sports featured mass participation until the late 1960s, when competition, aided by Title IX legislation, became the primary goal.
- The children's play movement expanded first because of a recreational emphasis for all and then because of a mania for fitness.
- As fitness for children became a national focus, starting in the 1950s, youth sports expanded from value-oriented programs to adult-controlled leagues.
- The federal government has mandated equal educational opportunity, including physical education, for individuals with disabilities.

The controversy concerning which system of gymnastics would best meet the needs of students in the United States continued into the early years of the twentieth century. Beginning in the 1920s, school physical education moved away from formalized gymnastics to curricula that included sports, games, aquatics, and outdoor activities with educational outcomes foremost. Two themes emerged in the middle of the twentieth century; education through the physical and education of the physical vied for advocates and influenced school physical education and sport curricula. Since the turn of the century, the popularity of athletics at all levels and for both sexes has expanded tremendously. Nonschool programs from mid-century until today offer sports competitions for individuals of all ages and skill levels, lifetime recreational activities, and fitness alternatives. Federal legislation mandating equal opportunity for participation in sports and physical activities for females and disabled individuals led to dramatic changes in school and nonschool programs. Today, people participate in physical activities to develop and maintain fitness and in lifetime sports for fun, fitness, and competition.

THE NEW PHYSICAL EDUCATION

The Battle of the Systems had not resulted in the adoption of any one gymnastics program by the end of the nineteenth century. The formal nature of the alternatives had failed to appeal to a broad base of physical educators and their students, who were seeking activities that offered competition, fun, and more freedom of expression.

Speaking at the International Congress on Education sponsored by the National Education Association in 1893, Thomas Wood articulated his vision for a new physical education. "The great thought in physical education is not the education of the physical nature, but the relation of physical training to complete education, and then the effort to make the physical contribute its full share to the life of the individual, in environment, training, and culture" (p. 621). The **new physical education** *focused on developing the whole individual through participation in play, sports, games, and natural, outdoor activities.* The curriculum and philosophy of this new physical education was heavily influenced by and consistent with educational and psychological theory developing simultaneously.

Psychologist G. Stanley Hall made Clark University a center for child study after publishing in 1904 his landmark book, *Adolescence,* in which he defined the educational significance of children's developmental stages. Other leaders in the study of the individual, many of whom influenced each other's work, included William James, Edward Thorndike, William Kilpatrick, and John Dewey. They successfully integrated scientific education, educational developmentalism, and social education. Educational developmentalism, also known as the psychological movement, used children's play and other natural activities for learning. Teachers College of Columbia University nurtured the development and popularization of the latter two educational themes through faculty members Thorndike and Dewey who were close associates of Hall.

Teachers College also contributed to the integration of educational developmentalism and social education into the new physical education. Thomas Wood taught there for 31 years. Rosalind Cassidy took a Teachers College degree, as did hundreds of physical educators in the middle decades of the 1900s. For 27 years Jesse Williams influenced Teachers College students to advocate education through the physical as proposed by Wood and Cassidy.

LEADERS IN THE NEW PHYSICAL EDUCATION

Luther Gulick and his roommate Thomas Wood discussed their mutual interest in physical education at Oberlin College, where they were influenced by Delphine Hanna. In 1887 Luther Gulick became an instructor at the YMCA Training School in Springfield, Massachusetts, and, two years later, was named superintendent. While at the YMCA Training School, he emphasized sports in the physical directors' curriculum and started the YMCA's Athletic League to promote amateur sports. Stressing unity in the development of body, mind, and spirit, he designed the YMCA triangle (Figure 9-1), emblematic of the all-around man. He then moved to New York and taught before accepting the position of Director of Physical Training for the New York City public schools. Although Gulick supported gymnastics as the basis of school curricula, he founded the Public Schools Athletic League to provide after-school sports opportunities for boys, especially in track and field activities.

Another Gulick legacy was his promotion of play. In 1906, he helped establish the Playground Association of America and served as its first president. He also advocated the provision of playgrounds and public recreation in this country, initiated the Campfire Girls in 1913, and led in the camping movement. In *A Philosophy of Play* he forcefully articulated the importance of play as an educational force and helped begin the play movement within physical education.

Thomas Wood, after directing the gymnasium work for men for two years at Oberlin College and receiving a medical degree at Columbia, developed his first undergraduate teacher training curriculum in physical education at Stanford University beginning in 1891. Ten years later, he joined the faculty of Teachers College of Columbia University, where he led in the establishment of the first masters (1910) and doctors (1924) degree programs in physical education. Also, he was instrumental in the development of health education as a separate field of study. *The New Physical Education,* which he co-authored with Rosalind Cassidy in 1927, provided the philosophical foundation for refocusing school programs from gymnastics to sports, games, dance, aquatics, and natural activities.

Rosalind Cassidy helped broaden and clarify the tenets of the new physical education during her professional career at Mills College in California. She helped develop and promote "education through the physical," *a leading theme for understanding physical education as the field that could uniquely contribute to the education of the whole person through physical activities.* Through her voluminous writings, she also redefined physical education as the study of human movement.

Clark Hetherington was taught and greatly influenced by Wood at Stanford University. This influence is evident from Hetherington's coining of the term "new

FIGURE 9-1
YMCA emblem.

physical education" and from his advocacy of organic, psychomotor, character, and intellectual development as descriptive of physical education's objectives. G. Stanley Hall, a second mentor for Hetherington, also emphasized educational developmentalism, which paralleled Hetherington's philosophy that play was a child's chief business in life. At the University of Missouri, the University of Wisconsin, New York University, and Stanford University, Hetherington helped establish undergraduate physical education programs. At New York University he led in the development of graduate degree programs.

One of the first graduates of New York University's Ph.D. program in physical education was Jay Nash. Nash had served as the California Assistant Supervisor of Physical Education under Hetherington before joining the faculty at New York University in 1926 as Hetherington's replacement. Nash stressed that recreational skills should be learned early in life and could then supplement satisfaction from work. Fearing an overemphasis on spectating in the United States, Nash stated that school programs should teach carryover, or lifetime, sports to encourage people to adopt active lifestyles; that is, people should be educated for leisure.

Influenced by Wood and Cassidy's concept of complete education through the physical and John Dewey's social education theories, Jesse Williams emphasized that the development of physical skills in the schools could be justified only if such activities helped to educate the total child. According to Williams' theories about "education through the physical," educating a child to live in a democratic society, through social and intellectual interactions within physical education, justified its inclusion in the schools. Through his 41 books and the students he influenced in the highly regarded graduate physical education program at Teachers College of Columbia University, Williams became one of the most influential leaders in physical education, especially between 1930 and 1960.

Figure 9-2 summarizes the influence of these new physical educators on each other. It is interesting that Nash signaled a change in the professional training of physical educators. Whereas Gulick, Wood, and Williams held medical degrees, Nash earned a Ph.D.

MAJOR DEVELOPMENTS IN PHYSICAL EDUCATION

Paralleling and building upon the emergence of the new physical education, several movements contributed to curricular expansion. These developments included the play movement, the rise of teacher training, the growth of women's physical education, the education of the physical movement, the growing emphasis on fitness, the focus on human movement, and the influence of the scientific movement, educational developmentalism, and social education in the schools. Many of the leaders in these developments are highlighted in the box on pages 208–209.

The Play Movement

Luther Gulick proclaimed the importance of play for children, especially outside of the schools. In New York, he established the Public Schools Athletic League's (PSAL) sports competitions for boys and the Girls Branch of the PSAL, which provided opportunities for girls to participate in folk dancing. Elizabeth Burchenal

DELPHINE HANNA
Anthropometrics
Individualized program

LUTHER GULICK
Play and athletics

THOMAS D. WOOD
Complete education and
The New Physical Education

JESSE FEIRING WILLIAMS
Education through the
physical

CLARK HETHERINGTON
Play is a child's chief
business in life

ROSALIND CASSIDY
The New Physical Education
and education through the
physical

JAY B. NASH
Recreation, especially
in lifetime sports

FIGURE 9-2

New physical educators.

directed the Girls Branch of the PSAL before founding and presiding over the American Folk-Dance Society.

As Supervisor of Physical Culture in the Detroit public schools for 14 years, Ethel Perrin stressed informal, coeducational classes that emphasized play, rather than formalized gymnastics. Under her leadership, Detroit led the nation in the provision of specially trained physical educators at all levels of instruction.

The play movement also influenced nonschool programs. Following the passage of child labor laws, children were taken out of the sweat shops and returned to their neighborhoods where playgrounds and parks were provided for them. There immigrant children were assimilated into the American culture. There they made friends, learned social skills, and learned how to win and lose. There they perfected their baseball, basketball, football, softball, and ice hockey skills. Cities and towns prioritized offering sports competitions and recreational activities first for children and later for adults to meet this inherent need to play.

Teacher Training

When physical education gained stature as a recognized subject by the National Education Association in 1891, it began to move from its association with medicine to allegiance with educational philosophies and curricula. Whereas many early physical educators, like Hitchcock, Sargent, Wood, and Williams, held medical degrees, after 1900 several universities offered professional preparation courses in physical education. Oberlin College, the Universities of Nebraska, Missouri, and California, and Stanford University developed the initial programs.

Most states established teacher training institutes, or normal colleges, to replace the private schools that had predominated in the late 1800s. While the state normal colleges changed into regional comprehensive universities in recent decades, most have retained their commitment to teacher education, including physical education.

The impact of teacher training has extended to nonschool settings as well. Physical educators, who were educated to use physical activities to teach sports skills and physical fitness, have moved into other careers. For example, physical educators have been leaders in training military personnel during wartime and times of peace. Physical educators have directed public and private recreational programs, coached sports teams for youth and adults, taught lessons in swimming, tennis, and golf at private clubs, and managed commercial and professional sporting events. Most of these individuals received their education at one of the physical education teacher education institutions.

Women's Physical Education

Not until the 1970s did most college physical education programs lose their separation by sex. Throughout most of the 1900s, women's physical education focused on preparing teachers with strict disassociation from competitive athletics. Curricula remained somewhat formalized; centered on minimal skill development, rather than on enhancement of the abilities of the highly skilled; and focused on value development, not winning, through sport.

Only gradually did women gain acceptance as equals within physical education. For example, Mabel Lee was elected the first woman president of the

TWENTIETH-CENTURY LEADERS IN PHYSICAL EDUCATION IN THE UNITED STATES

Luther Halsey Gulick (1865–1918)

Served as instructor (1887–1900) and superintendent (1889–1900) of the Department of Physical Training at the YMCA Training School

Directed physical training for the New York City public schools (1903–1908)

Established the Public Schools Athletic League in New York City (1903)

Helped establish the Playground Association of America (1906)

Influenced by Delphine Hanna and Thomas Wood

Thomas Denison Wood (1864–1951)

Taught at Stanford University (1891–1901)

Taught at Teachers College of Columbia University (1901–1932)

Formulated the philosophical cornerstone for the "new physical education"

Appointed first professor of health education at Teachers College of Columbia University

Influenced by Delphine Hanna, Luther Gulick, and Rosalind Cassidy

Clark Wilson Hetherington (1870–1942)

Directed physical training and athletics at the University of Missouri (1900–1910)

Established a Demonstration Play School at the University of California, Berkeley (1913–1917)

Taught at the University of Wisconsin (1913–1918)

Served as state supervisor of physical education for California (1918–1921)

Taught at New York University (1923–1929)

Taught at Stanford University (1929–1938)

Influenced by Thomas Wood and G. Stanley Hall

Jay Bryan Nash (1886–1965)

Taught at New York University (1926–1953)

Promoted recreation and carryover sports

Influenced by Clark Hetherington and extended his theories as well as those of Luther Gulick and Thomas Wood

Jesse Feiring Williams (1886–1966)

Taught at Teachers College of Columbia University (1911–1916 and 1919–1941)

Stressed educational values, social education, and education through the physical

Became a dominant influence in physical education (1930–1960)

Influenced by John Dewey

Rosalind Cassidy (1895–1980)

Taught at Mills College (California) (1918–1947)

Taught at the University of California at Los Angeles (1947–1962)

Led in writing about and promotion of the new physical education, education through the physical, and physical education as human movement

Influenced by Thomas Wood

TWENTIETH-CENTURY LEADERS IN PHYSICAL EDUCATION IN THE UNITED STATES (CONTINUED)

Elizabeth Burchenal (1876–1959)

Served as Executive Secretary of the Girls' Branch of the Public Schools Athletic League (1906–1916)

Founded and served as first president of the American Folk-Dance Society (1916–1929)

Became first chairperson of the Committee on Women's Athletics of the American Physical Education Association (1917)

Influenced by Luther Gulick and Melvin Gilbert (in dance)

Ethel Perrin (1871–1962)

Supervised physical culture in the Detroit public schools (1909–1923)

Provided leadership with the executive committee of the Women's Division of the National Amateur Athletic Federation (1923–1932)

Served as assistant/associate director of health education for the American Child Health Association (1923–1936)

Influenced by Amy Morris Homans

Robert Tait McKenzie (1867–1938)

Taught (1891–1904) and served as Medical Director of Physical Education (1896–1904) at University Medical College (Canada)

Taught as professor on medical faculty and directed physical education (1904–1931) and served as professor of physical therapy (1907–1931) at the University of Pennsylvania

Depicted hundreds of athletic events in works of sculpture that showed the aesthetic harmony of bodily proportion and expression

Mabel Lee (1886–1985)

Directed physical education for women at the University of Nebraska (1924–1952)

Elected first woman president of the American Physical Education Association (1931–1932)

Led the profession as a proponent of wholesome sport for women and as an author

Influenced by Amy Morris Homans

Charles Harold McCloy (1886–1959)

Worked for the YMCA in the United States and internationally (1908–1930)

Served as a research professor in physical education at the State University of Iowa (1930–1954)

Stressed the development of skills and organic vigor as the primary objectives of physical education (education of the physical)

Eleanor Metheny (1908–1982)

Taught at Wellesley College and at the Harvard Fatigue Laboratory (1940–1942)

Taught at the University of Southern California (1942–1971)

Led in the study of meaningful movement experiences

Influenced by Charles McCloy

Mabel Lee, the first female president of the American Physical Education Association.

American Physical Education Association (APEA) 46 years after it was established. Within the APEA, Lee, Burchenal, and other women fought to preserve an educational model for women's participation in sport.

Education of the Physical

Charles McCloy led the fight against a primary emphasis on educational outcomes as advocated by Wood, Cassidy, and Williams. Instead of supporting Williams' claim that physical education merited inclusion in the schools because it helped attain social, emotional, and intellectual goals, McCloy affirmed his belief in "education of the physical." This referred to a belief that *physical education's unique contribution within education should be to develop individuals' physical fitness and sport skills.* During his more than 20 years with the YMCA and especially in his tenure at State University of Iowa, McCloy stressed organic and psychomotor development as the most important objectives for physical education. He stated that the uniqueness of physical education depended on the development of skills. He encouraged the teaching of sports skills and the measurement of progress through standardized tests.

An extension of this philosophical approach to physical education was the growth in the use of tests and measurements, which paralleled the scientific movement in education. Built on the importance of anthropometric measurements in the late 1800s, early twentieth-century physical educators developed numerous physical tests. The Public Schools Athletic League initiated achievement tests to reward boys' successful performances. College achievement tests measured cognitive knowledge, motor ability, endurance, and sports skills. David Brace's Motor Ability Test, Frederick Cozens's test of general athletic ability, Frederick Rogers' Strength Index and Physical Fitness Index, and Charles McCloy's Motor Quotient were among the most notable measures developed.

Fitness

Fitness as a curricular emphasis usually surfaced during wartime or times when peace was threatened. Certainly this characterized physical education during the years surrounding World Wars I and II. One of the greatest advocates for the importance of physical training to the war effort was R. Tait McKenzie. Although recognized more for his outstanding sports sculptures, during World War I McKenzie used his training as a physical educator and physician in England, his native Canada, and the United States. Many male and female physical educators served as physical training instructors or consultants to the Armed Forces.

Within schools and colleges, mass calisthenics and the development of fitness formed the basis of the curricula. Males and a few females fought in the wars, while stronger females during the 1940s were needed to staff industrial production for combat. Soon after both wars, fitness lost its emphasis.

An exception occurred during the Cold War years of the late 1950s. First, many felt threatened by the rising prominence of the Union of Soviet Socialist Republics (USSR). Second, the United States was embarrassed by the 1953 results of the Kraus-Weber Test that showed American children inferior to European children. This minimal muscular fitness test included six items: (1) in supine position, execute one straight leg sit-up; (2) in supine position, do one bent-knee sit-up; (3) in supine position, hold extended legs above the floor for ten seconds; (4) in prone position, pull the head, shoulders, and chest off the mat and hold for ten seconds; (5) in prone position, raise the extended legs off the mat and hold for ten seconds; and (6) from a standing position, bend until fingertips touch the floor without bouncing or bending the knees and hold this contact for three seconds.

As an immediate response to this report and following a national conference on the topic, President Eisenhower established the President's Council on Youth Fitness. This Council promoted a minimum of 15 minutes a day of vigorous activity for all children and distributed thousands of copies of *Youth Physical Fitness: Suggested Elements of a School-Centered Program*. The American Association for Health, Physical Education and Recreation (AAHPER) stimulated fitness through its 1958 Operation Fitness project that included the AAHPER Youth Fitness Test.

Human Movement

Rosalind Cassidy and Eleanor Metheny helped revolutionize the conceptual base of physical education. Metheny, a student of Charles McCloy, was acclaimed for her insightful writings and her inspirational speeches on this topic.

Movement education, especially as influenced by Rudolf Laban from England, significantly impacted elementary school curricula. Movement education, *a child-centered curriculum, emphasized presenting movement challenges to students and encouraging them to use problem solving and guided discovery to learn fundamental skills.* To some, the developmentally appropriate subject matter for children should focus on their free expression of movements in response to challenges or problems. Advocates favored individualized learning of locomotor, non-locomotor, and perceptual-motor skills.

Scientific Movement, Educational Developmentalism, and Social Education

Public school physical education in the 1900s reflected and was directly influenced by the scientific movement, educational developmentalism, and by social education. Athletic and motor ability achievement tests, measurements of posture, and the use of statistical analyses are three examples of techniques resulting from the scientific movement. The justification of play for children led the way for the playground and recreation movement that carried over into the schools. Educational developmentalism influenced the passage of state laws requiring physical education as an integral part of each child's school experiences. The popularity of sports within physical education curricula contributed to achievement of social education outcomes, including social skills such as cooperation, habits and attitudes of good citizenship, and values and ethical conduct.

In more recent years, however, school physical education programs have experienced numerous attacks, partially as a result of administrators with limited resources attempting to cut any programs viewed as nonessential. The likelihood of such attacks increased when physical educators were unable to demonstrate the achievement of educational standards. Another causal factor was the national call to improve and reform education in response to the belief that the economic predominance of this country was threatened. An examination of *AMERICA 2000: An Education Strategy,* released in 1991, verified the lack of centrality of physical education. The health and physical well-being of children was not valued enough to receive any mention.

Understanding the history of physical education and sport as a field can help professionals respond to such attacks. Certainly these major developments in physical education have overlapped and are interwoven, thus shaping today's programs.

LEADERSHIP FROM THE NATIONAL ASSOCIATION

In the early 1900s, the American Physical Education Association (APEA) was dominated by Easterners who attempted to build a strong profession through the exchange of ideas and shared projects. James McCurdy, who served as editor of the APEA's *American Physical Education Review* for 23 years, was one outstanding leader during the early years.

In the early 1900s, dancing and athletics were frequently added to school and college programs, challenging the former supremacy of gymnastics. Besides these two, frequently discussed topics at the annual meetings of the APEA included school hygiene, the value of gymnastics, skill and fitness testing, and standards for teacher preparation and graduate education. There was a proliferation of professional preparation in physical education between 1920 and 1927: 70 new college programs were begun.

Following the combination of the Midwest Society, a regional group of physical educators, with the national APEA in 1930, Elmer Mitchell assumed the editorship of the profession's two major publications, the *Journal of Health and Physical Education* and the *Research Quarterly,* and served in this capacity for 13 years. The Department of School Health and Physical Education of the National Education Association merged with the APEA in 1937, to become the American Association for Health and Physical Education (*recreation* was added to its name (AAHPER) in 1938). The national organization was subsequently configured into six geographical districts.

After World War II, the AAHPER sponsored numerous conferences focusing on facilities, undergraduate professional preparation, graduate professional preparation, fitness, and other interest areas. In 1974, it was restructured into an alliance composed of seven (now six) associations (see Chapter 4) to allow greater autonomy in providing leadership and programs for its diverse interest areas. The addition of *dance* to its current acronym (AAHPERD) occurred in 1979.

In 1985, the Alliance's centennial celebration focused on recalling its service and leadership to health, physical education, recreation, dance, and sports. The April 1985 issue of the *Journal of Physical Education, Recreation and Dance* traced 100 years of the profession by highlighting special events and notable leaders. The message conveyed in this publication and through the centennial convention was that the Alliance, through its membership, had enriched programs for many diverse populations. In the twentieth century, the six national associations focusing on health, leisure and recreation, dance, fitness, physical education, and sport have gained greater autonomy under the Alliance umbrella, enabling each specialized area to serve the unique needs of its members more effectively.

TEACHER PREPARATION

A perennial concern of the AAHPERD and its preceding organizations has been the inconsistencies among professional preparation programs for teachers. Each normal school, as it developed, was free to pursue its own course of study, with little relationship to what was being taught at the others. When four-year degree programs were developed in colleges and universities, each institution had the latitude to design and implement its own curriculum. Since, in the early 1900s, there were no **accreditation** procedures or standards, great program diversity resulted. In the 1930s, the Department of School Health and Physical Education of the National Education Association established a committee to evaluate teacher education curricula and to establish standards. In 1948, the National Conference on Undergraduate Professional Preparation in Health Education, Physical Education, and Recreation recommended standards and programs in teacher preparation. The AAHPER voted, in 1960, to accept the National Council for Accreditation of Teacher Education (NCATE) as the official accrediting agency in its fields of study. This led to many state departments of education certifying only teachers who graduated from NCATE-approved institutions. In the 1970s, many state departments began to require that certain competencies be met in professional course work before future teachers would be certified. Each of these developments enhanced the quality of the graduates of teacher education programs.

In the 1980s, many people expressed concern about the lack of standards for or credentials of individuals engaged in various sports and fitness programs. For example, there was no national certification for aerobic dance instructors. Seemingly anyone with a leotard and coordinated tights and leg warmers who could enthusiastically motivate people to exercise to the resounding beat of the latest hit tunes could teach. Knowledge about human anatomy, exercise physiology, first aid, cardiopulmonary resuscitation, psychology, and teaching progressions was not a prerequisite. This lack of standards led to repeated injuries, some serious; high dropout rates; and a general lack of accountability on the part of the instructors and the sponsoring groups. Certification programs for fitness instructors and leaders, such as through the American College of Sports Medicine, have filled the gap in this area, but still such training often is optional rather than mandatory. Unless sports like scuba diving, weight training, karate, and racquetball regulate their own instructors' training, anyone is free to teach these or other activities outside the schools.

AMATEUR AND COLLEGIATE SPORTS

The popularization of sports in the twentieth century has been phenomenal. In addition to becoming the nucleus of physical education programs, sports are organized for competition both inside and outside the schools.

Intramurals

Most college athletic teams and some physical education programs in the late 1800s and early 1900s evolved out of interclass competitions organized by male students. As athletics and physical education developed their own separate programs, a need still existed for recreational activities for students. In 1913, the University of Michigan and Ohio State University appointed the first intramural directors. At Michigan, beginning in 1919, Elmer Mitchell led in the development of sports opportunities for students who were not varsity athletes but who wanted more competition than was available in physical education classes. Originally in the colleges and after the mid-1920s in the schools, **intramurals** offered league and class, or homeroom, competition in individual and team sports. In the 1940s, the introduction of coeducational activities became popular. The greatest expansion in combined male-female activities occurred in the 1970s.

Today, many intramural programs operate as campus recreation programs, having greatly expanded the scope of their activities. In addition to competitive leagues and coeducational recreation, club sports, extramural competitions, faculty-staff programs, instructional clinics, fitness classes, special events and tournaments, and free-play opportunities have been offered. Over the years, many of

Leisure-time activities, such as soccer, are offered by recreation departments, YMCAs and YWCAs, corporate recreation programs, and school intramural programs.

these intramural recreational sports programs have moved from receiving funds first from athletic departments and then from physical education departments to being supported by students' fees. At the school level, where intramural activities vary from traditional competitions to unusual contests and events, and where these events are squeezed into times throughout the day, physical educators normally provide the expertise while school budgets provide the equipment. Intramural programs in business, industry, and the military also have become popular.

Outside of the schools, this same concept of intramurals, or sports competition within the walls, has provided innumerable opportunities for physical activity. Many corporations offer sports leagues and competitions in volleyball, bowling, softball, and many other sports for their employees at all levels of the organization. These leisure-time activities help build camaraderie among employees as well as help them live healthier lifestyles.

Collegiate Sports for Men

In the early 1900s, concerns in collegiate sports focused on football primarily because of the injuries and deaths that occurred with shocking regularity. While President Theodore Roosevelt expressed concern, college presidents threatened to ban intercollegiate football. As a direct result of football injuries and deaths, today's National Collegiate Athletic Association (NCAA) was formed in 1906. Although composed of a small group of faculty representatives with power only to recommend, the NCAA attempted to control the roughness and brutality of football by revising its rules. Gradually, football overcame these problems and emerged as the major collegiate sport. Baseball in colleges, though rivalled by the professional major leagues, retained a degree of popularity secondary to the pros and to football, while intercollegiate competitions in boxing, golf, tennis, track and field, and wrestling began but never seriously challenged the supremacy of college football. Basketball did emerge as the second leading collegiate sport, but not until the 1950s.

College football in the 1930s. (Photo courtesy North Carolina Collection, UNC Library at Chapel Hill.)

SPORT GOVERNANCE ORGANIZATIONS

Boys and Men

1888	Amateur Athletic Union (AAU)
	*1879—National Association of Amateur Athletes of America
1910	National Collegiate Athletic Association (NCAA)
	*1906—Intercollegiate Athletic Association of the United States
1922	National Federation of State High School Associations (NFSHSA)
1938	National Junior College Athletic Association (NJCAA)
1952	National Association of Intercollegiate Athletics (NAIA)
	*1940—National Association of Intercollegiate Basketball

Girls and Women

1974	National Association for Girls and Women in Sports (NAGWS)
	*1917—Committee on Women's Athletics
	*1927—Women's Athletic Section
	*1932—National Section on Women's Athletics
	*1953—National Section on Girls and Women's Sports
	*1958—Division of Girls and Women's Sports
1971	Association for Intercollegiate Athletics for Women (AIAW) (ceased 1982)
	*1966—Commission on Intercollegiate Athletics for Women

First Championships Offered for Girls and Women:

1916	Amateur Athletic Union
1976	National Junior College Athletic Association
1980	National Association of Intercollegiate Athletics
1981	National Collegiate Athletic Association

*Earlier name of the same organization.

The NCAA continued as the sole voice of and controlling organization for college athletes until 1938, when the National Junior College Athletic Association (NJCAA) was founded to provide competitive opportunities for students in two-year institutions, and 1952, when the National Association of Intercollegiate Athletics (NAIA) began to sponsor championships for the small colleges (it sponsored an annual basketball tournament for men starting in 1940). The box above lists these and other major sports organizations for men and women.

Collegiate athletics for men in the 1990s are very different from what they were in the 1940s. Under faculty control by representative vote, the NCAA remained primarily an advisory organization during its first 40 years. Control rested with each institution, where most frequently athletic councils composed of alumni, faculty, and students exercised authority over athletics. Institutions that held membership in conferences agreed to follow additional regulations and guidelines. Other than standardizing the rules and providing championships, the NCAA had not been granted power by the institutions to legislate or to mandate rules. Beginning with the national acceptance of athletic grants-in-aid in 1952, the role of the NCAA changed dramatically during the next decade, because institutions were willing to relinquish some of their autonomy to the NCAA to ensure that other institutions would comply with the regulations governing grants-in-aids and recruiting. A second development began with the first negotiation of a television contract in 1951, thus providing the NCAA with enforcement leverage. Subsequently, the NCAA could penalize an institution economically by disallowing television appearances. The NCAA, with a budget over $225,000,000, has become the most powerful amateur sports organization in the United States and possibly the world.

Collegiate Sports for Women

During the early 1900s, sports for women were strictly controlled by women physical educators, who consistently followed societal expectations. Caution about a potential overemphasis on competition or on unladylike behavior led to modified rules in several sports. Mass participation in class exercises, field days, play days, and sports days, rather than competitive athletics, became the norm. Physical education, because of its healthful benefits, was stressed for girls in schools and for women who attended colleges. Outfitted in middy blouses and bloomers, the traditional gymnasium costume of the day, these women exercised in mass drills, engaged in therapeutic Swedish gymnastics, and enjoyed sports such as archery, basketball, field hockey, rowing, and tennis. Field days were normally conducted once or twice a year on campus, and all students were urged to participate. Play days, beginning in the 1920s, provided for social interaction as women students met and formed teams composed of representatives from several institutions. These teams played one or more sports before reassembling for a picnic or other social event. Evolved from these play days were sports days, during which college teams competed, frequently in only one sport, but still with the emphasis on social interaction and fun.

In 1917, a Committee on Women's Athletics was established by the American Physical Education Association (today's AAHPERD) to establish standards and policies that advocated mass participation while vigorously opposing varsity competition. The Women's Division of the National Amateur Athletic Federation, between 1923 and 1942, also opposed highly competitive sports, including those in the Olympic Games, as inappropriate for women.

In the 1960s, a gradual change in societal attitudes regarding women in sports paralleled a liberalized philosophy displayed by women leaders in physical education. As long as the welfare of the athletes was guaranteed and high standards were maintained, competitions were permitted and even encouraged, especially beginning in 1969, when the Commission on Intercollegiate Athletics for Women began the sponsorship of national tournaments. Two years later, the Association for Intercollegiate Athletics for Women (AIAW), an institutional membership organization, assumed this responsibility. During the next 11 years, the AIAW provided championships and established standards and policies governing women's intercollegiate athletics. With equal opportunity mandated by Title IX of the 1972 Education Amendments, colleges and schools financed increased sports competitions for girls and women. In 1976, the NJCAA and, in 1980, the NAIA began offering championships for college women; these smaller institutions benefitted financially from having one membership fee, one governance structure and set of rules, and similar sport schedules for all athletes.

1890s

1890s to early 1900s

Changes in women's sports attire. (Lower photo courtesy Basketball Hall of Fame.)

1920s to 1930s

1940s

Late 1940s to early 1950s

The NCAA initially opposed Title IX of the 1972 Education Amendments claiming that its requirement for equal opportunity in all educational programs would end men's intercollegiate athletics. The NCAA lobbied the Department of Health, Education and Welfare for exclusion of athletics from Title IX, campaigned in support of the Tower Amendment in the Senate to exclude revenue sports from Title IX jurisdiction, and turned to the courts arguing the inapplicability of Title IX to athletics on constitutional grounds. Each of these approaches were unsuccessful.

Claiming Title IX mandated that the NCAA govern both men's and women's athletics, in 1981, the NCAA began to offer championships for women. Thus, a head-to-head confrontation with the AIAW was staged. The AIAW in the previous decade had grown to provide 41 championships, in three competitive divisions, in 19 sports. But without a large financial base, the AIAW could not match the NCAA's payment of expenses for women's teams participating in its championships, its waiver of membership dues for women's athletic teams if their men's programs were members, and its contract to televise both the men's and the women's (directly opposite the AIAW's title game) basketball finals. The AIAW's educational model for athletics ceased to exist in June, 1982. Although a few women have gained some status in NCAA, such as Judith Sweet, the first female to serve as president, the NCAA is predominantly governed by men. They hold most coaching and administrative positions of women's athletics within the NCAA as well as the NAIA and NJCAA.

Amateur Sports

The amateur sports scene in the United States outside the colleges remained largely under the direction of the AAU through the 1970s, since this organization sponsored a great diversity of sports competitions for people of all ages. Basketball, boxing, swimming, and track and field especially attracted thousands of participants. Because championships in these sports were offered by NCAA institutions, the two organizations frequently clashed. Repeatedly, when the time arrived for the selection of Olympic teams, controversies raged. In 1922, the National Amateur Athletic Federation was formed to mediate this dispute, with few positive results. The conflicts inevitably affected the athletes as the two associations often refused to sanction events, to certify records, or to permit athletes to participate in each other's events. The Amateur Sports Act, passed in 1978, resolved some of these problems by requiring that each Olympic sport have its own (single-sport) governing body and by establishing guidelines governing the selection of these organizations.

The spirit of the Olympics promoted by Pierre de Coubertin, founder of the modern games, and perpetuated by the governing International Olympic Committee, prevailed during the first half of the twentieth century. The five interlocking rings symbolized friendship among the athletes of the world. Competitive superiority remained the ideal until the Olympic Games became the stage for displaying the supremacy of one's national ideology starting in the 1952 Helsinki Games with the entry and beginning dominance of athletes from the USSR. Commercialism illustrated by product displays and lucrative television contracts forever changed the image of these competitions. Media attention and the potential of leveraging medals into endorsements played significant roles, too. The highly

Jim Thorpe, a Native American, won gold medals in the 1912 Stockholm Olympic Games in the pentathlon and decathlon.

Mildred (Babe) Didrikson in the 1932 Los Angeles Olympic Games won gold medals in the 800-meter hurdles and the javelin throw and a silver medal in the high jump.

commercialized 1996 Atlanta Games offered competitions for athletes, most of whom were professionals.

The original events of the modern Olympic Games paralleled the popular activities of the turn of the century such as track and field, gymnastics, fencing, and tennis. These and other Olympic sports had minimal impact on school curricula. While many Olympic sports were associated with elitist clubs for men, including shooting, rowing, yachting, and equestrian clubs, the entry of college males in track and field, swimming, and wrestling broadened the composition of the teams from the United States and thus may have attracted participants from

Many states offer amateurs competitive opportunities through "state games." (Photo courtesy Maggie McGlynn.)

throughout society. Few women, primarily in swimming (starting in 1912) and track and field (starting in 1928), competed in the Olympics until the number of sports opened to them increased. The recent popularity of gymnastics, basketball, and volleyball certainly has been enhanced through the showcasing of Olympic competitions. However, only the growth in gymnastics can probably be linked specifically to the Olympics.

PLAY TO RECREATION TO FITNESS

Play

The playground movement continued apace in the early 1900s, as the Playground Association of America (PAA), founded in 1906 by Luther Gulick and Henry Curtis, provided the necessary leadership. Gulick served as its first president and was instrumental in the publication of its monthly magazine, *The Playground*. The provision of adequate playgrounds throughout the country was also enhanced by the support of President Theodore Roosevelt. Clark Hetherington supervised the writing, in 1910, of *The Normal Course in Play*, the book used to prepare recreation leaders. Joseph Lee, as president of the PAA, helped expand the play concept to include the value of play and recreation for all ages, leading to the reorganization of the PAA in 1911 and its new name, the Playground and Recreation Association of America (PRAA).

Recreation

In 1930, the PRAA became the National Recreation Association (which became the National Recreation and Park Association in 1965), verifying the importance of the worthy use of leisure time by people of all ages. The Depression years suddenly gave people large amounts of leisure time, but many had limited financial resources. The federal government helped in two ways. Federal agencies, such as the Works Progress Administration, provided jobs by funding construction of camping sites, golf courses, gymnasiums, playing fields, and swimming pools, and once completed, these were opened for recreational use by everyone. Especially popular sports during the 1930s were bowling and softball.

War production brought the United States out of the Depression. At the same time, sports competitions and recreational programs were initiated to revive the spirits and bodies of soldiers and factory workers. While the armed services used sports for training and conditioning soldiers, industries began to provide sports teams and competitive opportunities for employees, realizing that such activities positively affected productivity and morale. Industrial recreation continued to expand even after the war crisis ended.

Outdoor education emerged as the recreational thrust of the 1950s. As the country became more mechanized and technological, the appeal of camping, hiking, and similar back-to-nature activities provided people with the chance to get away from daily stress and routine. Some schools and colleges began to offer backpacking, rock climbing, spelunking, winter survival, ropes courses, and orienteering, which have maintained their popularity in programs in the 1990s.

Jay Nash, as early as the 1930s, promoted carryover, or lifetime, sports within the curriculum. By the 1960s, this philosophy gained numerous supporters and affected programs. Led by the Lifetime Sports Foundation with joint sponsorship by the American Association for Health, Physical Education and Recreation,

Backpacking is one of several popular outdoor activities. (Photo courtesy Jim Kirby.)

archery, badminton, bowling, golf, and tennis were introduced into many schools. Slowly, programs expanded from offering only team sports to the inclusion of these and other lifetime sports.

Fitness

A mania for fitness began in the 1970s, with joggers leading the boom. In 1970, the lonely runner was suddenly joined by thousands of marathoners and road racers of all ages and both sexes, while tennis participants multiplied and swimming became more popular. The pervasiveness of this fitness mania could be verified by observing not only the sport paraphernalia that enthusiasts used and wore but also the popularity of sporting attire for everyone. This fitness phenomenon has continued into the 1990s as aerobic dance, racquetball, and weight training have remained favorite activities outside and sometimes inside the schools. However, the people most involved in getting and keeping in shape have come from the middle and upper classes, rather than being drawn equally from all economic levels. Also, many school-age children, rather than becoming fitness advocates, have preferred to watch television, play video games, or become sports spectators.

Fitness for Children   When the results of the Kraus-Weber Minimal Muscular Fitness Test were published in 1953, European children demonstrated greater fitness (only 9% failed) than children in the United States (57.8% failed). Since the six-item Kraus-Weber Test primarily measured flexibility and abdominal strength, and thus received criticism that it inaccurately assessed fitness, the physical education profession developed the AAHPER Youth Fitness Test. To the dismay of professionals, the 1958 results of this eight-item test battery still showed that children in the United States had low levels of fitness. This test included pull-ups (for boys), flexed-arm hang (for girls), straight leg sit-ups, the shuttle run, the standing broad jump, the softball throw, the 50-yard dash, and the 600-yard run-walk. Between 1958 and the second national administration of this test in 1965, teachers promoted fitness through daily physical education classes, periodic testing, and an increased consciousness of the importance of fitness. These efforts were rewarded with improvement by all age groups in all skills, except for 17-year-old girls in the softball throw. Unfortunately, these vigorous efforts lapsed, so poor fitness levels of school-age children were reported again in national studies in 1985 and 1987.

In response to widespread criticism that the AAHPER Youth Fitness Test failed to measure the major components of fitness, in 1981 the AAHPERD introduced the Health-Related Lifetime Physical Fitness Test. Its items measured strength with sit-ups, flexibility using a sit-and-reach, cardiovascular endurance in a 1.5-mile or 12-minute run, and body composition by taking skinfold measurements. While more accurately measuring the recognized components of fitness, these test norms only reconfirmed the lack of fitness of school-age children in the 1980s.

In 1994, the American Alliance for Health, Physical Education, Recreation and Dance (AAHPERD) joined with The Cooper Institute for Aerobics Research (CIAR) in a collaborative physical fitness education and testing program. AAHPERD's educational approach to fitness helps motivate students to change their

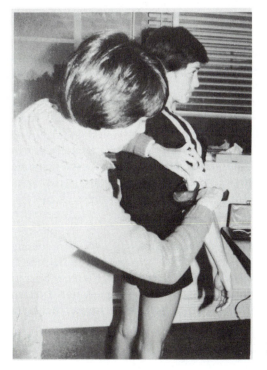

Body composition is an excellent indicator of overall fitness. (Photo courtesy Diane Victorson.)

behaviors and commitment to lifetime fitness. The Physical Best educational materials teach students to set their own individualized fitness goals and by monitoring, reporting to parents, and recognizing achievement the program helps students incorporate the cognitive, affective, and psychomotor components of fitness into their lives. The Prudential FITNESSGRAM, developed by The CIAR, is designed to assess aerobic capacity (1-mile walk/run or pacer for young children), body composition, muscular strength, and endurance (curl-ups, push-ups, or alternatively pull-ups, modified pull-ups, or flexed-arm hang and trunk lift), and flexibility (back-saver sit-and-reach). The FITNESSGRAM program recognizes achievement, improvement, and behavior change through its awards, while the Physical Best recognition system reinforces the importance of attaining individual goals and participation in extracurricular physical activities. The latest data on the fitness of American youth come from the National Children and Youth Fitness Study I and II. These studies revealed that the fitness levels of American youth need improvement. The need for improvement in youth fitness comprise a part of *Healthy People 2000* goals as discussed in Chapter 1.

Although some local and state assessments of the fitness levels of children have been conducted, no replication of the national study has occurred. Data, however, do show that the youth fitness goals in *Healthy People 2000* have not been achieved. In the wake of the 1996 publication of *The Surgeon General's Report on Physical Activity and Health* and the identification of physical inactivity as a primary risk factor contributing to coronary heart disease, the nation's interest in the physical well-being of parents and children alike has never been stronger. Schools, public recreation programs, and private businesses need to combine their efforts in providing greater opportunities for physical education and sport activities for children.

Fitness for All Ages   An emphasis on aerobic fitness for individuals of all ages may trace its initial stimulus to the 1968 publication of Kenneth Cooper's *Aerobics*. This book described a program that showed how each individual could attain and maintain physical fitness by compiling a minimum of points each week by participating in favorite activities. Since the 1970s, many Americans have renewed regular physical activity by playing tennis, racquetball, and golf, running road races and marathons, in-line skating, wind surfing, and skiing, and purchasing millions of dollars of home exercise equipment. Women, many for the first time ever, joined classes in aerobic dance, step aerobics, water aerobics, and several other variations of exercise combined with music. Health and fitness clubs offer aerobics classes, individualized weight training programs, aerobic machines such as stair climbers, treadmills, stationary bikes, and rowing machines, tennis, racquetball, and golf instruction, leagues, and tournaments, massage, sports medicine consultation, and nutritional counseling. Some people have suggested that these clubs have replaced social events and bars as the preferred places for meeting and interacting with others. The appearance of fitness is certainly vogue when looking at fashions—so many Americans are trying to achieve a level of fitness that both looks and feels good.

YOUTH SPORTS PROGRAMS

In the 1920s, the popularity of sports in the United States led many people to expect the schools to provide competitive sports for children. Some junior and most senior high schools assumed this responsibility, because physical educators believed that students in these age groups were physiologically and psychologically prepared for competition. For elementary-age children, educators widely believed that the negative outcomes from competitive sports outweighed the positive benefits. This belief did not prevent the development of youth sports programs, however; communities, private associations, and civic organizations, seeing sports as potential deterrents to delinquency, tools for social control, promotional devices, and fun for the boys, got involved. Local as well as national programs such as Little League Baseball, Pop Warner Football, and Biddy Basketball expanded until today they involve millions of young athletes and adult organizers and billions of dollars.

Although many physical educators philosophically disagree with highly competitive youth leagues, these sports enterprises are deeply inculcated into American society. Parents have favored youth sports programs for several reasons: (1) their children have fun through participation; (2) these programs offer opportunities for learning sports skills; (3) these experiences enhance socialization abilities like cooperation and teamwork and development of values; (4) sports involvement contributes to physical development and fitness; and (5) youth sports programs provide children wholesome alternatives for the use of their time, thus lessening misbehavior or unattended hours at home watching television. Additionally, many value youth sports because the family can participate together—as players, coaches, cheerleaders, and volunteers to prepare the competitive facility or to sell concessions.

Children have varying reasons for their participation in youth sports. The leading motivators are to have fun, to learn or improve sports skills, to stay in shape or get exercise, to associate with friends, and to have something to do. Unfortunately, joining a team or continuing participation may occur just to please one's parents. After years of success as a young athlete, motivators may change to winning; seeking valued rewards, awards, and popularity; and, for the few, qualifying for college grants-in-aid or professional careers.

When youth sports programs remain focused on the aspirations of the children and when parents' attitudes and behaviors are kept in perspective, millions benefit. When winning surpasses all other goals, exploitation of the children and an erosion of values reign. For example, the 1992 champions of the Little League World Series from the Philippines had to forfeit the title when it was determined that the coach had used eight ineligible players. This incident illustrates that adults, who write the rules (often to control the potential misbehavior of other adults), design and call the plays, dispute officials' calls, and berate their athletes, are the culprits.

Numerous occurrences in youth sports call attention to the prevalence of exploitation. Pressures to win, commercialization, elimination of less competitive players, injuries from overuse, violence, overspecialization, cheating, and lack of value development are but a few examples of the resulting concerns. As more and more educators promote and provide coaching education programs, these problems may be reduced. Parent orientation sessions are also important deterrents to placing excessive pressures on children and to adult misbehavior.

FEDERAL LEGISLATION

Although early leaders of this country, such as Benjamin Franklin and Thomas Jefferson, were promoters of physical education, not until recent years has the federal government become involved. Legislation that directly influences physical education includes mandates for equal opportunity for both sexes and for the disabled.

Coeducational Physical Education

Title IX of the 1972 Education Amendments required equal opportunity in all educational programs and stated as its basic principle that "no person in the United States shall, on the basis of sex, be excluded from participation in, be denied the benefits of, or be subjected to discrimination under any education program or activity receiving federal financial assistance." In relation to physical education, this statement meant it was illegal to discriminate against either sex in curricula content, equipment and facility usage, teacher quality, or other program areas.

Although equitable treatment, which mandated mixed classes except in sex education and contact sports, was the law, some schools and colleges resisted change. Often this resistance was due to teachers' refusal to instruct students of the opposite sex or to the administration's lack of insistence on compliance. Many institutions maintained class rolls of boys and girls but offered single-sex

An increasingly popular school elective in physical education for both girls and boys is weight training. (Photo courtesy Bob Hilliard.)

instruction and activity. As attitudes and behaviors gradually changed, some teachers instructed mixed classes but refused to allow girls and boys to compete with and against each other.

Despite such resistance, Title IX led to substantial changes. Elementary school children accepted as the norm classes composed of both girls and boys. As they participated with and against each other during the developmental years, the differences in their levels of performance lessened. Teachers assessed abilities and evaluated performances to ensure fair standards and groupings. Increasingly, students in the secondary schools accepted combined classes, learning respect for the capabilities of those of the opposite sex. Gradually acceptance and appreciation of girls and women actively participating in sports led to recreation and fitness programs that welcomed all who sought to enjoy activity and develop their physical capabilities.

Adapted Physical Education Programs

Historically, physically disabled students were not given opportunities to participate in activity classes or were assigned to corrective or remedial classes, with a resulting social stigma. The development of adapted programs led to a more individualized approach. *Adapted physical education is for exceptional students who are so different in mental, physical, emotional, or behavioral characteristics that, in the interest of quality of educational opportunity, special provisions must be made for their proper education.* Yet, not all schools made such provisions for students' special needs; therefore, the federal government became involved.

Inclusion places physically-challenged children into regular classes.
(Photo courtesy Bob Hilliard.)

Section 504 of the Rehabilitation Act of 1973 specified that "no otherwise qualified handicapped person shall, on the basis of handicap, be excluded from participation in, be denied the benefits of, or otherwise be subjected to discrimination under any program which receives or benefits from Federal financial assistance." Thus every student was guaranteed access to the entire school program, including physical education. The Education Amendment Act of 1974 mandated that all children must be placed in the least restrictive environment (LRE), or the setting in which their optimal learning and development could occur.

The Education for All Handicapped Children Act of 1975 (Public Law 94-142) was the first law to specifically mandate physical education in its guidelines. Generally it required that physical education, specially designed if necessary, must be provided for every disabled child in the public schools within regular physical education classes, unless the student has unusual restrictions; any unusual restrictions are to be provided for through the development of an Individualized Education Program (IEP). This IEP must be a written plan that has been designed by a representative of the public agency (school) who is qualified to provide or to supervise special education, the child's teacher, one or both of the child's parents, the child (when appropriate), and other individuals selected at the discretion of the parent or school. One problem in the development of IEPs has been the frequent failure to involve physical educators, even though Public Law 94-142 specifies that the children's physical needs must be met.

Each IEP must contain the following:

1. A statement of the child's present levels of educational performance;
2. A statement of annual goals, including short-term instructional objectives;
3. A statement of the specific special education and related services to be provided to the child, and the extent to which the child will be able to participate in regular educational programs;

INDIVIDUALIZED EDUCATION PROGRAM

Student: Chris Miller   Age: 9   Grade: 3
School: Eastwood Elementary   Height: 42″   Weight: 62
Placement: Least Restrictive Environment Date of annual review: August 1997

Present level of performance: Chris is mildly mentally retarded and lacks balance and eye-hand coordination skills; prefers sedentary to vigorous activity; can toss and catch a rubber ball thrown from 12 feet, 3 times out of 10; can do two bent-knee sit-ups and comes within 6 inches of touching her toes with her legs slightly flexed.

Annual goals:

1. Increase abdominal strength
2. Increase flexibility
3. Increase eye-hand coordination
4. Increase balance

Sample performance objectives	Sample activities	Evaluation measure	Completion date
1. Perform 10 bent-knee sit-ups without stopping	1. Teacher-assisted sit-ups daily; leg lifts held for 1 to 10 seconds	1. Observation	1. August 1997
2. Touch toes with fingers without bending knees and hold for 2 seconds	2. Lower and upper leg stretches; teacher-assisted toe touches	2. Observation	2. August 1997
3. Toss and catch a 20-inch rubber ball, at 20 feet, 6 times out of 10	3. Self-toss, wall toss, and partner toss from 10, 15, and 20 feet	3. Observation	3. August 1997
4. Walk 6 feet on a 4-inch balance beam placed 6 inches off the floor	4. Walk on a 4-inch line on the floor; teacher assistance while on balance beam	4. Observation	4. August 1997

Date: _____   Teacher: _____

4. Projected dates for initiation of the services and anticipated duration of the services; and
5. Appropriate objective criteria and evaluation procedures and schedules for determining, on at least an annual basis, whether the short-term instructional objectives are being achieved.

The box above provides a sample IEP. In 1990, the Education for All Handicapped Children Act of 1975 and its 1983 and 1986 Amendments, which extended benefits to infants and preschool children, was renamed Individuals with Disabilities Education Act (IDEA), or PL101-476.

Inclusion refers to the integration of children with disabilities into classes with nondisabled students. Full inclusion means that regardless of whether a child can do the appropriate class work or keep up with the achievements of other students, this disabled child is placed in a regular educational setting. Advocates of full inclusion emphasize that being near and interacting with nondisabled peers, primarily to foster social skills and to build self-esteem or self-image, far outweigh any liabilities. The principles of full inclusion rest upon the rights of children to attend their home schools, instead of being isolated in special programs. Critical to the success of inclusion classrooms are well-prepared teachers, supplementary aids and services, and support personnel.

Another approach that complies with federal legislation is the use of the least restrictive environment. Each child is placed into the educational setting most appropriate for his or her learning and development. Placement and curricular decisions are based on individuals' abilities and needs, with a continuum of alternatives available from full inclusion to total isolation. Special classes, such as adaptive physical education, should be provided if needed to enhance the learning of each child. Although students may learn from one another, disabled students may also negatively affect the academic environment of other students by increasing class sizes or by making the teacher's job more difficult. Rather than automatically including all disabled children in a regular classroom, each child should be placed in the setting where optimal learning can occur. This least restrictive environment varies from child to child. Whether mentally retarded, learning disabled, emotionally disturbed, or physically handicapped, all disabled children can benefit from having individualized programs that are appropriate for their developmental levels.

SUMMARY

Built on the gymnastics programs of the early 1900s, curricula in physical education provide a blend of play, fitness, health, intramurals, recreation, and sports. The new physical education, beginning in the 1920s, led in this transition, demonstrating that physical education contributed to the complete education of students. The box on pp. 232–233 highlights many of the significant occurrences in physical education and sport in the twentieth century.

Besides the new physical education, major developments impacting physical education in the 1900s included the play movement, the rise of teacher training, the growth of women's physical education, the education of the physical movement, the growing emphasis on fitness, the focus on human movement, and the influence of the scientific movement, educational developmentalism, and social education. Intramural programs developed to meet the needs of students desiring sports competition outside of physical education classes yet at a lower level than athletics. Leadership from the national association, such as through professional journals or at conferences, and standards for teacher preparation helped solidify physical education into a recognized profession.

Collegiate sports for men expanded from their student-organized status into multimillion-dollar business enterprises with extensive regulations and media exposure. Women's sports in the colleges focused on a philosophy of mass participation until the 1970s when the AIAW encouraged competition. The most visible amateur sports competitions were the Olympic Games. The play movement for children expanded into recreational activities and then fitness for families and workers.

SIGNIFICANT EVENTS IN TWENTIETH-CENTURY PHYSICAL EDUCATION AND SPORT

1900   Grammar School Athletic League of Philadelphia created

1903   Public Schools Athletic League formed in New York by Luther Gulick (Girls' Branch began in 1905)

1906   Playground Association of America founded

1909   Publication of Jesse Bancroft's *Games for School, Home, Playground, and Gymnasium,* Clark Hetherington's *The Normal Course in Play,* and R. Tait McKenzie's *Exercise in Education and Medicine*

1910   Teachers College of Columbia University offered the first master's degree with a specialization in physical education

1913   First departments of intramural sports started at the University of Michigan and Ohio State University

1916   New York became the first state to appoint a director of physical education, Thomas A. Storey

1919   Fred Leonard published *Pioneers of Modern Physical Training*

1919   Eastern District of the APEA founded

1924   National Association of Physical Education of College Women started

1924   James H. McCurdy's *Physiology of Exercise* and Elmer Mitchell's *Intramural Athletics* became the first books published on both subjects

1924   Teachers College of Columbia University conferred the first Ph.D. with a specialization in physical education

1926   American Academy of Physical Education founded

1927   *The New Physical Education: A Program of Naturalized Activities for Education toward Citizenship* authored by Thomas D. Wood and Rosalind Cassidy

1928   Southern District of the APEA founded

1930   First publication of the *Journal of Health and Physical Education* and the *Research Quarterly*

1931   Mabel Lee elected first woman president of the American Physical Education Association

1931   Northwest District of the APEA founded

1934   Central District and Midwest District of the APEA established from the former Middle West District

1935   Southwest District of the APEA founded

1937   American Physical Education Association merged with the Department of School Health and Physical Education of the National Education Association to form the American Association for Health and Physical Education

1938   The AAHPER established a national headquarters at the National Education Association in Washington, D.C.

1947   The AAHPER published *A Guide on Planning Facilities for Athletics, Recreation, Physical and Health Education*

1948   National Conference on Undergraduate Professional Preparation in Health Education, Physical Education, and Recreation held

1950   National Conference of Graduate Study in Health Education, Physical Education, and Recreation held

1953   Results of the Kraus-Weber Minimal Muscular Fitness Test published

1955   AAHPER began an Outdoor Education Project

1955   *Physical Education for High School Students* published by AAHPER

1956   President's Council on Youth Fitness established

1956   AAHPER Fitness Conference held

1958   Administration of the AAHPER Youth Fitness Test began

1959   The International Council on Health, Physical Education, and Recreation established

1965   Lifetime Sports Foundation established

1971   Association for Intercollegiate Athletics for Women established

1972   Education Amendments (including Title IX) passed

SIGNIFICANT EVENTS IN TWENTIETH-CENTURY PHYSICAL EDUCATION AND SPORT (CONTINUED)

1972	National Conference on Professional Preparation of the Elementary Specialist held
1974	National association restructured into the American Alliance for Health, Physical Education and Recreation, comprising seven associations
1975	The Education of All Handicapped Children Act passed
1978	Amateur Sports Act passed
1980	AAHPERD moved into its headquarters in Reston, Virginia
1980	AAHPERD initiated the Lifetime Health-Related Physical Fitness Test
1984	Second National Conference on Preparing the Physical Education Specialist for Children held
1985	Centennial convention of the American Alliance for Health, Physical Education, Recreation and Dance held
1988	AAHPERD introduced Physical Best, physical fitness assessment and education program

The current mania for fitness impacted children in the 1950s when school programs started to test for and promote fitness. Throughout the twentieth century, though, American children have tested poorly on fitness. Instilling in children a commitment to lifetime fitness is a primary goal of education. Youth sports programs also potentially can benefit the participants, although adult-controlled leagues may threaten the intended outcomes. The federal government has attempted to ensure that all Americans have equal opportunities to become physically educated, by legislating that all school children, including those with disabilities, have the right to physical education.

JESSE FEIRING WILLIAMS
(1886–1966)

EDUCATION
A.B., Oberlin College
M.D., Columbia University

BACKGROUND

Jesse Feiring Williams has been called the dominant physical educator between 1930 and 1960. Espousing objectives in harmony with those of education, he emphasized that the development of the individual was physical education's *raison d'être* and that physical education was obligated to equip students to live in and to contribute to society. Through his voluminous writings and the students he taught, his philosophical influence spread throughout the country.

Williams obtained his bachelor's degree at Oberlin College and while still an undergraduate served as Director of Athletics and as a coach and a tutor at Oberlin Academy. For the majority of his career (1911–1913 and 1919–1941), he taught at Teachers College of Columbia University; after 1923, he also served as head of the department. Numerous students at Teachers College, one of the foremost institutions for graduate study in physical education in the United States, were influenced directly by Williams' philosophy. The most significant of his 41 books was *The Principles of Physical Education,* which was published in eight editions between 1927 and 1965. In addition, Williams authored numerous articles published in the *Journal of Health and Physical Education, Journal of Higher Education, School and Society, Teachers College Record,* and other professional journals.

ACCOMPLISHMENTS

Throughout his writings, Williams emphasized that the role of education, and hence physical education, should be to prepare children to live in a democratic society. He stressed that physical education merited its inclusion in the educational realm because it provided opportunities for equality of learning opportunity, for developing personal worth and individual responsibility, and for realizing self-fulfillment. The development of social values, such as a sense of belonging, working together as a member of a group, and group responsibility, reinforced Williams' belief that physical education should help individuals adjust to and serve society.

Programmatically, Williams opposed formalized gymnastics because they thwarted, rather than enhanced, the learning of moral and social values. In contrast, sports and games provided the mechanism through which values such as initiative and self-discipline were learned. In his advocacy of this change in curricular content, he paralleled the ideas of Thomas Wood, who also taught at Teachers College.

Williams reiterated constantly that humans were unified beings. To overemphasize physical development distorted harmony and acknowledged a mind-body dualism. He insisted that physical education must concern itself with developing proper emotional responses, personal relationships, group behavior, mental learning, and other related outcomes. To achieve these objectives, he advocated that more time be devoted to class discussions, even at the expense of activity.

CONTRIBUTIONS TO PHYSICAL EDUCATION

Heavily influenced by the social and educational theories of John Dewey, Williams' philosophy answered an especially timely concern. Namely, he stated that the objectives of education and physical education were inextricably interwoven. Education's mission must rest on inculcating students with society's values, and physical education provided a vital laboratory for learning these lessons. So forceful were his writings that he convinced the profession that it should afford opportunities for individuals and groups to learn mentally and socially as well as physically.

REVIEW QUESTIONS

1. What were the philosophies of the new physical educators of the 1920s? How are these philosophies different from or similar to those of your teachers?

2. What was the significance of any two developments in physical education, other than the new physical education, during the 1900s? Who were the key leaders in these developments?

3. What is the difference between Jesse Williams' "education through the physical" and Charles McCloy's "education of the physical"?
4. What are several programs for which the American Alliance for Health, Physical Education, Recreation and Dance has provided leadership?
5. Why were intramural programs begun? Why did they flourish in the colleges?
6. How are the National Collegiate Athletic Association's influence and power different today from what they were in its earlier years?
7. Why were the sports opportunities provided for girls and women from the 1920s to the late 1960s different from those provided for boys and men?
8. What recreational developments have highlighted each decade since the 1930s? How popular has each been?
9. What have been the major developments in the promotion of youth fitness since the 1950s?
10. What were the major changes that resulted from passage of the following federal legislation: Title IX, Section 504 of the Rehabilitation Act of 1973, and the Education for All Handicapped Children Act of 1975.

STUDENT ACTIVITIES

1. Interview someone in the sports information office, athletic department, library, or news bureau who can help you learn about the earliest intercollegiate men's and women's sports at your institution. Based on this and on information that you can obtain from other sources, write a two-page description of each of these two programs.
2. Write a three-page comparison of the philosophies and major contributions of the "new physical educators."
3. Learn about the test items of the Prudential FITNESSGRAM. Divide into groups and administer these test items to each other.
4. Ask your professors who they think have been the most important physical educators of the twentieth century. Based on their responses and your reading, summarize the career and contributions of one of these persons in a two-minute class presentation.
5. Select one personality from a decade (1900s, 1910s, 1920s, 1930s, 1940s, 1950s, 1960s, 1970s, or 1980s). Write a three-page description of his or her contributions to physical education and sport.
6. Conduct a class debate about whether the most appropriate theme for physical education should be "education through the physical" or "education of the physical."
7. Select one theme each for school and for nonschool physical activity programs for the first half and second half of this century. Develop a position statement to explain the value and impact of each on the field of physical education and sport as it enters the twenty-first century.
8. Write a five-page paper comparing the major developments in men's and women's intercollegiate sports in the twentieth century.

REFERENCE

NEA Proceedings, 32:621, 1893, National Education Association.

SUGGESTED READINGS

Bandy S: Clark Wilson Hetherington: a pioneering spirit in physical education, *JOPERD* 56(1):20, 1985. Throughout his many years of service at Missouri, Wisconsin, New York University, and Stanford and in other professional positions, Clark Hetherington stressed achieving educational objectives and reinforced his advocacy of play.

Davenport J: Thomas Denison Wood; physical educator and father of health education, *JOPERD* 55(8):63, 1984. Stressing educational outcomes, Thomas Wood, at Stanford and Teachers College of Columbia University, initiated bachelor's degree programs in professional physical education. At the latter institution, he also started masters and doctors degree programs in physical education and undergraduate health education programs.

English EB: Charles H. McCloy: the research professor of physical education, *JOPERD* 54(4):16, 1983. Charles McCloy led in producing a scientific body of knowledge for physical education, especially in the area of strength tests, cardiovascular measures, classification indices, anthropometric scores, and character/social traits.

Gerber EW: The ideas and influence of McCloy, Nash, and Williams. In Bennett BL, editor: *The history of physical education and sport,* Chicago, 1972, The Athletic Institute. These three leaders of the profession displayed diverse philosophies of physical education and emphasized quite different objectives and program concepts. The period of 1930 to 1960 showed physical education to be an amalgamation of Jesse Williams' social goals, Jay Nash's lifetime activities, and Charles McCloy's advocacy of physical development.

Hardy, D, (ed): Girls' and women's sports—it is our season, *JOPERD,* 61(3):45, 1990. This nine-article feature emphasizes that the time is now for females to get involved in sports—at the grassroots level, in leadership positions, as coaches, in networking, in marketing and promotions, and in public relations.

Kozar A: R. Tait McKenzie: a man of noble achievement, *JOPERD* 55(7):27, 1984. Canadian R. Tait McKenzie throughout his life contributed significantly in the fields of physical education, medicine, and art.

Massengale J, Swanson R: *History of exercise and sport,* Champaign, 1996, Human Kinetics. This book provides a comprehensive history of the development of exercise and sport programs.

Miller SE: Inclusion of children and disabilities: can we meet the challenge?, *Phy Educ* 51(1):47, 1994. The impact of the Education for All Handicapped Children Act on physical education classes is presented along with the challenges that are presented in inclusion classrooms.

NAGWS Title IX toolbox, Reston, VA., 1992, American Alliance for Health, Physical Education, Recreation and Dance. This notebook includes reprints of legislation, litigation reports, articles, and quotes from leading individuals for use in the fight against sex discrimination in education-related athletics.

Stein JU: Total inclusion or least restrictive environment?, *JOPERD* 65(9):21, 1994. This article describes the principles of total inclusion and the least restrictive environment (LRE). It includes an explanation of the basic legislative requirements relevant to the LRE.

UNIT THREE

Issues, Trends, and the Future of Physical Education and Sport

The Changing Nature of Physical Education and Sport

KEY CONCEPTS

- Specializations and careers in fitness and exercise and sport science appeal to many students.
- School programs reflect their sports and games heritage, with the addition of the concepts of movement education, a renewed fitness emphasis, and a focus on the development of lifelong activity behaviors.
- Changes are occurring in certification requirements, competencies expected of teachers, and accreditation standards.
- Teachers of physical activity must understand and practice their legal obligations.
- An expansion of research by specialists in physical education and sport and technological advances contribute to an expanding knowledge base.
- Changes in competitive sport such as sport specialization, rule violations, pressures to win, and overcommercialization threaten the integrity of programs.

Traditionally, physical education has focused primarily on teaching sports and games to school children. Today, fitness specialists and exercise and sport scientists in various settings work with adults to help them establish and maintain lifelong activity programs. There have also been changes in school programs to guarantee that there are opportunities for all persons to meet their unique needs while engaged in progressively challenging experiences. Calls for a national curriculum and daily physical education for students, changes in certification requirements, competencies of teachers, and accreditation standards are related to efforts to improve the quality of education for students. The threat of lawsuits and the high risk of injuries mandate that individuals working in physical activity settings avoid negligent behavior by acting responsibly. Specialization, research, technology, and the scholarly pursuit of knowledge also furnish stimuli in this process of change. The integrity of physical education and sport programs is threatened, however, by an overemphasis on winning which has replaced value and skill development in sport.

FITNESS AND EXERCISE AND SPORT SCIENCE

The most dramatic change in physical education and sport has occurred in the proliferation of exercise and sport science majors as more and more students are choosing to pursue careers related to physical activity but outside of educational settings. The study of human movement and the application of its principles has broadened beyond the classroom while the field has grown more specialized as the quantity and quality of knowledge has expanded exponentially.

Colleges and universities responded to the decrease in physical education majors preparing to teach in the 1970s and 1980s by offering specializations. Students were attracted to these majors because they sought careers in the emerging areas of athletic training, corporate and commercial fitness, and sport management. Most of these graduates were attracted to positions that allowed them to work with adults participating in fitness and sports programs by choice. The diversity of career options and opportunities for advancement, travel, economic security, research, and management also appealed to many.

Career options in fitness and exercise and sport science have increased in recent years due to the media-reinforced appeal of cosmetic fitness, concern about health conditions related to lifestyle such as coronary heart disease and obesity, and skyrocketing health care costs. Those most likely to participate in fitness programs are the upper class, young adults, males, whites, suburban residents, and those with more education, although fitness enthusiasts occupy every demographic strata. Fitness specialists find their greatest challenge in trying to motivate individuals to initiate and maintain activity programs through self-discipline. The two most frequent explanations for not exercising are lack of time and poor motivation or discipline.

Fitness programs have expanded in private and public health and sports clubs, recreation departments, retirement homes, work sites, rehabilitation clinics, hotels, and resorts. Many have joined clubs specifically to receive instruction and encouragement from fitness leaders in aerobics and weight training. Besides teaching, individuals in these careers are expected to prescribe safe exercise programs, monitor members' progress, provide nutritional guidance, manage the facility, and sometimes supervise other personnel. Many fitness specialists and exercise and sport scientists are expected to provide smoking cessation classes, information about injury prevention and care, and exercises for the reduction of low back pain. Undergraduate students need to receive instruction to prepare them to handle these diverse responsibilities.

Increasingly, graduates of exercise and sport science curricula are working with adults and sometimes children in health and fitness programs. As described in previous chapters, these professionals are challenged to direct and manage programs that help unfit Americans develop and maintain personal fitness, to provide recreational opportunities in a wide variety of sports and games, and to offer leisure-time activities that may include spectator events, cruises, and theme parks.

Exercise and sport scientists may prescribe swimming as part of an aerobic conditioning program for clients. (Photo courtesy Bob Hilliard.)

Personal trainers, sport managers, recreation directors, and aerobics leaders are examples of how the graduates are changing the face of physical education.

Many college graduates will be required to obtain certifications and licensure in order to work in exercise and sport science positions. For example, exercise physiologists in Louisiana are required to hold a license in order to prescribe exercise programs. More and more health and fitness clubs are expecting their employees to hold certifications as personal trainers, aerobics leaders, or program directors. Almost all individuals responsible for providing emergency care to athletes in sports competitions are expected to have training in basic first aid and cardiopulmonary resuscitation, while persons serving as athletic trainers must hold certifications. Expectations for credentials verifying one's knowledge and skills will increasingly be mandated by states and employers to ensure that only qualified individuals work in physical activity situations.

Another phenomenon within careers in fitness is that program participants want to develop all-around wellness. While physical activity provides the setting, individuals are increasingly seeking emotional, spiritual, intellectual, and social benefits along with physical fitness. Many want to find balance through their workouts leading to the management of stress, self-esteem, development of friendships, and peace of mind. This means that program and exercise leaders must prepare themselves to address the whole person, not just their bodies. The expansion in program offerings in health and fitness clubs to include massage, yoga, nutrition counseling, stress management workshops, and musical and artistic outings along with personal fitness plans reflects this broadening focus.

ELEMENTARY SCHOOL PROGRAMS

Since the early 1900s (see Chapter 9), elementary school physical education programs have focused on teaching fundamental skills that led directly to the ability to play sports and games. Curricula that evolved during this century stressed a balanced and varied range of activities progressing from simple to complex through the grade levels. These activities included stunts, tumbling, simple games and relays, rhythmic activities, basic sport skills, lead-up games, and game play. Professional preparation courses and textbooks suggested the importance of progressions, percentages of time for each major category of activity, and instructional methodology.

In the 1960s, an alternative subject matter for elementary physical education was introduced in the United States. It was based on the concepts of spatial and body awareness; movement qualities of flow, force, space, and time; and relationships to others or to objects, as taught by Rudolf Laban. Students learned about their own space—relative to body size, movement task, and equipment—thereby gaining insights into their own capabilities and becoming more skilled movers.

Movement education has stressed these concepts. First, the lessons are both activity centered and student centered; each child determines specific movement patterns within parameters established by teachers, and the emphasis is on experimenting through moving, not on following instructions. Second, children are encouraged to analyze and to explore space, their bodies, and various uses for pieces of equipment, with the focus on self-directed or individualized learning, rather than on group drills and class goals. Third, problem solving and guided discovery are incorporated using challenges that students may respond to in many ways. The teacher guides students through movement experiences by imaginatively and creatively involving both their minds and their bodies. Fourth, children, independently and at their own rates of development, think about the challenges and then move in response. Since many solutions are possible and no

Elementary school students should be encouraged to learn fundamental movement skills. (Photo courtesy Bob Hilliard.)

group goals exist, each child is evaluated individually. Fifth, informality in class structure allows children to create freely and to learn at their own levels of achievement.

Today, in addition to selecting elementary physical education curricula that match their own philosophies, teachers must be aware of national guidelines and state requirements. The Council on Physical Education for Children (COPEC), a substructure of the National Association for Sport and Physical Education (NASPE), in its *Guidelines for Elementary School Physical Education,* identifies eight components that contribute to quality in each instructional program. The council recommends that each child develop motor skills and efficient movement patterns, achieve a high level of physical and health-related fitness, learn to express and communicate through movement, learn safe practices, gain self-understanding and acceptance, interact socially, and learn how to handle risk-taking, winning, losing, and other challenges. COPEC also advocates that elementary school children participate in an instructional program of physical education for a minimum of 150 minutes per week, exclusive of time allotted for free play and supervised play.

Whether movement education or a more traditional curriculum is the basis of an elementary physical education program, each is centered on the concept that movement is a child's first expressive opportunity. Since it is through movement experiences and challenges that the world is discovered, these must be developmentally appropriate for the age, size, and maturational level of each child. For example, parallel and cooperative activities are developmentally appropriate for five- to seven-year-olds, whereas team sports are not. Dodgeball, relays, musical chairs, and kickball are contraindicated games because they emphasize hitting classmates with balls, stress speed over technique, involve too little activity, and eliminate, rather than include, student participation. COPEC's document "Developmentally Appropriate Physical Education Practices for Children" describes these concepts in greater detail (the box on p. 243 provides examples).

MIDDLE SCHOOL PROGRAMS

The emergence of middle schools occurred in response to the unique developmental needs of students during this transitional period of physical, social, emotional, and intellectual growth. Students between the ages of 10 and 14 should have already been taught fundamental movement skills and basic fitness concepts. If so, they are ready to learn lead-up games, specific sports skills, and cooperative and competitive games and sports. Interest and ability grouping, rather than gender-role stereotyping, are essential during these pivotal years. Title IX of the 1972 Education Amendments mandates coeducational physical education classes; thus teachers are challenged to meet the social and physical needs of all their students equally.

Middle school students should participate in daily physical education classes of at least 50 minutes. Although seasonal team sports like volleyball, basketball, and softball may make up a portion of the curriculum, these young people need

DEVELOPMENTALLY APPROPRIATE PHYSICAL EDUCATION PRACTICES FOR CHILDREN

Appropriate practices	*Inappropriate practices*

Component: curriculum

The physical education curriculum has an obvious scope and sequence based on goals and objectives that are appropriate for all children. It includes a balance of skills, concepts, games, educational gymnastics, rhythms and dance experiences designed to enhance the cognitive, motor, affective, and physical fitness development of every child.

The physical education curriculum lacks developed goals and objectives and is based primarily on the teacher's interests, preferences, and background rather than those of the children. For example, the curriculum consists primarily of large group games.

Component: physical fitness tests

Ongoing fitness assessment is used as part of the ongoing process of helping children understand, enjoy, improve and/or maintain their physical health and well-being.

Test results are shared privately with children and their parents as a tool for developing their physical fitness knowledge, understanding, and competence.

As part of an ongoing program of physical education, children are physically prepared so they can safely complete each component of a physical test battery.

Physical fitness tests are given once or twice a year solely for the purpose of qualifying children for awards or because they are required by a school district or state department.

Children are required to complete a physical fitness test battery without understanding why they are performing the tests or the implications of their individual results as they apply to their future health and well-being.

Children are required to take physical fitness tests without adequate conditioning (e.g., students are made to run a mile after "practicing" it only one day the week before.)

Component: forming teams

Teams are formed in ways that preserve the dignity and self-respect of every child. For example, a teacher privately forms teams by using knowledge of children's skill abilities or the children form teams cooperatively or randomly.

Teams are formed by "captains" publicly selecting one child at a time, thereby exposing the lower-skilled children to peer ridicule.

Teams are formed by pitting "boys against the girls," thereby emphasizing gender differences rather than cooperation and working together.

Component: equipment

Enough equipment is available so that each child benefits from maximum participation. For example, every child in a class would have a ball.

Equipment is matched to the size, confidence, and skill level of the children so that they are motivated to actively participate in physical education classes.

An insufficient amount of equipment is available for the number of children in a class, (e.g., one ball for every four children).

Regulation or "adult size" equipment is used which may inhibit skill development, injure, and/or intimidate the children.

Girls and boys in middle school physical education often participate in games to develop their sports skills. (Photo courtesy Maggie McGlynn.)

instruction in the skills of throwing, catching, striking, and running independently and within lead-up games. Inclusion of various dance forms, tumbling, outdoor adventure activities, and games chosen by students will enrich the curriculum. Despite limited facilities and equipment, skill heterogeneity, and large class sizes, physical educators need to creatively design and implement broad curricula that meet the interests and needs of their students.

Vital components of middle school curricula are health-related physical fitness and sport skill-related fitness. Students in this age group are capable of taking greater responsibility for establishing personal goals for enhancing their cardiovascular endurance, muscular strength and endurance, and flexibility as well as goals for developing skill-related fitness. School programs should creatively reinforce the achievement of these goals using honor rolls on bulletin boards, schoolwide announcements, newsletter features, assembly recognitions, "I'm Fit" t-shirts, or opportunities to lead or select class fitness activities.

Motor skill, fitness, and cognitive standards should guide the development of sequential and progressive instruction. Assessments should be used periodically to ensure the attainment of these standards. Whenever possible, the physical education specialist, who is a certified physical education teacher, should integrate the instructional material with other subjects. With these standards in place, physical education programs of quality will be valued by middle school students, their parents, and school administrators. NASPE's Middle and Secondary School Physical Education Council's (MASSPEC) guidelines describe standards for these programs. (See the box on p. 245.)

SECONDARY SCHOOL PROGRAMS

Too often secondary school students are placed into physical education classes where they again are taught volleyball, basketball, and softball. Most would prefer receiving instruction in lifetime sports like bowling, golf, and tennis and in

MIDDLE SCHOOL PHYSICAL EDUCATION CURRICULUM

Physical activity programs should be comprehensive and well-balanced for the purpose of enhancing the psychomotor, cognitive, and affective development of individuals through the means of body movement. It has been long recognized that middle school students need quality physical experiences on a regular basis. The unique contribution of movement to the development of youth indicates that the middle school curriculum should provide for systematic instruction in a wide variety of activities. These offerings should include activities and concepts in the areas of conditioning and physical fitness, individual and dual sports, team sports, gymnastics, rhythms and dance, track and field, aquatics, and outdoor activities.

These physical education experiences must be planned and implemented in ways that will maximize the potential contribution to the overall goals of education. Basic concepts in physical education should be identified and integrated through a wide variety of activities. Therefore, we believe that middle school physical activity programs should:

- Allow students to participate in physical education on a regular basis equivalent to five times per week.
- Have philosophy and program goals consistent with the educational goals of the school system and reflective of the needs of middle school students.
- Represent a transitional progression from the elementary program to the high school program by providing the opportunity to participate in short explanatory units as well as longer units of instruction.
- Have specific instructional objectives for each activity.
- Have each activity developed on a continuum so that students can progress on an individual basis.
- Provide a variety of physical education activities for all students regardless of their level of physical development.
- Allow students to assess and evaluate their physical and social selves.
- Provide opportunities for the remediation of motor and fitness skills.
- Provide experiences that would promote motor skill development and fitness throughout life.
- Provide opportunities for students to be more self-directing in the selection of and performance in activities.
- Reflect a multimedia, multispace approach with opportunities for individual learning in skill acquisition and fitness development.
- Provide for interaction and coordination with other disciplines in the school curriculum.
- Provide the concepts and skills to pursue personal wellness for a lifetime.
- Develop skills that would enable them to apply technology to the development of personal wellness.
- Develop an appreciation of physical activity and its effect on total well being.

(*Guidelines for Middle School Physical Education,* 1992, National Association for Sport and Physical Education.)

fitness activities such as aerobics or weight training. Facility and equipment limitations can be overcome by using community lanes, courses, and courts and by
getting students to bring personal sports equipment. School gymnasia can be
used for a variety of aerobic activities, badminton, rock climbing and rappeling,
dance, one-wall racquetball, martial arts, and target archery. Weight training
equipment and aerobics machines, such as stationary bicycles, stair climbers, and
rowing machines, purchased for community use in the school or recreation center on weekends and evenings, could be used by students during the school day.
States and local educational agencies would be more likely to require or to offer
more elective courses to secondary school students if this broadened curricula
were available. Learning skills in sports that they can participate in enjoyably
throughout their lives should be a primary focus of secondary physical education
programs.

In secondary school physical
education, students can be
introduced to activities that
they may participate in during
their leisure hours and later in
life. (Photo courtesy Maggie
McGlynn.)

Volleyball may make up a part of the school curriculum,
but . . . (Photo courtesy Lisa Sense.)

. . . so should tennis, country and square dancing, and bowling. (Photo courtesy Lisa Sense.)

A second area of emphasis should be the opportunity to develop and implement individualized physical fitness programs. While these may be incorporated into aerobic or weight training classes, students should be encouraged to establish fitness goals using activities that they find personally satisfying. Secondary school students are capable of learning how to initiate and sustain fitness programs that they enjoy and are likely to continue throughout their adult lives.

Secondary school physical education classes should meet daily and be equal in length and class size to other subjects. (The box on p. 248 provides curricular guidelines for this and other secondary school programs.) Yet most states require less than annual physical education for high school graduation. Sometimes these classes are taught by individuals who focus their time and energy on their coaching responsibilities, thus shortchanging their students in physical education. Other issues challenging secondary school programs are too little instructional time, large classes, discipline problems, apathetic students, and meeting the needs of heterogeneous students by sex, race, and disability, while balancing the emphasis on competitive and cooperative activities. Relevant curricula, committed professionals backed by supportive administrators and parents, and instructional quality can alleviate many of these problems.

NATIONAL CURRICULUM

Even though education has been and continues to be considered first a state and then a local prerogative, rather than a national directive, some people have called for the establishment of a national curriculum. They advocate specified subject matter for kindergarten through grade 12 to replace the smorgasbord curricula

SECONDARY SCHOOL PHYSICAL EDUCATION CURRICULUM

- Students should be given the opportunity to participate in physical education on a regular basis equivalent to five times per week.
- The instructional program in physical education should not be confused with various cocurricular activities such as marching band, cheerleading, drill team, ROTC, or athletics.
- Instructional activities should be selected to realize the potential of achieving established program goals.
- Instructional activities should follow a scope and sequence within each unit of instruction, as well as from unit to unit, and year to year.
- Students should be introduced to a variety of physical activities to enable all students to meet appropriate individual goals.
- The curriculum should be structured to include a variety of fitness activities and to enable all students to meet appropriate individualized health-related fitness standards.
- Students should have opportunities to develop intermediate and advanced skills in personally selected activities.
- Students should have opportunities to develop participatory skills in adventure and other challenge activities.
- Students should be self-directed in conducting their individual lifelong physical activity programs.
- Students should have opportunities to develop skills that would enable them to apply technology to the development of personal wellness.

(*Guidelines for Secondary School Physical Education,* 1992, National Association for Sport and Physical Education.)

existing today. All content areas would be progressively and sequentially developed with measurable behavioral objectives.

Supporters of a national curriculum argue that it would provide a common educational foundation for all students and the progressive achievement of educational goals by meeting essential standards. They add that federal financial support would increase if a national curriculum were mandated. Opponents argue that only local leaders know what is the best education for their children; local control permits educational creativity. Also, state and local autonomy leads to greater funding with certain school districts.

If a national curriculum were adopted, the content for physical education would likely include physical fitness, sports skills mastery, and an integration of cognitive knowledge with motor skills and fitness. Activities would focus on preparing students to take responsibility for living active, fit lives.

In 1987, the 100th United States Congress, as a result of the persistent support of numerous legislators and vigorous lobbying efforts, passed the Physical Education Resolution, or House Concurrent Resolution 97 (box p. 249). Although not a national mandate, it encourages states and local educational agencies to provide quality, daily physical education for all children in kindergarten through grade 12. Although this resolution has no force of law, it is being used nationally

HOUSE CONCURRENT RESOLUTION 97

To encourage State and local governments and local educational agencies to provide high quality daily physical education programs for all children in kindergarten through grade 12.

Whereas physical education is essential to the development of growing children;

Whereas physical education helps improve the overall health of children by improving their cardiovascular endurance, muscular strength and power, and flexibility, and by enhancing weight regulation, bone development, posture, skillful moving, active lifestyle habits, and constructive use of leisure time;

Whereas physical education increases children's mental alertness, academic performance, readiness to learn, and enthusiasm for learning;

Whereas physical education helps improve self-esteem, interpersonal relationships, responsible behavior, and independence of children;

Whereas children who participate in high quality daily physical education programs tend to be more healthy and physically fit;

Whereas physically fit adults have significantly reduced risk factor for heart attacks and strokes;

Whereas the Surgeon General, in *Objectives for the Nation,* recommends increasing the number of school mandated physical education programs that focus on health-related physical fitness;

Whereas the Secretary of Education in *First Lessons—A Report on Elementary Education in America,* recognized that elementary schools have a special mandate to provide elementary school children with the knowledge, habits, and attitudes that will equip the children for a fit and healthy life; and

Whereas a high quality daily physical education program for all children in kindergarten through grade 12 is an essential part of a comprehensive education: Now, therefore, be it

Resolved by the House of Representatives (the Senate concurring), That the Congress encourages State and local governments and local educational agencies to provide high quality daily physical education programs for all children in kindergarten through grade 12.

to lobby state legislators and district board members to require daily physical education for all school children.

CHANGES IN CERTIFICATION REQUIREMENTS

State control of education has resulted in the establishment of certification standards for public school teachers. Most state departments of education (or the equivalent) specify the number of college or university hours or credits that must be completed before a person can teach. This requirement includes specific courses in the theory and application of instructional methodologies and in educational and developmental psychology and also includes a period of supervised student teaching. Physical education programs include disciplinary content, specialized methodology of teaching, and application of knowledge to students.

More and more states are requiring that students in all disciplines, including physical education, take the *Praxis Series: Professional Assessments for Beginning Teachers* to ensure that they possess both the general and the specialized knowledge necessary to teach. The *Praxis Series* includes assessments of academic skills (general for all teachers), subject matter, and classroom performance. Some states have developed their own competency tests. Many states have reciprocity agreements with other states, so that certification in one is equivalent to certification in the other. Certification in a nonreciprocating state requires the teacher's completion of one or more courses.

The most common requirement for interscholastic coaches is a teaching certificate, required for all coaches in about half of the states. For those states with no established standards and for those that commonly grant exceptions to the state regulations, liability concerns are paramount. Also a trend of hiring non-teachers to coach has developed because a number of coaching job openings do not have corresponding teaching positions. The lack of professional preparation in spite of the importance of providing educationally sound and safely conducted programs resulted in the development of a coaching certification position paper by the National Association for Girls and Women in Sport (NAGWS) and the National Association for Sport and Physical Education (NASPE).

COMPETENCY-BASED TEACHER EDUCATION

The conceptual basis of **competency-based teacher education** (CBTE) is that every teacher must possess certain competencies to be successful, and since a college's or university's faculty teaches and evaluates these competencies, its graduates qualify for certification. The box on pages 251–253 lists such competencies. In practical terms, CBTE in physical education requires attainment of disciplinary competencies such as knowledge of the oxygen transport system, the learning curve, feedback, motor skill acquisition, and the demonstration of minimal skills. The college or university is responsible for ensuring that all specified competencies are evaluated.

ACCREDITATION STANDARDS

Although not under the jurisdiction of state or federal governments, accreditation standards help ensure optimal quality education for teachers. Based on established criteria or standards, accreditation in teacher education, as enforced by the National Council for Accreditation of Teacher Education (NCATE), makes institutions accountable for program content. Although compliance is voluntary, many schools require that prospective teachers graduate from NCATE-accredited programs. Some institutions, however, choose not to seek NCATE accreditation believing that they can best monitor the quality of their programs.

For physical education, NASPE has been given the responsibility for ensuring that physical education undergraduate and graduate programs meet the minimal disciplinary standards. Each college or university must submit its curricula with accompanying explanatory documents to NASPE on a periodic basis. A national panel of reviewers assesses whether that program is in complete compliance. If it is not, changes are mandated.

COMPETENCIES REQUIRED OF PHYSICAL EDUCATION AND SPORT TEACHERS

General

1. Understand the scientific and philosophical bases of physical education and sport.
2. Develop a comprehensive knowledge about analyzing movement.
3. Develop a wide range of motor skills, especially those related to the area of teaching.
4. Study the teaching-learning processes specifically related to the area of physical education and sport.
5. Become knowledgeable about planning, organizing, administering, supervising, evaluating, and interpreting various aspects of a balanced physical education and sport program.

Elementary School Physical Education Teacher

We believe that:

1. Professional preparation for the elementary school physical education teacher should focus on the child in preschool through grade six. The curricula should result in the prospective teacher being competent in:

   a. Understanding child growth and development, with an emphasis on motor development
   b. A knowledge of and appreciation for the structure and function of human movement
   c. Observing and assessing children and their movements
   d. The knowledge and assessment of health-related and skill-related aspects of physical fitness
   e. A knowledge of learning processes, teaching strategies, and factors that affect motor learning
   f. Developing curriculum with emphasis on curriculum designs and strategies appropriate for elementary school programs
   g. Assessing and working with children who have special needs
   h. Personal skills and teaching skills in the content areas of fundamental movement patterns, games/sports, dance, gymnastics, and aquatics to meet the needs and interests of children in kindergarten through grade six

2. In addition, teacher preparation/staff development will provide:

   a. Laboratory and field experiences that are directed and supervised throughout the teacher preparation program
   b. Opportunities to become acquainted with a variety of elementary school organizational structures and the administration of physical education within those settings. The professional preparation curricula should culminate in certification specific for teaching children in the elementary grades

3. Preparation for the classroom teacher should include an understanding of the relationship of physical growth and motor development to the total development and learning experience of the child. Course work in movement skills, methods, and content of elementary school physical education programs should be required. Laboratory assignments which provide for experiences with children in physical education are essential.
4. Continuous staff development opportunities should be provided to meet the individual needs of educators concerned with physical education programs for children. Teachers in the field should be involved in the planning of such programs.
5. Personnel concerned with teacher preparation and staff development in physical education should have continuous interaction with children. They need also to be aware of current research and legislation and be able to interpret them for application.

Guidelines for Elementary School Physical Education, 1988, National Association for Sport and Physical Education.

(Continued)

COMPETENCIES REQUIRED OF PHYSICAL EDUCATION AND SPORT TEACHERS (CONTINUED)

Middle School Physical Education Teacher

Preparation of teachers should include courses and teaching experiences that pertain to the education of middle school students. The in-service education program for physical education teachers is imperative to assure skilled and knowledgeable teachers to administer the varied programs required for middle schools. Administrative support is necessary to encourage and to provide opportunities to attend workshops, meetings, and conventions which keep physical education personnel current on materials and information.

Educational programs should prepare teachers who:

- Have an understanding of the middle school concept
- Possess teaching certification in physical education
- Avoid gender-role discrimination and gender stereotyping by grouping students according to interest and ability levels
- Understand the physical, social, emotional, and intellectual characteristics that are unique to middle school youth
- Possess a positive self-concept and demonstrate respect for the dignity and worth of all individuals
- Have knowledge and skills of developmentally appropriate practices to work with students on a one-to-one basis
- Are familiar with a wide variety of skills and activities in order to implement the exploratory qualities of the program
- Apply various teaching styles and modify rules, equipment, and instructional stations to conform to the needs of the learner
- Continually strive to increase their knowledge and understanding to meet the changing needs of middle school students and their learning environment
- Can interact with students and fellow teachers in a way that is supportive of the special needs of the middle school student
- Will assume leadership in providing for the expanding physical experiences for all students in the school
- Are able to interpret the goals and objectives of the activity programs to students and their parents
- Use instructional strategies based upon the developmental and skill level of the student as well as the nature of the activity
- Are able to maintain and manage record-keeping systems for planning sequential instruction

Guidelines for Middle School Physical Education, 1992, National Association for Sport and Physical Education.

Secondary School Physical Education Teacher

Educational programs should be conducted by certified physical education teachers who:

- Serve as positive role models of personal health, fitness, skill, and enjoyment of participating in physical activities
- Are knowledgeable in curriculum and instruction, demonstrate sportsmanship and sensitivity to students' needs
- Know and apply effective teaching strategies that provide maximum student time on task

COMPETENCIES REQUIRED OF PHYSICAL EDUCATION AND SPORT TEACHERS (CONTINUED)

- Apply various teaching methods and instructional strategies that personalize physical education classes and allow students to attain optimum personal growth
- Provide for equitable instruction and participation with regard to individual needs of the student
- Demonstrate professional commitment through membership and involvement in professional organizations and other enrichment experiences
- Plan program activities that promote understanding of cultural diversity
- Accommodate the needs of exceptional students in regular physical education classes
- Understand that the instructional program and athletics are separate and distinct and strive to keep a balanced perspective between the dual role of teaching and coaching
- Use recognized assessment and evaluation instruments in planning for accountability of the instructional program
- Apply technology in their teaching on a regular and continuing basis

Guidelines for Secondary School Physical Education, 1992, National Association for Sport and Physical Education.

Two phases basic to accreditation are the institutional self-study and the peer evaluation. Nationally established standards and an institution's stated purposes and goals provide the measuring devices for the self-study. After a comprehensive examination of each institution's governance, curricula, faculty, students, physical resources, self-evaluation, program review, and long-range planning, the accreditation committee documents the degree of adherence to the standards. Next, a visiting team of evaluators conducts an objective study to determine the accuracy of the report. Its judgments are submitted in writing to the accrediting agency, which decides to grant or to deny accreditation for a five-year period. Thereafter, continuing accreditation is granted every five years if a visiting team positively evaluates the program quality.

Accreditation standards apply in nonschool physical activity settings, too. As described in Chapter 6, certifications are offered by several organizations because employers are requiring that sport and exercise leaders attain a specified level of competence. Whether leading group exercises, serving as a personal trainer, teaching aquatics activities, providing athletic training, or coaching youth sports, increasingly certifications are mandated. Individuals want to participate in programs that are conducted at standards of quality that ensures that accurate and up-to-date information and activities are provided.

The importance of accreditation for quality assurance and the desire of the teaching profession to govern itself have resulted in the establishment of separate commissions for accrediting secondary schools and elementary schools.

LEGAL LIABILITY

The risk of injury in physical education and sport settings necessitates that teachers, leaders, supervisors, and administrators understand and comply with their responsibilities. This compliance is especially important because of the predisposition of many to seek legal redress for real or perceived mistreatment. *Negligence,* the most frequent claim, occurs with the teacher's or director's failure to act as a reasonable and prudent person should, resulting in injury to another person. Four factors must exist for negligence to be proven:

- Presence of a duty (such as providing supervision of a class)
- A breach of that duty (failure to act as a reasonable and prudent person would under similar circumstances)
- Proximate cause of the injury (the action or failure to act caused the subsequent injury)
- The substantial nature of the injuries (Were the injuries substantial?)

There are two legal defenses against negligence:

- Assumption of risk by program participants (however, they must know, understand, and appreciate these risks).
- Contributory or comparative negligence by the person injured. Contributory negligence refers to behavior by the plaintiff that contributed to the injury. Sometimes contributory negligence can bar recovery for the injury. Comparative negligence apportions damages between a negligent plaintiff and a negligent defendant. Some states have adopted contributory negligence, while others use comparative negligence.

In order to avoid liability for negligence, you must act reasonably by recognizing potentially hazardous conditions or situations and by protecting your students and clients from them. First, general supervision is always required when activity occurs. This responsibility includes knowing what to look and listen for, where to stand, how to move around, and what to do when a problem arises. The more dangerous the activity, such as a gymnastics class or a stress test, the closer the specific supervision mandated. Second, not only do you have a responsibility to eliminate hazards of which you had *actual notice,* or known hazards, but also those of which you had *constructive notice,* those that any reasonable and responsible person should have noticed, such as broken glass on a floor. This responsibility requires informing your supervisor of the necessity of repairing or removing objects or situations that might cause injury. Third, the person in charge should make regular inspections, involve participants in taking the responsibility for their own safety, do preventive maintenance, and post warnings about using facilities. Fourth, every participant should be warned about potential risks; specifically, each person must know, understand, and appreciate the risks and potential for injuries in the activity. The box on page 255 summarizes some of the guidelines to avoid the charge of negligence.

One recommendation for helping students and activity participants know, understand, and appreciate risks and safety rules is the use of an *agreement to participate.* This is not a waiver, parental consent form, or guarantee against lawsuits. However, an agreement to participate may help instructors in one of the defenses against negligence because it articulates what assumption of risk means. An agreement to participate, written specifically for each activity, should describe the specific skills required for safe participation, the possible injury consequences, and the important rules for safe participation. On this form, the participant should be questioned about any preexisting physical condition and specifically about any limitation. A reminder that a student may discontinue activity due to discomfort or stress also may be included. The final statement signed by the participant should specify a knowledge, understanding, and appreciation of the risks involved in the activity. In preparing an agreement to participate, the instructor should ensure that it is consistent with the legal concept of the defense of assumption of risk.

Several other steps can also be taken to avoid liability. First, provide instruction to all students in the proper techniques for skill execution. Meeting this responsibility requires preparation of and adherence to sequential and progressive instructional plans that clearly show that no students are expected to attempt skills that they are incapable of executing safely. Second, ensure that students' fitness, conditioning, and ability levels are sufficient to participate in the day's activities. Failure to ascertain students' limitations or apprehensions may lead to injuries for which the teacher is liable. Third, enforce safety rules and regulations. Strict compliance with school, club, or corporate policies, including those governing the reporting of accidents and injuries, is critical.

Fourth, when injuries occur, instructors, who should hold current cardiopulmonary resuscitation and first aid certifications, must respond appropriately. For

One liability issue is what are appropriate sports activities for school and college curricula. (Photo courtesy Lisa Sense.)

MANAGEMENT STRATEGIES TO AVOID THE CHARGE OF NEGLIGENCE

- Follow the guidelines established by the school, employer, and state for safe programs.
- Prepare a statement of safety procedures and distribute it to the program director and to parents, if appropriate.
- Establish an operational system of emergency care in the event of a serious injury.
- Establish a system for identifying, treating, reporting, and recording all injuries.
- Purchase the best equipment that the budget will allow from reputable dealers.
- Make sure that all facilities are safe and free of hazards.
- Follow sound practices and program-approved activities that specify appropriate skill progressions.
- Learn and teach using the latest and the best instructional techniques.
- Closely supervise all activities.
- Carry liability insurance with broad coverage.

example, any person suffering from a possible neck, head, or back injury should not be moved without the emergency responders' supervision. Fifth, do not use inadequate, ill-fitting, or defective equipment. The instructor must regularly inspect all equipment, removing any in need of repair or replacement. Sixth, only qualified persons should supervise physical activity. Teachers' aides, student teachers, personal trainers, aerobics instructors, and tennis or other sport professionals, when responsible for one or more students, are held responsible for their welfare.

Closely adhering to each of these suggestions and the risk management strategies listed in the box on page 255 not only will help you to meet your obligation to those you instruct, but will also greatly reduce the likelihood of your becoming the defendant in a negligence lawsuit. Also, unless your employer provides adequate insurance protection for you, you should purchase liability insurance.

GENERALISTS REPLACED BY SPECIALISTS

Traditionally physical educators were generalists who could teach a dozen or more sports, coach two or three teams, and still have time to sweep the gymnasium floor. They proudly considered themselves generalists who focused on the practical field of teaching. Students majoring in physical education were exposed to its breadth. Today, students are more likely to specialize and study in-depth one of the applied sport sciences.

The knowledge explosion in recent years has influenced all subject areas. Expanded research efforts, technological advances, and computer-assisted data generation and analyses have aided this proliferation. The quality and quantity of information has led to increasing specializations for two primary reasons. First, the sheer volume of books, research, reports, and scholarly papers makes it difficult for individuals to gain a comprehension of any entire discipline. Second, a greater understanding of a subdiscipline encourages people to specialize in an area of particular interest. For example, the coach who prefers treating athletes' injuries and helping them rehabilitate to develop game strategies can now become a full-time athletic trainer. The physical education generalists who taught everything but really enjoyed teaching weight training may choose a career involving only this specialty.

As a result of the popularity of physical activity and sport throughout society, diverse careers have emerged. Colleges and universities have responded by broadening the types of majors offered. Most students today choose to specialize in athletic training, sport management, fitness, or exercise and sport science because these areas interest them and because of the availability of jobs. When hired, they will be expected to remain knowledgeable in their specialty, not the entire field of physical education and sport.

Graduate degree programs at the masters and doctors levels are increasingly specialized. For example, graduate students with career goals of becoming exercise physiologists or sport psychologists study specific content areas, like biochemistry and experimental psychology, respectively. Corporate fitness directors, club managers, head athletic trainers in universities, and marketing directors for

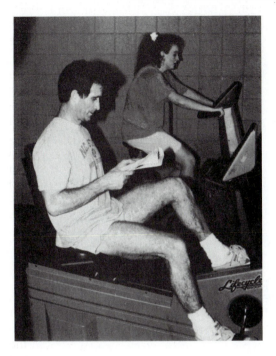

Aerobic conditioning can be attained and maintained by exercising on a stationary bicycle.

professional sports teams often must have master's degrees because of the scope of their responsibilities, which often include personnel and financial management.

College faculty are required to have the minimum of master's degrees, while university professors must have earned doctorates. Both groups are usually expected to teach in their areas of specialization. Most universities also require scholarly productivity of faculty including research-based presentations at professional conferences and publications in peer-reviewed journals. Most of this scholarship is focused on one area of specialization as faculty interests in teaching and research narrow.

PROLIFERATION OF RESEARCH

Within the past decade, the quantity of scholarly publications and presentations has been overwhelming. Responding to university mandates, specialists dedicated to the expansion of knowledge in their areas are eagerly conducting research and reporting their findings. For many, the surging tide of scholarly research is becoming the primary justification for physical education's existence within institutions of higher education. Physical education and sport professionals in non-traditional settings, such as corporate fitness centers, recreation programs, and fitness and health clubs, are also conducting research on their clientele and about their programs and sharing their findings.

Another growing area of research in physical education focuses on pedagogy. Studies in this disciplinary area include observations of teaching, analyses of time-on-task and academic learning time, and observations of how students' performances match expectancy efforts or how a teacher expects them to

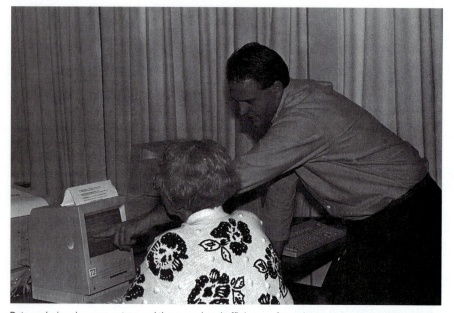

Data analysis using computers and the speed and efficiency of word processing enables the quality of increasing numbers of research projects.

respond or to execute. Although a relatively new area, the research in this specialization has the potential to affect dramatically the quality of instructional classes in all settings.

Technology contributes to the proliferation of research in physical education and sport. Within sports medicine, athletes can recover faster as a result of advanced surgical techniques and computer-monitored rehabilitation programs. Data collection on the incidence and cause of injuries can be used to redesign conditioning and practice drills to both reduce injury and speed rehabilitation. Sport psychologists use biofeedback and relaxation techniques to enhance performance; biomechanists apply computer technology to skill execution in order to both improve technique and reduce the risk of injury. Computer analyses of blood lactates, oxygen exchange, workloads, and drug effects are invaluable to exercise physiologists' understanding of how the body functions under the stress of exercise.

Library retrieval systems and CD-ROMs help researchers in all disciplines keep abreast with the burgeoning of information and data, allowing them to replicate studies or to build upon the findings of colleagues. Electronic mail assists researchers' collaboration in a timely fashion. Without the use of personal computers for word processing, access to data analyses on mainframe computers, and readily available information on the Internet, the productivity of today's university, corporate, and community researchers would be slowed tremendously. Increasingly in the future, physicians, sport psychologists, sport biomechanists, exercise physiologists, and athletic trainers will share their expertise and research to the benefit of school students and the general public as well as world-class athletes.

A frequently mentioned criticism of researchers in physical education and sport is their failure to apply their findings. Technology can help to alleviate at least part of this problem by focusing on practical as well as theoretical studies, by disseminating new information more widely, and by focusing on specific situations in need of change rather than on generalities. Physical educators who could benefit from the findings also have a responsibility to work with researchers to apply new information in a timely fashion. Versatile equipment, data processing, and assistance with thorough and accurate experimental design in studies are but a few of the contributions that technology can make to close the research-to-practice gap.

CHANGES IN COMPETITIVE SPORT

Specialization in one sport, circumvention of rules to gain competitive advantages, pressures to win, and overcommercialization are the major changes pervading competitive sport from the youth to the collegiate level. Due to these negative factors, many of the lofty values associated with sport, like fair play, have eroded.

The rationale for early and continued specialization in one sport is that only focused training can lead to victories and attainment of long-term goals such as Olympic medals, professional contracts, or college grants-in-aid. While children aspire for what over 99% will never achieve, they miss the enjoyment of playing various sports and risk overuse problems, such as epiphyseal injuries. Interscholastic athletes are increasingly advised by coaches and parents to focus on only one sport, which again reduces fun and leads to overuse injuries. While some high school students still earn multiple varsity letters, the college dual sport athlete is almost an anachronism. The time and training required of intercollegiate athletes usually precludes participation in multiple sports.

Coaches often instruct their athletes in how to circumvent game rules, especially without getting penalized. At early ages, youth and school sport participants learn that faking an injury to get the clock stopped, calling an opponent's ball out when it helps you win, and lying about one's legal guardian in order to play on

Competitive opportunities in sport include cycling and triathlons.
(Photo courtesy Craig Premo.)

a desired team are acceptable, and even praised, behaviors. Later athletes may take anabolic steroids, accept money from a booster to ensure attendance at a certain university, or cheat on a test to maintain academic eligibility because these actions may contribute to victories.

Pressures to win are exerted on athletes of all ages by coaches, parents, and fans. In some coaches' overzealousness for victories, they excessively stress youngsters' arms and bodies, verbally and physically abuse children, and teach and model unethical behaviors. They also emphasize winning so much that by age 12 over 50% of all youth sport participants drop out because they are no longer having fun and developing skills. Too many parents try to live through their children by taking fulfillment from their youthful sports achievements. Others may even withhold love from children who do not perform to parental expectations. Families have moved or separated and other children have been neglected in the pursuit of potential lucrative professional sports careers. Fans adore and reward athletes who win; yet, they speak disparagingly about and disassociate themselves from the less successful.

Commercialization in sport is both a reality and a necessity in our capitalistic society. Corporate and community funding, fans' financial support, and the media are not inherently bad. Problems occur, however, when these factors outweigh developmental and educational values. Communities may seek recognition and status through winning age-group Pop Warner National Championships or state basketball titles. Corporate sponsorships help youth, school, and college sports teams pay their expenses, yet how much control should these sponsors have in the hiring or firing of coaches or in the awarding of advertising space in sports arenas? Similarly, fans who donate huge sums of money to athletic programs often want more than preferential seating and parking. Television already dictates, or at least strongly influences, who gets broadcasted and when and where the teams compete. Many wonder how long television can charge sponsors increasingly higher prices for advertisements.

While certainly not the only changes, sport specialization, rule violations, pressures to win, and overcommercialization have impacted competitive sport at all levels. Combined they pose threats to the integrity of these programs unless they are moderated or potential abuses are controlled.

SUMMARY

Physical education and sport programs will continue to change during your career. Increasingly, public and private health and sports clubs, worksite programs, rehabilitation clinics, and retirement homes will meet the fitness and activity needs of adults, thus calling for specialists in these areas. While school programs reflect their sports and games heritage, they have broadened to include movement education, fitness, and lifetime activities and sports. Educational reforms with an emphasis on standards, discussion about a national curriculum, and the congressional call for daily physical education may significantly affect funding for school programs and lead to important changes. Tougher standards for state certification and accreditation seem inevitable as accountability requirements increase. The call for coaching certification may be answered because of liability concerns as well as the responsibility to meet young athletes' needs. Teachers must take seriously their responsibilities to provide safe environments for learning and to act responsibly when injuries occur. A virtual knowledge explosion in physical education and sport, accompanied by expanded research activities and technological advances, has widespread implications for the future. Essential for all programs are the dissemination of the latest research findings and the utilization of this information by practitioners in all settings. Coaches, parents, and fans need to moderate their emphasis on winning to deter the harmful effects of sport specialization, rule violations, pressures on athletes, and overcommercialization.

RENÉ REVIS SHINGLES
Assistant Professor
Central Michigan University
Mount Pleasant, Michigan

EDUCATION
B.A., Health and Physical Education, University of North Carolina at Chapel Hill
M.S., Physical Education: Athletic Training/Sports Medicine, Illinois State University
Ph.D., Candidate in psycho-social aspects of sport, Department of Physical Education and Exercise Science, Michigan State University

JOB RESPONSIBILITIES AND HOURS

As a university assistant professor and certified athletic trainer, René teaches in a sports medicine/athletic training curriculum accredited by the Commission on Accreditation of Allied Health Education Programs. Courses taught include Introduction to Athletic Training, Therapeutic Exercise, and Athletic Training Practicum: Lower Extremity. In her supervision of the Injury Care Center, René coordinates the schedule, the evaluation of the student staff, the budget, the inventory, the record keeping, and the reports. Her typical work hours are 8:00 A.M. to 6:00 P.M. Some evening and weekend hours are also required for class preparation, student evaluations, and center supervision.

SPECIALIZED COURSE WORK, DEGREES, AND WORK EXPERIENCES NEEDED FOR THIS CAREER

NATA certification and experience as a volunteer, intern, or employed athletic trainer are essential prerequisites to teaching in this applied science. Licensure as an athletic trainer is required in some states. René states that all athletic training courses, sport sciences classes such as exercise physiology, and courses that taught instructional methodology have been beneficial in her current position. A master's degree is the minimal academic credential for a college position, although a doctoral degree in sports medicine or a related area is preferred.

SATISFYING ASPECTS

René enjoys developing relationships and sharing experiences with students who want to be athletic trainers. She finds it rewarding to work with and mentor future professionals.

JOB POTENTIAL

She holds a tenure track position that carries with it the opportunity to advance from assistant to associate to full professor. Depending upon experience and academic degrees held, assistant professors at her university start with salaries between $27,000 and $32,000. Research, scholarly publications, and teaching proficiency are required for promotion in rank and tenure. Salary increases and additional responsibilities usually are associated with this advancement.

SUGGESTIONS FOR STUDENTS

Obtaining a terminal (doctorate) degree is essential for teachers to advance in higher educa-tion. She advises students to get involved in professional organizations (e.g., the NATA and AAHPERD) and to appreciate and cultivate relationships with mentors.

REVIEW QUESTIONS

1. Why do more students choose to specialize in fitness and exercise and sport science than to prepare to teach physical education in the schools?
2. What are the differences between a traditional elementary school curricu-lum and a movement education program?
3. How should middle school and secondary school physical education and curricula differ?
4. Why are teachers expected to achieve and demonstrate certain compe-tencies?
5. How do accreditation standards affect school and nonschool programs?
6. What four factors must exist for negligence to be proven?
7. What are several risk management strategies that you should take to ensure that the rights of all participants in your program are being protected?
8. What is the difference between a generalist approach and a specialized approach to physical education?
9. How has technology changed research in physical education and sport?
10. What four changes have significantly affected competitive sport at all levels?

STUDENT ACTIVITIES

1. Ask a faculty member at your institution who led in the development of undergraduate specializations why these programs were established?
2. Secure a copy of the local elementary, middle school, and secondary school standards and curricula for physical education; analyze them to determine if the standards are being achieved through a progressive and sequential program.
3. Make a list, using library resources or information obtained through inter-views, of the competencies that professionals in physical education-related careers should demonstrate.
4. Read two articles in any professional journals or popular magazines that describe how an expanded knowledge base and technology in physical education and sport have positively affected nonschool programs. Summa-rize these impacts in two or three sentences each.

5. Read two articles about negligent behavior by people in physical education-related careers. What action did they take or fail to take? What was the outcome of the litigation if there was litigation?

6. Do a risk management assessment of a physical activity program, a sporting event, or a sports facility. List all potentially unsafe actions or situations.

SUGGESTED READINGS

Conn JH, editor: The litigation connection—perspectives of risk control for the 1990s, *JOPERD* 64(2):15, 1993. This seven-article feature examines civil rights, employment issues, supervision, the duty to properly instruct, proper classification, establishment and enforcement of rules and regulations, and legal obligations relative to facilities.

Cotton DJ: What am I getting myself into? Agreements to participate, *Strategies* 5(4):13, 1992. This article recommends the use of agreements to participate to inform students of the nature of the class activity, the behaviors expected of them, and the risks involved in the activity. The agreement should include statements about the nature of the activity, the possible injury consequences, and the behavioral expectations and physical condition of the participant; it should conclude with a statement affirming the knowledge, understanding, and appreciation of the risks involved in the activity.

Graham G, editor: Developmentally appropriate physical education for children, *JOPERD* 63(6):29, 1992. In this nine-article feature, the authors describe the components of a developmentally appropriate program for elementary children, which includes sequencing of games, dance, gymnastics, and fitness. Activities that should be excluded are also described.

Graham KC, Stueck P, editors: Decisions for middle and high school physical education, *JOPERD* 63(7):65, 1992. This six-article feature argues that practitioners, supervisors, and professional preparation faculty need to work together more effectively for excellence in secondary physical education and suggests ways to promote cooperation.

Gray GR: Safety tips from the expert witness, *JOPERD* 66(1):18, 1995. This paper informs physical educators and coaches about how to avoid negligent actions and decisions through an understanding of what expert witnesses will testify in liability cases.

Hutchinson GE: Gender fair teaching in physical education, *JOPERD* 66(1):42, 1995. To remove gender-based inequities, physical educators must use inclusive teaching behaviors, instructional strategies, and management approaches. Recommendations for gender equitable programs are suggested.

Lirgg CD: Effects of same-sex versus coeducational physical education on self-perceptions of middle and high school students, *Res Q* 64(3):324, 1993. In a study of a 10-lesson basketball unit, middle school students preferred same-sex classes and high school students preferred coeducational classes.

Placek JH: Rethinking middle school physical education curriculum: an integrated thematic approach, *Quest* 44(3):330, 1992. After reviewing current approaches, the author suggests that physical education should be integrated into the core curriculum of middle schools.

Stroot SA: Contemporary crisis or emerging reform? A review of secondary school physical education, *J of Teach in PE* 13(4):333, 1994. A review of the literature reveals three themes that describe current perceptions about secondary school physical education. These include restructuring and reform, curriculum and instruction, and contextual factors in the secondary school setting.

Tannehill D, O'Sullivan M: Teacher certification testing in physical education, *J of Teach in PE* 9:227, 1990. This article reports that state AHPERD officers and state directors of physical education are minimally involved with teacher testing. The call is made for greater leadership in the assessment of teaching effectiveness.

Trends and Issues in Physical Education-Related Careers

KEY CONCEPTS

- The benefits of a fitness lifestyle should be made available to persons of all ages who will become active participants.
- Consumers need to be aware of unfounded claims as they purchase sporting goods and services.
- Effective public relations includes influencing decision makers about the importance of quality physical activities programs and advocating for healthy lifestyles.
- Professionals face several challenges, such as demographic and economic changes, in meeting the recreational and leisure services needs of all groups.
- Career burnout can be alleviated by recognizing and managing contributing factors and by providing appropriate recognition for competence, for example, through job security and merit pay.
- Issues facing physical educators include standards and assessment, instructional challenges, program threats, an identity dilemma, and role conflicts for teachers and coaches.
- A major health need facing Americans of all ages is the importance of attaining and maintaining a level of fitness that contributes to a positive quality of life. For professionals working in physical activity settings, our challenge is to lead those we serve to value physical fitness and health.

This chapter examines a few of the issues and trends impacting physical education-related careers in addition to the importance of physical activity for all. Consumer education plays a part as individuals seek out fitness equipment, products, programs, and services. The role of public relations includes the publicizing of quality programs as well as advocating for the value of living healthy lives.

Providers of recreational and leisure services must adapt to changing demographics, family, work, and economic factors, while promoting the quality of their programs.

Maintaining one's competence as a physical educator is critical to successful teaching and to job security which depends on the competent completion of established, and sometimes changing, job responsibilities. Merit pay is one way that has been proposed to reward and promote exemplary job performance and to prevent burnout. Issues impacting school physical education and sport programs include standards and assessment, instructional challenges, program threats, identity dilemma, and teacher-coach role conflict.

THE VALUE OF PHYSICAL EDUCATION ACTIVITY FOR EVERYONE

Physical education is for everyone, but convincing all the various publics of this fact remains a major challenge. The objectives of physical education in the schools include learning and applying fitness concepts, learning motor and fundamental sports skills and lifetime sports, gaining knowledge about sports rules and strategies, and enhancing social and emotional values and behaviors. As discussed in Chapter 1, these objectives can only be met when teachers focus on them and teach to ensure their achievement. Teachers must provide quality programs and promote the value of these programs to school administrators, legislators, and parents.

Children and youth must learn healthful living habits while in the school, because many will not attend college or be able to afford sport club memberships or expensive private exercise equipment. During the critical elementary years, students need to learn how to develop cardiovascular endurance, focusing on the frequency, intensity, and duration of exercise. They need to learn to walk, jog, swim, cycle, and jump rope as methods of developing aerobic endurance. They need to learn how to attain and maintain muscular strength, endurance, and flexibility, because these health-related fitness components will enhance not only how they feel but also their ability to study, work, and play more easily and productively. Closely aligned with these needs is the importance of teaching children sports skills that they can use throughout life. Basic throwing, catching, striking, and locomotor movements are easily transferable to tennis, golf, bowling, dance, and other lifetime activities. Teachers should demonstrate and positively reinforce development of cooperative behavior, teamwork, fair play, and the ability to be a follower and a leader. Individually, students nurture self-confidence and self-worth by being successful in achieving personal goals. Concurrently with these psychomotor and affective outcomes, teachers should ensure that children are provided information about nutrition, diseases, environmental concerns, and the harmful effects of drugs.

After ensuring that quality experiences are offered to their students, teachers should invite school administrators, legislators, and parents to observe what physical education really is. Hosting PTA/PTO programs, parents' nights, mall demonstrations, and other special events signifies that physical education is vital to the health and well-being of students. Parents should be encouraged to participate more fully in the education of their children.

At the high school level, there should be a continuation of the emphasis on fitness development, lifetime sports, and health issues such as smoking, drugs, sex education, and nutrition. At this level especially, it is important to give students some options for what sports and activities they want to learn. Although some consumer information may be relevant earlier, the teen years lend themselves well to consumer education. Adolescents need to learn how to differentiate between the facts and fallacies of fitness ads. Although some home exercise equipment is beneficial, such as rowing machines or exercise bicycles, belts that rub off fat or machines that supposedly help a person lose weight without effort blatantly misrepresent the truth. What are the caloric and nutritional components of the average fast-food meal? Are any diet centers or diet programs safe or worth the money? Should a high school athlete take anabolic steroids? Should a person smoke cigarettes or marijuana? What are the effects of alcohol on the body and its fitness? Where can a person find a qualified aerobics instructor? Given these important questions that demand answers and the potential benefits of school physical education, it is imperative that the schools fund physical education and health curricula.

Those who refuse to provide this funding claim that physical education is nonessential. The poor fitness levels of school-age American children, which may currently be the worst ever, speak otherwise. Another argument is that community programs and interscholastic athletics can provide students with adequate sports opportunities. However, because of cost, poor skills, jobs, and other factors, many students, especially those who drop out of school, never participate in these programs. And, in most of them, competition rather than instruction is stressed.

Many colleges and universities have retained their required programs on the basis of the importance of educating the poorly skilled and those who have had poor physical education and sport experiences in the schools. While some colleges and universities have reduced their requirements because of budget limitations, many others have been able to keep some required courses, often taught by graduate students. In many of the institutions with elective programs only, these programs have had to become entirely self-supporting; students elect any activity course available, but they pay instructional, facility usage, and equipment rental fees. On other campuses, this pay-as-you-participate approach applies only to some off-campus or nontraditional offerings. This type of program is limited to those who are genuinely interested in a particular activity or sport and who can afford to enroll in it. However, in elective programs, those who need physical education the most may not choose to enroll.

One trend that may help school physical education is that parents who realize the importance of living fit lifestyles may demand that the schools help their children learn these habits. Parents must be convinced of the importance of developing the fitness parameters themselves; by making lifestyle changes at home, they can reinforce school and college learning. Again, the involvement of parents in the education of their children is vital to their learning and the usage of knowledge and skills.

In 1992, the American Heart Association added physical inactivity to high blood pressure, smoking, and high blood cholesterol as the significant contributors to heart disease. To thwart the effects of these, many inactive, overweight adults are changing their habits. As middle-aged and senior citizens join the millions of

PROGRAM ADHERENCE FACTORS

- Set realistic goals.
- Implement an individualized and progressive program that is safe.
- Ensure proper supervision that includes education and motivation.
- Be patient—developing fitness takes time.
- Ensure convenient access to facilities at convenient times.
- Provide periodic assessments and feedback.
- Provide family and peer group encouragement and reinforcement.
- Participate in fun and satisfying activities.

others who are walking to stay fit, these segments of the population reinforce being physically active. To help prevent their becoming the next coronary statistics, older Americans are quitting smoking, reducing alcohol consumption, ridding their diets of many sources of cholesterol, and exercise walking, swimming, and cycling. Other popular activities include fishing, camping, aerobic exercises, and bowling. For those restricted by age or physical limitations, retirement homes, recreation departments, churches, and hospitals are increasingly providing appropriate opportunities for movement, sports, and recreational pastimes. In fact, providing for the leisure needs of this age group may open up the greatest number of physical education-related jobs in the next century.

Related to the issue of the value of physical education is the challenge of how to get individuals who have begun exercise programs to continue them. Adherence is a pervasive concern of everyone who prescribes exercises and activities. Whether the corporation or the individual is paying for the program prescription, the desire is for positive outcomes that are lasting. The box above lists several factors that contribute to activity adherence. Most adult exercise programs emphasize similar strategies to enhance lasting and positive lifestyle changes. Most importantly, all people need appropriately designed programs that they understand, important goals that are feasible and monitored, and positive experiences that will encourage them to participate.

Thus, physical education and sport really can be a part of everyone's life regardless of age or capability. The earlier you can teach others the value of being physically fit, the greater the quality of their lives. As physical education and sport professionals, you are challenged to serve as advocates never ceasing to proclaim and demonstrate through your lives the values of fitness that can be learned in activity classes in various settings.

CONSUMER EDUCATION

As more people engage in physical activity or are forced to make lifestyle changes for health reasons, consumer education becomes critical. Leading sporting goods manufacturers are marketing giants seeking greater market shares. Multimillion-dollar advertisements bombard the television screen and print media. Besides marketing ploys focusing on attracting consumers to purchase designer footwear or clothing, there are advertisements for every imaginable fitness aid. Charlatans have sold shoddy playground equipment to schools. Get-rich-quick scams have left well-intentioned people with broken fitness equipment and a disillusionment about activity. It sometimes seems like everyone wants to sell a new aerobics tape, a "take off pounds quickly" gadget, or a five-year membership to a fitness club that never seems to deliver promised services. Consumers must beware. The prospective jogger should investigate various types of shoes and individual foot characteristics and movement patterns before investing in an expensive pair of shoes. When considering joining a health or sport club, questions about monthly and add-on charges, the availability of activity classes or individualized instruction, and services guaranteed should be asked and adequate answers provided before you write out a check.

Any program device or pill that promises immediate and unbelievable results should be automatically suspect. For example, the only way to reduce body weight is to either increase caloric expenditure or decrease caloric intake. Passive exercises or belts to pound off fat simply will not work. Besides being deceitful, some touted health aids, like the use of rubber suits, can be dangerous.

Consumers also need to be aware of subliminal messages in advertisements. The use of the sports star testimonial is a popular approach. The fact that an outstanding professional athlete endorses a product (for a large fee) does not guarantee it will meet your needs. Many times sporting goods ads sell sex as much as they do a product since the sex appeal of the fit athlete or model attracts many purchasers. Some individuals are willing to pay for the most sophisticated fitness equipment with the latest technology, but such screens and monitoring devices will only work when you exercise.

PUBLIC RELATIONS

Physical educators must recognize the necessity of convincing decision makers of the vital importance of physical activity, especially critical when faced with program elimination and financial cutbacks. Many states have either increased or retained school and community programs specifically through the use of public relations strategies. The National Association for Sport and Physical Education's SPEAK (Sport and Physical Education Advocacy Kit) includes data and information in defense of school physical education programs, news releases, and other promotional materials to assist states, associations, and individuals in these efforts. Jump Rope for Heart is a joint project of the American Heart Association and American Alliance for Health, Physical Education, Recreation and Dance. This program, with its demonstration teams and enhancement of the cardiovascular condition of participants, serves an effective public relations purpose as well as a fund-raising project for heart research.

What does this mean to you personally? Many school and recreational programs face financial cutbacks. In some cases this is a small loss of funding; in others, entire programs may be eliminated. Frequently, this occurs because physical activity is considered noncritical, because its purposes are misunderstood, or because decision makers have not been informed about the positive outcomes

American Heart Association

FIGURE 11-1

Jump Rope for Heart is a national project of the American Heart Association (AHA) and the American Alliance for Health, Physical Education, Recreation and Dance (AAHPERD).

for participants. Regardless of the reason, it is vital that an educational process occurs. Professionals in physical education-related careers must convince state legislators and members of school boards that physical activity is essential to each person's well-being. Otherwise, monies will be cut even more severely than they have been, or new programs will not be initiated.

Public relations efforts are critical in nonschool fitness and recreation programs. Corporate executives, company and club stockholders, taxpayers, and other key decision makers must be informed about the value of these activities to those served. Every program should have clearly articulated goals and standards that can be evaluated to prove effectiveness. Accountability for dollars spent applies regardless of the setting.

RECREATION AND LEISURE SERVICES

Several social factors are influencing the provision of leisure services. These factors include demographic changes, altered family and work patterns, environmental concerns, and the economy. In addition, laws, societal accountability, and a human services focus mandate significant changes in this field.

An increasingly diverse ethnic mix in the population of the United States signals that business as usual will no longer be acceptable. African-Americans, Native Americans, Asian-Americans, Hispanics, and other ethnic groups are demanding recreational and artistic programs that appeal to their unique cultural backgrounds. The former melting pot concept has given way to an encouragement of diversity throughout society, including leisure programming.

Demographic changes also reflect the graying of America. As life expectancies increase, older adults are expecting to have their recreational needs met

Golf is a favorite sport for seniors. (Photo courtesy Jerry Wachter.)

along with those of younger groups. Senior citizens are often physically vigorous; plus, they possess considerable political clout and financial resources. While some may require only passive activities in a retirement center, other retirees robustly play golf and tennis, walk and hike, travel and tour, and swim and cycle. Many careers in the twenty-first century will serve the recreational and leisure needs of this population, as well as younger individuals.

The traditional 1950s family of a working father, a homemaking mother, and two or three children characterizes what is the norm to less than half of today's school-age children. Divorced parents, broken homes, and absent or unknown fathers leave about one out of every two children in single-parent homes before they reach adulthood. While almost all of these parents work, many dual-career families exist, too.

Child care has become a major issue for these parents with associated concerns about cost and quality. Meeting the developmental play needs of preschool children challenges those who offer in-house or commercialized child care services. Schools, churches, and public centers offer after-school care for children, which may or may not include recreational play opportunities.

Many adolescents and sometimes preadolescents have become latchkey kids. At whatever age the parent selects, children return from school to empty homes every afternoon. These unattended children may be required to lock themselves in the house because playing outside is unsafe. Often, such constraints lead to seemingly unending hours of viewing television and eating junk food. Lack of supervision may also permit youthful experimentation with alcohol, tobacco, other drugs, sex, and law-breaking activities.

Most cities and towns through schools, recreation departments, and private clubs provide numerous alternatives to unsafe, inactive, and delinquent behaviors. Competitive youth sports teams, children's fitness clubs and programs, adventure activities, cooperative games, and creative playground opportunities are a few of these options. While some parents can afford to enroll their children in private dance, gymnastics, swimming, or tennis lessons, many rely on the public programs for facilities, equipment, and instruction.

Threats to the environment also threaten the resources available for recreation and leisure. Efforts to protect natural resources and open spaces from abusive individuals and encroaching real estate developers raise environmental issues. Rock climbers, hikers, and campers are increasingly expected to leave nature exactly as they found it. Industries are expected to no longer pollute the air, water, and land without penalty. Despite limited resources, cities and states seek to acquire land for recreational purposes both to preserve an adequate amount for the future and to address existing demands.

Increased budget constraints, however, raise economic issues. People are taxed for municipal services, including recreation, yet there never seems to be enough money, space, or programs. To meet their budgets, many recreation departments must charge entry or participation fees, which may eliminate those unable to pay. Vandalism, security costs, and lawsuits have sharply increased expenses for these agencies, too. The Americans with Disabilities Act specifies that recreational programs and facilities must be provided for individuals with limitations. Although essential, enlarging doorways, locker rooms, courts, and fields to provide equal access is costly. Specialized recreational equipment and personnel also may be needed.

Recreation and leisure services are among the human services industries that have proliferated in recent decades. Everyone choosing a career in national and state parks, boys' and girls' clubs, commercial and corporate fitness, sport clubs, and recreation must focus on customer or client satisfaction. In order to accomplish this, you must determine the goals of participation for those you serve. For example, those pursuing backpacking, rock climbing, and canoeing may have

Canoeing has become a popular leisure-time activity for individuals of all ages.

these goals in mind: (1) to learn outdoor skills, (2) to challenge ability limits, (3) to enjoy risk-taking achievements, (4) to develop cooperative or self-reliant behavior, and (5) to appreciate nature. Knowing these goals, you can propose or help guide a person through an individualized or group program.

Active lifestyles can take myriad directions. The recreation specialist's challenge is to help promote and provide activities that match each person's age, economic, family, social, time, ability, and interest needs.

CAREER BURNOUT

A combination of discipline problems: apathetic students; the repetitiveness of teaching; the lack of adequate facilities, equipment, and other resources; and inadequate administrative support leads to stress that can result in burnout. In addition, many physical education teachers realize that, because of reduced turnover, fewer new teachers are being hired; also, they feel isolated from other teachers, lack professional mobility, and face threatened spending cuts or verbal attacks by the public about education. Thus, many display the signs and symptoms of **burnout** listed in the box below. Persons in physical education careers other than teaching may also find their jobs unrewarding intrinsically and extrinsically, frustrating because of a lack of change or too much innovation too fast, unchallenging or too routine, confining in hours and work required, or lacking in potential for advancement.

Often burnout occurs as a result of a combination of these factors. For example, a beginning physical education teacher often is hired to teach a full load of classes and to coach one to three sports. Lesson plans, grades, reports, student-monitoring responsibilities, and associated teaching duties combine with year-round planning, practices, competitions, and administration of the teams to fill most days and nights. One of four patterns usually then develops:

- A tenured teacher-coach decides that the small coaching supplement is not worth the time demands, so he or she resigns from coaching, but keeps teaching.

SIGNS AND SYMPTOMS OF BURNOUT

- Constant tension from too little or too much stimulation
- Less enjoyment of work and even leisure activities
- Bodily changes, such as fatigue, high blood pressure, insomnia, digestive disorders, or increased heart rate
- Overeating or under eating
- Excessive drinking or abuse of drugs
- Frustration with job-related factors such as task repetitiveness, lack of recognition, overwork, and impossibility of advancement
- Anxiety and depression

- The teacher-coach concentrates on coaching putting little effort into teaching because it is viewed as repetitive and unrewarding.
- The teacher-coach becomes apathetic about both jobs, just going through the motions instead of being committed.
- The teacher-coach changes careers.

The coaches who resign may display signs of burnout partially because of the pressures placed on them by parents and school administrators to win. This teacher-coach conflict is aggravated because of the higher recognition and rewards for coaching compared with those for teaching.

The chronic, job-related stress resulting from role conflict or role ambiguity that leads to teacher-coach burnout can be reduced but probably not eliminated, since this person holds two somewhat incompatible positions simultaneously. Suggestions for reducing potential burnout are listed in the box on page 275.

Since anxiety, frustration, and stress are often causes as well as consequences of burnout, combatting them becomes essential to career survival. Job satisfaction necessitates taking a positive approach toward work responsibilities. Financial reward, job challenge, observation of and work with others, promotion, variety in responsibilities, and in-service development may contribute to job satisfaction. Also vital is receiving positive feedback: if people are constantly bombarded by negative comments, they cannot continue to function effectively. Recognition and praise for completion of responsibilities often lead to positive changes and enhanced self-motivation.

Excessive work demands may lead to job-related stress and eventually to burnout.

REDUCING TEACHER-COACH BURNOUT

1. School administrators should define, evaluate, and reward the teaching and coaching roles separately.
2. The athletic director should specify team responsibilities and lines of authority to preclude potential conflicts between teaching and coaching duties.
3. School administrators and the athletic director should work together to relieve the excessive pressures placed on coaches by athletes, parents, and team supporters.
4. The coach should seek to balance the time and energy spent in meeting the responsibilities of both jobs.

When individuals are given the opportunity to take part in the planning process, a greater allegiance to the resultant programs or goals is readily evident. Finally, physical education and sport professionals should interact with others both on the job and by attending seminars, workshops, and conferences. At least once a year, everyone needs to rejuvenate commitment to and enthusiasm for job responsibilities.

Work-related stress probably cannot be avoided, yet each of us should understand what causes stress and how to eliminate as much as we can and how to counteract the rest. Physical educators have a definite advantage in the latter case, because they know that exercise reduces stress. We need to attain and maintain a personal level of fitness that not only positively affects our productivity and quality of life but also allows us to serve as role models for others.

Participation in physical activity, like volleyball, can help relieve stress and lessen the possibility of career burnout. (Photo courtesy Lisa Sense.)

MERIT PAY

Directly associated with avoiding burnout in the workplace is the concept of **merit pay**, whereby the employee is paid on the basis of quality of performance rather than years of service and a general salary scale. Although not a new issue, merit pay is a volatile one for many states and school districts. Proponents emphasize that merit pay rewards teachers for superior service and ability, thus encouraging effective teaching and professional productivity. Opponents stress the difficulty of evaluating quality teaching fairly, administering a merit pay system, and dealing equitably with all teachers interpersonally as well as financially. For any merit pay plan to work, each school district and state, with teacher involvement, should examine all the possibilities and devise the plan that best meets its local and state needs.

A merit pay system is based on the retention and advancement of productive and exemplary employees and the elimination of those who do not contribute at a high level. Free-lance sport journalists or sport photographers readily accept the merit pay concept: they are paid for their work that is published. Periodic evaluations or assessments based on job performance criteria are essential for the implementation of an equitable merit pay program. Monetary reward, although certainly not the sole motivator, is important to most people.

Instead of merit-based pay, some states have adopted the career ladder approach. Outstanding teachers enjoy career advancement into more challenging and intrinsically rewarding jobs rather than receiving large monetary rewards. These jobs may include coordinator positions, such as program head or lead teacher, or administrative roles, such as principal or district supervisor.

JOB SECURITY

Job security is a concern for many physical educators, especially those in schools and colleges. Competent completion of job responsibilities in most cases results in continued employment, but this is not always guaranteed. When teacher-coach burnout appears, some physical educators seek to resign from their coaching duties only to find that they must lose their teaching positions, too. Also, many first-year teachers are learning that their contracts are written so that they can keep their teaching jobs only if they coach. Many current coaches, especially basketball and football, are being told subtly or overtly that they must annually produce winning teams to retain their jobs.

In addition, many nontraditional physical education careers do not offer secure futures because they depend on public demand and payment for services rendered. One reason membership sales are so important in commercial fitness programs and sport clubs is that without enrolling a significant number of new members, jobs may be lost. Because city and community recreation departments are funded based on the volume of program participants, the level of staffing is variable. In these and similar positions, job security may be tenuous during times of recession or budgetary retrenchment. As expected, the best insurance for job retention and advancement is exemplary performance.

Teaching jobs have traditionally offered security in the form of tenure after the successful completion of three to seven years of service to a school district.

Tenure guarantees academic freedom and provides a safeguard from political pressure, while providing a buffer to job uncertainty for professionals. However, after receiving tenure some persons may stagnate as ineffective teachers, making it impossible to hire those who are more competent. The initiation of post-tenure review in colleges and universities grew out of the call for accountability faculty to ensure continual improvement and the upgrading of knowledge and skills.

Job security in entry-level physical education and sport careers is based on demonstrated knowledge and skill as well as the willingness to enhance these abilities. Diligence, responsibility, eagerness to learn, dependability, and cooperation are among the characteristics that most employers are seeking.

STANDARDS AND ASSESSMENT

A major trend in public education is the standards and assessment movement. Although a component of the overall call for educational reform, standards serve as the foundation upon which each subject or discipline is established. A **standard** is *a uniform criterion or minimum essential element for the measurement of quality.* Educational standards determine what all children should learn and know.

The mandate for educational standards emerged as schools were attacked for graduating illiterate or ill-prepared individuals after 13 years of class attendance. State legislators sought proof that the millions of dollars allocated for education resulted in learning. In some states, like Arkansas and Tennessee, incremental state funding was tied to meeting and surpassing standards. Based on these demands, schools needed comparative measures, or assessments, for determining whether the standards were being achieved.

The seven content standards for physical education were developed by the National Association for Sport and Physical Education (see box below). The

---

CONTENT STANDARDS FOR PHYSICAL EDUCATION

- Demonstrates competency in many movement forms and proficiency in a few movement forms.
- Applies movement concepts and principles to the learning and development of motor skills.
- Exhibits a physically active lifestyle.
- Achieves and maintains a health-enhancing level of physical fitness.
- Demonstrates responsible personal and social behavior in physical activity settings.
- Demonstrates understanding and respect for differences among people in physical activity settings.
- Understands that physical activity provides opportunities for enjoyment, challenge, self-expression, and social interaction.

National Association for Sport and Physical Education.

school and college professionals who developed these content standards provided examples of outcomes for grades K, 2, 4, 6, 8, 10, and 12. Although not a national curriculum, these benchmarks can be used to guide the development of local and state physical education curricula and assessments, as well as physical activity programs in a variety of settings.

Quality, in education, business, and government, is stressed increasingly today. Parents, employers, and politicians demand that all educational systems document that students are learning and that they graduate with the knowledge and skills necessary to become contributing members of society. Demand for accountability of resources and time has led to a national call for standards in all disciplinary fields and for assessment of whether these standards are being met.

Competence as a teacher may include assessing whether students learn proper movement skills such as throwing. (Photo courtesy Lisa Sense.)

Standards are important for instructional programs at all levels. (Photo courtesy Lisa Sense.)

Quality in school physical education can only result when several components are in place and functioning properly. Every physical education class should be designed and taught by a competent and certified physical education teacher. Unfortunately many classroom teachers in the elementary grades do not have the requisite knowledge, skills, or interest to instruct children in fundamental movement activities. High school coaches hired to provide competitive sport experiences for adolescents and then assigned to teach physical education classes without adequate physical education background will not meet this first requirement for quality either.

Like every other school subject, physical education should include sequenced learning activities characterized by objectives, instructional strategies, developmental levels, and standards of achievement. Performance-based assessment (see box below) lists four criteria for ensuring that students learn. Objectives should be identified by grade level, and specified outcomes should be assessed at each level by valid and reliable measurements. Quality physical education will help students of all abilities develop physical fitness and motor skills, gain knowledge and understanding, enact appropriate social behavior, and value a healthy lifestyle.

Achievement of these objectives cannot occur when children and adolescents receive only one or two days of physical education per week. The National Association for Sport and Physical Education recommends that children from kindergarten through the fifth grade receive physical education instruction 30 minutes per day and students in grades 6 through 12 receive 50 minutes per day. To achieve outcomes that focus on quality, students must be physically active for at least 50% of class time.

Quality experiences in sport and physical activity programs outside of the classroom also are important. Whether a recreational youth sport league, a senior citizens' walking club, or a commercial fitness program, appropriate objectives, standards, and assessments will help ensure fun, program adherence, and maintenance of a healthy lifestyle. For example, a corporate fitness program might include the following:

- All personnel prescribing exercise programs must be certified such as by the American College of Sports Medicine.
- All activity instructors must be certified in basic first aid and cardiopulmonary resuscitation.

PERFORMANCE-BASED ASSESSMENT

- Define content standards and learning outcomes.
- Establish criteria for assessing student performance.
- Design curriculum to ensure that students achieve content standards and learning outcomes.
- Plan and deliver instruction to ensure that all students achieve content standards and learning outcomes.

- Each participant, following a fitness assessment, will establish personal goals that will be monitored regularly.
- Incentives, such as leave from work, free exercise clothing and shoes, and recognition in corporate newsletters, will be given to those who meet their goals.
- Employees will help select and facilitate a variety of physical activity programs for co-workers and their families.

INSTRUCTIONAL CHALLENGES FACING SCHOOL PHYSICAL EDUCATORS

School teachers, including those in physical education, face many challenges. Among these are insufficient resources for facilities and equipment, apathetic students, drug use and abuse, lack of parental and family support for education, heterogeneous students in large classes, and discipline problems. Despite these factors that negatively affect students' readiness to learn and the instructional environment, teachers are held accountable for sequential learning.

Limited facilities and equipment need not dissuade physical educators from expanding their programs. The gymnasium provides a setting for rock climbing,

Tennis remains a popular leisure-time sport for players of all ages.

badminton, and aerobics as well as traditional team sports. Community courts, driving ranges, and lanes are often available for tennis, golf, and bowling instruction and participation. Additional equipment can be brought by students, borrowed from recreational departments, leased from companies, and even received free from some organizations seeking to promote their sports. Ask students and parents to help construct goals, net supports, weights, and playground apparatus.

Apathetic students who do not want to dress out, participate, try, or behave present an even greater challenge to teachers. Since each student is unique, teachers need to use whatever resources or people they can to determine the causes for this apathy. Only then can the physical educator appeal to these students' interests and needs. Replacing dodgeball or unpopular activities with weight training or aerobics may be the only change needed. Rewarding appropriate behavior, rather than simply punishing misbehavior, may lead to some changes. Teaching relevant content, ensuring equal opportunity for all students, and making classes enjoyable may not attract every student, but the number of apathetic ones will certainly diminish. Keeping students busy is not necessarily education. Teaching must make learning enjoyable.

When students attend school under the influence of alcohol or purchase and use drugs on school grounds, the teaching-learning process is severely tested. Drug education classes and enforcement of school policies for drug-free campuses are two ways to help reduce the incidence of these problems. The physical educator should use every opportunity to discourage drug use by showing how it adversely affects physical performance and well-being.

The lack of parental and family support for education is partially caused by the changing demographic and socioeconomic nature of this country. Over half of American children will spend a portion of their developmental years in single-parent homes. Most children with two parents will still find no one at home after school because both parents work. About a quarter of today's children live in households with incomes below the poverty level. Children of minorities already exceed the number of whites in some schools; this population shift will continue. Teachers must overcome this lack of parental support by helping students learn to value education themselves. One way is to help them take more responsibility for their own education. For example, the physical educator can use an after-school fitness club to instill in a child self-worth, confidence, discipline, and responsibility. These abilities can be nurtured in physical education and other classes.

Many states dictate maximum class sizes, but too often exceptions are granted for physical education. When school administrators believe that only play, not instruction or cognitive learning, occurs, physical educators may be expected to teach 50 to 60 students in one class. The first objective is to educate your principal about your curriculum and to invite decision makers to observe the quality of your program. Working with other professionals, you need to lobby against this exception to maximum class size. The best rationale is the lack of safety especially due to inadequate supervision and crowded instructional and activity conditions. Even with a normal size class, physical educators still face students with heterogeneous abilities. Skill grouping, use of lead-up or progressive games, and curricula that include both cooperative and competitive activities help meet these students' diverse needs.

Discipline problems may be the most recurring issue facing teachers. Rather than dissipating in an activity setting, these problems may be exacerbated. Some students with histories of misbehavior may be attracted to physical education so they can dominate or show off. Physical educators must establish, with student input, gymnasium policies and then enforce them consistently. Using time-outs, rather than exercises or laps as punishment, teaches respect for the rules. Rewarding appropriate behaviors with the opportunity to participate in favorite activities is more effective for most students than is in-school suspension.

As can be seen from this long list of trends, physical educators must be prepared to do a lot more than just teach their favorite sports and games. However, they have bountiful opportunities to positively affect the lives of many troubled youth.

ISSUES FACING PHYSICAL EDUCATION AND SPORT

The issues facing physical education and sport today include program threats, an identity dilemma in name and image, role conflicts between physical educators and coaches, and the poor fitness levels of most Americans. Each of these situations and some suggestions for actions that can be taken to ameliorate them will be briefly described.

Program Threats

The greatest challenge for most physical education and sport programs rests with inadequate resources. No longer can schools and colleges expect to receive budgetary increases. In many states, educational budgets have been cut, some substantially. During tight economic times, the so-called nonessential subjects, such as physical education, art, and music, are reduced, if not eliminated. Corporate fitness programs, public recreation agencies, and even private clubs may reduce their leagues, operating hours, and staff to withstand financial shortfalls or zero-growth budgets. No longer can leaders in our field expect an ever-increasing revenue stream. Rather, we must expect to meet our goals on the same or fewer resources. We may have to eliminate excesses in big-time college athletics or simply be more frugal with our meager equipment allocation through careful maintenance and repair. We may have to charge increased fees for participation, while always providing alternative payment methods for those who would otherwise be excluded. We may have to market our programs better to increase participation volume and donations.

Identity Dilemma in Name and Image

The field is no longer unified by its traditional name—*physical education*. Although schools continue to use the term, many people disparagingly refer to the instruction occurring in its classes as "gym," "phys ed," "recess," or "play." Many fail to respect the profession because physical educators have failed to teach its skills, knowledge, and values.

Most colleges and universities, in attempting to align themselves with a multidisciplinary content that is recognized as academic, have chosen names such as *kinesiology, human performance,* and *exercise science*. This disassociation from physical education has also grown out of the dramatic shift in students' major fields of study from preparing to teach physical education in the schools to specializing in exercise science, athletic training, and sport management. Although many outside the schools educate others in performing physical activities, they prefer titles such as tennis pro, aerobics leader, personal trainer, exercise physiologist, athletic trainer, and coach.

Changing the public's perception of physical education rests squarely on the shoulders of those in the field. School physical educators must design and teach quality programs that they proudly demonstrate to parents, school administrators, school board members, and legislators. College physical education instructional programs also must provide quality instructional opportunities for their students in a variety of activities. These may become the only two groups that retain the name of *physical education.*

College academicians will continue to conduct research and to educate their students in specialized subdisciplines such as exercise physiology, sport psychology, and athletic training. As long as the focus remains on enhancing the physical well-being of those served, the name probably is irrelevant. What is essential, though, is that each specialist, regardless of the title, demonstrates a commitment to physical activity for all.

Role Conflicts Between Physical Educators and Coaches

Many physical educators in the schools and small colleges also coach. In fact, some obtain degrees in physical education to increase the likelihood of obtaining coaching positions. Because of the overlap in instructional knowledge and skill content, this joint career seems most appropriate. When these individuals commit equally to teaching students of heterogenous ability levels and to coaching the highly skilled, all students benefit.

Conflicts occur because of time and energy constraints, unequal rewards, self-imposed and external pressures, and personal preferences. Most physical

Teacher-coach conflict is often associated with the time required to fulfill practice and game responsibilities. (Photo courtesy Maggie McGlynn.)

educators are expected to teach a full class load and then to coach after school. This schedule results in long days. For those coaching multiple sports, these long days seem to never end. Some coaches rapidly experience burnout, causing them to quit. Others compensate by losing enthusiasm and not preparing for one of their roles—usually their classes.

Compensation for the teacher-coach varies widely. Teaching salaries are usually established by the school district based on years of experience and academic degree(s). Coaching stipends usually are salary supplements. In small colleges, there will likely be more equity in salary and workload for the teacher-coach. Fringe benefits, such as bonuses or deals with sporting goods companies, always relate to a person's coaching duties.

Pressures to win, whether self-imposed or from external sources, accompany sports competitions. Although most people have no interest in the quality of instruction provided by the teacher-coach, hundreds or even thousands may pass judgment on one's ability to develop a successful team. Accompanying these pressures, which in the worst case may cause one to be fired, are the public prestige and status of being a coach.

Another potential source of conflict is preference for one role. Often, the teacher-coach finds coaching the highly skilled and building a solid team more rewarding than the daily routine of teaching, especially when many students, unlike most athletes, do not want to learn. A personal preference often leads to the disproportionate allocation of time and energy to the coaching role.

Resolution of this role conflict is difficult because the conflict usually develops gradually. The teacher-coach needs to continually assess the commitment given each responsibility to ensure that it is equitable. Regardless of the pressures, rewards, constraints, and preferences, the teacher-coach as a professional is ethically expected to serve competently in both roles. The box on pages 285–286 elaborates on this conflict and suggests strategies to ameliorate some of the problems.

Poor Fitness Levels of Americans

The publication of the *Surgeon General's Report on Physical Activity and Health* in 1996 urged Americans of all ages to participate in moderate amounts of physical activity. This clarion call reported that too many Americans are negatively impacting their health and quality of life through inactivity. The consequences of such lack of physical activity include greater risk of dying of heart disease, the leading cause of death in the United States, and of developing diabetes, colon cancer, and high blood pressure. Sedentary individuals also are more likely to become overweight and obese.

According to this report, more than 60% of adults in the United States fail to exercise regularly, including 25% who never exercise. Only 22% of adults engage regularly in sustained physical activity of any intensity. Approximately 50% of the youth (ages 12–21) of this country are not vigorously active on a regular basis. Distressingly, physical activity declines dramatically during adolescence. One contributing factor to this decline is a reduction in daily enrollment in physical education classes among high school students from 42% in 1991 to 25% in 1995. About 14% of American young people are inactive.

THE ROLE OF THE TEACHER-COACH IN SECONDARY SCHOOLS

Coaching of athletic teams in the secondary schools in this country is no longer provided exclusively by teachers of physical education. Athletic programs, prompted by societal demands, have become a powerful element in all secondary schools.

Proliferation, intensification, and staffing of the athletic program have produced a dilemma that is not easily resolved. Keeping the role of the physical educator, (or any other teacher), in perspective as it relates to the demands of the coaching assignment is fundamental to this dilemma.

The basic question then is, does quality physical education instruction have to be compromised at the expense of a quality athletic program? The following belief statements, recommendations, and strategies for implementation may answer that question. These recommendations are directed towards those who make educational decisions for their communities.

Belief Statements

The physical educator should be held accountable to the same high standards of teaching as in any other instructional area. Coaching prowess is not to be allowed as an insulator from commitment to the physical education program. Performance should be comprehensively evaluated with superior teaching performance appropriately recognized.

Physical education classes and athletic programs must share the very same educational philosophy to which all school personnel are held accountable.

The role of coach is distinct from the role of the physical education teacher. While the two are similar in certain ways, disparities in the time necessary for each role, resources available for each role, recognition, goals, the performance abilities of each population and their expectations clearly differentiate between the two roles and argue for their separability.

Recommendations

Education

Undergraduate and graduate teacher education programs should consider the teaching and coaching roles. For example, time requirements, differential rewards available through each role, the varying expectations, support systems, and contrasting norms of behavior associated with the teaching and coaching role should be studied. Such study could complement a "coaching practicum" which should be part of the student's preparation for athletic coaching.

Liberal Education

The broad scope of the educator's responsibilities requires a well-rounded education; that is, one which addresses values as well as technology, and the humanities as well as the arts and sciences— a growing awareness wholly consistent with the historical roots of physical education. The liberal education protects against the dangers of overspecialization.

Staff Development

Physical education faculty should continue to develop their teaching skills through a variety of professional activities (e.g., convention attendance, workshops, institutes, conferences, teacher exchanges, mentorship, independent study, etc.). Part of this development should include education regarding the teacher-coach roles. Supervisory personnel evaluating job performance should be similarly educated as to the multiple requirements of dual roles.

Performance

Teaching is the primary responsibility of those hired to teach physical education. Supplemental assignments for other components of the educational process, such as coaching, are not to interfere in any way with conducting this primary responsibility. The philosophy of the district/institution

(Continued)

THE ROLE OF THE TEACHER-COACH IN SECONDARY SCHOOLS (CONT'D)

establishes teaching expectancies which should result in competent performance. These expectancies should be made clear to all candidates for the teacher-coach position. The following guidelines are offered as criteria for assessment:

- Planning instruction
- Implementing instruction
- Developing pupil competencies
- Developing pupil self-concept
- Assessing and evaluating student progress
- Demonstrating professional skills
- Accountability through written, oral, and on-sight actions

The same evaluation process for all teachers, coupled with appropriate staff development sessions for supervisors, will provide the framework for the consistent assessment of the teacher-coach performance.

General guidelines for the assessment process should include:

- Preconferences to establish mutually agreed upon objectives
- A series of observations
- Postconferences for sharing the effectiveness of the teaching-learning process
- Including the teacher's self-appraisal as well as the evaluator's assessment

The cooperative leadership of the board of education, the school administration, and the teacher association will enhance the quality of the teaching-learning process.

The Time Factor

As cited in a survey by Locke and Massengale (1978), and confirmed by the National Federation of State High School Activities Association (1987), the most prevalent problem of the teacher-coach is the inordinate amount of time demanded by the responsibilities of both positions. Research indicates that time overload contributes to teacher-coach stress and anxieties which could affect job performance, i.e., teacher-coach burnout and commitment to roles.

School administrators should carefully review and evaluate the number of contests, and the length of season and off-season participation relative to educationally justifiable criteria. The philosophical position of the school district may warrant participation at a number less than the state maximums. Administration staffs need to explore creative methods to minimize the time commitment of the teacher-coach, i.e., not more than two coaching assignments, not more than one head coaching assignment, and the monitoring of assistant coach expectations. Administrators could also consider rotating departmental assignments with other qualified faculty members during coaching seasons to assure continual competency in teaching physical education. When financially feasible, a teacher-coach may have a reduced teaching load during the coaching season, e.g., a qualified physical education teacher shall be hired on a part-time basis.

National Association for Sport and Physical Education.

Yet, the positive effects of physical activity on health and disease are unquestioned. Regular physical activity helps prevent disease and premature death and adds to quality of life by helping individuals maintain normal muscle strength and joint function. Stress management and enhanced mental health are additional outcomes. At no time in history has there been a greater emphasis on self-responsibility for cardiovascular fitness and healthful living.

SUMMARY

Physical activity programs are for everyone; they help people learn fitness and sports skills and incorporate them into their daily lives. It is hoped that students and exercise participants of all ages will increasingly enjoy activities, reach their goals, and adhere to their appropriately designed programs. However, demographic, family, work, and economic factors are altering the provision of recreational leisure services. Public relations efforts on the part of physical educators in all settings may bolster exercise adherence while encouraging greater support and funding for physical activity and sport in the schools, recreational settings, and fitness programs.

   Accountability is inextricably linked with all of the issues discussed in this chapter and especially the standards and assessment movement. Although instructional constraints threaten the teaching-learning process, competent teachers must creatively find ways to surmount these barriers. Physical educators in all careers must fulfill their job responsibilities competently to maintain employment, to receive awards, and to ensure financial support. Individuals must overcome limitations associated with their jobs, yet they should expect to receive appropriate levels of recognition, such as merit pay and job security. Professional involvement and interchange among colleagues are two of the ways to combat job stress and career burnout.

L. FRANKLIN RAGAN
Deputy City Manager for Operations
City of Aurora, Colorado

EDUCATION
B.S., Recreation and Parks Administration, North Carolina State University
M.S., Recreation Resources Administration, North Carolina State University

JOB RESPONSIBILITIES AND HOURS

Frank oversees five departments within the city of Aurora, i.e., Planning, Utilities, Public Works, Fitzsimons Army Base Redevelopment, and Parks and Open Space. The responsibilities reflect the reorganization of a city with tremendous quality growth opportunities. An objective of this right-sizing structure was to group the major planning and infrastructure components of the municipal government under one leader with the overt intent to gain greater effectiveness and efficiencies with citizen-supported services and facilities. With a previous nineteen-year career focused on the field of parks and recreation and the resultant experience gained in overall leadership and management skills, the opportunity and resultant challenge to assume more responsibilities, albeit more difficult, came more fluidly than Frank had imagined. Although his present responsibilities involve broader areas of citywide planning, development, and management oversight, the various functional departments operate through the same fundamentals of management common to all park/recreation and related public service organizations. Accountability to the citizens who finance local government operations, as well as your pay-check, has become more challenging in recent years. Participatory management and commu-nity government are the trends of today and the orientation of local government to the future.

The hours of commitment to public service can vary widely, dependent upon one's initia-tive and the characteristics of the organization for which one works. Frank's weekly schedule of hours devoted to the job can vary from 50–70, with an average around 55. Certainly, 40-hour weeks are nonexistent. While there is some semblance of cycles throughout the year, i.e., budget preparation, long-range capital improvements planning, infrastructure development activities, etc., the pace of an institution and one's desire to either keep up, fall behind, or get out in front of the pack is a strong determinant of hours on the job. With that said, there is a critical need within this profession, and any other for that matter, to balance career goals with other, some-times more important, goals. Public sector officials work hard to ensure that everyone has the opportunity to enjoy a good quality life, however, these same people sometimes fail to enjoy it themselves. It can be a difficult lesson learning how to balance a career with personal life.

SPECIALIZED COURSE WORK, DEGREES, AND WORK EXPERIENCES NEEDED FOR THIS CAREER

Frank states that his most valuable courses were those with a strong business orientation. He encourages students to take diversified courses with a strong liberal arts background. While both his undergraduate and graduate degrees were within Parks and Recreation, which was quite appropriate for careers within the field, it is somewhat difficult to move into a city or county manager's office without an M.B.A., Masters in Public Administration, or closely related degree. Good, recognized experience can overcome some educational preferences by fields outside the mainstream of one's educational orientation. Educational preparation should include courses aimed at information technology, sociology, psychology, research methodol-ogy, personnel management, finance/accounting, horticulture, design, planning, zoology, chemistry, and a variety of other courses filling out a broad spectrum of learning activities.

A couple of courses Frank begrudgingly took when he was in college focused on park and recreation facilities maintenance. They ended up being two of the most practical courses to prepare him for real world responsibilities. Keeping communities clean and beautiful does take some "grunt work." Understanding the various functions and possessing some working knowledge of what makes things work throughout one's organization, even with the least spec-tacular jobs, leads to a better understanding of the people whom you need to fill those posi-tions and meet your mission. Understanding and listening to people is critical in this business and life in general. Unlike what he felt while attending North Carolina State University, Frank found that virtually every course on his transcript helped in some way or another over the many years of his movement and progression within local government management.

It may be superfluous to mention the role in which information technology is now playing within this field, as it is within most fields. There are space-age technologies being utilized within the public works and community services portion of Frank's city, Aurora, Colorado. From maintenance programming incorporating pinpoint accuracy recording of street pothole loca-tions via utilization of satellites and computer voice recognition, to the entire mapping of infra-structure, demographics, and other data deemed important, to efficient, effective delivery of services, the application of technology into everyday work planning and operations is becom-ing more routine and essential. Certainly, one cannot learn too much in this field of activity regardless of one's career destination.

SATISFYING ASPECTS

Of most importance to Frank is seeing the direct results of his organization's work and the noticeable, tangible impact made upon individuals' quality of life. He adds that there are few fields of endeavor where the efforts of one's lifework are so evident in day-to-day living. He takes particular pride in working with economic development and redevelopment projects which are major contributing factors to a community's financial prosperity, hence providing stability to the overall health of a community and its interdependent, diversified neighborhoods.

JOB POTENTIAL

Opportunities within local government are great, if one is willing to make some sacrifices. The flexibility to relocate to different parts of the country are imperative for those who want to advance quickly to departmental director positions or higher management/administrative positions. Such drastic moves are unnecessary at lower level positions due to greater availability of positions within a given geographic area, particularly within more urbanized areas of the country. Generally, salaries will tend to be proportionate with the size of the community and the resultant priorities and reflective budget of that jurisdiction. Salaries can also differ significantly in different parts of the country. Costs of living can vary just as greatly, and as a result, one should do research to truly establish whether positions are promotional or more lateral.

SUGGESTIONS FOR STUDENTS

Frank recommends that those considering a career in local government interview people in positions of interest to them. Of particular value is "shadowing" a person during a typical workday and/or evening as the case may be, to directly see what that job or career involves. Once you have chosen a field, he stresses the importance of getting volunteer, part-time and/or seasonal work experiences prior to graduation. Internships are valuable, particularly when you have the opportunity to work with people in a progressive, creative agency who take time to work with interns rather than just take advantage of their budgeted hours. Frank also believes in a strong variation of work experiences and recognizes that the diversity of one's experiences and the professional references drawn from them are often significant and deciding factors when going for that first full-time position and everything else that follows. One's opportunities are enhanced exponentially once within a good organization that values and rewards its achieving performers. The responsibility of recognizing good opportunities resides with each person, as well as the requisite education and experiences deemed essential to taking full advantage of them.

REVIEW QUESTIONS

1. What are desirable outcomes of physical activity programs for people of all ages?
2. What are the four contributing factors to heart disease according to the American Heart Association?
3. What are three examples of fitness frauds that consumer education could expose?
4. What strategies should physical educators use to get financial support for physical education and sport programs from legislators?
5. What are several challenges facing professionals in recreation and leisure services?
6. What are five contributing factors to career burnout?
7. What are two advantages and two disadvantages of merit pay?
8. What are the issues facing the school teacher-coach and the college professor relative to job security?

9. What is a standard? What is the standards and assessment movement?
10. What are several issues facing school physical educators?

STUDENT ACTIVITIES

1. Talk with five of your friends about any individual exercise programs that they formerly participated in or in which they are currently involved. Summarize the factors that led to their quitting or adhering to their programs.
2. Find two examples of fitness frauds in magazines—machines, foods, or programs that claim outcomes of questionable validity.
3. Write a press release for a newspaper or a letter to a legislator explaining and justifying why physical education should be required in grades K to 6, 7 to 9, 10 to 12, or in college.
4. Find examples of five nontraditional recreational opportunities in the place where you live. For whom are these programs provided?
5. Describe two actual examples of people who have suffered from career burnout. What changes would you have recommended that might have prevented these situations from occurring?
6. Conduct a class debate addressing the continuation (or discontinuation) of physical education in schools.
7. Write a one-page paper about your personal accountability in a job you have held in a physical education-related field, such as lifeguard, sport official, camp counselor, or sales person. (If you have not had any of these experiences, talk with those who have and report their experiences.)

SUGGESTED READINGS

Barrett KR: What does it mean to have a developmentally appropriate physical education program?, *Phy Educ* 49(3):114, 1992. This article suggests what teachers must know about developmentally appropriate physical education, such as that change occurs in an orderly, sequential fashion and that appropriate activities are age- and experience-related, and how teachers must be skilled observers of movement and its purposes.

Butt KL, Pahnos ML: Why we need a multicultural focus in our schools, *JOPERD* 66(1):48, 1995. Teachers can help shape how their students perceive and respond to students who are different to ensure equity and a respect for diversity.

Gidding SS, et al: Improving children's heart health: a report from the American Heart Association's Children's Heart Health Conference, *J of Sch Health* 65(4):129, 1995. At this 1994 conference, recommendations were made to promote the cardiovascular health in children in the areas of physical activity, nutrition, and avoidance of tobacco.

Hardy S: SMQ profile/interview, *Sp Mrk Q* 5(3):5, 1996. Matt Levine shares his successful innovative sport marketing strategies implemented with the Golden State Warriors and San Jose Sharks, including the use of audience audits, focus groups, market research, and Web site.

Melograno V: Quality physical education: setting the standards step by step, *Strategies* 5(6):15, 1992. The author identifies standards for quality physical education programs in the areas of curriculum, instruction, teachers, and administration. Strategies for implementing the proposed standards are included.

Siedentop D, et al: Don't sweat gym! an analysis of curriculum and instruction, *J of Teach in PE* 13(4):375, 1994. School physical educators need to move away from the traditional methods of instruction if they are to change how physical education is accepted within the curriculum.

Spink KS, Carron AV: Group cohesion and adherence in exercise classes, *J Sp & Ex Psy* 14:78, 1992. This investigation found that selected aspects of group cohesion influenced female exercise participants' adherence behavior.

Strand B, Reeder S: Using heart rate monitors in research on fitness levels of children in physical education, *J of Teach in PE* 12(2):215, 1993. This study of heart rate intensity levels of middle school students as they participated in a variety of activities revealed that heart rate monitors have considerable potential in assessing fitness achievements of children.

Sylvester C: Therapeutic recreation and the right to leisure, *Ther Rec J* 26(2):9, 1992. The author defends the right to leisure as the purpose for the field of therapeutic recreation.

Tannehill D, Zakrajsek D: Student attitudes toward physical education: a multi-cultural study, *J of Teach in PE* 13(1):78, 1993. This study reported that while cultural differences surfaced, none were significant. Overall, students considered physical education important to their overall education and liked physical education for fun and enjoyment, but they had negative attitudes toward fitness.

CHAPTER 12

Issues in Sports

KEY CONCEPTS

- Girls and women are increasingly involved in sports and have been aided by Title IX in these advances.
- Minorities, senior citizens, and disabled individuals, while enjoying greater activity, still struggle for equality in sports.
- Rather than emphasizing winning, the benefits and developmental goals of community youth sports and interscholastic athletics must be reinforced.
- As many intercollegiate athletic programs are besieged with problems associated with commercialized sports, colleges and universities must strive to ensure the attainment of educational outcomes.
- The Olympic Games provide opportunities for friendship among athletes of the world who are seeking to prove their physical superiority; yet, they are characterized by politics, nationalism, and overcommercialization.

Sports participants seek to win. "We're number one" seemingly has become the United States' motto as sports from Little League to professional teams have become big businesses. To produce the best teams, athletes are often expected to specialize in one sport, to accept coaches' dictates without question, to practice and train with deferred gratification, to excel or face elimination, and to circumvent the rules when necessary. Ethical behavior often is disdained or negatively rewarded by coaches, teammates, and spectators, since winning surpasses it in importance.

Contrastingly, cooperation, discipline, emotional control, fair play, self-esteem, and teamwork are often outcomes of sports, if those in leadership roles seek the development of these in participants. Athletes can learn to respect their opponents both on and off the field and can be taught to accept the officials' decisions without dispute. Even spectators are sometimes beneficiaries of these values by learning from the athletes. Models are especially important for young people, who imitate the attitudes and behaviors of school, college, professional, and Olympic athletes.

Sports are fun. Sports provide a setting for people to develop their own identities by learning about their capabilities and their limitations. A genuine satisfaction results from maximal effort when the outcome is not overemphasized. A revitalization of body, mind, and spirit through sports can renew one's perspective on life. The potential for value development is present, although overly competitive and overcommercialized sports undermine it. Administrators, coaches, athletes, and fans must ensure that experiencing the positive side of sports is the right of everyone by working to maintain its values.

Sports, although a part of most school physical education programs, when highly organized and competitive take on new dimensions and face unique challenges. Girls and women, minorities, senior citizens, and disabled persons, while being treated more equitably in sports today, still face discriminatory practices and biases. Public and private youth sports organizations, interscholastic programs, and elite competitions at the collegiate and international levels share some common problems and conflicts. Several controversial issues and some proposed solutions are discussed in this chapter to show the importance placed on sport in the United States.

GIRLS AND WOMEN IN SPORTS

Even though the Greeks excluded women from the ancient Olympic Games, and the founder of the modern Olympic Games viewed their role as cheering spectators, there has been a gradual acceptance of girls and women as sports participants. Traditionally, both physiological and societal factors contributed to the discriminatory treatment many girls and women experienced when they initially sought to compete in sports. Even though males beyond puberty have advantages in sports emphasizing speed, strength, and power, this does not justify the past virtual exclusion of females from sports. Research provides evidence that most females are not as strong, are shorter and lighter, have lower maximum oxygen uptakes, and because of their size have smaller lung capacities, vital capacities, and cardiac outputs. Yet, many female athletes have surpassed the prejudicial limitations placed on them by running and swimming faster and longer, competing professionally against and with males, achieving high levels of muscular strength and endurance, and becoming proficient in sports skills once the domain of males only. The physical potential of girls and women is not yet known, since girls and women must first have equal opportunities in sports to achieve maximally. Contrary to the writings of the early 1900s, women do not risk sterility when they train strenuously and compete aggressively. Like males, females benefit in multiple ways when they achieve physically.

Societal attitudes change slowly: sports have traditionally been viewed in the United States as masculine—for males only. Familial and environmental influences affix a sex identification to sports. For example, boys are usually given balls and outdoor toys, while girls usually receive dolls or quiet and passive toys. Early in life, girls learn that if they participate in sports they risk being called a tomboy or being viewed as less feminine or less attractive. Peer group pressure results in a role conflict, making choosing sports more difficult; therefore, many girls opt out. The more determined ones may compensate by always emphasizing a feminine appearance, by deemphasizing their athletic involvement (and their successes), and by selecting a sport that is viewed as more acceptable, such as golf, gymnastics, swimming, or tennis. The other alternative is to participate actively in sport, regardless of the consequences. Although few chose this route in the past, the situation is changing.

Television commercials that portray women as sports enthusiasts still include sexist overtones and innuendos. Newspapers and periodicals that publish sports stories on women (even on the sports pages, rather than in the society news as in earlier decades) seldom use them as lead stories and never cover them as extensively as they do males' sports stories. Since women have lower salaries (today women in the same jobs earn slightly over 70% of what men earn), they have less discretionary income to spend for sporting equipment and fitness club memberships. With over 50% of American women working outside the home, they usually enjoy less leisure time for recreational activities because of a combination of work, family, and housework obligations. Because of traditional programming and less interest of women in sports in the past, they have yet to receive equal access in public or private facilities.

Today, city recreation programs and private clubs are trying to attract more women, and the emphasis on fitness stimulates greater acceptance of women who not only look and dress fit but are fit. Myths die slowly, and prejudicial attitudes are even more resistant to change. As girls' and women's sports performances improve and as each generation of parents senses that equity is desired, this issue in sports will come closer to resolution.

One leading reason girls and women are enjoying expanded opportunities to play and to compete has been Title IX of the 1972 Education Amendments. (The box on pages 295–296 describes its effects.) Because of this federal legislation (reemphasized by the 1988 Civil Rights Restoration Act, which overrode the Supreme Court opinion in 1984 that weakened its application), thousands of school and college females have achieved greater equity in sport. In 1992, the

Joan Benoit won the initial Olympic marathon for women in 1984. (Photo courtesy Kathy Davis.)

IMPACT OF TITLE IX ON SPORTS FOR FEMALES

High Schools*

Number of Participants†

	1971	1977–1978	1984–1985	1990–1991
Girls	300,000	2,000,000	1,700,000‡	1,900,000
Boys	3,700,000	4,400,000	3,300,000‡	3,400,000

Most popular girls' sports: Basketball
Track and field
Volleyball
Softball (fast-pitch)
Tennis
Soccer
Cross country
Swimming and diving
Field hockey
Golf

National Association of Intercollegiate Athletics§

Average number of sports for women: 4.07

Most popular sports: Basketball
Volleyball
Softball
Tennis

Female head coaches of women's teams: 41.4%

Female assistant coaches of women's teams: 53%

Full-time female head coaches of women's teams: 45.5%

Full-time female assistant coaches of women's teams: 4.4%

Females holding all types of coaching positions of women's teams: 45.0%

Female administrators of women's programs: 13.4%

National Collegiate Athletic Association ‖

Average number of sports for women:

1978: 5.61

1982: 6.59

1986: 7.15

1990: 7.24

1992: 7.09

1996: 7:50

Most popular sports: Basketball
Volleyball
Tennis
Cross country
Softball

(*Continued*)

IMPACT OF TITLE IX ON SPORTS FOR FEMALES (CONTINUED)

Female coaches of women's teams: (Since 1986, the number of head coaching jobs increased by 1003; of these, women were hired for 333.)

1972: over 90%

1978: 58.2%

1982: 52.4%

1986: 50.6%

1990: 47.3%

1992: 48.3%

1996: 47.7%

Female administrators of women's programs: (Females hold 35.9% of all administrative jobs in women's programs; yet, no females are involved in the administration of 23.8% of women's programs.)

1990: 15.9%

1992: 16.8%

1996: 18.5%

* Data from the National Federation of State High School Association.
† Numbers have been rounded.
‡ Change in method of collection of data may have accounted for these decreases.
§ Data from 1992 study conducted by Virginia Neal and Peggy Anderson.
‖ Data from 1996 study by Vivian Acosta and Linda Carpenter.

Supreme Court ruled in *Franklin v. Gwinnett County Public Schools* that monetary damages are available under Title IX. Since victims now can be compensated for their injuries for the first time, this powerful incentive may force schools and colleges to eradicate discrimination. (The box on page 297 lists the most important events related to the impact of Title IX on girls' and women's sports.)

Title IX's provisions relative to athletics have not been uniformly implemented because of gender biases, limited budgets and facilities, lack of coaches, and resistance to change. Largely, though, women benefitted by receiving approximately one-third of colleges' athletic budgets for extensive team travel, recruiting, coaches' salaries, medical treatment, publicity, and athletic grants-in-aid. School girls, too, have gained more teams, better-paid coaches, access to facilities, and other program support such as equipment and uniforms.

As these programs expanded, however, control shifted to men. Today, a much smaller percentage of women coach girls and women than before Title IX, and few women administer athletic programs for females (see box on pages 295–296). Among the factors leading to the increasing number of men coaching girls and women are the following: too few women with expertise or interest in coaching; more equitable salaries for coaches of female teams than was the case prior to Title IX; unwillingness of many women to coach highly competitive teams; and hiring practices in which male athletic directors and school principals prefer to hire male coaches. When female and male athletic programs were combined, usually on the premise of equal opportunity, men were inevitably named to the

TITLE IX TIME LINE

1971	Establishment of the Association for Intercollegiate Athletics for Women.
1972	Congress passes Title IX of the Education Amendments.
1975	Federal government publishes guidelines to explain application of Title IX.
1976	Schools required to be in full compliance with Title IX specifications.
1978	Colleges required to be in full compliance with Title IX specifications.
1979	Congress adopts its policy Interpretation of Title IX.
1984	United States Supreme Court rules in *Grove City College v. Bell* that Title IX is applicable only to educational programs that directly receive federal funding (this ruling results in the dropping of 100 pending claims of violation of Title IX in the Office of Civil Rights).
1988	Congress passes (over presidential veto) the Civil Rights Restoration Act, which states that Title IX applies on an institutionwide basis, including athletics.
1992	United States Supreme Court rules in *Franklin v. Gwinnett County Public Schools* that plaintiffs can sue for compensatory and punitive damages in cases alleging intentional discrimination. This means that monetary compensation for lost athletic opportunities can be received.
1993	National Collegiate Athletic Association releases the report of its Gender Equity Task Force (women comprise 35% of the varsity athletes; receive 30% of the athletic grants-in-aid dollars; are allocated 17% of the recruiting dollars; receive 23% of the operating budget dollars; have access to 37% of the athletic opportunities for participation).
1996	Females comprise 42% of the United States' Olympic team competing in Atlanta. They win 38% of the medals awarded to athletes from the United States.
1997	United States Supreme Court refuses to grant *certiorari* and hear the appeal of *Cohen v. Brown University,* thus indicating that schools and colleges must provide varsity athletic positions for males and females matching the overall percentage of the student body.

top positions either because of seniority or because of the belief that they knew athletics better. Occasionally, though, a female is hired to administer an athletics program that competes at the highest collegiate level. Thus, a major issue confronting athletic programs is the need for more qualified female coaches and sport administrators.

EQUALITY FOR MINORITIES

Members of minority groups have found themselves sports outcasts throughout most of this nation's history. Prior to 1950, sports were rarely integrated, with a few exceptions, such as Jack Johnson, Joe Louis, Paul Robeson, Satchel Paige, Jackie Robinson, and Jesse Owens. Following the Supreme Court's *Brown v. Board of Education* decision in 1954, school desegregation slowly began to open more school and college sports programs to minorities.

Throughout the years, minorities have experienced blatant discrimination in the form of quota systems (only a small number allowed on a team), position stacking (minorities competed for only a limited number of positions because certain others were unavailable to them), social exclusion from clubs and parties, disparity in treatment by coaches, weak academic counseling, and little tutorial help. Sometimes, minority athletes, because of their cultural and educational backgrounds, were ill-prepared for the academic demands of college; their athletic prowess had gotten them through a technical, rather than college-preparatory, high school. Many failed to earn college degrees, thus eliminating themselves from possible coaching positions when their dreams of professional stardom failed to materialize or ended quickly.

Many minorities oppose the National Collegiate Athletic Association's rule that requires first-year athletes at its Division I institutions to have attained a minimum

Wilma Rudolph, in 1960, became the first American woman to win Olympic sprint gold medals in the 100 meters and 200 meters.

Carl Lewis, shown here receiving the baton (lane 5) in the gold-medal-winning 4 x 100 meter relay in the 1984 Los Angeles Olympic Games, has been called by some the greatest athlete ever. (Photo courtesy Paula Welch.)

score of 820 on the Scholastic Aptitude Test (SAT) or 68 on the American College Test (ACT) and to have achieved a minimum standard of 2.50 grade point average in 13 core high school courses (although a sliding scale allows prospective student-athletes to quality for grants-in-aids and competition with a GPA down to 2.00, with test scores up to 1010 on the SAT and 86 on the ACT). They argue that the SAT and the ACT are culturally biased against minorities and, therefore, the test requirements prove that the predominantly white institutions want to limit the domination by minorities on some of their sports teams.

Whether the discrimination against minorities in sports is subtle or overt depends on the school or college, the team, and the leadership of both. Many interesting questions persist. Why are the starters on football and basketball teams predominately minorities when the student bodies are predominantly white? Why are minorities seldom members of tennis, swimming, golf, and gymnastics teams? Why do fewer minority team members who are marginal athletes receive athletic scholarships than comparably skilled whites? What is the status of the minority female athlete? Why are almost all head coaches white?

Are minority athletes bigger, stronger, and generally more highly skilled than white athletes? Research does not substantiate this. However, it is factual that minority athletes' opportunities in elite and expensive sports have traditionally been limited, resulting in their devoting greater amounts of time and energy to the school-sponsored sports of football, basketball, and baseball. These three sports also offer the potential for professional careers. Coaches often experience pressure to win. For them, recruiting the best athletes becomes imperative; yet in traditionally white institutions they also may receive encouragement to have as

Formally underrepresented groups, when given the opportunity, often become dominant forces in sports. (Photo courtesy Maggie McGlynn.)

many white players as possible which may result in athletic scholarships being given disproportionately to marginal white athletes who play as substitutes, if they play at all.

The cost and the fewer opportunities for participation and competition have traditionally prevented many minorities from pursuing tennis, swimming, golf, and gymnastics. Private lessons, expensive equipment, club memberships, and travel requirements for quality competition discourage most minorities from entering these sports; the virtual absence of role models only reinforces the status quo. The minority female athlete must overcome both racial and sexual barriers to equity of sports opportunity.

Minority athletes, regardless of sex, sport, or level of competition, deserve to be treated fairly and equally. All athletes should be expected to complete their academic work in schools and colleges and to earn their degrees in preparation for later life. Because of past discrimination, minorities may deserve to receive counseling to help them derive the most from their education and to learn marketable skills. Since prejudicial attitudes change gradually, everyone must work together to eliminate discrimination in athletics. Coaches must not allow mistreatment of minorities on their teams, and administrators must ensure equity for all.

EQUALITY FOR SENIOR CITIZENS

Senior citizens have had to face discriminatory biases to gain sporting opportunities. As the average age of the United States population increases, a greater awareness of the needs of seniors to exercise and to compete emerges. Persons past 60 years of age are walking, cycling, hiking, swimming, lifting weights, and engaging in a large number of sporting activities with the blessings of their physicians, who favor such activities as preventive medicine. This enthusiasm for exercise and activity has rekindled in many a desire to compete. The United States Senior Games and masters events in national, state, regional, and local competitions are providing opportunities for former athletes and newly aspiring older athletes to achieve in sports in unprecedented ways. Whether competing for recognition or personal satisfaction, these older Americans are beneficiaries of enhanced strength, flexibility, endurance, and balance, factors that directly improve the quality of their lives. This activity also reduces the stress of lost spouses and friends and replaces loneliness with new friends and social opportunities.

EQUALITY FOR DISABLED INDIVIDUALS

In recent years, disabled persons have increasingly desired equal opportunity to participate and compete in sports. The Amateur Sports Act of 1978 specified that the competitive needs of disabled athletes must be accommodated. The Education for All Handicapped Children Act of 1975 mandated that athletics be provided to disabled school students, and the 1990 Americans with Disabilities Act called for access to public activity facilities for those previously denied it. These factors and an eagerness and determination to treat everyone equitably have led

In 1984, the Olympic Games showcased the athletic achievements of disabled athletes. (Photo courtesy Paula Welch.)

to a proliferation of organizations and competitions. Through the International Games for the Disabled, individuals beginning on the local level compete for recognition as highly skilled athletes.

The Paralympic Games, which began in 1948, offer international competitions in athletics (track and field), archery, basketball, boccie, cycling, equestrian, fencing, goalball, judo, lawn bowls, power lifting, seven-a-side soccer, shooting, swimming, table tennis, tennis, and volleyball. Over 3500 athletes competed in the 10th Paralympic Games held in Atlanta in 1996.

The Special Olympics, since 1968, has provided competitive opportunities for mentally retarded individuals. Although experts initially questioned this program, the overwhelming success of personal training and state, national, and international competitions have verified the importance of giving individuals the chance to achieve and to be recognized as winners. Official Special Olympics sports include aquatics, athletics, basketball, bowling, equestrian events, gymnastics, rollerskating, football (soccer), softball, volleyball, alpine skiing, cross-country skiing, figure skating, speed skating, floor hockey, and poly hockey.

YOUTH SPORTS

Around 35,000,000 children and adolescents (ages 4 to 18) participate annually in youth sport competitions sponsored by cities, companies, and local and national organizations. These youthful athletes ride derby cars, horses, and dirt bikes; throw baseballs, softballs, footballs, basketballs, and bowling balls; hit golf balls, tennis balls, racquetballs, and table tennis balls; kick soccer balls; break boards; turn flips; swim; dive; wrestle; run; and compete in triathlons and many more sporting events. This proliferation of youth sports has been fueled by television, money, civic pride, the desire to produce national champions, parental overzealousness, and professional sports models.

The major issues facing youth sport programs are an overemphasis on winning, poorly trained coaches, parental interference, and eroded ethical values. When winning becomes the primary objective, other potential outcomes are lost. Coaches are usually the ones initially caught up in this win-at-all-costs attitude. To fulfill their own ego needs, coaches too often pressure their young players to play while injured, to violate the rules to their advantage, and to quit if they are not good enough. Also, coaches' lack of preparation may result in poorly taught skills, improper treatment of injuries, and inability to understand and to deal with children's developmental needs.

Parents, while usually well intentioned, often impose their wishes on their children as they force them to play a particular sport or several sports to fulfill parental aspirations to succeed in sports, rather than the children's needs, because these adults either were or were not successful themselves. Children may experience considerable guilt because their parents invest huge amounts of time and money in lessons and competitions, and thus these young athletes want desperately to succeed. Parents too often reward results rather than effort and improvement. Interrelated with these problems are misplaced values. Coach and parental role models may reinforce cheating to win, abusing officials and opponents, circumventing the rules, and outcome (winning) over process (having fun and developing skills).

With such a long list of problems, why do youth sports continue to grow in popularity? First, children in America have a genuine interest in and enthusiasm for sports. Second, the positive outcomes in most programs exceed the negative aspects. There are leagues, organizations, coaches, and parents who emphasize fun and participation and who ensure positive outcomes for the children physiologically and psychologically.

Soccer is a popular sport for children. (Photo courtesy Winkie LaForce.)

Through orientation programs, parents learn about program goals and how to help their children benefit most from their experiences. Program administrators are more aware that elimination of children from teams, overspecialization, extrinsic awards, and total adult control need replacing by a system in which everyone plays in every event and in rotating positions, certificates of participation and team outings are given as rewards instead of huge trophies and championship playoffs, and children are asked what they want from their sports experiences to ensure attainment of these aspirations. Coaches and parents should stress and reinforce cooperation, teamwork, and sportsmanship. Outcomes such as individual skill development, participation of everyone, development of intrinsic motivation, learning and playing several sports in varied positions, safe participation, and fun should be guaranteed.

Each year millions of girls and boys ages 8 to 18 years compete in the largest amateur sports program in the United States, the Junior Olympics, which are organized by the Amateur Athletic Union and recognized by the United States Olympic Committee. These amateur athletes compete in more than 3000 local meets, the state championships, the regional events, and the national finals. The benefits from being a part of the Junior Olympics include making friends, having opportunities to travel, gaining a sense of achievement, and enjoying the excitement of the competitions. Youth also compete in state games, such as the Empire State Games (New York) and the Keystone State Games (Pennsylvania), which provide a variety of sports opportunities for children of all ages. Most of the athletes in these state games have developed their skills through youth and school athletic programs.

INTERSCHOLASTIC ATHLETICS

The National Federation of State High School Associations promotes interscholastic athletics as an integral part of the educational experiences of high school students. Most physical educators traditionally have favored and supported interscholastic athletics. They believe, however, that adolescents are better able developmentally and emotionally to compete than are children. School administrators stress the beneficial outcomes of fitness, sportsmanship, cooperation, self-discipline, and other values for the participants. From a broader perspective, interscholastic athletics enhances school spirit and, in many locales, enlists strong community support for the school. The Sport and Physical Education Advocacy Kit (SPEAK) developed by the National Association for Sport and Physical Education in PART III of the Kit provides some excellent information about the benefits of interscholastic sports programs.

Today, though, many interscholastic athletics coaches have not been properly prepared to coach. Several factors have contributed to this problem:

- Elimination of some physical education requirements and teacher positions;
- More specialized requirements for prospective physical education teachers, thus reducing coaching-related courses in colleges;
- Physical educators not choosing to combine teaching and coaching careers;

- Physical educators ceasing to coach;
- More school sports teams, especially for girls, requiring coaches;
- Teachers of other school subjects seeking coaching positions.

One way to address this need is through the Program for Athletic Coaches' Education (PACE), which provides generic, practical information appropriate for beginning level interscholastic coaches. Basic principles and procedures are presented in the areas of philosophy, growth and development, sports medicine, psychology, litigation and liability, and sport management.

An overemphasis on winning is the major criticism of high school sports in the United States. Indicative of this compulsion are year-round conditioning programs and practices, students specializing in one sport, students playing while hurt, and coaches' jobs depending on winning records. Advocates of year-round conditioning programs stress that they are needed to develop proper skills, to stay competitive with other teams' athletes, and to increase chances for college grants-in-aid. Arguments against single-sport specialization include athletic burnout and overuse injuries; denied opportunities to acquire other skills, to play with other athletes, and to learn from other coaches; and exploitation by coaches concerned only with their teams.

The confusion for the teacher-coach who must try to meet the demands of two full-time jobs is compounded when school administrators, parents, and local team supporters mandate winning. Coaching supplements are low when compared with these pressures, and the time expectations are high, although personal satisfaction and community and school recognition may compensate somewhat.

Another controversial issue facing interscholastic athletic programs is the "no pass, no play" policy adopted by some states. Generally, this policy requires obtaining passing marks in all courses taken during the previous grading period.

Basketball had become a popular school sport nationally by the early 1900s (Raylon School, Texas). (Photo courtesy Thomas L. Ward.)

Supporters state that the purpose of schools is education. Thus, participation on a team, or in any other extracurricular activity, is a privilege earned by those who achieve in the classroom. Advocates also claim that this policy will motivate students to achieve academically on a consistent basis. Lawmakers, school administrators, and most parents applaud the effectiveness of this policy because students' performances in their class work overall have improved. Opponents disagree. They claim that extracurricular activities, and especially sports, encourage some young people to remain in school. Experience, though, has shown that although a few students may only continue their education because of the appeal of sports participation, many students seem to be taking their schoolwork more seriously because of the "no pass, no play" policy.

The abuse of drugs is all too pervasive in the schools. Most adolescents and children, including athletes, have ready access to tobacco, alcohol, marijuana, amphetamines, cocaine, and other drugs. Unless coaches educate their athletes about the harmful effects of these drugs on their bodies, and hence their performances, many interscholastic athletes will succumb to peer pressure and use these drugs. Underage drinking, cigarette smoking, and use of smokeless tobacco occur among interscholastic athletes. They also may use anabolic steroids, resulting in immediate and irreparable physiological damage. Taken to increase muscle bulk and size for appearance and performance purposes, large dosages of anabolic steroids may interfere with normal growth and development, lead to overly aggressive and irrational behaviors, cause sterility, and even kill the user.

School athletic programs also face other problems such as spectator violence, unsportsmanlike conduct by coaches and athletes, cheating on academic eligibility, and program threats. Because of skyrocketing costs, due somewhat to injury and liability insurance and the provision of athletic programs for girls and disabled persons, many schools can no longer afford to provide athletics as a right. Many high schools are adopting a pay-for-play policy, which means that no longer will educational allocations finance athletic teams; instead, any student who desires to participate on a team will have to pay for the experience. Although this policy excludes from athletics students who are unable to pay, this is an increasingly popular trend, especially in private schools.

INTERCOLLEGIATE ATHLETICS

Ever since the proliferation of college athletic programs for men in the late 1800s, college faculties and administrators have been concerned about the potentially detrimental effects of athletics on academic work. Associated problems then and now include students missing classes because of competing and traveling, receiving unearned grades, and being admitted even though underqualified. The National Collegiate Athletic Association (NCAA), the National Association of Intercollegiate Athletics (NAIA), and the National Junior College Athletic Association (NJCAA) have all attempted to administer intercollegiate athletics on the basis of educational principles, although regulations concerning these issues largely rest with each institution. The problem that each college faces is how to deal effectively with regulations when winning is almost synonymous with survival, especially at the larger institutions.

Winning teams appeal to spectators and lead to increased interest. More fans bring in larger gate receipts. More money contributes to hiring coaches with winning reputations and to recruiting and awarding grants-in-aid to better athletes, who combine to win more games. This cycle (winning = fans = money = winning = fans = money) repeats itself and spirals larger and larger. The resultant overcommercialization changes college athletics from an extension of the institution's educational mission to a business venture. When winning becomes the most important objective, rules frequently are violated, both during play and in the recruiting of athletes; sportsmanship, character development, and other values are often lost or at least deemphasized in the process. Increasingly, college and university presidents are addressing these problems by emphasizing academic outcomes over athletic goals, despite opposition by some coaches.

Why do intercollegiate athletics continue to thrive? There are three major justifications. First, intercollegiate athletics reflect American attitudes, beliefs, and values. Many people advocate that colleges have the responsibility to offer athletic teams for students to play on for the love of the game, and they defend the concept that sports participation helps prepare the athletes for life by developing physical, intellectual, social, and moral skills. Second, the benefits already mentioned exceed the liabilities. Many people think that the problems listed above are sporadic rather than pervasive. They add that participants and spectators experience a cathartic release of tension and have fun, while college spirit and allegiance are greatly enhanced. Third, athletic teams are valuable public relations tools for institutions. College enrollments often increase as a result of successful athletic programs, especially in football and men's basketball. The provision of entertainment attracts large numbers of spectators to college athletic

Intercollegiate football teams have become multimillion-dollar businesses in major institutions, thus challenging the accuracy of the concept of the student-athlete. (Photo courtesy UNC Sports Information Office.)

contests, with an accompanying surge in college loyalty that many claim positively affects legislative appropriations and private donations to academic departments, in addition to generous support for athletics.

Realistically, intercollegiate athletics, regardless of the extent of the challenges, will continue to thrive because of its entertainment value and benefits. To accentuate the positive and to reduce the negative, the following actions are recommended:

1. Sanction intercollegiate coaches and athletes who violate athletic regulations, especially in the areas of recruiting and scholarships, for the first offense; place violators on a two-year probation from coaching and from competing for the second offense; ban violators from college coaching and from intercollegiate competition for life for the third offense.

2. Withhold for five years from an institution one grant-in-aid for every athlete who does not graduate within six years.

3. Require that coaches of nonrevenue-producing sports be employed full-time (either within athletics or some other aspect of the institution).

4. Base coaches' job security and salaries not on their won-lost records but on the fulfillment of their other job responsibilities and the provision of positive experiences for their athletes.

5. Restrict schedules of all sports to no more than two days of competition per week while classes are in session.

6. Excuse athletes from classes no more than five days per academic year for travel and competition.

7. Admit only those athletes who meet the academic standards of admission to the colleges they attend.

8. Limit grants-in-aid to tuition, fees, and books, and award them only on the basis of need.

If some or all of these suggestions are implemented, intercollegiate athletics might become a more positive, educational experience for athletes.

The abuse of drugs by college athletes and the desire by the NCAA to curtail their use has led to drug testing at football bowl games and NCAA Championships. Although only a few athletes have been barred from competition because of their use of banned drugs, many claim that this testing and institutional drug-testing programs have deterred many athletes from the use of performance-enhancing drugs. Still, too many college athletes are guilty of perjury when they sign the pledge required by the NCAA stating that they do not use these substances. Even the drug education programs offered by colleges and universities have failed to eradicate this blemish on the reputation of intercollegiate athletics.

The use of anabolic steroids is especially dangerous. Besides providing unfair advantages physically, anabolic steroids can severely harm those who abuse them. These drugs may cause the users to behave violently on and off the field. Their abuse is often linked with an obsession to earn a starting position, to become a star player, or to get drafted into a professional league. Amphetamine abuse may also occur under the guise of increasing one's aggressiveness and effort. Cocaine, marijuana, tobacco, and alcohol are more likely to be used socially or for relaxation. As with other college students, most athletes' drug of choice is alcohol, even though most are underage drinkers. Coaches, therefore, face the challenge of educating their athletes about the negative efforts of drug abuse as well as about the rules and values violated through their use.

To preserve the integrity of intercollegiate sports, coaches and athletic administrators must also resolve issues of institutional control. Several institutions have failed to keep overeager supporters from giving money, cars, clothes, and other benefits to athletes. Although not illegal, these actions violate NCAA rules governing payments to athletes. In the intense recruiting battles for blue-chip athletes, coaches may convince admissions committees to lower entrance standards. Many institutions have been criticized for the low graduation rates of athletes, especially African-Americans.

Some athletes' conduct also undermines the educational value of athletics. For example, actions such as taunting opponents and excessive celebrations illustrate that such behavior runs counter to the goals of fair play and respecting one's opponents. Coaches' physical and emotional abuse of players is another example of such destructive behavior. In addition, misdemeanors and felonies, such as driving under the influence of alcohol, assault, drug dealing, and rape, have negatively affected the image of athletes and institutions. Booster clubs or athletic foundations also repeatedly have paid off the contracts of coaches with whom they have become disillusioned for not winning enough games. Such actions always raise the question of who is in control of athletics. These examples describe situations at only a few of the nationally prominent universities that have failed to maintain institutional control over their big-time athletic programs.

●   ●   ●   ●

Both high school and college athletes can take advantage of their state games and of the United States Olympic Festival as ways to further develop their sports prowess. This latter opportunity, through its qualifying events and annual competitions (except in Olympic years), gives developing athletes chances to demonstrate their skills against the other top athletes in their sports. The United States Olympic Festival often serves as the qualifying event or training ground for athletes in several sports.

INTERNATIONAL SPORTS

Elite athletes around the world have numerous opportunities to compete in championship events annually as well as in special events, such as the Pan-American Games, the Asian Games, the British Empire and Commonwealth Games, and the World University Games. These events, open to athletes from the countries implicit in the games' titles, are conducted every four years except for the World University Games, which are held every two years. All of these are important competitions, but the most prestigious internationally are the Olympic Games (patterned after the ancient Greek spectacle). Since 1896 (and 1924 for the Winter Games) athletes from around the world have competed every four years (except during World Wars I and II) under the direction of the International Olympic Committee (IOC) (see the box on pages 310–311). Starting in 1994, the Winter Games have been held in even-numbered years alternating with the Summer Games.

The Olympic Games have been subjected to numerous threats to their ideals, with politics being the chief detractor. From the inception of the Games through the attempt by the Nazis to prove Aryan supremacy in 1936 to the boycotts of 1976, 1980, and 1984, countries have attempted to use the Olympics to influence public opinion. The worst political situation occurred during the 1972 Munich Olympic Games when Arab terrorists massacred eleven Israeli athletes. The banning of some countries and the nonrecognition of others prove that the Olympic Games remain political. Athletes competing as representatives of their nations, the playing of national anthems during the awards ceremonies, national medal counts, team sports, and national uniforms constantly reinforce nationalism. Governments, financially and ideologically, continue to increase their involvement because international prestige and promotion of their political ideologies are at stake. Judging irregularities often result from political alliances, while increased use of drugs verifies the importance placed on winning.

Commercialism has grown exponentially. For example, the 1968 Mexico City Games cost $250 million to stage, while the 1980 Moscow Games reportedly cost over $2 billion. CBS paid $660,000 to broadcast the 1960 events; NBC televised the 1996 Olympic Games at a cost of about $800 million worldwide. The athletes are not immune to commercialism either. Although the Olympic Games were begun for amateur athletes competing for the love of sport, today most athletes are openly professionals, with each sport's governing federation specifying what competitors are allowed to accept monetarily. Many athletes receive money from their countries based specifically on how many and what types (gold, silver, or bronze) of medals they win. The list could continue, but the point is that few, if any, Olympic athletes are amateurs in the sense of never having profited from their athletic skill.

In spite of these problems, the Olympic Games thrive and continue to increase in popularity. The development of friendships and the attainment of personal athletic goals are two of the many positive outcomes. Most disdain the boycotts, political maneuvering, unfair judging, and drug abuse, since these incidents only detract from but do not destroy the Olympic Games. Commercialization of the overall staging and of the athletes themselves seemingly is a nuisance to be tolerated, rather than a reason to end the competitions. Many people advocate either reducing the numbers of events and entries or lengthening the Games and

Jesse Owens, a Big Ten champion from Ohio State University, won four gold medals in the 1936 Berlin Olympic Games. (Photo courtesy the University of Michigan.)

MODERN OLYMPIC GAMES*

	Year	City	Nations	Events	Sports	Males	Females	Athletes
I	1896	Athens, Greece	13	42	9	311	0	311
II	1900	Paris, France	22	60	17	1319	11	1330
III	1904	St. Louis, MO	12	94	14	681	6	687
V	1908	London, England	22	104	21	1699	36	2035
V	1912	Stockholm, Sweden	27	106	13	2490	57	2547
VI	1916	Berlin, Germany (canceled WWI)						
VII	1920	Antwerp, Belgium	27	154	21	2543	64	2607
VIII	1924	Paris, France	45	137	17	2956	136	3092
IX	1928	Amsterdam, Holland	46	120	14	2724	290	3014
X	1932	Los Angeles, CA	37	124	14	1281	127	1408
XI	1936	Berlin, Germany	49	142	19	3738	328	4068
XII	1940	Tokyo, Japan (canceled WWII)						
XIII	1944	London, England (canceled WWII)						
XIV	1948	London, England	59	138	17	3714	385	4099
XV	1952	Helsinki, Finland	69	149	17	4407	518	4925
XVI	1956	Melbourne, Australia	67	145	16	2958	384	3342
		Stockholm, Sweden (equestrian only)	29	6	1	145	13	158
XVII	1960	Rome, Italy	84	150	17	4738	610	5348
XVIII	1964	Tokyo, Japan	94	162	19	4457	683	5140
XIX	1968	Mexico City, Mexico	113	172	18	4750	781	5531
XX	1972	Munich, Germany	122	196	21	6659	1171	7830
XXI	1976	Montreal, Canada	92	199	21	4915	1274	6189
XXII	1980	Moscow, USSR	81	200	21	4320	1192	5512
XXIII	1984	Los Angeles, CA	140	223	21	5458	1620	7078

XXIV	1988	Seoul, Korea	160	237	23	6963	2438	9421
XXV	1992	Barcelona, Spain	171	257	25	7555	3008	10563
XXVI	1996	Atlanta, GA	197	271	26	7061	3683	10744
XXVII	2000	Sydney, Australia						

WINTER OLYMPIC GAMES

	Year	City	Nations	Events	Sports	Males	Females	Athletes
I	1924	Chamonix, France	16	13	5	281	13	294
II	1928	St. Moritz, Switz.	25	13	6	366	27	393
III	1932	Lake Placid, NY	17	14	5	277	30	307
IV	1936	Garmisch-Parkenkirchen, Germany	28	17	5	680	76	756
V	1948	St. Moritz, Switz.	28	24	6	636	77	713
VI	1952	Oslo, Norway	30	22	5	624	108	732
VII	1956	Cortina d'Ampezzo, Italy	32	24	5	687	132	819
VIII	1960	Squaw Valley, CA	30	27	5	502	146	648
IX	1964	Innsbruck, Austria	36	34	7	758	175	933
X	1968	Grenoble, France	37	35	7	1063	230	1293
XI	1972	Sapporo, Japan	35	35	7	927	218	1128
XII	1976	Innsbruck, Austria	37	37	7	1013	248	1261
XIII	1980	Lake Placid, NY	37	39	7	1012	271	1283
XIV	1984	Sarajevo, Yugoslavia	49	40	7	1127	283	1490
XV	1988	Calgary, Canada	57	46	7	1270	364	1634
XVI	1992	Albertville, France	65	57	7	1313	488	1801
XVII	1994	Lillehammer, Norway	67	61	7	1302	542	1844
XVIII	1998	Nagano, Japan						
XIX	2002	Salt Lake City, UT						

*Courtesy of the United States Olympic Committee.

increasing the numbers of sites and sports. Several support reductions in the symbols of nationalism.

As other nations emphasized Olympic sport success, the United States found its traditional dominance lessening, often because of other nations' subsidization of elite athletes. A restructuring of amateur sports in the United States seemed appropriate. Following the passage of the Amateur Sports Act of 1978, the United States Olympic Committee (USOC) established the United States Olympic Training Center in Colorado Springs, Colorado. It offered to National Governing Bodies (NGBs) for each Olympic sport its resources and facilities as training sites for athletes. The USOC has received some federal funding but relies largely on corporate sponsorships and private donations to support its work. Increasingly NGBs and athletes in the lesser-known sports receive funding from the USOC to continue training.

SUMMARY

Sports opportunities for girls and women and for minorities of race, age, or ability, while often limited in the past, are today more equitable, although some barriers exist that only time and effort will remove. Youth sports too often overemphasize winning, as do high school sports. Yet most parents support their children's participation in sport because the positive outcomes outweigh the negative risks. Balancing educational values with business concerns remains the dilemma facing major college sports today. Abuses abound, yet the public continues to expect colleges to offer athletic programs as entertainment. Similarly, the Olympic ideals, whether real or imagined, seem to ensure people's support of the Olympic Games, as politics, nationalism, and commercialization provide insufficient reasons to cancel the spectacle. The pervasiveness of sports in the United States means that people believe that sports contribute far more to society than they detract from it. It is the responsibility of those of us who work in any of these sports arenas to ensure that the values of sport are realized by all.

LEMONT JONES
Head Boys Basketball Coach and Assistant Football Coach
Englewood High School
Jacksonville, Florida

EDUCATION
B.S., Physical Education, Lenoir-Rhyne College, Hickory, North Carolina

JOB RESPONSIBILITIES AND HOURS

Lemont teaches weight training classes that focus on developing the fitness, strength, and agility of students, who are also athletes. Because of the number of sports he coaches, his season is year-round. His duties as head coach of two sports make him responsible for practice planning; administrative details such as facilities, equipment, and budget; and competition management and strategy. Lemont's typical teaching day begins at 6:50 A.M. and ends at 2:10 P.M. He starts coaching at 2:50 P.M. and continues to work until at least 6:00 P.M.

SPECIALIZED COURSE WORK, DEGREES, AND WORK EXPERIENCES NEEDED FOR THIS CAREER

The undergraduate courses that Lemont has found most beneficial include concepts of physical education, prevention and care of athletic injuries, and human growth and development. His current position requires a degree in physical education plus a coaching certification.

SATISFYING ASPECTS

Lemont enjoys staying fit, being around kids, and serving as a role model for what he teaches.

JOB POTENTIAL

From a teaching standpoint, the only job potential is being a role model. Having students come back and say "Thanks for everything" means more than anything. The longer he teaches, the more he realizes how important his job really is. In Florida, a teacher starts at over $20,000, with compensation for coaching responsibilities.

SUGGESTIONS FOR STUDENTS

Lemont states that in this career, one must enjoy kids, have a lot of patience, and be able to work with flexible hours. He stresses the importance of surrounding oneself with a positive school atmosphere and good people, which will help one enjoy the job immensely.

REVIEW QUESTIONS

1. What are three ways in which social factors inhibit girls' and women's involvement in sports?
2. What have been the positive and negative effects of Title IX on sports and opportunities for females?
3. How have minorities faced discrimination in sports?
4. What are three common problems facing youth and interscholastic sports programs, and how would you recommend solving them?
5. What do "no pass, no play" and "pay-for-play" policies mean in relation to interscholastic sports?
6. What are three general justifications for college sponsorship of athletics?
7. What are three major problems facing intercollegiate athletics today, and how would you recommend solving them?
8. What is the meaning of the winning = fans = money = winning = fans = money cycle in sports today?

9. What are the three major issues facing the Olympic Games today?
10. How can sports contribute to value development?

STUDENT ACTIVITIES

1. Interview students about their attitudes toward women in sport. Ask them what financial support women should receive, which teams they should have, who should coach them, as well as other related questions. What changes have they observed in society's acceptance of women in sport?

2. Interview two minority athletes on your campus. Ask them whether they have experienced any discrimination during their sports careers and, if so, to describe it. Have they seen or experienced any changes in how they are treated today as opposed to how they were treated when they first began playing their sports on the college level?

3. Based on your attendance at a youth sport event, what were the philosophy and values of that program? What should they have been? Was winning emphasized too much? If so, how was winning stressed too much?

4. Discuss whether the intercollegiate athletic program at your institution is a business or a component of education. Can it be both? If so, how?

5. List several possible changes that could improve the Olympic Games. Which of these are realistic alternatives?

6. Interview senior citizens who have participated in Senior Games or masters events or who are active sports participants. What are their reasons for competing and for being active? Has their involvement been lifelong, or is it a recent lifestyle change?

7. Stage a class debate addressing the topic "Athletics does/does not have a place in our educational system."

8. Attend a youth sports practice session and tabulate the number of times the coach(es) provide positive and corrective feedback, the amount of time spent on task such as in drills and observing skill demonstrations, and the methods used for learning motor skills.

9. Locate in a newspaper or magazine an illustration of biased journalism in the coverage of girls and women in sport. Discuss how this article depicts these athletes.

10. Identify an issue facing sports today and find a current article in a magazine or newspaper that discusses this issue. Present a brief overview of this issue in class.

SUGGESTED READINGS

Aicinena S: Youth sport readiness: a predictive model for success, *Phy Educ* 49:58, 1992. Readiness for organized sport participation in the proposed model is based on an interaction of sport-related fundamental skill development, motivation, socialization, and sport-specific knowledge.

Davis RW: The 1996 Atlanta Paralympics, *JOPERD* 67(6):59, 1996. The Paralympics, begun in 1948, have grown into quadrennial competitions in 17 events for over 3500 international athletes with physical and sensory impairments.

Fejgin N: Participation in high school competitive sports: a subversion of school mission or contribution to academic goals?, *Soc of Sp J* 11(3):211, 1994. Data from a national sample of 10th graders about the impact of athletic sports participation revealed positive effects on grades, self-concept, and educational aspirations and a negative effect on discipline problems.

Fox C, editor: Title IX at twenty—mature programs or still toddling? *JOPERD* 63(3):33, 1992. The seven articles in this feature examine the progress, or lack of it, made by females in coaching, athletic training, officiating, and athletic administration. Opportunities for minority women in sports and the power and limitations of Title IX are also discussed.

Gerdy JR: Blow the whistle on athletic coaches, *Trusteeship* 3(6):22, 1995. This article calls for reform in the role of college athletic coaches in the areas of better hiring processes, meaningful professional development, and better evaluation.

Rotella RJ, et al: Burnout in youth sport, *Elem School J* 91(5):21, 1991. Children, due to stress, burn out in sports and then withdraw from participation. The study of burnout includes a cognitive-affective model that contains situational, cognitive appraisal, physiological, and behavioral components. The authors suggest ways to prevent and treat burnout.

Sherrill C, Pizarro A, Barnes L: A gathering of families: issues and concerns of Special Olympics International 1991, *Palaestra* 8(2):8, 1992. This article celebrates the purpose, mission, and philosophy advocated by those who gather annually to support the achievements of Special Olympians.

Thornton JS: Springing young athletes from the parental pressure cooker, *Phys & Sp Med* 19(7):92, 1991. Some child athletes use pain and injury to escape excessive parental pressure. Physicians are encouraged to recognize the characteristics of pushy parents and to intervene in these destructive relationships.

Wilde TJ: Seeking equitable distribution of opportunities for intercollegiate athletic participation between the sexes, *J of Sp Mgmt* 9:3300, 1995. This article describes Title IX case law and relevant legal principles before examining selected gender-equity initiatives. A three-for-one proposal is suggested as a way to satisfy the athletic interests and abilities of both genders.

Wolff A: The slow track, *Sp Ill* 77(13):53, 1992. Through a colloquy with his football-coaching uncle, the author builds a case for the elusiveness of equity in high school and college sports. Despite the two decades that have elapsed since the passage of Title IX banning gender discrimination, myths like "football makes money," "girls and women are not interested in playing sports," and "the only way to provide teams for females is to cut males' teams" are still firmly espoused.

CHAPTER 13

Living in the Twenty-First Century

KEY CONCEPTS

- Life in the twenty-first century will differ dramatically from today's world and significantly impact the role of physical activity programs.
- A new name for the field of physical education reflects its changing image.
- The promotion of physical activity is essential in helping broaden participation levels.
- Physical activity is a valued part of life.

INTRODUCTORY SCENARIO I—LIVING IN 2050

By the mid-point of the twenty-first century most Americans' lives will be completely different from those lived by earlier generations, even as recently as a half-century earlier. Every school child's education is totally computer-based and individualized according to his or her learning style. Within this somewhat sterile learning environment, physical education, including dance and sport, has become essential for developing children's social, emotional, and physical skills. These daily school programs for youth from age 3 to 20 focus on individualized fitness programs, environmentally-safe outdoor activities, and cooperative sports in addition to games developed and initiated by the students.

Parents are infused into the school environment—in the classroom and gymnasium—because the year-round school day starts at 7:00 A.M. and continues until 7:00 P.M. With more single-parent, non-Caucasian families, schools provide continuing education for parents, enrichment activities in extended-day programs for children, and leisure-time activities for all ages. Social service and governmental agencies work with and through the schools to provide health care and counseling, recreational programs, and career education.

Within this technological society, a huge gap has developed economically. Those without advanced skills and knowledge provide services; those with these skills work in technology-based careers expanding the boundaries of knowledge as they lead the Information Age. Menial tasks, such as manufacturing, are completed by robots or through other nonhuman technologies. Restaurants have been replaced by food packets and pills to save time and money. Americans' fascination with the automobile has been eradicated and replaced by fast, efficient mass transit. Work requirements have increased with most employees choosing to spend an average of 50 hours per week on the job. Despite these work hours, with less time needed for transportation and eating, there is greater leisure time, which is being spent mostly in inactive pastimes such as conducting most business and personal activities through the Internet and watching over 100 television channels.

The threat of heart disease, increasingly the number one killer, has finally begun to catch Americans' attention. Within the past decade, the percentage of adults engaged in physical activity has risen 50%, while 75% more school children are physically active. Extended school programs, private fitness and health centers, and the use of home exercise equipment have been credited with these dramatic improvements. The challenge for physical educators, exercise physiologists, recreation directors, health educators, dance specialists, and sport leaders is to promote the value of physical activity for all.

INTRODUCTORY SCENARIO II—LIVING IN 2050

At 7' 7", 275 pounds, Jimmy broke every national high school scoring and rebounding record during the 2049–2050 season. A basketball phenomenon, he touched off a recruiting frenzy that quickly exceeded sports fans' wildest imaginations. But, to get Jimmy, everyone had to go through James, Sr., who had genetically engineered his son and then incessantly conditioned, fed, and trained him physically and mentally using the latest technologies and drugs. James, Sr. announced to the world, Jimmy's talents could be obtained only for a huge price.

State University offered Jimmy a new car and a condo of his choice, a $100,000 per year salary, and a bonus to rename the basketball arena in his father's honor if Jimmy helped the semi-pro Golden Knights win the NCAA Championship.

The New York Kings, the leading professional basketball franchise, tried to entice Jimmy to leap to its league directly out of high school. They implored James, Sr. to allow Jimmy to sign a $5,000,000 per year, 20-year, no-cut contract. As an incentive, the Kings added a $10,000,000 bonus for each season Jimmy won the league Most Valuable Player Award.

The NRA conglomerate (formerly Nike, Reebok, and Adidas) promised to introduce the Jamming Jimmy autograph shoe one month later if Jimmy signed its $1,000,000 per week endorsement agreement. Jamming Jimmy clothing and sports equipment would be marketed within six months, if he signed.

International Sports Marketing (ISM), however, succeeded in getting James, Sr. to grant it monopolistic control over Jimmy's career. Jimmy would play for State University for one year before joining the Kings. He would sign with NRA immediately and wear his autograph shoe at the University, but defer the $1,000,000 and other endorsements until he joined the Kings. All of the promised payouts were guaranteed; plus, ISM would negotiate for Jimmy an additional $1,000,000 per year in endorsements managed by ISM.

Are you ready for life in the twenty-first century? Do these scenarios accurately predict reality a half-century from now? This chapter's purpose is to project what living in the twenty-first century may be like. This chapter will focus on building upon the field of physical education and sport as described previously to help prepare you for the future.

Physical educators have often followed, rather than led, in Americans' participation in sports and activities. As a result, the importance and prestige of physical education in the schools and sports for all have suffered. Survival of school programs and educationally-based sports programs may be in jeopardy. To take a leading role in the sports and fitness movement, physical educators and sport professionals in various settings need to improve the quality of their programs and better publicize the potentially valuable outcomes of these programs. Fitness leaders must publicize and document the benefits of active lifestyles for all segments of the population. To add credibility to this advocacy, physical education and sport professionals must become good role models of fitness.

Physical education and sport professionals can guarantee accountability in instructional quality by making curricula and programs more humanizing to meet students' and clients' needs, keeping abreast of the knowledge explosion and applying this research-based information, providing equal opportunities for diverse populations, and refocusing athletics to ensure that educational outcomes are imperatives for the future.

PROJECTIONS FOR THE TWENTY-FIRST CENTURY

The world in the twenty-first century will be different, with numerous changes in the field of physical education and sport from what we know today. Following are several projections based upon the continuation of current trends and divided into the categories of school programs, higher education, athletics, and sport and fitness careers. Consider whether these proposed changes and trends will become reality. How will they affect society and you and your career? Are these possibilities desirable? If not, what can be done to avert any undesired outcomes?

School Programs

- Physical education will achieve the established standards for student achievement and through performance assessment respond to the call for educational accountability.

- Physical education curricula will emphasize fitness development and maintenance as well as learning psychomotor skills and enhancing social and emotional skills.

- Physical educators will incorporate technology and computer skills into their programs to enhance learning.

Just as the pole vaulter focuses on the goal ahead, physical educators and sport professionals must focus on preparing to contribute in the twenty-first century. (Photo courtesy Maggie McGlynn.)

- Significantly more minority teachers will be recruited and retained to serve as role models for an increasing number of minority students.
- Coaching certifications will be required of all interscholastic coaches.
- Competency entrance and exit tests will be required of prospective teachers.
- Physical educators will continuously upgrade their instructional abilities and content knowledge.
- An appropriate reward system will be implemented to recognize excellence in teaching and coaching.
- Performance, more than longevity, will determine merit pay and career advancement.

Higher Education

- Five-year teacher education programs will become the standard, while increasingly advanced education and certifications (beyond bachelor's degree) will be required of sport and exercise practitioners.
- The number of graduates with specializations in fitness, exercise physiology, health education, athletic training, and sport management will increase.
- Elective physical education activity programs focusing on aerobic activities, weight training, outdoor activities, and lifetime sports will continue to thrive.

- College students will be older, more career oriented, and more diverse in background.
- College professors will specialize even more in the applied sciences.
- More minority faculty members will be recruited and retained to serve as teachers of and mentors for minority students.
- Increased research productivity will be required for promotion and tenure, although scholarship will be defined more broadly.

Athletics

- Coaching certifications will be required of all youth sport coaches.
- The emphasis on winning in sports at all levels will intensify because of lucrative rewards.
- Value development will still be espoused, although only marginally attained.
- College athletics programs will become more commercialized and more dependent on financial subsidies from educational institutions, sponsors, and donors.
- College athletes in the revenue-producing sports will be paid salaries.
- Drug abuse will increase in athletics at all levels.
- The use of technological advances will enhance athletes' skills and performances.

Sport and Fitness Careers

- Sport and fitness instructors and managers will help change participation levels of adults leading to significant lifestyle changes.
- Physical activity and sport programs for senior citizens will expand dramatically.

Sports increasingly will attract females who welcome the chance to display their skills. (Photo courtesy Maggie McGlynn.)

- Businesses will increasingly provide fitness programs for their employees to help control escalating health care costs.

- Technology will significantly improve sport and fitness equipment, facilities, and programs.

- Extended day sport and physical activity programs for children, adolescents, and their parents will proliferate.

- Outdoor activities will continue to attract new enthusiasts.

- Consumers will become more discriminating in their purchases of fitness equipment, selection of sports to participate in, and nutritional choices to reduce calories, fat, and cholesterol.

- Baccalaureate and master's degrees, continual upgrading of skills and knowledge, and advanced certifications will be required of instructors and managers in sport and fitness careers.

THE TWENTY-FIRST CENTURY PHYSICAL EDUCATION SPECIALIST

In education, those who follow you at your college or university will probably have to complete five years of course work if they choose a teaching career in the schools. Such a requirement is a likely outgrowth of the emphasis on obtaining a liberal arts education before becoming certified as a teacher. Everyone, in all careers, will be expected, yes required, to continually retrain, upgrade, and recertify to keep abreast of the knowledge explosion. If you do not have the sophistication mandated by the Information Age, such as computer literacy for evaluating health risk profiles and prescribing and monitoring exercise programs, then you may not be competitive in the job market beyond 2000.

You must not only be an astute consumer yourself in this era of marketing mania, but you will be called upon to help those you teach or direct to discriminate between fact and fallacy. You must teach athletes what food or drugs to take or training regimens to follow in their quest for success. You must be prepared to differentiate between effective and ineffective exercise equipment and diets. Questions will be asked of you concerning whether certain behaviors in sports are ethical, whether the exercises provided by a certain fitness program or instructor are appropriate, and whether the schools, communities, or both should provide fitness programs for school-age children. You may need to become an advocate for "truth in advertising" because quackery in fitness, exercise, health, and nutrition abounds. Because of the increasing popularity of this broad field, many charlatans will eagerly take consumers' money and even cause them to risk their health and well-being unless you help the buyer beware.

Social issues continuing to influence our lives, such as aging and technology, will call for our involvement. Meeting the leisure needs of an older American populace will demand that fitness, recreational, and educational leaders develop and implement programs that are appropriate for their needs. We will not categorize people of retirement age or older as nonproductive or as nonenergetic. This segment of the population will demand to have its fitness needs met through seniors or masters competitions, daily walks in the malls, aerobics, bowling leagues, or golf. Also, it will be important to provide inexpensive recreational opportunities for those on fixed incomes.

The technology of the twenty-first century will probably astound each of us. Incorporating technology into fitness programs through the use of blood pressure and heart rate monitors on exercise equipment, the use of computers to assess health risks and dietary problems, and the use of videotaping and computer analysis to improve sports performance allows technology to contribute to exercise safety and skill enhancement. Televised and videotaped exercise classes for home use, for school-age children, at the work-site, and in retirement homes may increase due to economic constraints and increased demand for fitness programs.

The environment also will concern many people as they consider what possible irreparable damages our lifestyles may be heaping upon future generations. Backpackers, rock climbers, canoeists, and hikers will be challenged to enjoy nature while leaving it untarnished for those who follow. Ensuring urban green space and protecting state and national parks will be other ways in which recreation specialists will be able to leave a legacy.

A NEW NAME AND CHANGING IMAGE

Before physical education can effectively meet the challenges of leading the sports and fitness movement, it must reestablish its identity and ability to provide leadership in physical education and sport programs. Throughout this book, the term *physical education and sport* has been applied to all of the various programs and careers that involve movement, play, recreation, athletics, and leisure. Part of the image issue facing physical education and sport as it seeks to lead into the next century is the accuracy of its name—does it describe what professionals in this field know and do? The term *physical education* is appropriate when it is used to describe educational programs in schools that focus on the development of the psychomotor dimension. Practitioners today in corporate, recreational, hospital, clinical, fitness, health, and sport settings, though, most often choose other descriptors, such as sport psychologists, fitness leaders, coaches, athletic trainers, exercise physiologists, and recreation directors.

Regardless of the name or setting, leaders must justify their chosen field's existence on its own merits or contributions, rather than on the basis of any traditional status or fad. While proclaiming the values and outcomes of activity programs, professionals in the field must also serve as positive role models—accepting responsibility for living healthy, fit lifestyles so that others may be positively influenced to adopt similar habits.

PROMOTING PHYSICAL ACTIVITY

Accountability for program content is essential and will continue to grow in importance. Without quality and benefits accruing to those served, no program merits continuation. If children, club members, athletes, senior citizens, or corporate employees are not being taught the skills and knowledge that they deserve in activity or sports programs, then elimination of the activity is warranted or at least replacement of the teacher or leader is mandated. Individuals hired to teach programs owe it to their participants to educate. Abdication of this responsibility will lead to others being hired to do these jobs. For example, accountability in school physical education necessitates that every student achieve content standards established by the National Association for Sport and Physical Education:

- Demonstrates competency in many movement forms and proficiency in a few movement forms;
- Applies movement concepts and principles to the learning and development of motor skills;
- Exhibits a physically active lifestyle;
- Achieves and maintains a health-enhancing level of physical fitness;
- Demonstrates responsible personal and social behavior in physical activity settings;
- Demonstrates understanding and respect for differences among people in physical activity settings;
- Understands that physical activity provides opportunities for enjoyment, challenge, self-expression, and social interaction.

Linked closely with accountability is the importance of public relations. Traditionally, the perspective taken by individuals in physical education and sport has been a willingness to serve but not a desire to publicize and, yes, even to market programs. Today, this attitude is archaic. Teachers and program leaders, regardless of setting, must publicize the benefits to those who participate in sport and physical activity. To enlist involvement and financial support, programs must be

Karate is an example of a nontraditional activity enjoyed by people of all ages. (Photo courtesy Don Ridgeway.)

attractive and successful in meeting perceived needs. An additional outcome of this concerted effort to tell others what physical education and sport can do for them is that it brings together, rather than drives apart, all physical activity programs. Some examples of ways to promote physical activity and sport could be:

- Get your Governor or Mayor to proclaim May as Physical Fitness and Sport Month in your state or city.
- Conduct special events like a family fitness night, community fun run, or mall exhibitions of physical education during Physical Fitness and Sport Month.
- Celebrate National Employee Health and Fitness Day in May.
- Initiate daily fitness programs in schools and businesses to encourage everyone to participate in 10 minutes of stretching and aerobic activities simultaneously.
- Develop public service announcements for local radio and television stations that promote physical activity and include fitness tips.
- Write and publish a newsletter or local newspaper articles about popular physical activities, sports, and fitness.
- Involve the community, such as through the PTA/PTO or a local service organization, in developing a fitness trail.
- Ask the school and city libraries to display books about physical activity, sports, and fitness.
- Involve senior citizens with school-age children in cross-generational walks, dances, or other recreational activities.
- Plan special events in schools, businesses, and public agencies to celebrate National Nutrition Month (March), Family Health Month (October), and Heart Month (February).
- Celebrate National Girls and Women in Sports Day (first Thursday in February).
- Initiate a sports attire day each month to encourage everyone to dress for activity and participate in it each month.

PHYSICAL ACTIVITY THROUGHOUT LIFE

The Madison Avenue promotion of physical activity has contributed to its overwhelming surge in popularity, especially for the middle and upper classes. Because of social needs and feelings of self-worth, people of all ages are motivated by the media to join exercise and sport programs. Designer sports clothing and the latest technologically advanced equipment are essential. Club membership, attendance at sport camps, and making business and personal contacts on the golf course, as a sport spectator, or after workout sessions are examples of this popular phenomenon.

The sports and fitness movement, recognized now as a part of the American way of life, rather than a fad, is initiating dramatic changes in physical education and sport programs. Consumer demand is readily evident for healthy lifestyles that seek to improve the quality of life through physical activity. Physical education and sport professionals must share their knowledge about physiology, nutrition, psychology, and fitness and skill development. They must conduct their programs at the worksite as well as in public facilities and private clubs. While helping the corporate executive, they must not neglect lower-income individuals, whose levels of productivity and lifestyles also can be enhanced.

The group whose needs probably will become paramount in the next century includes individuals 65 years of age and older. Between 1982 and 2050, the percentage of people in this age category will almost double (to over one-fifth of the population). As Americans live longer, they need lifetime recreational activities not only to prevent disease and degeneration, but also as a way to enjoy happier, healthier lives.

Advances in medicine and technology not only help us live longer, but they greatly change our lives in other ways. Cures for cancer, AIDS, and other diseases, advances in heart surgery to prevent coronaries, and electronically stimulated movement of paralyzed limbs are but a few medical breakthroughs that elongate and invigorate life. Fewer and fewer household and mundane tasks demand our time and energy, as machines free us from routine jobs. Although only some of our free time is currently spent developing fitness and enjoying sports and other leisure-time activities, free time will increase in the future. Technological advances directly influence these pursuits, too. Better designed running shoes, exercise cycles equipped to monitor fitness levels, biomechanical analyses of tennis strokes or other sport skills, and individualized training paradigms already exist. Undoubtedly, advances in sporting equipment, clothing, and facilities will continue to enhance performance as well as pleasure.

The twenty-first century will expand the Information Age. Handheld personal computers, cellular phones, and satellite transmissions are only the beginning. With a service economy based on and mandating communications skills and technology as the norm, we will increasingly turn to sport, fitness, and leisure activities during nonwork hours for rest and stress reduction.

Computer technology already permits exercise and sport scientists to assess fitness levels, to prescribe exercise paradigms designed to meet individualized needs, and to monitor the attainment of personal fitness goals. Using database

Senior citizens have become enthusiastic participants in road races.

management computer software, corporate fitness leaders can determine the impact of each exercise program offered by using attendance numbers and by recording fitness parameters measured periodically. Sport managers can use computers to generate ticket sales solicitations and target marketing campaigns. Computer graphics, desktop publishing, financial forecasts for athletic programs and clubs, students' fitness report cards for parents, biomechanical analyses of athletes' skill performances, and computer-based play calling are a few examples of technological advances impacting our programs.

The realm of space travel and the establishment of space colonies broadens our perspective from this country to the importance of viewing how physical education and sport can influence the entire world. Our enthusiasm for sports and fitness is already altering attitudes in other countries. Many professionals share their sports expertise with people in other countries. Successful businesses worldwide model their corporate fitness programs on ours. All of these contribute to greater international understanding through the sharing of activity.

SUMMARY

Future physical activity leaders hold the keys to the acceptance and promotion of physical activity and sport programs for all. Improved curricula based on standards that focus on meeting all students' fitness and lifetime sports and activity skill needs are imperative. The power and potential of physical education and sport, by whatever name, is based on a commitment to physical activity, and our nation's health, and maybe even its existence, depends on this. Through technological advances, we must strive to improve the quality of life for ourselves and for others worldwide in the twenty-first century.

WINIFRED WARREN LAFORCE
Director, Sports and Venue Management
1999 Special Olympics World Summer Games
Research Triangle Park, North Carolina

EDUCATION
B.A., Education, University of Florida
M.A., Reading and Language Arts, University of North Carolina at Chapel Hill
M.A., Physical Education with specialization in Sport Administration, University of North Carolina at Chapel Hill

JOB RESPONSIBILITIES AND HOURS

The job responsibilities of the Director of Sports and Venues Management for an enterprise the size and scope of the Special Olympics World Summer Games are huge. Winkie manages the sports competitions for over 7000 Special Olympians from over 150 countries around the world and venues in Raleigh, Durham, and Chapel Hill. She coordinates staff members and volunteers who plan and conduct the competitions and directs the personnel who prepare and operate sites for all sporting events. Scheduling and hosting competitions for Special Olympians of various ages requires extensive organizational expertise, patience, and negotiating acumen. Winkie's experience includes serving as a director with the U.S. Olympic Festival '87, President and Executive Director of North Carolina Amateur Sports, which conducts the State Games of North Carolina, and Director of Special Events and Projects in the Sports Department for the Atlanta Committee for the 1996 Olympic Games. The demands of all of her sport management positions have required long hours with the focus on doing whatever it took to get the job completed successfully.

SPECIALIZED COURSE WORK, DEGREES, AND WORK EXPERIENCES NEEDED FOR THIS CAREER

Although no specific degree is required for a sport management career, experiences that include managing people and details are vitally important. Winkie believes that management and business courses that include learning about motivation and goal setting are critical to successfully fulfilling job expectations.

SATISFYING ASPECTS

Winkie loves to work with people and to see the culmination of their combined efforts in a successful event. Managing sporting events requires working with hundreds of people including community leaders, staff members, and volunteers who coordinate the competition sites and the sports and with corporate sponsors who support the events.

JOB POTENTIAL

Given the increasing popularity of sporting events, opportunities abound for sport managers who are willing to gain skills and knowledge starting in entry-level positions. Salary increases, job security, and career advancement depend on experience, proven performance, and networking.

SUGGESTIONS FOR STUDENTS

Winkie suggests that you willingly start at a low salary in order to "get your foot in the door." Make yourself invaluable to your employers by working hard (including weekends). With such diligence, you can move to the top. Since sport management careers remain male oriented, says Winkie, women have to work harder and longer to be recognized for their merit; however, when this recognition is achieved, a woman may have an advantage in this professional environment.

REVIEW QUESTIONS

1. What factors will influence society and you in your career as you enter the twenty-first century?
2. What changes are projected for school programs in the twenty-first century?
3. What changes are projected for college and university programs in the twenty-first century?
4. What changes are projected for athletic programs in the twenty-first century?

5. What changes are projected for sport and fitness programs in the twenty-first century?
6. How will technology affect physical activity programs in the future?
7. How can physical education change its image? Will a name change help?
8. Why is the achievement of standards the most important component in accountability?
9. Why are even more physical activity programs for senior citizens essential in the future?
10. What is the greatest challenge you will face in your career within the next few years?

STUDENT ACTIVITIES

1. Find five magazine advertisements that validly use physical activity or fitness in marketing their products. Find five magazine advertisements that make outlandish claims about their fitness-related products.
2. Interview three people who teach physical activities in any program. Ask them what they think the problems and challenges are for people in their careers or similar careers. What suggestions for improvement do they have?
3. Describe the program offerings of an elementary school, secondary school, college activity program, health club, or recreation department that you think meets the needs of the individuals currently being served. Will these needs differ by 2010? If so, how will these needs be met?
4. Write a two- or three-page paper describing "Living in the Year 2020" when you will be around the midpoint of your career.

SUGGESTED READINGS

Chinworth SA: A physical education Christmas carol (with apologies to Charles Dickens), *Phy Educ* 52:114, Fall, 1995. Sue, a student in physical education, is visited by the ghosts of physical education past, present, and yet to be. Built on the history of this field and current threats, the future of physical education depends on gaining and applying greater knowledge.

Clumpner RA: Teaching physical education—strategies for improving instruction, *JOPERD* 62(1):28, 1991. Since initiating change in teachers is difficult, administrators must use strategies such as self-analysis, peer analysis, conferences and workshops, and evaluations to support teachers in improving their effectiveness.

Edginton CR, Davis TM, Hensley LD: Trends in higher education: implications for health, physical education, and leisure studies, *JOPERD* 65(7):51, 1994. Access, delivery systems, privatization, curricular innovation, accountability, strategic thinking, and entrepreneurship are among the trends that will impact the future of health, physical education, and leisure studies programs.

Jones CJ, Rikli RE: The gerontology movement—is it passing us by? *JOPERD* 64(1):17, 1993. The authors suggest changes in HPERD curricular development and professional preparation to educate students for careers within the field of gerontology.

Jordan D, (ed): Promoting active lifestyles—a multidisciplinary approach, *JOPERD* 64(1):34, 1993. This seven-article feature describes an Exercise and Nutrition for Lifetime Wellness course; facilities and equipment designed for children, seniors, and people with disabilities; changing perceptions of aging; fear as a constraint to females' activity; teaching students with disabilities; aquatic programs; and assessment. These all affect the promotion of active lifestyles.

Kraus R: Tomorrow's leisure: meeting the challenges, *JOPERD* 64(4):42, 1994. Six challenges face leisure service providers in the year 2000 and beyond: multiculturalism, the environment, leisure education and values-oriented play, conflicts in goals and strategies, agency coordination and professional development, and work perspectives.

McBride RE (ed): Critical thinking . . . an idea whose time has come! *JOPERD* 66(6):21, 1995. This feature includes five articles that describe the importance of teaching critical thinking in all levels of physical education classes.

Newell KM: Kinesiology: the label for the study of physical activity in higher education, *Quest* 42:269, 1990. The author defines kinesiology as the study of movement or physical activity. It is argued that this term should be acceptable to those favoring the disciplinary, professional, and activities dimensions of this field.

Smith TK, Cestaro N: Saving future generations—the role of physical education, *JOPERD* 63(8):75, 1992. Two physical educators recount the modifications in their school's physical education program to focus on lifetime fitness and to incorporate multidisciplinary concepts.

Washington SJ: Diversity education for professional practice, *JOPERD* 67(2):42, 1996. Educating for diversity can occur in a variety of settings and includes being more inclusive, respectful, and appreciative of diversity in order to affect social change.

Appendix A

PROFESSIONAL JOURNALS RELATING TO PHYSICAL EDUCATION AND SPORT

Journal	Publisher and Address	Focus
Academy Papers	American Academy of Kinesiology and Physical Education Human Kinetics Publishers, Inc. Box 5076 Champaign, IL 61825-5076 1-800-747-4457	Papers presented at annual meetings of the Academy
Adapted Physical Activity Quarterly	Human Kinetics Publishers, Inc. Box 5076 Champaign, IL 61825-5076 1-800-747-4457	Teaching and research including case studies
American Fitness	Aerobics and Fitness Association of America 15250 Ventura Boulevard, Suite 200 Sherman Oaks, CA 91403 1-800-446-2322	News and information concerning aerobics, health, and fitness
American Health	19 W. 22nd Street New York, NY 10010 212-366-8900	Research-based news magazine for health, fitness, and medicine
American Journal of Public Health	American Public Health Association 1015 Fifteenth Street, NW, Suite 300 Washington, DC 20005 202-789-5600	Diverse types of articles for health professionals
American Journal of Sports Medicine	American Orthopaedic Society for Sports Medicine 230 Calvary Street Waltham, MA 02154 617-736-0707	Sports medicine articles and information

Journal	Publisher and Address	Focus
Athletic Administration	National Association of Collegiate Directors of Athletics P.O. Box 16428 Cleveland, OH 44116 216-892-4000	Articles and administrative materials
Athletic Business	1846 Hoffman Street Madison, WI 53704 608-249-0186	Articles about facilities, management, and financing
CAHPER Journal	Canadian Association for HPER Place R. Tait McKenzie 1600 James Naismith Dr. Gloucester Ont. KIB 5N4 Canada 613-748-5622	Articles for all aspects of HPER fields
Clinical Journal of Sport Medicine	Canadian Academy of Sport Medicine Liptencoct-Raven 1185 Avenue of the Americas New York, NY 10036 212-930-9500	Research articles, clinical reviews, case reports, and new procedures in sport medicine
Dance Magazine	33 West 60th Street New York, NY 10023-7990 212-245-9050	Articles focus on dance performance
Health Education Quarterly	Society for Public Health Education John Wiley and Sons, Inc. 605 3rd Avenue New York, NY 10158 212-850-6000	Articles advocate promoting health through improved health education, medical practice, and research
IDEA Personal Trainer	International Association of Fitness Professionals 6190 Cornerstone Court East, Suite 204 San Diego, CA 92121-3773 1-800-999-4332	Popular articles about fitness
International Journal of Sport Biomechanics	Human Kinetics Publishers, Inc. Box 5076 Champaign, IL 61825-5076 1-800-747-4457	Research and theoretical articles

Journal	Publisher and Address	Focus
Interscholastic Athletic Administration	National Federation of State High School Associations 11724 NW Plaza Circle P.O. Box 20626 Kansas City, MO 64195-0626 816-464-5400	Administrative concerns about high school athletic programs
Journal of Applied Sport Psychology	Association for the Advancement of Applied Sport Psychology c/o Vikki Krane Bowling Green State University HPER, Eppler Center Bowling Green, OH 43403 419-372-7233	Research articles about sport psychology
Journal of Athletic Training	National Athletic Trainers' Association 2952 Stemmons Freeway, Suite 200 Dallas, TX 75247-6103 1-800-879-6282	Practical articles about various components of athletic training
Journal of Health Education	American Association for Health Education of the American Alliance for Health, Physical Education, Recreation and Dance 1900 Association Drive Reston, VA 22091-1599 1-800-213-7193	Informational and practical articles
Journal of the International Council for Health, Physical Education and Recreation, Dance and Sport	American Alliance for Health, Physical Education, Recreation and Dance 1900 Association Drive Reston, VA 22091-1599 703-476-3486	Teaching and research articles
Journal of Leisure Research	National Recreation and Park Association 2775 S. Quincy Street, Suite 300 Arlington, Va 22206-2204 703-820-4940	Research and empirical reports in leisure

Journal	Publisher and Address	Focus
Journal of Motor Behavior	Heldref Publications 1319 Eighteenth Street, NW Washington, DC 20036-1802 202-296-5149	Articles about human movement
Journal of the Philosophy of Sport	Philosophic Society for the Study of Sport Human Kinetics Publishers, Inc. Box 5076 Champaign, IL 61825-5076 1-800-747-4457	Philosophical articles concerning sports
Journal of Physical Education, Recreation and Dance	American Alliance for Health, Physical Education, Recreation and Dance 1900 Association Drive Reston, VA 22091-1599 1-800-213-7193	Informational and practical articles for educators
Journal of School Health	American School Health Association P.O. Box 708 Kent, OH 44240 216-678-1601	Education and promotion of health articles
Journal of Sport and Exercise Psychology	Human Kinetics Publishers, Inc. Box 5076 Champaign, IL 61825-5076 1-800-747-4457	Basic and applied research articles
Journal of Sport History	North American Society for Sport History 101 White Building Penn State University University Park, PA 16802-3903 814-238-1288	Scholarly research about sport history
Journal of Sport Management	North American Society for Sport Management Human Kinetics Publishers, Inc. Box 5076 Champaign, IL 61825-5076 1-800-747-4457	Theoretical and practical articles

Journal	Publisher and Address	Focus
Journal of Sport and Social Issues	Sage Periodicals Press 2455 Teller Road Thousand Oaks, CA 91360 805-499-0721	Articles about prominent issues in sport
Journal of Strength and Conditioning Research	National Strength and Conditioning Association Human Kinetics Publishers, Inc. Box 5076 Champaign, II 61825-5076 1-800-747-4457	Research relative to conditioning of athletes
Journal of Teaching in Physical Education	Human Kinetics Publishers, Inc. Box 5076 Champaign, IL 61825-5076 1-800-747-4457	Research in teaching and teacher education
Medicine and Science in Sports and Exercise	American College of Sports Medicine Box 1440 Indianapolis, IN 46206-1440 317-637-9200	Research into the scientific bases of sports and exercise
National Coach: The Voice of High School Coaches in America	National High School Athletic Coaches Association P.O. Box 5020 Winter Park, FL 32793-5020 407-679-1414	Practical articles for coaches
NIRSA Journal	National Intramural-Recreational Sports Association 850 SW 15th Street Corvallis, OR 97333 507-737-2088	Practical articles for college intramural professionals
Palaestra: The Forum of Sport, Physical Education and Recreation for the Disabled	Challenge Publications, Ltd. 549 Meadow Drive P.O. Box 508 Macomb, IL 61455 309-833-1902	Results of competitions and practical articles
Parks and Recreation	National Recreation and Park Association 2775 S. Quincy Street, Suite 300 Arlington, VA 22206-2204 703-820-4940	Articles about research and its application in the leisure services

Journal	Publisher and Address	Focus
Perceptual and Motor Skills	Psychological Reports Box 9229 Missoula, MT 59807-9229 406-728-1710	Experimental and theoretical articles dealing with perception and motor skills
The Physical Educator	Phi Epsilon Kappa 910 W. New York Street Indianapolis, IN 46202 317-637-8431	General articles in the broad aspects of the field
Physical Therapy	American Physical Therapy Association 1111 North Fairfax Street Alexandria, VA 22314 703-684-2782	Practical and research articles for physical therapists
The Physician and Sportsmedicine	McGraw-Hill Healthcare Group 4530 W. 77th Street Minneapolis, MN 55435 612-835-3222	Theoretical and practical articles about the medical aspects of sports, exercise, and fitness
Quest	National Association for Physical Education in Higher Education Human Kinetics Publishers, Inc. Box 5076 Champaign, IL 61825-5076 1-800-747-4457	Articles about critical issues in higher education
Research Quarterly for Exercise and Sport	American Alliance for Health, Physical Education, Recreation and Dance 1900 Association Drive Reston, VA 22091-1599 1-800-213-7193	Scholarly articles
Scholastic Coach	Scholastic Inc. 555 Broadway New York, NY 10003 212-343-6100	Practical articles for coaches
Sociology of Sport Journal	North American Society for the Sociology of Sport Human Kinetics Publishers, Inc. Box 5076 Champaign, IL 61825-5076 1-800-747-4457	Practical and theoretical papers

Journal	Publisher and Address	Focus
The Sport Psychologist	International Society of Sport Psychology Human Kinetics Publishers, Inc. Box 5076 Champaign, IL 61825-5076 1-800-747-4457	Scientific articles on the psychological aspects of sport and physical activity
Sport Science Review	International Council of Sport Science and Physical Education Human Kinetics Publishers, Inc. Box 5076 Champaign, IL 61825-5076 1-800-747-4457	Articles that promote scientific studies in physical education and sport
Strategies: A Journal for Sport and Physical Educators	National Association for Girls and Women in Sport and National Association for Sport and Physical Education of the American Alliance for Health, Physical Education, Recreation and Dance 1900 Association Drive Reston, VA 22091-1599 1-800-213-7193	Articles to improve teaching and coaching
Strength and Conditioning	National Strength and Conditioning Association Human Kinetics Publishers, Inc. Box 5076 Champaign, IL 61825-5076 1-800-747-4457	Theoretical and practical articles
Therapeutic Recreation Journal	National Recreation and Park Association 2775 S. Quincy Street, Suite 330 Arlington, VA 22206-2204 703-820-4940	Articles of practical use
Women's Sports and Fitness	2025 Pearl Street Boulder, CO 80302 303-440-5111	Popular and practical articles
Youth Sports Coach	National Youth Sports Coaches Association 2050 Vista Parkway West Palm Beach, FL 33411-2718 1-800-729-2057	Practical articles for coaches of youth sports

Appendix B

CERTIFYING ORGANIZATIONS

Aerobics and Fitness Association of America
15250 Ventura Boulevard, Suite 200
Sherman Oaks, CA 91403
1-800-446-2322

American Sport Education Program
Box 5076
Champaign, IL 61825-5076
1-800-747-4457

American College of Sports Medicine
Box 1440
Indianapolis, IN 46206-1440
317-637-9200

American Council on Exercise
5820 Oberlin Drive, Suite 102
San Diego, CA 92121
1-800-825-3636

American Red Cross (National Headquarters)
431 Eighteenth Street, NW
Washington, DC 20006
202-737-8300

Cooper Institute for Aerobics Research
12330 Preston Road
Dallas, TX 75230
1-800-635-7050

Exer-Safety Association
3785 West Commodore Cove
Reminderville, OH 44202
216-562-8280

National Athletic Trainers' Association
2952 Stemmons Fwy., Suite 200
Dallas, TX 75247-6103
214-637-6282

National Dance-Exercise Instructor's Training Association
1503 S. Washington Avenue, Suite 208
Minneapolis, MN 55454
1-800-237-6242

National Federation of State High School Associations
11724 NW Plaza Circle
P.O. Box 20626
Kansas City, MO 64195-0626
816-464-5400

National Youth Sports Coaches Association
2050 Vista Parkway
West Palm Beach, FL 33411-2718
1-800-729-2057

United States Water Fitness Association
P.O. Box 3279
Boynton Beach, FL 33424
407-732-9908

Young Men's Christian Association
101 North Wacker Drive
Chicago, IL 60606
312-977-0031

Glossary

Academic discipline   a formal body of knowledge discovered, developed, and disseminated through research and inquiry

Accreditation   process of measuring institutions' attainment of established program standards to ensure quality

Adapted physical education   program for exceptional students who are so different in mental, physical, emotional, or behavioral characteristics that, in the interest of quality educational opportunity for all students, special provisions must be made for their proper education

Affective objective   educational outcome that focuses on the development of attitudes, appreciations, and values, including both social and emotional dimensions

Agoge   educational system for Spartan boys

Allied fields   the areas of dance, health, and recreation that share some purposes, programs, and professionals with physical education and sport

Applied sciences   the areas of adapted physical education, exercise physiology, motor development, motor learning, sport biomechanics, sport history, sport management, sports medicine, sport pedagogy, sport philosophy, sport psychology, and sport sociology, which constitute the discipline of physical education and sport

Arete   all-around mental, moral, and physical excellence valued by the Greeks

Athletics   organized, highly structured, competitive activities in which skilled individuals participate

Battle of the Systems   controversy raging in the 1800s over which system of gymnastics was most appropriate for Americans

British Amateur Sport Ideal   belief in "playing the game for the game's sake"

Burnout   decreased performance quality and quantity resulting from stress, job repetitiveness, lack of support and reward, and overwork

Calisthenics   term used in the 1800s to describe Catharine Beecher's program of exercises designed to promote health, beauty, and strength; also used synonymously with general exercises today

Cognitive objective   educational outcome that emphasizes the acquisition, comprehension, analysis, synthesis, application, and evaluation of knowledge

Competency-based teacher education   the theoretical basis that every teacher must possess certain competencies and skills to be successful

Dance   bodily movements of a rhythmic and patterned succession usually executed to the accompaniment of music

Ethics   the branch of philosophy that deals with good and bad, moral duty and obligation, and principles of conduct

Exercise   to practice, to strengthen, or to condition through physical activity

Exercise physiology   the study of bodily functions under the stress of muscular activity

Existentialism   twentieth-century philosophy that centers on individual existence and advocates that truth and values are arrived at by each person's experiences

Games   activities ranging from simple diversions to cooperative activities to competitions with significant outcomes governed by rules

Greek Ideal   unity of the "man of action" with the "man of wisdom"

Gymnasium   site for intellectual and physical activities for Greek citizens

Gymnastics   term used to describe Greek athletics, European systems of exercises with or without apparatus, and a modern international sport

Health   soundness of body, mind, and soul, or one's general well-being

Hygiene   the science of preserving one's health

Idealism   philosophical theory that advocates that reality depends on the mind for existence and that truth is universal and absolute

Inclusion   the integration of children with disabilities into classes with nondisabled students

Intramurals   recreational and competitive activities participated in by students within an institution or employees within a company

Kinesiology   the scientific study of human motion that focuses on the art and science of how the body moves

Leisure   time free from work or responsibility that may be used for physical activity

Light gymnastics   Dio Lewis' program based on executing Beecher's calisthenics along with handheld apparatus

Merit pay   rewarding quality performance financially

Motor development   the maturation of the neuromuscular mechanism that permits progressive performance in motor skills

Motor learning   the study of cognitive processes underlying motor acts and associated with skill acquisition through practice and experience

Movement education   child-centered curriculum emphasing movement challenge and encouraging problem solving and guided discovery

Nationalism   pervasive theme stressing promotion and defense of one's country that was the desired outcome of several European systems of gymnastics in the 1800s

Naturalism   a belief that the scientific laws of nature govern life and that individual goals are more important that societal goals

New physical education   curriculum focused on developing the whole individual through participation in play, sports, games, and natural outdoor activities

Normal school   an institute for the training of teachers

Paidotribe   the first physical education teacher who taught Greek boys wrestling, boxing, jumping, dancing, and gymnastics at a palaestra

Palaestra   Greek wrestling school where boys learned wrestling, boxing, jumping, dancing, and gymnastics

Pancratium   an event in Panhellenic festivals that combined wrestling and boxing skills into an almost-anything-goes combat

Pentathlon   a five-event competition that included the discus throw, javelin throw, long jump, stade race, and wrestling

Philosophy   the pursuit of wisdom

Physical activity   all movements that can contribute to improved health

Physical education   a process through which an individual obtains optimal physical, mental, and social skills and fitness through physical activity

Physical fitness   combination of cardiovascular endurance, muscular strength and endurance, flexibility, body composition, agility, balance, neuromuscular coordination, speed, and power

Play   amusements engaged in freely, for fun, and devoid of constraints

Pragmatism   American movement in philosophy emphasizing reality as the sum total of each individual's experiences through practical experimentation

Profession   a learned occupation that requires training in a specialized field of study

Realism   philosophical system that stresses that the laws and order of the world as revealed by science are independent from human experience

Recreation   refreshing or renewing one's strength and spirit after work; a diversion that occurs during leisure hours

Renaissance   a period from the fifteenth to seventeenth centuries marked by a renewed appreciation for classical culture

Sport   physical activities governed by formal and informal rules that involve competition against an opponent or oneself and are engaged in for fun, recreation, or reward

Sport biomechanics   the study of the effects of natural laws and forces on the body through the science and mechanics of movement

Sport history   descriptive and analytical examination of significant people, events, organizations, and trends that shaped the past within the social context of the time

Sport management   the study of the management of personnel, programs, budgets, and facilities in various sports settings

Sport pedagogy   the study of how to enhance instructional content, the learning process, and the achievement of learning outcomes

Sport philosophy   the search for and interpretation of truth and values in sport

Sport psychology   the study of human behavior in sports, including an understanding of the mental processes that impact motor skill performance

Sport sociology   the study of the social units and processes within the social context

Sports medicine   the study and application of the prevention, treatment, and rehabilitation of sports injuries

Standard   a uniform criterion or minimum essential element for the measurement of quality

Thermae   facilities in Rome for contrast baths of varying water temperatures and other leisure activities

Wellness   mental, emotional, spiritual, nutritional, and physical factors that lead to healthy behaviors

Credits

CHAPTER 1

P.10, Reprinted with permission of the American Alliance for Health, Physical Education, Recreation and Dance, 1900 Association Drive, Reston, VA 22091.

CHAPTER 2

P. 42, Box, Reprinted with permission of the *Journal of Athletic Training*, Dallas, TX 75427.

CHAPTER 3

P. 68, Photo, Reprinted with permission of the University of Tennessee Press. From Kozar AJ: R. Tait McKenzie, the sculptor of athletes, 1975, The University of Tennessee Press.

CHAPTER 4

P. 75 but not the Box, Reprinted with permission of the American Alliance for Health, Physical Education, Recreation and Dance, 1900 Association Drive, Reston, VA 22091.
P. 79 but not the Box, Reprinted with permission of the American Alliance for Health, Physical Education, Recreation and Dance, 1900 Association Drive, Reston, VA 22091.
P. 81, Box, Reprinted with permission of the Southern District of the American Alliance for Health, Physical Education, Recreation and Dance, 1900 Association Drive, Reston, VA 22091.

CHAPTER 7

P. 174, Puzzle, Reprinted with permission of Jane Jenkins.

CHAPTER 8

P. 177, Reprinted with permission of Human Kinetics Publishers, Inc., Champaign, IL 61825-5076. P. 191, This article is reprinted with permission from the *Journal of Physical Education, Recreation, and Dance,* April 1960, p. 27. The journal is a publication of the American Alliance for Health, Physical Education, Recreation and Dance, 1900 Association Drive, Reston, VA 22091.

CHAPTER 9

P. 203, *NEA Proceedings,* 32: 621, copyright 1893, National Education Association. Reprinted with permission.

CHAPTER 10

Boxes on pages 243, 245, 248, 251, 252, and 253, Reprinted with permission of the National Association for Sport and Physical Education, 1900 Association Drive, Reston, VA 22091.

CHAPTER 11

P. 270, Fig. 11-1, Reprinted with permission. ©Jump Rope for Heart, American Heart Association. Boxes on pages 277 and 285–286, Reprinted with permission of the National Association for Sport and Physical Education, 1900 Association Drive, Reston, VA 22091.

CHAPTER 12

P. 295–296, Box, National Federation of State High School Associations. (1992). (available from 11724 NW Plaza Circle, P.O. Box 20626, Kansas City, MO 64195-0626). Neal, V., and Anderson, P. (1992). 1992 NAIA sports program survey; administrators and coaches of varsity teams (available from the first author, Lewis and Clark College, 0615 S.W. Palatine Hill Road, Portland, OR 97219-7899). Acosta, R.Y. and Carpenter, I.J. (1996). Women in intercollegiate sport—a longitudinal study nineteen-year update 1977–1996 (available from the authors, Brooklyn College, Brooklyn, NY 11210). P. 310–311, Data provided by the United States Olympic Committee and the International Olympic Committee.

CHAPTER 13

P. 323, Reprinted with permission of the National Association for Sport and Physical Education, 1900 Association Drive, Reston, VA 22091.

Index

A

Academic discipline
  components of, 51–52
  physical education/sport programs
    as, 52–53
Academic preparation
  scope of, 128–129
  See also Physical education/sport
    training; Teacher education
Academy Papers, The, 80
Accountability, criteria for, 323
Accreditation, 213, 250, 253
  requirements for, 253
  standards, 250, 253
Adams, Jane, 191
Adapted physical education
  career opportunities in, 103
  legislation related to, 228–231
  nature of, 54–55
  training in, 89
Aerobics, 226
Aerobics and Fitness Association of
    America (AFAA), 83
  certification from, 135
Affective objectives, of physical
    education/sport programs,
    12–13, 17
Age of Enlightenment, physical
    activity in, 162
Agility, 15
Agoge, 148
Agreement to participate, 254–255
Amateur Athletic Union (AAU),
    84, 192, 303

Amateur sports
  historical view, 192–194, 220–222
  organizations for, 193
Amateur Sports Act, 220, 300, 312
*AMERICA 2000: An Education
    Strategy,* 212
American Alliance for Health,
    Physical Education, Recreation
    and Dance (AAHPERD), 10,
    73, 190, 212
  associations of, 75–78
  district associations, 78
  Health-Related Lifetime Physical
    Fitness Test, 224
  membership applications, 79
  periodicals of, 75
  Youth Fitness Test, 211, 224
American Association for Health
    Education (AAHE), 76
American Association for Leisure and
    Recreation (AALR), 76
American Association for the
    Advancement of Physical
    Education (AAAPE), 191
American College of Sports Medicine
    (ACSM), 82
  certifications from, 133, 134
American Council on Exercise
    (ACE), 83
  certification from, 135
American Physical Education
    Association, 10, 212, 217
*American Physical Education
    Review,* 191
American Red Cross, certifications
    from, 133

349

E

Eclecticism, 43
Educational protagonists, 162–163
Education Amendments of 1972.
    See Title IX
Education and training. *See* Physical
    education/sports training;
    Teacher education
Education for All Handicapped
    Children Act (PL 94–142), 229,
    230, 300–301
Egyptians, and physical activities, 147
Electromyography, uses of, 59
Elementary school programs, 240–242
    development/scope of, 241–242
    recommendations for, 242
Empire State Games, 303
England, English sport, rise of,
    168–171
Environment, and leisure
    activities, 272
Ethics, 37–42
    code of professional practice, 42
    definition of, 38
    deontology, 41
    ethical choices in sports, 40
    moral reasoning, 39
    teaching ethical standards, 41–42
    teleological theories, 39, 41
Exercise, meaning of, 6
Exercise physiology, nature of, 55–56
Existentialism, 35–36

F

Family, and career choice, 97–98
Feltra, Vittorino de, 36, 162, 163
Fitness
    components of, 14–15
    and consumer education, 268–269
    demographic factors, 270–271
    educational specialization in, 88
    as goal of educational programs,
        13–15
    lack in American adults, 284, 286
    lack in American youth, 224–225
    and lifespan, 324–326
    program adherence factors, 268
    and public relations, 269–270

FITNESSGRAM, 225
Fitness movement
    for children, 224–226
    historical view, 210–211, 224–226
Flexibility, 14–15
Follen, Charles, 184
*Franklin v. Gwinnett County Public
    Schools,* 296
Froebel, Friedrich, 163

G

Gambling, 194
Games, nature of, 6
Generalists, versus specialists,
    256–257
German gymnastics system, 164–165
    in United States, 179, 181,
        185–187
Girls. *See* Women
Gladiators, 159
Goal setting, and personal goals,
    127–128
Graduate education, 137–140
Greeks, 147–148, 149–156
    Athenians, 149–151
    Greek ideal, 148, 161, 169–170
    Homeric era, 148
    Olympics, 151–157
    sports participation of, 59, 68
*Guidelines for Elementary School
    Physical Education,* 242
Gulick, Luther, 204, 208, 222
GutsMuths, Johann, 164, 165
    biographical information, 172–173
Gymnasiums, Greeks, 150
Gymnastics
    German system, 164–165, 179, 181
    light, 182
    Swedish system, 166–167, 183–184
    United States, 179, 181, 182,
        183–184

H

Hall, G. Stanley, 203, 205
Hanna, Delphine, 185, 187, 190, 204
Hartwell, Edward, 184, 185
Health, definition of, 9
Health education, status of, 15–17